Human Rights for the 21st Century

U.S.–Post-Soviet Dialogues

Human Rights for the 21st Century

for the 21st Century
Foundations for Responsible Hope

A U.S.–Post-Soviet Dialogue

Edited by
Peter Juviler & Bertram Gross
with
Vladimir Kartashkin & Elena Lukasheva

Routledge
Taylor & Francis Group

LONDON AND NEW YORK

First published 1993 by M.E. Sharpe

Published 2015 by Routledge
2 Park Square, Milton Park, Abingdon, Oxon OX14 4RN
711 Third Avenue, New York, NY 10017, USA

*Routledge is an imprint of the Taylor & Francis Group,
an informa business*

Library of Congress Cataloging-in-Publication Data

Human rights for the 21st century, foundations for responsible hope :
a U.S.–post-Soviet dialogue / edited by Peter Juviler . . . [et al.].
p. cm. — (U.S.-post-Soviet dialogues)
Includes index.
ISBN 1-56324-044-0 (C). — ISBN 1-56324-110-2 (P)
1. Human rights.
I. Juviler, Peter H.
K3240.6.H8765   1993
341.4'81—dc20
92-33908
CIP

ISBN 13: 9781563241109 (pbk)

To the memory of Andrei Dmitrievich Sakharov

Contents

About the Contributors

Elena Bonner, medical doctor and World War II veteran, human-rights champion, spouse of the late Andrei Sakharov, author of numerous articles on human rights and the political situation in the USSR. She was administratively exiled to Gorky (recently renamed Nizhnyi Novgorod), with Academician Sakharov from 1980 until 1986, when Mikhail Gorbachev invited them back to Moscow.

Viktor Chkhikvadze, Corresponding Member, Russian Academy of Sciences, former director of the Institute of State and Law, founder and former head of its Human Rights Division, author of many books developing the past Soviet views on human rights.

Norman Dorsen, Stokes Professor of Law, New York University Law School, former General Counsel then President of the American Civil Liberties Union, author of many works on civil rights and liberties including (with others) *Civil and Political Rights in the U.S.,* editor of *Our Endangered Rights* and other leading surveys.

Riane Eisler, founder of the Los Angeles Women's Center Legal Program, author of *The Equal Rights Handbook* (1978), *The Chalice and the Blade: Our History, Our Future* (1987) (a study of the influence on the social system of the relations between women and men), and "Human Rights: Toward an Integrated Theory of Action," *Human Rights Quarterly,* August 1987.

David Forsythe, Professor of Political Science, University of Nebraska, and President of the International Organization Section of the International Studies Association, author of *The Internationalization of Human Rights* (1991), *Human Rights and World Politics* (2nd ed., 1989), *Human Rights and U.S. Foreign Policy: Congress Reconsidered* (1988), and *Humanitarian Politics: The International Committee of the Red Cross* (1977), and editor of *Human Rights and Development: International Views* (1989).

Paula Garb, Ph.D., is a researcher and lecturer at the University of California, Irvine, in Global Peace and Conflict Studies where she focuses on the former Soviet republics. Garb received her training in anthropology at Moscow State University and at the USSR Academy of Sciences, and conducted extensive field work throughout the former Soviet Union. Between 1975 and 1990 she worked as a translator for Novosti Press Agency, Radio Moscow, Progress Publishers, and CBS News. She is the author of *Where the Old are Young: Long Life in the Soviet Caucasus*, *They Came To Stay: North Americans in the USSR*, and several articles on these and related subjects.

Bertram Gross, Distinguished Professor Emeritus, Urban Affairs and Political Science, Hunter College, CUNY. Visiting Professor, St. Mary's College, Moraga, CA 1982–; and University of California, Berkeley, 1985–. Author (with Ned Schneier) *Legislative Struggles* and *Legislative Strategy* (forthcoming); *Friendly Fascism* (1982), *The Legislative Struggle* (1978), winner of the 1954 Woodrow Wilson Award, American Political Science Association, best book in American government; *Organizations and Their Managing* (1968), and *The State of the Nation: Social Systems Accounting* (1966); Co-editor and contributor, *Unemployment: A Global Challenge*, (special issue of *The Annals*, July 1987). Executive Secretary, Council of Economic Advisers to the President, 1946–52. Helped draft Employment Act 1946, Full Employment and Balanced Growth Act 1978, current Human Rights Education Act H.R. 3077.

Charles Henry, Professor, Afro-American Studies Department, University of California at Berkeley; past member Amnesty International Board and Board of Directors, Amnesty International, USA; author of numerous works on race in politics and society including *Growing Down: Culture and Black Politics*, and co-author, *The Chitlin' Controversy: Race and Public Policy in America* (book of the year, National Association of Black College and University Students, 1978).

Susan Heuman, Ph.D., Columbia University in Russian History, Associate Professor of History (Adjunct), Manhattanville College; author of "Severed Roots: Liberal Legal Thought in Russia Before the Revolution," in *State and Law* (Moscow), "Perspectives on Legal Thought in Pre-Revolutionary Russia," in Piers Beirne, ed., *Revolution in Law: Contributions to the Development of Soviet Legal Theory* (1990); "A Socialist Conception of Human Rights: A Model from Pre-Revolutionary Russia," in Adamantia Pollis and Peter Schwab, eds., *Human Rights: Ideological and Cultural Perspectives* (1979), and numerous other writings including the book *Transforming Subjects into Citizens: Bogdan Kistiakovsky and the Search for Constitutionalism in the Russian Empire* (forthcoming).

Peter Juviler, Professor of Political Science, Barnard College, co-director of the Columbia University Center for the Study of Human Rights; U.S. coordinator, International Dialogue for Human Rights; consultant to Lawyers Committee on Human Rights, co-editor and contributor for books including *Gorbachev's Re-*

forms: U.S. and Japanese Assessments (1988); author of *Revolutionary Law and Order* (1976); co-author of a report on human rights in Central America (1984), author of numerous articles and chapters on human rights.

Dr. Vladimir Kartashkin, doctor of laws. Leading Research Fellow in the Human Rights Division, Institute of State and Law, Professor of International Law, Lumumba University, Moscow. He served in the Human Rights Division of the United Nations from 1969 to 1973, and from 1979 to 1985 in the legal department of the United Nations. Works on international law and human rights include *International Protection of Human Rights* and *Human Rights and International Security,* compiler (with Dr. Ernest Ametistov) of *Human Rights: Basic International Documents.* Dr. Kartashkin has written a number of popular pamphlets and articles in such leading newspapers such as *Izvestiia, Literary Gazette, Soviet Russia,* and *Komsomolskaia pravda* as well as in magazines including *Ogonek* and *Raduga.* His reform proposals received wide circulation in an interview on human rights, legislative processes, and emigration rights published in *Ogonek* in January 1989.

Stanley Katz, President, American Council of Learned Societies, Professor of Constitutional History, Woodrow Wilson School, Princeton University, author and editor of numerous works on U.S. history and constitutional development.

Vladimir Kudriavtsev, Academician, former USSR People's Deputy, Vice President, Russian Academy of Sciences, formerly director, Institute of State and Law, author of numerous works on law and criminology.

Irina Lediakh, senior research fellow, Division of Human Rights, Institute of State and Law. Like most of the other members of the Human Rights Division, Dr. Lediakh participates, as writer and consultant, in the present process of Russian reform. A co-author of *The Socialist Conception of Human Rights,* she is a major contributor to a special supplement on "Perestroika and Human Rights" of the widely read *New Times.*

Pavel Litvinov, physicist; grandson of the wartime Soviet ambassador to the U.S. and Foreign Minister Maxim Litvinov; underground editor and writer during the Brezhnev days; compiler with commentary, *The Trial of the Four: A Collection of Materials on the Case of Galanskov, Ginzburg, Dobrovolsky and Lashkova 1967–1968.* Near that work's completion, Litvinov was arrested while participating in a silent protest on Red Square against the Warsaw Pact invasion of Czechoslovakia, and was sentenced to five years' Siberian exile. Litvinov is now a U.S. citizen.

Elena Lukasheva, doctor of laws, member of the Soviet delegation to the 45th session of the U.N. Commission on Human Rights, and to Meetings of Experts,

Commission on Security and Cooperation in Europe (CSCE). She holds the leading academic post in human rights in Russia as head of the Human Rights Division, Institute of State and Law, Russian Academy of Sciences. Parliamentary consultant on legal reform. Author of numerous works on human rights, international cooperation in their achievement, legality and legal consciousness, Dr. Lukasheva is the leading author of *The Socialist Concept of Human Rights* and *The Realization of Human Rights in Soviet Society* and the author of such other works as *Socialist Law and the Individual*, and *Law, Morality and the Individual*.

Andrei Sakharov (1921–1989), Academician, physicist, "father of the hydrogen bomb," specialist in thermonuclear reactions and theoretical physics. In the late 1950s he warned of environmental dangers of nuclear testing and dropped military work in 1968, the year he wrote to Brezhnev his seminal long essay, *Reflections on Progress, Coexistence and Intellectual Freedom*. Leading figure in the movement for human rights despite harassment and exile; co-founder of the Moscow Human Rights Committee in 1970; awarded the Nobel Peace Prize in 1975, accepted in his name by Elena Bonner. Elected USSR people's deputy by USSR Academy of Sciences in 1989. Author of many works on physics and human rights and *Memoirs*, published in 1990. Founder of Fund for the Survival and Development of Humanity, he was an advocate of further democratization and rights of the nationalities until the last day of his life, December 14, 1989.

Richard Schifter, former Assistant Secretary of State for Human Rights and Humanitarian Affairs.

Henry Shue, Professor of Philosophy, Director of the Program on Ethics in Public Life, Cornell University; author of *Basic Rights* (1980).

Evgenii Skripilev, Doctor of Laws, Senior Research Fellow, Institute of State and Law.

Vasilii Vlasikhin, head of legal studies, Institute of the USA and Canada, Harvard Law School visiting scholar 1977; expert on human rights in Soviet delegation during Shultz-Shevardnadze negotiations in 1988; author of works on U.S. constitutional law and criminal justice, including *Prosecutorial Services in U.S. Law and Politics*; *Constitution of the USA: Political and Legal Commentary* (co-author with August Mishin); *Two Hundred Years of U.S. Constitutionalism* (with August Mishin, in English); *Governmental System of the USA*.

Oleg Vorobiev, Research Fellow, Human Rights Division, Institute of State and Law, specialist on rights of free speech.

Acknowledgments

We are grateful to Mr. Gennadii Kaliamin, a leading editor at Progress Publishers, and the editor in charge of our book, for his helpful input at meetings and his unflagging and patient interest. Thanks go to Anne C. Stephens for help in preliminary editing and for conference organizing in New York in 1991, and for her long peaceful coexistence with this book in the making, and to the skilled and helpful editors at M. E. Sharpe: Patricia Kolb, Elizabeth Granda, and Kathleen Hamel Peifer.

The Soviet–U.S. Dialogue on Human Rights and the Future, active since 1989, has met in conferences annually since 1989. It is sponsored by the American Council of Learned Societies (ACLS) and the Russian Academy of Sciences through the Institute of State and Law, and included by IREX as an exchange of its subcommission on law. We thank Dr. Stanley Katz of ACLS for his ever attentive encouragement and his endorsement of the Dialogue. We thank also Dr. Wesley Fisher, formerly of IREX, for his accessibility and suggestions. Co-coordinators for the ACLS have been Bertram Gross and Peter Juviler. The Soviet coordinators have been Elena Lukasheva and Vladimir Kartashkin. The initial conference, in August of 1989, was hosted by the University of California at Berkeley through its Peace and Conflict Studies Program. We thank Dr. Sheldon Margen, its director, and Joan Levinson of the program, as well as Rita Maran of Human Rights Advocates and the many students of the university who pitched in. The 1989 conference at which this book originated was funded by the Ford Foundation and the Chancellor of the University of California at Berkeley as major donors, and by Henry Daking and the Soros Foundation. The initiation of the Dialogue was made possible in part by a grant from IREX, with funds provided by the Andrew W. Mellon Foundation, the National Endowment for the Humanities, and the U.S. Department of State. None of these persons or organizations is responsible for the views expressed here.

Translations from Russian texts are by Peter Juviler.

Foreword

When Bertram Gross and Peter Juviler began their "dialogue" on human rights with Soviet colleagues nearly five years ago, I acceded to their request for sponsorship in the belief that the American Council of Learned Societies should support serious, well-intended international humanistic activities. I was of course particularly interested in the human rights project both because of my own scholarly concerns and because of the long-standing exchange relationship of ACLS and the Academy of Sciences in Moscow.

It never occurred to me that the human rights dialogue would be transformed from a colloquy among humanitarian academics into a project on the cutting edge of international legal and political change. But so it has turned out. In my wildest dreams I could not have imagined my friend Vladimir Kudriavtsev, formerly the head of the Soviet Academy's Institute of State and Law, coauthoring a chapter entitled "Postcommunist New Thinking on Human Rights." But so he has. Nor could anyone have predicted that this volume would conclude with Peter Juviler's important statement on "Rethinking Rights Without *the* Enemy."

For most of those who attended what sometimes seemed an endless series of east-west conferences on human rights, common ground seemed an unachievable goal. The discussions always revolved about the ritual western assertion of the primacy of civil and political rights and the socialist insistence on the superiority of social and economic rights. Since there were both intellectual and political reasons why both sides were right, and why neither side could compromise, all participants shared an unusual sense of frustration during and after these formal exercises. Privately we could agree that there was something to be said for the other side of the coin, but not in public.

It is greatly to the credit of the organizers of the dialogue that they were determined to break through the impasse by creating an atmosphere of mutual respect out of a shared commitment to some version of human rights—and a willingness to look at one's own rights theories with a critical eye. Here we must be especially grateful to Elena Lukasheva and her Soviet colleagues for agreeing to participate—the risks for them were much greater than for the Americans.

The essays in this volume constitute the first extensive, multinational attempt to come to terms with the future of human rights in the post-Soviet world. They apply some of the newest human rights thinking (such as Philip Alston's notion of "solidarity" rights) to the new situation. And they involve not only some of the most important human rights thinkers in each country, but also some of the most important actors in human rights negotiations.

It takes nothing away from the historic dimensions of this volume to say that its authors do not provide solutions to the most pressing problems of human rights conceptualization. The conflict between positive and negative rights, the apparent incompatibility of individual and collective rights, and tension between democracy and self-determination will be with us into the foreseeable future. But the thinking represented here will help both citizens and policy makers to discuss human rights more clearly and more usefully.

This book was created as part of a dramatic process, a dialogue between an informal group of scholars from two countries with diametrically opposed ideologies, though both ostensibly committed to the protection of rights. *Perestroika* and *glasnost'* have altered the ideological terms so that it is now possible for the group (which intends to continue its efforts) to think more positively about a regime of human rights which can realistically be recommended to both countries—and elsewhere.

Many readers will surely welcome the authors' emphasis on universal human rights education, the duties allied with all rights, and the overarching concept of international human rights law as a living force that grows and adapts to new challenges. In a world now suffering from far too much hopelessness, more thought and action along these lines could help build stronger foundations for responsible hope.

Stanley N. Katz
President, American Council
of Learned Societies

Human Rights
for the
21st Century

1

Golden Opportunities, Huge Obstacles

Bertram Gross and Peter Juviler

All human beings are born free and equal in dignity and rights. They are
endowed with reason and conscience and should act towards one another in a
spirit of brotherhood.

(Article 1, Universal Declaration of Human Rights, 1948)

The contributors to the three-year dialogue that resulted in this book have been
active participants in the movement toward a shared understanding of human
rights. That understanding figured prominently in the ending of the cold war. We
believe that human rights continue to pose the basic issues for this century and
the next. This book is at once living history and an attempt to get outside it, to
look back in order to see further ahead.

When we opened the dialogue leading to this book, we agreed to lay bare all
the obstacles in our path. At that time Soviet troops were still bloodying Afghanistan; U.S.-backed contras were trying to overthrow the Nicaraguan government;
NATO and Warsaw Pact missiles were targeted at each other. Because of these
facts, and the ongoing diplomatic impasse over human rights, some onlookers
criticized us for being too far ahead of our time. Others criticized us for being
behind the times; human rights, they said, no longer figured as issues. Our critics
were wrong on both counts. A common ground could be worked out among
these writers. As for the rest of the world, that is a different story.

In this age of uncertainty and difficulties over democratization, we look to the
year 2000 as the possible dawn of a human rights era. We envision a twenty-first
century whose opening years might become historic turning points in
humankind's halting progress toward genuine civilization.

No one reading this book will accuse us of dreaming of a utopian millennium.
We point to the huge obstacles along the way. But we intend this book to help us
become aware of the obstacles and seize the opportunities to move effectively
against the *real* enemies of human rights: ignorance and indifference; inexperience with democracy, fossilized bureaucracies, and economic stagnation; reces-

sion and depression; militarism; poverty in rich countries and greater poverty (along with elite opulence) in poor countries; and widespread uncertainty and hopelessness.

No one, moreover, can miss the paradox that while peoples of the world have never been more closely linked and interdependent, many countries are being torn apart by ethnic or religious extremism. This book responds to another paradox: that in our present "information age," most people in the world are little informed, or misinformed, about human rights, their relevance to our needs, their violation, and their fulfillment.

Somewhat less obvious but no less widespread is the difficulty we all face in keeping up with rapid change and accepting limitations on national sovereignty and personal interests. Elena Lukasheva's section of this preface conveys strikingly her experience of rethinking on rights, the lessons learned from their past violations, and the shockingly rapid breakup of her country.

In working together on the three parts of this book to cover the former USSR, the United States, and the future for human rights, the participants assume a triple responsibility. We try to show the world as it *has been* for human rights; we analyze the world as it *is*, in its myriad combinations of progress and regress; we look ahead, as pragmatic idealists, to what *could be*. New thinking and new actions for human rights such as we propose would require the cooperation of the United States, the Soviet successor states, and other countries, all working through a strengthened United Nations and regional organizations.

The first part of the book opens with a discussion among leaders in the human rights struggle which took place in 1989 at a public forum of our first human rights conference. Richard Schifter describes the battle of new and old in the USSR, noting that whether the reformers would succeed was "not at all clear." It still isn't. Viktor Chkhikvadze, formerly a high official from Georgia and now an academic specialist on human rights, characterizes his own past writing and that of other academic human rights specialists as "not representing reality in any way whatsoever."

Elena Bonner states that not law, as Chkhikvadze said, but lawlessness permitted the exile without trial to Gorky of herself and her husband, Andrei Sakharov, from 1980 to 1986. Both she and the late Andrei Sakharov note the political educational importance of the first frank and open sessions of the reformed parliament in 1989. "The entire population" saw on TV "for itself without embellishment what we really are." Andrei Sakharov conveys the picture of a poverty-stricken country, medically ill-served, bureaucratically exploited, and living in a despoiled environment. In a prescient talk, Academician Sakharov recalls the dissident movement's fight in defense of "the fundamental principles necessary to democratic development." He deplores the slow pace of reform and prescribes more democracy, more minority rights and less bureaucracy, long-overdue privatization, and more aid from the west. Pavel Litvinov, the exiled dissident, rejects recriminations against Chkhikvadze and urges him and the other Soviet legal experts who are lending their expertise to legislation for human rights "to take the next step and open to people who have been monitoring human rights in the Soviet Union for all these years." Years later, this process of networking with independent monitors is only just beginning.

The end of the cold war and the outcome of *perestroika*—the breakup of the very Union it was to revitalize—have particularly reshaped the chapters on the former USSR. These chapters record the legacy and decline of centralized absolutism and confront the new threats and opportunities following on the USSR's breakup. Chapter 4 and chapters 6 to 8 convey the long struggle between absolutism and the imperatives of modernization that had been hospitable to the ideals of freedom, democracy and the rule of law but were wiped out by Bolshevism and are making a difficult comeback today in the post-Soviet successor states.

In chapter 5, Elena Lukasheva writes passionately about the costs of totalitarian repression and deceit, and of the dangers to democracy and rights in the rapid but as yet superficial democratization of anarchic post-Soviet society. The paradox emerges: Although people are as yet not ready to internalize rule of law, the Commonwealth of Independent States and its member countries must build a "legal mechanism for protecting human rights on the territory of the commonwealth." Finally, Paula Garb's timely analysis draws attention to the need for legal protections of the rights of foreigners working in the former USSR.

Bertram Gross's opening chapter for Part 2 argues that the United States is still a beacon of freedom for a topsy-turvy world despite continuing violations of human rights within the United States and abroad. In Chapter 11, Irina Lediakh and Oleg Vorobiev share with other contributors the view that economic and social rights in the United States fall short of international human rights standards and western practice generally, with bad results also for political rights. Norman Dorsen, specialist on civil liberties and former long-serving president of the American Civil Liberties Union, notes the evolution in and strains on U.S. civil liberties and writing. He finds in human rights norms as interpreted in the United States the lack of a community of rights. (Mary Ann Glendon, a Harvard law professor, has also emphasized the relative lack of a sense of community of rights and responsibilities in the United States, in her book *Rights Talk: The Impoverishment of Political Discourse*.) Vasilii Vlasikhin notes in chapter 13 that Soviet experts, himself included, used to misrepresent the U.S. constitutional system, whose protections of liberty he now emphasizes. Chapter 14 contains Vladimir Kartashkin's critique of U.S. foreign policy for its inconsistency as regards human rights and for its history of linking human rights with other interests. He also makes proposals for future cooperation toward international rule of law. David Forsythe comments on the U.S. Congress's role in human rights policy abroad, noting that it was "neither totally determined by the executive" nor "totally characterized by blatant double standards." He looks to a western European influence on human rights in central Europe and the former

Soviet Union and supports continuing pressures on the United States to give full legal recognition to international human rights standards.

Part 3, "Toward the Twenty-first Century," opens with Vladimir Kartashkin's keynote vision of a common global home, "common" because it would achieve one single legal space, one shared understanding of human rights and interests. Charles Henry develops proposals for an outreach approach to education for human rights in the new world order. Riane Eisler integrates feminist thought and comparative data on women's status and rights (or lack of rights) into her concept of genuine partnership in both private and public life as essential to the realization of human rights. Bertram Gross sees hope for a healthier United States, not in domestic reform alone, but in an international give-and-take on human rights, and in the untapped potential of the poor.

Henry Shue continues his philosophical contributions to understanding human rights with a reminder that one person's rights are some other person's or institution's duties, and with his clear distinction between negative and positive duties. In the closing essay, Peter Juviler suggests a rethinking on human rights that rests on redefining security in a world without *the* enemy; a reinterpretation of human rights to include firmer recognition of solidarity rights (such as the right to a safe and healthy environment) and of ethnic groups' collective rights of self-determination; and the facilitation of increased cooperation within the human rights community through the formation of human rights associations on the national, regional, and global levels.

Some will say that it is impossible to realize our vision for the beginning of the twenty-first century. Yet our views are grounded in years of interchange as well as analysis of many developments in the United States and the former USSR that also had been regarded as impossible. One thing we are sure of is that genuine progress cannot emerge without vigorous, action-oriented debates on what is to be done and undone. Such debates should be conducted, we believe, with full awareness of the world's potential for both unpredictable horrors and surprising initiatives for human betterment.

2

Witness to Upheaval

Elena Lukasheva

Our cooperation began in 1988. In the course of making arrangements, we came to understand that we had to overcome obstacles, prejudices, and stereotypes that had built up over many years. Soviet society, embarked on restructuring, declared its commitment to universal human values, democracy, legality, and human rights. It was the breakthrough to new political thinking which opened the way to the Soviet-American dialogue on human rights. Leaving confrontation behind, we decided to look at the human rights situation in our countries objectively and without bias.

Abandoning the accustomed stereotypes is a very difficult process. Therefore we decided that the authors of this book would write parallel chapters on human rights in our respective societies, each as seen through the eyes of Soviet and American writers.

When we began work, it was difficult to foresee how complicated that task would be. This applies particularly to the analysis of the past and present state of human rights in the former Soviet Union. While U.S. society is characterized by stability and settled legal principles and mechanisms for realizing human rights, the changes taking place in the USSR compelled us at every step to overcome customary approaches and abandon traditional standards. To keep up with the rush of events, the authors had to revise their work many times.

After the announcement of restructuring—*perestroika*—directed toward the revolutionary renewal of society, Soviet people experienced a euphoria, a hope for renewal and rapid change. However, many underestimated the inertia of the administrative-command system and its capacity to resist change. We looked to a rapid victory, broad democratization, the affirmation of human rights. But these processes ran up against stiff opposition. Reforms proceeded slowly, with half measures, and therefore failed to achieve their objectives. The reasons for this are to be found not only in the resistance of the totalitarian system, but also in the lack of a correct strategy of transformation.

At first, this centered on the needs for democratization and for the liberation of the economy from excessive regulation. Talk of the market as a necessary prerequisite for all the transformations began quite a while later, when time had already been lost. Moreover, since democracy did not rest on a market structure, it remained truncated and halting, not liberating the individual but limiting his or her autonomy and their possibilities for free choice and self-determination. The development of democracy and of market relations should go on at the same time, otherwise society finds itself in a dead end.

In the absence of a new mechanism of economic regulation, the delay in developing a market led to the deformation and disruption of old economic links, to chaos, disorganization, and sharp drops in production. Society suffered short-ages, growing insecurity, and political and economic instability. The present state of society results not only from more than seventy years of domination by the authoritarian-command system, but also from the miscalculations, errors, and delays that characterized the period known as *perestroika*. All this complicated the process of developing human rights and strengthening their guarantees. The situation was aggravated by sharply escalating nationality conflicts. Dissatisfac-tion and uncertainty spread throughout society.

Conservative forces utilized this situation in their attempted coup of August 19 to 21, 1991. They counted on people not to oppose the establishment of a dictatorship, tormented as they were by shortages and endless queues, wearied by the growing difficulties. Characteristically, the putsch-makers' first step was to clamp down on civil liberties—freedoms of expression, meetings, demonstra-tions, and the press and other mass media.

The resistance to the putsch-makers showed that six years had not passed in vain, that a significant segment of society could no longer be returned to the old dictatorial order, and that the process of democratization was irreversible, how-ever difficult its road ahead. Democratic forces had won. And their victory confirmed the need for a decisive course of political and economic reforms.

However, the difficulties keep growing. The uncontrollable collapse of the Union continues to intensify economic chaos, breaking economic links built over decades. Production had been distributed over the country with a single economy in mind, but the unrestrained and heedless sovereignization of the former repub-lics weakens or sunders those links. Economic agreements must be activated rapidly in order to preserve interrepublic links and to halt the fall in production. The situation now may well rule out guarantees of citizens' economic rights; it is also leading to the overthrow and curtailment of democracy within the former Union. We already see the emergence of authoritarian regimes in some former Union republics.

At present, a growth of national consciousness is taking place. That is a salutary process. Unfortunately, however, it is often accompanied by the growth of nationalism and intolerance of other peoples who have lived next door for centuries. And that leads directly to the violation of the rights of citizens of nonindigenous nationalities in sovereign national states and the appearance of hundreds of thousands of refugees. Of course, democracy and human rights are the first to suffer in times of political, economic, and national instability.

The events occurring in our country show how unsteady the ground was under the Union's governmental, national, and economic structures, prompting a reappraisal of the historic past of Soviet society.

From the start, the tragedy of Soviet society lay in setting goals that were utopian and unreal for a country with a backward economy, weak democratic traditions, and human rights that had been buried in oblivion. The struggle for these goals was carried out by violent methods which could and did lead to the formation of a totalitarian regime. The Soviet Union had not known even a short period favoring the development of human rights. Today, one of the most urgent questions is how, in our present dramatic situation, to prevent a curtailment of human rights and to humanize our life. Events in this land are unfolding stormily and unpredictably. One would like to hope that we can cross this historical divide without new losses, that democratic processes are irreversible, and that human rights will occupy a worthy place in society.

The authors studied with great interest the historic experience and contemporary processes taking place in the former USSR and the United States. However, the paths they followed toward the assessment of the situation were different. U.S. scholars were free and unfettered in their approaches and opinions. It was not easy for the Soviet authors to overcome settled stereotypes, but the course of events in their country impelled them to reassess their accustomed interpretations of history and current happenings.

The group of authors strove for objective analysis of the real situation for human rights in our countries. How successful they were in this, life itself will show.

Part 1

The Ex-USSR:
Endings and Beginnings

3

Actors in the Drama Speak Out
(Berkeley, California, August 10–11, 1989)

Richard Schifter, Viktor Chkhikvadze, Elena Bonner, Andrei Sakharov, Pavel Litvinov

Richard Schifter

For many decades, the Soviet Union's political drama was played off-stage. There would be an occasional public announcement as to the final moments of a particular scene, such as news of the death of a general secretary, but neither the potential domestic nor the foreign audience knew what was really transpiring. All we knew was that the cast performing in this drama was small and highly select.

Now, it would seem, we are treated to a very truly public spectacle, much of it in living color on television. The cast numbers in the thousands, with the audience joining the act.

The response to this spectacle outside the Soviet Union has been varied. There are those, like Fidel Castro, who view these developments as a betrayal of the cause. Other apologists for the *ancien régime* prefer to avert their eyes or to offer some embarrassed and incomprehensible explanation for the turn of events in the motherland of socialism. At the other end of the political spectrum are those who say it is all a farce, a huge Potemkin Village designed to mislead the west, to cause it to end its vigilance against aggressive Soviet designs.

To lay the foundation for another interpretation of developments in the Soviet Union, let me take you back to the year 1903: A relatively obscure group of Russian revolutionaries holds a convention in Brussels. It styles itself as the leadership of the Russian Social Democratic party. Concerned about the scrutiny of the Belgium police, it recesses and reconvenes in London. Like other social democratic parties throughout Europe, the Russian Social Democrats are inspired by the teachings of Karl Marx. Like these other social democrats, they have internal disagreements and argue over the proper interpretations of Marxist teachings. But unlike the others, they have differences so profound that they divide the party. It is a split that will cast a shadow over the remainder of the century.

In spite of all the blood and thunder in the writings of Karl Marx and his colleague Friedrich Engels, Europe's social democrats were, by and large, a rather benign lot. Though committed to end the rule of the bourgeoisie, they had wishes to do so in keeping with the principles of social organization developed by the Enlightenment, that is, by majority vote and with respect for the rights of the individual.

But the Russian Social Democratic party leadership had a member who marched to a different drummer. Vladimir Il'ich Ulianov, whom the world came to know as Lenin, did not believe that the better world envisaged by Karl Marx could be attained if Marxists played by democratic rules. Iron discipline, the total disregard for what he referred to as bourgeois morality, the seizing and maintaining of control by force, and the imposition of dictatorial rule in both the party and the socialist-led state were his prescription for the attainment of the Marxist Utopia of a just and fair society.

Lenin's theses divided the Russian Social Democratic party in 1903 and, after the Bolshevik accession to power in Russia, the world socialist movement. It is the sharp difference in the evolution of the two wings of world socialism in the last eighty years which may shed light on developments during the late 1980s in the Soviet Union.

It was as long ago as 1908 that the term "revisionism" was coined to describe the modifications in Marxist precepts advocated by the German social democrats such as Kautsky and Bernstein. To see how far revisionism has taken the social democrats, we need only to take a look at France of the 1980s. France is, after all, governed by the Socialist party, the ideological descendants of the men and women who in 1903 were the comrades of Russia's Mensheviks.

Revisionism has meant the continual testing of doctrine and principle against experience and reality. When reality taught that nationalization of the means of production and distribution did not necessarily improve a society's productive capacity, the policy was abandoned. So, ultimately, was an identification with the teachings of Karl Marx. What remained of the original program was a commitment only to the objective to use the state to advance the general welfare of the population. This goal came to be shared with other democratic parties. Today, programmatic differences between social democrats and nonsocialist parties are over the extent of state involvement in economic management, not over fundamental principles concerning the basic relationship between the state and the individual.

The other wing of the movement, by contrast, remained frozen in time. Lenin's precepts became immutable doctrine. Their elaboration took the form of articles of faith. Leninism developed its own hierarchy, its own rituals, and committed itself to total intolerance of all other beliefs.

There are those who contend that this is not what Lenin had envisaged, that there is evidence that toward the end of his life he wanted to steer a somewhat different course, that his New Economic Policy of 1921 is evidence of his pragmatism. But Lenin was incapacitated by stroke in 1923 and died in 1924. Whether he would have modified his prescriptions is an interesting question for students of communist history, but objectively speaking it is irrelevant. It is in his name and on the basis of his theories that the Soviet Union, for decades, maintained a system of government and economic management which was not only brutally repressive but increasingly out of touch with the reality of world-wide economic and social development.

There were past efforts to break out of this iron mold. The first of these is associated with the name of Nikolai Bukharin [party theoretician, advocate of concessions to private trade and farming during the New Economic Policy, purged to death by Stalin in 1938—Ed.] and the second with Nikita Khrushchev [post-Stalin Communist party leader from 1953 until his ouster in 1964—Ed.]. Both efforts, as we know, failed. And now, I submit, we are dealing with the third attempt to align the precepts governing the politics and economics of the Soviet Union with events in the real world.

Today's gap between the stubborn convictions of the orthodox communists and the generally accepted understanding of what works and what does not in economics and politics is far greater than it was during the days of Bukharin and Khrushchev. Bukharin was a believer to the very end. So was Khrushchev, who predicted that the communist system would "bury" the capitalist. That is no longer the prevailing sentiment.

Much of the change during the late 1980s in the Soviet Union was, of course, associated with the name of Mikhail Gorbachev. And rightly so. His most significant role to date can be equated with that of the young child in the fairy tale "The Emperor's New Clothes." He came forward to say bluntly that the command system had failed. Those who knew all along that the emperor had no clothes but were afraid to say so are now speaking up. And others who had talked themselves into believing that the emperor was wearing clothes or that they were not seeing too well are now joining the chorus. (In this analogy, I have, to be sure, omitted the role of the dissidents. But the general Soviet public began to pay new attention only when the general secretary started to say what Andrei Sakharov had been saying for decades.)

As the reformers among Soviet political scientists and economists seek to break out of the Marxist-Leninist mold in which they had been encased, they resort to differing verbal formulas. But they all seem to have the same idea in mind. What most of them are fully aware of is that mere tinkering with the system will not do, that a total overhaul is required. The term which has been used to describe this commitment is "radical *perestroika*." Critics of radical *perestroika* contend that the reformers are abandoning socialism and are intent on reconstructing the Soviet Union in the image of the west. As far as one can tell, the reformers have stopped arguing the point. They have also stopped using old-time terminology; they have clearly discarded the old-time doctrine. They are looking around to see what works. With all its problems, its warts and its blemishes, the democratic west works. And that is what these reformers see and what now guides their thinking.

Leninist theory did not see any inherent good in dictatorship by a single leader or a small group or in suppression of human rights. These were all means to an end, the end being the communist workers' Paradise. Now that it has become clear that the road traveled these last seventy-two years did not lead to that end, there is clearly no justification for the means employed toward it. Thus, we see Soviet reformers aligning their views with those whose notions on government are founded on the ideas of the Enlightenment, as reflected in such documents as our own Declaration of Independence.

But these reformers are by no means home free. The Soviet population is in many respects socially conservative. The challenge to authority, the sense of uncertainty, and the increase in criminality, which are associated with the reduction in state authority, are unsettling to a great many Soviet citizens. There is also fear of a private-incentive system among those who believe that they will not be able to hold their own if the state stops guaranteeing employment for all. These supporters of the status quo form the natural base of support for those in leadership positions who do not want to surrender their power and their privileges.

And so the drama is acted out, the contest between the reformers and the stand-patters; or, to call a spade a spade, between democrats and adherents to communist orthodoxy.

Much has been accomplished during the late 1980s toward loosening the shackles of Soviet citizens. Political prisoners have been released. There is now greater freedom of expression than at any time in more than sixty years. The campaign against religion is being brought to an end. And in spring 1989 we witnessed honest-to-goodness free elections in some parts of the Soviet Union.

Regrettably, however, political reform has not yet been accompanied by economic reform of the kind that would really matter. The goal—the introduction of a market economy—is clear, but how to get there is not. Effecting the changes which make a sluggish system of production function efficiently has proved far more difficult than the advocates of *perestroika* initially believed. Yet success in improving the performance of the economy is of critical importance if the political moves toward a more open society are to be sustained.

Whether the Soviet reformers will succeed is not at all clear. What is clear is that if they do, it will bode a better future for the Soviet people, for the United States, and, given our respective roles in the world, for the rest of humanity.

Viktor Chkhikvadze

Ladies and gentlemen, distinguished friends, I should like to commence my remarks by saying how deeply gratified I am over the participation in this panel along with Elena Bonner and Academician Andrei Dmitrievich Sakharov. I have every reason to claim this honor of being by their side. Sakharov is extremely well known as an outstanding scientist, not only in our country but also by the whole scientific world. He's also very well known as a brave warrior, as a bold defender of human rights and of the rights of peoples. I happen to be a member of that very same Academy of Sciences where for many years Academician Sakharov has been working. Neither in the academy nor outside its confines is there a scientist—or was there ever any scientist—who so openly, courageously, fearlessly defended his positions in all matters, especially in the realm of human rights. That is why it is with every justification that we can call him a man of high conscience, of great righteousness and integrity, and of extreme courage. We're all aware of the great suffering he had to bear—not only he, but also his dear wife.

It is a shameful thing to admit—it is shameful for me as a lawyer to say this, but facts are facts: Those persecutions and limitations of freedoms imposed upon Elena Bonner and Andrei Sakharov were in fact implemented on the basis of laws. In saying this, I wish to stress how hypocritical many of our laws turned out to be, these laws which on the one hand proclaimed the defense of rights and freedoms, while on the other were put to use to persecute a person for a courageous struggle in the defense of human rights.

If, some seventy years after the establishment of Soviet power, I now were to write a new volume on human rights, I would entitle that book *Disappointment and Perestroika*. I have done a great deal of writing on human rights issues, but I think we all know by now that what I wrote and what my colleagues wrote in their day were the fruits of a limitless praising of Soviet democracy, of excessive praise for our legislation in the human rights field—of lavish praise—but something not reflecting realities in our country in any way whatsoever. I use the word disappointment in full awareness of what I'm saying, and I use it because, throughout all of the history of Soviet power, we did set about to limit and infringe upon human rights. In some cases to a greater extent were these rights violated; in other instances, there was less infringement and violation. But violations of human rights did continue on and on, and in fact they are still continuing.

I would also mention *perestroika* in the title as I noted, because it is precisely this setting of *perestroika*—its context—that has loosened our tongues and has opened up before us an opportunity to say openly and frankly what we really think, what we really want, in which matters we agree with our government, in which matters we differ from it. Now such a book would of course have in it a due place for the program, for the stances, for the approaches advocated and maintained by Academician Andrei Sakharov in the field of both Soviet and international human rights defense. Thank you very much.

Elena Bonner

This is the first time I come to Berkeley, and this is the first time I'm with representatives of the Institute of State and Law. It is, indeed, quite interesting from my point of view because we—with my husband—we find ourselves in a very odd situation today. It is indeed a pleasure for me to sit with and to see the people who have been saying those words for a good many years.

I will not engage in particularities of this issue. All I'm trying to say is that my colleague and my right-hand neighbor [Chkhikvadze] makes a mistake when he says that the persecution of Sakharov and some other dissidents has been realized on the basis of the Soviet law. They were realized because the state and the government apparatus would not recognize its own laws. Sakharov, let me remind you—and I'm sure many people remember it—was exiled to the city of Gorky without any trial. And the Soviet Constitution flatly states that no one can be subjected to any punishment without a fair trial. Only a trial, that is the only way. So I'm sorry, my friend, that I must remind you that this is in the Constitution.

I will not talk in particularities. Moreover, I won't be talking about human rights within the usual frame of mind which we're entertaining today; or the understanding of the ideology which we shall call the ideology of the protection of human rights and which already for decades has been a common, global thinking. No political or social activist can afford to continue to be an administrator or a politician without devoting substantial time to this issue.

The government of the Soviet Union understood it quite late, but once they understood it, they started to use the same terminology as the west did. But, until quite recently, behind these words and the terms that were used there was no substance, there were no deeds. We are living in a time when we can hope that indeed the reality of human rights will be brought about by the Soviet government and politicians who are responsible for observing human rights; and we are hoping that at this time there will be some deeds behind the words. We are quite hopeful for that.

But I would like to talk about something else. My husband and I came to the west immediately after the termination of the meeting in Moscow of the Congress of People's Deputies. It seems to me that the congress that took place in Moscow has not been given its due in the west. This Congress of Deputies was one of the most important historical moments in the life of our nation. The people, who for decades could not be involved in politics—who actually forgot how to be involved, who weren't able to handle the government—underwent total metamorphosis during the two weeks of this congress; they learned about politics, real politics. The meetings were fruitful, the results were quite optimistic; and we are witnessing right now what has been brought about in the Soviet Union.

Everything that takes place at the level of people, I believe, gives reason to look at the whole thing quite optimistically, particularly the strikes. I am not afraid that sometimes I might be called extremist by some people, but it turned out, for us and for the country as a whole, that the people in the Soviet Union are alive, not dead; that the people in our country do not always need official leadership and stewardship, and can themselves handle and do things and be leaders within their own movements.

One of the results of the People's Congress in Moscow was that the whole country witnessed hundreds of people—totally independent people, clever, well educated—who are troubled over the fate of their land, and who are suffering, but not because their salaries or some privileges are infringed upon, not at all, not for their own working place. It turned out that there are quite a few Sakharovs in our country, and the people who are called dissidents these days have grown in knowledge and in number. Everyone who is interested in the survival of the Soviet Union and wishes it would become a normal country in the world community must make a deep bow and say thank you to the people they used to call dissidents for their initiative, their unbreakable faith, and sometimes even for the sacrifice of their lives. I'm sure that the older people will raise a new generation of people who will soon be in charge of the USSR.

It is true, *perestroika* started from above, but this is just a half truth. It is true that *perestroika* produced *glasnost'* [openness], but again this is only a half truth. *Glasnost'* before *perestroika* produced the *Chronicle of Current Events* [dissident *samizdat*—underground—publication—Ed.], for instance, and various other magazines. *Glasnost'* then also pressed into use the typewriter, which can make four carbon copies. And *perestroika* itself did not give us the freedom of speech. Until now we had to take freedom of speech forcefully for ourselves.

Returning to the Congress of People's Deputies: On one side, the congress may be looked upon as an occasion for pessimism because it resulted in the demise of the illusions that people had held. It turned out that as a country we are not a conglomerate of peaceful people and nations. It turned out that we're the country which is the most environmentally, ecologically contaminated. It turned out that the population of our nation has the worst medical care and in child and infant mortality is in fifty-third place in the world. It turned out our no-fee education, especially at the lower level, the high schools, is quite authoritarian, that it suppresses the human spirit, if you will. And that the agricultural junior high schools and grade schools produce quite uneducated children. It turned out that the population of our country is the poorest in terms of housing, although officially there are no homeless people in our country. It turned out that our country, that our state, is the cruelest exploiter in the world. The ratio of salaries to GNP is low compared with that in all countries in the developed part of the world. We also have unemployment. It differs from your joblessness because our unemployed get no funds to live on once they are jobless.

One more point, a very interesting point which no country has encountered—perhaps only in Orwell's *1984* can you read anything analogous to this: It turned out that we are a country that is lacking its own history. Our nation has no history, and what to do about it no one knows, including the historians. The only conclusion we came to is to simply renounce the history being taught in schools and not to have examinations on historical subjects at all for the time being. This is the result of the development of a state that is now to cooperate in the development of human rights. This is the country I am talking about.

I believe that this collapse of illusion is very important and quite a positive factor. Finally, the entire population saw for itself, without any beautification, what actually we are, how lacking in social protections our society is, And what privileges we are running up against in our society; not just to hear of it but actually to witness it with their own eyes—who is what, who protects what—is extremely important. I wouldn't even be afraid to say that it's created a people, the people who are of a common way of thinking in certain aspects. Every day, while sitting in my car waiting for my husband to come out of the congress meetings, near the police who would not let the people walk on the Red Square, I thought back to when I was a girl, when the Seventeenth Congress [1934] took place at Stalin's time. And at that time Red Square was not guarded by police. This is the first time that Red Square was cordoned. And the delegates, the delegates who we believe are progressive, as we use the term, would be walking out into the city. People would come and approach them on the street as they walked, and they would start a conversation. There were delegates whom people loved and wanted to praise and talk to—delegates who were national heroes, not in some back country, but in the Kremlin Hall. And there were some delegates who would step out from the conference and would take off their badges, because they were afraid that people disliked them intensely. This is a fantastically symptomatic event which I witnessed myself while sitting and waiting for my husband. The country lost its illusions. I believe that a total crash has taken place. I think it's a useful and fruitful event, because the people, by means of strikes or of pressure, can force the government to carry out what they call *perestroika*, because the government is just scratching its head.

But now it's up to the west, I feel, and Berkeley in this sense is very important. *Your* illusions must be shattered. You must understand that socialism—whether you call it real or well-developed socialism—so far socialism has produced nothing as far as people are concerned, except for books, utopian books by St. Simon, Fourier. This is very important for the west to understand. Once it does, the west will understand how to help *perestroika*, how to help the Soviet Union, and what we are to do in the future. Thank you very much.

Andrei Sakharov

I am also extremely pleased about the fact that I have the opportunity to address you, even though I must say that I always have some difficulty in speaking along with and after my dear wife. She's managed to preempt virtually everything that I had intended to say. Each of us has his or her own personal experience. Each of us also has the experience of one's country behind them. Indeed, this recent congress has the enormous importance of having seen the merging into a single current, into a single monolith, of the experience of the entire country. All of the country's past seemed to come together there. This renders that congress even more significant than all of the four years, of *glasnost'*, the period when the press began to say more and more, to be increasingly more truthful, until it now covers virtually all matters except for those particularly delicate matters where we do see an iron fist coming down and clamping over its mouth. We also saw such violations of the right to speak, the right of expression, at the congress.

We dissidents, it has been said, commenced by working on a very narrow range of problems. Those problems concern a small number of people and that is why we were reproached for worrying about defending one another, this little clique which maintained its own momentum. Of course, that was not the case at all. In fact, the dissident movement in the sixties and seventies was fighting in defense of the fundamental principles necessary to democratic development. That was the main significance of our work then. In our actual activities, of course, we did struggle to defend particular individuals and their right to express their own views, their right to say things which no one but that particular individual or individuals, free of fear, rare as they might be, dared to say. And as was correctly noted by my wife, *glasnost'* grew out of a publication under the title *Chronicle of Current Events.*

But now the human rights issue is something that we must attack far more broadly. We now are able to tackle problems which we didn't even dare to contemplate earlier. And we are now thinking in terms of the entire range of problems having to do with human rights, not only of Article 19 [freedom of expression] and Article 12 [privacy of home, correspondence, protection of honor and reputation] of the Universal Declaration of Human Rights, but of all of the articles of that declaration taken together. This is particularly important in view of the fact that we now recognize all of the fallacy of Soviet propaganda. It asserted that the first things were such material things as the right to work, the right to education, the right to social justice; it claimed that these rights had been fully satisfied and responded to in the Soviet Union, so that all talk which held that the Soviet Union was a country wherein human rights were violated was false and superficial. Quite the contrary. Those particular rights were the rights most significantly violated in our country. And now we're thinking of this in an integrated way, looking at things against the background of thinking about what is going to happen and must happen in our country.

And we understand full well, as we do this thinking, that first and foremost, the question of questions is the question of power, because any changes in our country, be they economic, social, or national, run up against the fact that power in our country is in real terms held by this double-headed entity, the Party apparatus on the one hand, and the administrative-command economic apparatus. And all of this is maintained by a third, behind-the-scenes power; of course I'm talking here about the secret police, the KGB [Committee of State Security]. In another way, the army brings its force to bear as an instrument in support of the existing order.

When we gathered at the congress, at our historical museum [at the en-trance to Red Square near the congress site—Ed.], we had an enormous placard which read, "All power to the Soviets." This was an October 1917 slogan, and it was that slogan which in its new, present-day interpretation might be construed as a formulation of our demands with regard to power. It is precisely the local councils, the local soviets, the grass-roots power—power from the bottom generated by grass-roots demands—which must become the real power in our country.

This implies a renunciation of Article 6 of the Constitution of the USSR [on the one-party monopoly of the Communist party until 1990—Ed.], which sets down constitutionally what already existed prior to the 1977 Constitution: the ubiquitous and all-penetrating power of the party apparatus. This implies likewise the adoption which I, in my statement at the Congress, called a decree on power. All legislative power in the USSR must be that of the Congress of People's Deputies as the body created or shaped by elections and not as a result of maneuvers by the Party.

This further implies the doing away with the system of offices, departments, agencies, and authorities, which is probably the greatest evil in our country. Everyone is aware that we had a Ministry of Water Resources. (It's called something else now, but there it was.) This was and is a gigantic empire closed in upon itself, a huge apparatus which over a period of ten years received subsidies of some hundred fifty billion rubles. Of those monies, two percent were spent for land reclamation—in other words, for the purpose for which the organization is supposed to exist. But the rest was spent on gigantic, mindless, economically senseless, and environmentally extremely harmful "projects of the century," as they were called. And it was claimed that those projects were necessary to maintain the further existence of that self-same ministry. Tens of thousands of scientists and their assistants—I think some sixty-six thousand scientists, assistants, and technicians—were working in the scientific research establishments run by that ministry, and they were the justification for those expenditures. Nobody could get a handle on the whole thing.

Needed further is a resolution of the problem of property. Officially, the Constitution says that everything belongs to all of the people. This is a lie. In fact, property in our country, in real terms now, is owned by the very numerous and very greedy and very stupid class of rulers, the "new class," Djilas called it. Now, these changes in the structure of property ownership may well serve to help us deal with social and economic problems in our country. Officially, we have seen proclaimed the possibility of other forms of ownership. For example, leasing of land in the countryside has been limited to only one percent of total land available. This is something quite unbelievable, but it is no accident. The leasing of land, the rental of land, passes via the *kolkhoz*, the collective farm, so the *kolkhoz* is, so to speak, your landlord. It garners to itself a considerable portion of your income, the tenant's income, and what you have is a parasitic relationship to the detriment of the tenant. This is, of course, a major obstacle we have to overcome. The leasing of land and the tenure of other property keep running into obstacles raised by the existing system. And we simply have to deal with this. We have to do away with it.

A similar situation obtains with regard to industry. The independence of enterprises is a fiction as of today. The lion's share of profits—practically all profits—is sucked up by the ministries and then redistributed in ways running counter to the welfare of the economy as a whole. This is a purely bureaucratic redistribution, whereby a considerable portion simply goes to the ruling class, whereas another major portion goes to dying plants, factories on their last legs. This is a sort of resuscitation technique, a kind of iron lung. But of course, it won't work either. The same thing goes on in regard to agriculture.

Finally, an issue which we were not able to go into too deeply in the 1970s, but which has now emerged onto the foreground, is the national question. Our constitutional provisions with regard to nationality are those of an empire, the last empire on this planet, probably. That empire must be transformed into a genuinely federative or federal state, where all national and social formations will enjoy the equal rights of independent republics and independent economic rights, which enter into a union with the possibility of secession should a given republic decide that it would be advisable to secede. It is only such a federal arrangement that can take our country out of that tragic crisis of conflicts and clashes between nationalities.

We know very well how all of this happens, we know of the horror of the things going on in the Caucasus [pogroms against Armenians in Sumgait, Azerbaijan, in February 1988—Ed.]. During the congress itself, as it was going on, there arose some unbelievably tragic events in the valley of Fergana, in Uzbekistan [demonstrations in 1989 by unemployed youths, directed in part against other ethnic Moslems youths, ending in violence—Ed.] which gradually spread into other areas of the Soviet Union, including Central Asia. These events were clearly the work of provocateurs, but those provocateurs could do their work only on the basis of the colonial yoke under which the people of Uzbekistan live. The cotton culture, the yoke of cotton, has condemned the population of that republic to virtual slavery on cotton plantations. It has condemned children to spending most of the year on these plantations instead of going to school, to being poisoned by all sorts of pesticides and insecticides with the result that about two-thirds of these kids are ill with liver and other systemic diseases. This cotton culture has condemned the population to famine as well, because nothing has been left; for instance, there's practically no meat left in the country. It condemned to ecological disaster the area around the Aral Sea. At the Congress we heard the story, the tragic story, of the ecological destinies of the Aral Sea. This is a huge area which is not only in a condition of environmental disaster, but whose population is facing the threat of physical demise.

Only by bringing down the authoritarian administrative system and the Stalinist constitutional system can we put an end to all of this. And once again, I'd like to remind you of the political problems of democracy: that *perestroika* began from the top. It was a top-to-bottom affair. It couldn't have been otherwise because the course of history itself had brought the country as a whole to a total impasse. We suddenly realized that for seventy years we had been marching in the wrong direction and had approached the edge of that precipice; since no one else but the people at the top could have changed anything, it was absolutely necessary that they pick up the gauntlet, that they manifest that initiative. Fortunately, there were such people who undertook to do this. But of course this was only the beginning. The continuation of this process is possible only through the merging of initiatives from the bottom and their follow-up from the top.

This is what happened in 1988, after the adoption of certain antipopular laws which were directed against freedom of expression, freedom of the press, and freedom to hold meetings and demonstrations. These attempts at lawmaking were subsequently rejected by the great majority of voters, but they contained within them the seeds of the cruelest possible repressive actions against the people. We saw what happened, for example, in Minsk, in Byelorussia, in Krasnoiarsk, in the Crimea—and the acme of all, the events in Tbilisi [the slaughter of peaceful demonstrators by Soviet troops in Tbilisi on April 9, 1989—Ed.].

For the moment, this time bomb under the framework has been diffused and it seems we have averted for now certain even more horrendous events. The reaction in the west to the Tbilisi events was extremely weak. And it is perhaps not by accident that what happened in China happened eventually—the events of the fourth, fifth, and sixth of June in Tiananmen Square, Beijing, and in other cities in China [hundreds of peaceful demonstrators were slaughtered, thousands arrested—Ed.]. There seems to be a link between the two. If the west and the world as a whole persist in refraining from reacting in an adequate manner to events such as those that occurred in Tbilisi and subsequently in China, then we will continue to live under the threat that something similar might occur again in the Soviet Union.

There you have it. Everything is twisted into a single scheme of events. Both our country as a whole and our country's leaders face a choice: that of emerging from a state of unstable equilibrium into something better, into something else. We have only one choice; we need to radicalize *perestroika*. Assistance from the west, pressure brought to bear from the west, influence being exercised from the west to see to it that people realize that only given such a turn of events [the radicalization of *perestroika*] is cooperation with the USSR feasible, is cooperation with China workable. Otherwise, a turn backward will be a disaster for all, both for those who cleave to the right and for those who hold leftist views. But I think people are basically sensible. Thank you very much.

Pavel Litvinov

It is very difficult for me to speak on the same issues, on the same panel, after Dr. Sakharov and Elena Bonner. I cannot say something more or stronger about what's going on in the Soviet Union. Of course I am not informed on the same level and was not for the last fifteen years in the middle of what is going on in the country where I was born. I have been here for fifteen years. But because of my experience, being in this country and trying to speak up for human rights in this country, I think that I can still say something important.

I spoke up primarily—not exclusively but primarily—for people who were arrested and persecuted in different ways in the Soviet Union. Both when in the Soviet Union and when I emigrated to this country, I also had many meetings and communications and I gave many speeches about human rights in the Soviet Union; and I think I learned, to some degree, what Americans think about these issues and what kinds of misconceptions are typical in addressing those issues. Of course there are many misconceptions, some greater than others.

Today, fortunately, I feel that there is not much need for me to defend human rights in the Soviet Union from abroad in the traditional way. In the past I would get up when I got a call from the Soviet Union, or from someone who had just come from the Soviet Union, and learn that my friend, or a friend of my friends or some human rights activist, was arrested; and I would knock at the door of American newspapers, television stations, the human rights office of the State Department or a nongovernmental organization like the International League or Amnesty International. Fortunately, human rights activists in the Soviet Union today are not arrested, at least not arrested on the same level—harassed and persecuted—as they were; they're not put into mental hospitals. Even so, human rights activists in this country would still find the conditions under which today's human rights activists in the Soviet Union work intolerable and probably would call them awful and fascistic. Still, if you put it in the right perspective, the situation is much improved, and I feel that there is no need for me to work as I once did. So the question now comes: What really are the issues and what can be done; what should those people who care about human rights do and how can people cooperate? That's the theme of our discussion today: cooperation.

We have guests today, a group of Soviet lawyers and scholars from the Institute of State and Law, who represent the so-called Sector of Human Rights in that institute. We met them and we heard them, and I was pleased to hear Dr. Chkhikvadze saying how many things he did wrong, how many things he would like to change in his life; he didn't say it, but he probably could say how many untruths he once had to say in defending certain actions of the Soviet government. Of course, we didn't come here—at least I didn't come here—for a kind of self-congratulation that something good happened, or for recriminations that someone did bad things and I didn't do them or I did fewer of them or that someone wrote certain things at some time and so on. I don't think it is an issue. It might bring some satisfaction for some people, but not for me.

My eyes look to the future—what can and what should be done. Today, both Dr. Sakharov and Dr. Bonner mentioned a magazine, the *Chronicle of Current Events*. It was a publication with which I was fortunate to be associated. One of the important things which I did in my life was to be one of the people who was involved in its beginnings. This magazine consisted strictly of plain information on what happened in the Soviet Union in the area of human rights, information that was of course collected completely unofficially, through networks of equally minded people who were interested in protecting human rights. It was started in 1968, and I remember how the first issue was done in my apartment in Moscow.

Very soon after that I was arrested, but not for the magazine, because the Soviet authorities at that time didn't pay attention enough to that magazine; I was arrested for organizing a demonstration against the Soviet invasion of Czechoslovakia. But the magazine continued. It was published in *samizdat*, which means that it was typed on a typewriter—Erika, the name of East German typewriters which were popular in the Soviet Union and better than any Soviet ones—which could make four copies. Sometimes it could make even twenty copies if you used onion-skin paper. That twentieth copy you almost could not read. You would hurt your eyes. But people who are hungry, who are starving for real information on what's going on in their country, would read these twentieth copies. The *Chronicle of Current Events* was all done by volunteers. Some couldn't even type well. Some would just help someone else or make a photographic picture of each copy—nothing like Xerox-type copiers were available for the people in the Soviet Union.

Of course people who were involved in this publication sooner or later were arrested. Many of them got years in labor camps or went to mental hospitals. Some died in labor camps and in milder cases lost their awards and any possibility of promotion in their jobs. It all happened during the last twenty years, in the life of one generation. It was the start of something which today is known as *glasnost'*. Actually, *glasnost'* was the word which was very widely used among dissidents of that first generation of the 1960s.

And now I come to the point of what can be done today. People in the Soviet Union are not arrested in most cases for publications today, but they still don't have access to presses. They still find the press is under complete government and state control. You should understand that *glasnost'* is still going on in the Soviet newspapers, Soviet television, and Soviet radio, all of which are owned and controlled by the government and by the Communist party. Of course, among members of the Communist party and the government, there are many liberal-minded people who don't mind doing many good things, and the times are such that many things are done. But still, the media are not under the people's control.

I think one of the most important things which has to be done today is that people in the west, in the spirit of cooperation, have to demand that all people in the Soviet Union have access to presses. What does this mean practically? It means getting some kind of independent presses, maybe brought from here—things like Xerox machines and computers—with the help of nongovernmental organizations, human rights groups. Basically, everyone, including nongovernmental organizations and the people, have to demand the Soviet government to permit independent and cooperative publishing houses.

Our guests from the Soviet Institute of State and Law are people who now want to do good things for human rights. But they are state employees, and that makes a difference between them and American human rights lawyers. American human rights lawyers or researchers can work for the government or can work for nongovernment organizations like Amnesty International or the League for Human Rights or the Lawyers Committee for the Defense of Human Rights, or any kind of group. They can be interested in defending the rights of these or those minorities, or everybody else, or be affiliated with the United Nations, or anything.

I would finish by addressing my remarks particularly to our Soviet guests who are government employees and who are now, in the spirit of what is possible to be done in the Soviet Union today, writing about laws, about future projects, the changes in the Soviet legal system: You have to take the next step. You have to open to the people who have been monitoring human rights in the Soviet Union for all these years. You have to use their experience and their information and try to incorporate their sources and information in your work.

Although I could say many more things which I believe important, I will finish by saying one thing, which was always symbolized for us by one of the founders of the human rights movement—a great friend of mine and friend of the Sakharovs— Larisa Bogaraz: In our human rights movement there were always many women. We never felt at that time, at least not in the beginning of the movement, that women's issues were important. Women and men worked together. When I came to this country, I realized how important women's issues are, and I'm very glad to be reminded about that. But in the Soviet Union, the idea of women's issues and women's rights have just begun to develop. And I think it's important, in that spirit of cooperation, to remind the Soviet Union how important women's issues are. Thank you.

4

Russia Turned Upside Down

Peter Juviler

There can be no doubt that the moment when political rights are granted to a people who have till then been deprived of them is a time of crisis, a crisis that is necessary but always dangerous.

(Alexis de Tocqueville, *Democracy in America*)[1]

The Gorbachev regime turned its back on five centuries of almost continuous tsarist Russian and communist absolutism. During the years 1985 to 1987 it turned to a course of democratization and universal human rights as prerequisites for its goal of economic revitalization. But economic reform faltered. In a climate of openness, this undermined Communist party rule and the Union which had existed since 1922. On December 25, 1991, Gorbachev resigned as president of the USSR. The white, blue, and red tricolor flag of the Russian republic replaced the hammer and sickle that had flown over the Kremlin. The Soviet Union was no more.

Will progress in human rights under *perestroika* carry on? It will not be impossible, but it will not be easy.

Communist absolutism held society accountable to the state rather than the state accountable to society, as amply affirmed by a myriad sources, from the late Andrei Sakharov, physicist and human rights defender, to the USSR Constitution, whereby rights were conditional on the state interests.[2] The governing power elite of communism, the *nomenklatura*, ruled *through* as it defined law, not *under* law. Might made rights. As this system began yielding to democracy *under* law, a new principle came into play: rights make might. Communism's demise provides the opportunity for the triumph of that principle. The problem lies with communism's difficult legacy of economic collapse, inexperience with democracy, and interethnic conflict.

For some, this legacy is insurmountable; the former USSR, they say, remains a captive of its despotic past. Others have suggested that the processes of modernization may liberate societies from absolutism; that modernization makes unacceptable the economic and human costs of absolutist rigidity and repression.[3]

During the difficult Soviet transitional struggle between tradition and democratic modernity, politics and lawmaking became embroiled in a battle over the future of a basic and interdependent set of rights—political, economic, and ethnic.[4] The triple task of political, economic and multinational development strained the new democracy. In 1990, the president of similarly challenged Yugoslavia summed it up: "In situations of political and economic instability and national bigotry, democracy falls as the first victim."[5] In sum, new democracy opens the path to human rights while some of the conflicts it unleashes endanger both human rights and democracy itself.[6]

We shall look for lessons and models in Russia's earlier experiment with democratization and individual rights under an absolutism that was brought down by its own rigidity. Our discussion then turns to the devastating impact of communism on human rights. Its rigidities and inadequacies in the face of the need to modernize leave deep problems for any regimes to follow. Finally, we cover the changes in political, economic, and nationality rights. We shall see how *perestroika* altered thinking on human rights and unleashed a groundswell of initiatives from below and outside the belated and hesitant responses of the former Union center. The decentralization and breakdown of the old Soviet Union diffused the responsibility for violating and protecting human rights, which in turn complicated their monitoring and advocacy just as new local dictatorships and ethnic discord were producing new repression, new victims, and new prisoners within the republics and across their borders.

The Fatal Rigidity of Absolutism

> To the Emperor of all the Russias belongs the supreme autocratic power. To obey his commands not merely from fear but according to the dictates of one's conscience is ordained by God himself.
>
> (Fundamental Laws of Russia, Article 4)[7]

> Give us sacred liberty.
>
> (Alexander Pushkin, "The Decembrists")

Russia's despotic past complicates but does not deny the quest for rule of law based on human rights. Masses of people eventually echoed Pushkin's call for "sacred liberty" when tsarist absolutism failed on all fronts: carrying out land reform, girding for war, and feeding and housing the burgeoning city population. Perhaps the larger lesson is that despotism carries within it the seeds of its own destruction in its rigidity; in its obsession with military power, defense, and expansion, for the sake of which it attempts to hold society in permanent mobilization and disregards a whole complex of societal interests and claims to national identity and culture; and in its incompatibility with needed yet politically subversive liberal reforms.

Russia suffered an identity crisis when Peter the Great (1689–1725) opened his "window on the west" with the building of St. Petersburg, the imperial capital from 1703 to 1918 (renamed Leningrad from 1924 to 1991). Through that window Peter imported western ways of war, science, administration, and dress, forcing them on a reluctant populace. If it was to be a great power, Russia needed Peter the Great's "window on the west," yet the winds of change brought fatal chills. As the Marquis de Custine concluded a century later, "The political system of Russia could not survive twenty years' free communication with the rest of Europe."[8]

Tsarism's rigid monopoly of power and its justified fear of openness put Russia ever further behind the west in modernizing the economic and political bases of power. This has happened once again with communism.

Until 1905, the tsar and his delegates had all the rights, the people all the obligations and precious few incentives. To support war, the government exacted taxes and service. Serfdom had bound peasants to village communes which fed the nobility and supplied money and soldiers for the tsars' campaigns. Industry, largely a state enterprise, clothed and armed and later moved the troops.

In tsarist Russia's economy, property rights and private enterprise played relatively limited parts, in comparison with their roles within the private capitalism of the west. Even after the emancipation of the serfs in 1861, when private capital burgeoned with rapid railroad-building, all went into state hands. "What the Bolsheviks took over in 1917," wrote Bertram Wolfe, "even before they had nationalized a single industry on their own, was the largest state economic machine in the world."[9] All in all, the empire was, as Nicholas I conceded, "too colossal for one man."[10]

Michael Karpovich has pointed to the striking contradiction inherent to Russian absolutism. The tsars wanted to import western techniques to increase national military power and cohesion. Inevitably, along with the importation of these techniques came political ideas that subverted the very order which the tsars sought to protect.[11] Absolutism paid the price of greater subversion when it relaxed its controls and the price of greater stagnation when it asserted them. Torn between the realization of the need for constitutional reform and the fear of it, tsars ultimately yielded to fear.[12] Nicholas I (1825–1855) had the distinction of producing Russia's first psychiatric patient of conscience, Peter Chaadaev. Chaadaev deplored Russia's intellectual isolation. He described Russian culture and religion as inferior to the west's. Nicholas I had Chaadaev declared insane and put under police supervision. For a year Chaadaev had to undergo daily visits by a physician and a policeman.[13]

In 1855, the Russian defeat by the allied European powers in the Crimean War showed up the weaknesses of the tsarist system and the necessity for change. The reign of Alexander II (1855–1881) brought the emancipation of the serfs in 1861 and reforms in local government, the courts, and the military in 1864. Riasanovsky considers that the judicial reform "proved to be the most successful of the 'great reforms.' Almost overnight it transformed the Russian judiciary from one of the worst to one of the best."[14]

Alexander II was about to approve the first representative consultative body when he was assassinated by the People's Will (Narodnaia volia) revolutionary organization. The People's Will terrorists typified many among the revolutionary intelligentsia—in their dedication, their intolerance, their elitism and concomitant belief that the ends justify the means, and their disdain for legal reform aimed at individual rights and freedoms.[15] They later served as ethical models for Lenin and his Bolshevik supporters.[16]

Absolutism and a modernizing society went onto a collision course under the reactionary Alexander III (1881–94) and Nicholas II (1894–1917). Russia's defeat in the Russo-Japanese War (1904–1905) triggered revolution and concessions to civil liberties which appeared in the manifesto of October 17, 1905, and led to the formulation of the Constitution of 1906 which established the State Duma. This national assembly had power too limited to shape reform or curb abuses and an impressive but unfulfilled bill of rights. By then the tsarist reforms, the excellent training of its legal functionaries, and the emergence of a legal profession of high quality made the end of absolutism and guarantees of individual rights a possibility.[17]

Rights without Democracy

> To avoid the possibility of administrative abuse, it is necessary to establish and maintain the principle of inviolability of person and home. No one should be subjected to search or restriction in his movements except by order of a court, independent in its authority. To achieve the above ends, it is necessary to provide for. . . civil and criminal prosecution of officials who violate the law.
>
> In order to make possible the complete development of the spiritual resources of the people, the full expression of public needs and the free expression of public opinion, the following are indispensable: freedom of conscience and religion, freedom of speech and press, freedom of assembly and association.
>
> All citizens of the Russian Empire should have equal personal (civil and political) rights.
>
> (Theses of the National Zemstvo [local government]
> Congress, November 1904)[18]

"In the Russian tradition," said U.S. Attorney General Richard Thornburgh, "law has always been the instrument of ruling elites."[19] But turn-of-the-century reform-minded members of Russia's ruling elites were influenced by the movements for individual rights. Segments of Russian imperial society, including high administrators, were aware of the meaning and advantages of constitutionalism and individual rights.[20]

By the early twentieth century, absolutism was on the wane, its successors waiting in the wings.[21] Some opponents of autocracy anticipated the thinking of human rights defenders well before Gorbachev; their programs such as the *zemstvo* theses above anticipated the legal reform program which began to unfold in the USSR in the late 1980s. Despite "the unfavorable political environment," recent research shows that "concern for civil rights was rather more apparent than historians have been inclined to believe."[22]

Imperial Russia's participation in World War I from 1914 to 1917 brought defeats at the front and hunger at home which finished the monarchy. Nicholas II abdicated in March 1917, after a week of revolutionary disturbances in Petrograd (as St. Petersburg was patriotically renamed in 1914). Officially, authority lay with the Provisional Government, which has been formed out of a committee set up by the dissolved Duma. While competing for power with the obstreperous Petrograd Soviet (the council of workers' and soldiers' deputies), the Provisional Government began legal reforms from above.

Five processes pushed in different directions: legal reform, remnants of absolutism, democratization, nationalist separatism, economic discontent including land hunger, and the continuing war on the side of the Allies (all but land hunger and war dogged reform again in the early 1990s). Amidst growing chaos, the government began to pull fragmented interests together and to inch toward democracy. From below, the soviets and other grass-roots organizations clamored for speedier land reform; and after Lenin's return to Petrograd in April 1917, the Bolsheviks demanded an end to the war and the overthrow of the Provisional Government.[23]

Belatedly, after decades of tsarist "Russification,"[24] nationality issues began to be resolved by legal reforms aimed at ending discrimination which had been especially serious against the Jews. Forced Russification stopped, though not the different nationalities' assertions of self-determination where they had been either loosely incorporated (Finland) or bound in closely and intolerably (the other western marchlands and the Caucasus). But, fatally, the government hung on in the war and moved only slowly toward arrangements for elections. It postponed the land question until the elected Constituent Assembly would meet.

Perhaps unwisely for its own interest, the Provisional Government abolished censorship, the *okhrana* (political police), and the *gendarmerie* (public security force). It replaced the old police with a state militia shorn of such repressive powers as extrajudicial arrest and administrative exile. Lenin had good reason in April 1917 to call Russia "the freest of all belligerent countries in the world."[25]

The Provisional Government eliminated special political courts, released political prisoners, ended capital punishment (reintroduced at the front in July), ended official discrimination against non-Christians and women in the legal profession, and restored lost features of the 1864 judicial and local government reforms for the sake of more impartial and accessible justice and local control.[26] During *perestroika*, Soviet reformers finally began to seek inspiration from the distinguished liberal jurisprudence and reformism of Russia's past. "Legal nihilism," says legal journalist Arkadii Vaksberg, "also springs from our lack of memory. Today we are starting with a blank slate when we argue whether or not a jury system is democratic, although this question was resolved in our country more than a hundred years ago!"[27] After seven ensuing decades of legal nihilism under the communists, it may take seven more to rebuild a profession to a quality comparable to that which was emerging during the interval of freedom without democracy under the Provisional Government.

Amid growing public alienation under that government, the Bolshevik promises of "peace, bread, land and freedom" appealed to increasing numbers of workers and peasants.[28] The Bolsheviks won over only a minority of support in the country at large: nevertheless, they used their popularity in the soviets and among soldiers and the workers' militia in the capital to take over Petrograd in an armed coup, while the former prime minister, Alexander Kerenskii, fled into exile.

In the Second All-Russian Congress of Soviets, the assembly of representatives from the local and hitherto unofficial soviets, the Bolsheviks had a majority. The Congress appointed a group of Bolsheviks headed by Lenin to be the Council of People's Commissars, Russia's "temporary government" until the convocation of the Constituent Assembly.[29] For the next seventy-three years this "temporary" communist government imposed its absolutist vision of individual rights in the service of the cause rather than individuals and their civil society.

Bolshevism, Scientific and Utopian

In a Democracy, the real rulers are the dexterous manipulators of votes. . . . The history of mankind bears witness that the most necessary and fruitful reforms—the most durable measures—emanated from the supreme will of statesmen, or from a minority enlightened by lofty ideas and deep knowledge, and that, on the contrary, the extension of the representative principle is accompanied by the abasement of political ideas.
(Konstantin Pobedonostsev, Procurator of the Holy Synod [Civilian Head of the Orthodox Church] and Adviser to the Tsar, 1898)[30]

It is natural for a liberal to speak of "democracy" in general; but a Marxist will never forget to ask: "for what class?". . . Take the bourgeois parliament. Can it be that the learned Kautsky [German Marxist] has never heard that the *more highly* democracy is developed, the *more* the bourgeois parliament is subjected by the stock exchange and the bankers?   (V.I. Lenin, 1918)[31]

Lenin did not have to look far for his antidemocratism, his distrust of a civil society—a society at once autonomous and politically empowered. It had prevailed both in the tsarist regime and among many of its opponents before 1905. For the philosopher Nicholas Berdyaev, whose works are once again widely read in Russia, communist messianic absolutism was but a "transformation of Russian messianism" and autocracy and in tune with Russian tradition, whereas liberalism was not. For him, the Bolshevik victory confirmed that "liberal ideas, ideas of right as well as ideas of social reform, appeared, in Russia, to be utopian. Bolshevism . . . showed itself to be much less utopian and much more realist."[32]

Berdyaev cites the war as a factor in the Bolshevik triumph. Its continuation with the support of the Bolsheviks' foes—the liberal Kadet (constitutional democratic) party and the moderate socialist Mensheviks and the Socialist Revolutionary party—opened the way to the Bolshevik coup. The non-Bolshevik parties would almost certainly have taken over were it not for the Bolshevik coup—the "October Revolution." The Bolsheviks won only twenty-four percent of the votes in the November elections which they permitted to be held for the Constituent Assembly, which they then forcibly dissolved.[33] Most of the rest went to candidates who stood for parliamentary democracy and individual rights.[34]

The costly utopianism of Lenin and the other communists consisted in believing, as Dr. Lukasheva describes, that one can and should reach the city of the sun through the valley of the shadow of death—through terror and the stifling of democratic freedoms and all spontaneous political life.[35]

Lenin recognized and learned something from his mistakes such as the forcible expropriations of peasant grain and the dispossession of richer peasants. He launched the economic concessions to private farming and commerce which became known as NEP, the New Economic Policy. But he never relented on the vanguard monopoly role of his party.

The first Soviet constitution, the 1918 Constitution of the RSFSR (Russian Soviet Federated Socialist Republic), listed rights of conscience, expression, assembly and association, the obligation to work, rights to education, equality under the law, and the right to asylum. But these were no "human rights." Electoral rights favored cities over villages (working class over peasants). The constitution disenfranchised "members of exploiting classes." Article 23 laid down the seventy-year Soviet principle of derivative rights, rights serving the cause as the government defines it:

> Article 23. Guided by the interests of the working class as a whole, the Russian Socialist Federated Soviet Republic shall deprive individuals and groups of rights used to the detriment of interests of the socialist revolution.[36]

The 1924 Constitution for the new Union of Soviet Socialist Republics which was formed on December 30, 1922, skipped a bill of rights altogether, leaving that to the constitutions of the union republics. The "Stalin Constitution" of 1936 ended class disabilities (the old classes and their rights essentially having been wiped out but for the bureaucracy). Chapter X restored a bill of rights again qualified by service to the cause and reference to the Communist party's vanguard role.[37]

In 1917 and 1918 and again in 1936, the Soviet government legislated on the side of social rights, giving formal equality and emancipation to women in the family and the economy. But these ideals of a new and humane system fell victim to the harsh times of dire scarcities. Bolshevism's "legal nihilism" and its disdain for "bourgeois legality" stripped the growing court system of the legal safeguards that had given citizens procedural rights against it.[38]

As for nationality rights, "proletarian internationalism" was to supersede narrow "bourgeois nationalism" and chauvinism, as socialist equality would erase their root causes. Faced with disaffected nationalities, Lenin favored autonomy for all national minorities, taking a much less centrist line than did Stalin, the People's Commissar for Nationalities. But under Lenin, the Soviet government reincorporated by force, where it could, the border regions of the Caucasus, the Ukraine, and Central Asia. Stalin, the overseer of this episode of "proletarian internationalism," reduced nationality self-determination to the shell of culture: "national in form, socialist in content."[39]

Totalitarianism with a Changing Face

There are no fortresses Bolsheviks cannot storm.

(Joseph Stalin)[40]

The higher the historical goal we set ourselves . . . and the greater our impatience to land in the society of endless happiness and endless progress, the lower the standards of legality fell and the fewer the rights and material comforts remained for those who were pulling the barge of progress.

(Aleksandr Tsipko)[41]

Might made right under Stalin more than ever before in Russia. Stalin rested his power on other bases than force alone. He appealed to patriotism and to the ambitious young upwardly mobile soviets. His record of social and economic rights seems impressive at first glance. He ended unemployment, sent a nation to school, opened up professional opportunities for millions of the poor and less educated. He even inspired a genuine mass movement of patriots and beneficiaries devoted to building "socialism in one country."

On the other hand, Stalin used repressive force to enserf the peasantry through collectivization at the cost of nearly ruining agriculture and millions of lost lives; his mass purges claimed millions more victims. Masses of the "employed" worked as virtual serfs on collective and state farms or as slaves in labor camps. Stratification and privilege increased. Witness the five grades of dining rooms at Magnitogorsk, the giant steel-making complex in the Urals, from the plush formal rooms for VIPs to canteens serving bread and thin gruel to convict laborers. The reintroduction of internal passports completed the enserfment of the whole country.[42]

Women suffered setbacks from the equality proclaimed in the Constitution of 1936. Between that year and 1944, Stalin elaborated a campaign to stimulate the birth rate and promoted the legal family as the foundation of the state. This brought a ban on abortions, made divorce difficult, and restored the notion of illegitimacy but without any rights of maternal claims against or legal recognition of the father in cases of extramarital births.[43] Women's employment plus the abortion ban, coupled with the need for women to replace conscripted men in the work force during World War II, increased women's double burden of work and motherhood and caused many to resort to the risks of illegal abortions.[44]

In 1948 Stalin began a purge of Jewish intellectuals and professionals. Apparently, he was planning the deportation of Jews when death, mercifully, took him on March 5, 1953.

Two years of jockeying for power between Politburo members Georgii Malenkov and Nikita Khrushchev from 1953 to 1955 brought a period of de-Stalinization, dubbed the thaw after Ilya Ehrenburg's novel by that title. Terror abated; police chief Lavrentii Beria and his circle were executed and their summary purging procedures were eliminated under an unpublished edict in September 1953. Khrushchev emerged as the Soviet leader by 1955.

Khrushchev's human rights record improved on Stalin's. He opened up expression and contacts with the outside world. He initiated mass rehabilitations of Stalin's victims, dead and living. Khrushchev's dismantling of special procedures, his condemnation of terror, his attack on Stalin, his rehabilitations, and his limited *glasnost'* all helped prepare the way for *perestroika* twenty years later. Gorbachev's recognition, on November 2, 1987, of Khrushchev's contribution to de-Stalinization ended twenty-three years of Khrushchev being regarded as a "hare-brained schemer" and a nonperson in Soviet history.[45]

On the other hand, Khrushchev left the GULAG camp system in operation—smaller than it had been but still grim.[46] He also preserved the Communist party's power monopoly and the 1936 Constitution with its conditional rights. He intensified religious repression, and although the repression of dissidence abated it did not disappear. Further, the trials for "economic crimes" and the retroactive death penalty for them had anti-Semitic overtones.

Khrushchev's record in social-economic rights was mixed as well. He did restore women's freedom of reproductive choice in 1955; but although he permitted debate on Stalin's antifeminist family legislation, he held up its reform. His efforts at egalitarianism in access to education succeeded in further politicizing colleges at the expense of quality. His secondary-school labor training and his inroads into what was left of peasant and urban private property smacked of impetuous social engineering, hurt the economy, and eroded what little was left of any potential material basis for autonomy from the government.

Brezhnev unseated Khrushchev in 1964. What he called "mature socialism," Gorbachev later preferred to call "stagnation," owing to the economic decline associated with Brezhnev's rule. Brezhnev brought more tolerance of corruption and less of dissent. Despite its fine language on human rights, his 1977 Constitution placed more conditions than ever on civil rights.[47] The KGB and the courts under Brezhnev sent a generation of dissident writers, human rights activists, nationalists, religious dissenters, and advocates of free trade unions to jail or psychiatric hospital or exile.

Women's rights, however, fared better under Brezhnev. A reform that became effective on January 1, 1966, eased divorce procedures and increased protection for pregnant divorcees. The 1968 Fundamentals of Family Law partially restored the recognition of extramarital paternity and of certain suits for paternal support. Yet in 1980, the KGB disbanded the small first feminist group in Leningrad.[48] Brezhnev undid some of Khrushchev's damage to peasant private-plot farming but left the collectivized sector intact. Pollution became an open secret; its threat to health became apparent from published statistics on mortality rates before a veil of secrecy fell over them once again.[49]

Brezhnev's successor, Yurii Andropov, began an economic *glasnost'* on the subject of the faltering economy during his brief term of leadership from November 1982 to February 1984. No supporter of general *glasnost* , however, Andropov might have been called the Deng Xiaoping of the USSR if he had had more time in office. The even frailer Konstantin Chernenko held on for thirteen months. His death opened the way at last for the leader who, intentionally or not, turned Russia upside down and—unintentionally—brought on the breakup of the very country he had sought to restore to the front ranks of the great powers.

The Communist Concept of Human Rights

Every Soviet leader made a distinctive impact on citizens' rights. But over the course of seventy-two years all of them kept to a set of basic principles regarding those rights. These serve us as a measure of the great changes taking place in the 1990s. The communist principles of rights held that:

1. *Rights are class entitlements, not universal claims of all people*; they are conditional on their service to the interests of a dominant class as defined in the USSR by the CPSU and the government it controls.

2. *The vanguard party should have a monopoly of leadership and truth under socialist democracy, a system more just and more protective of working people's rights than is a multiparty bourgeois parliamentary democracy.* Parliamentary democracy always serves some hidden interests, so why not replace "bourgeois democracy," which serves the exploiters, with socialist democracy, which serves the working people?

3. *Political rights to freedom and security must protect a mobilized and unified society, not an autonomous, pluralized civil society.* The spontaneity of civil society has been an alien and disturbing concept.

4. *Collective economic and social rights have priority over private economic rights and public political ones.*

5. *Nationality rights must reflect proletarian and socialist internationalism rather than "bourgeois nationalism" and narrow ethnic-group interests.*

6. *The Communist interpretation of rights will triumph worldwide over the "bourgeois liberal" interpretation of universal human rights.* Its triumph will bring the first and only genuine universalism.

Democracy: Breakthrough or Breakdown?

In place of totalitarian power, we have a vacuum of power.

(Mikhail Gorbachev)[50]

Gorbachev entered the office of CPSU General Secretary (then the leadership post) on March 11, 1985. He faced a grim "crisis of effectiveness" of the system. Externally expansionist, the USSR had been stagnating internally under its bureaucratic centrist rule.[51] He made many initial mistakes, including the demoralizing and unpopular antialcoholism campaign and the long postponement of real economic and nationality reform.

As he combated stagnation, Gorbachev moved step by increasingly reluctant step toward the end of communist absolutism. Before turning to the meaning of this for human rights, we should review the communist conception of them. New thinking on human rights since 1987 by legal theorists and the Gorbachev leadership laid the foundation for the revolution of democratization.[52] Out went several of the communist principles of human rights which had justified such repression in the past. The new thinking, as discussed more fully in Elena Lukasheva's chapters:

• conceded that international norms of human rights had *not* been observed in the USSR and should be, under real guarantees of the rule of law and democratic accountability;[53]

• rejected the principle of class-oriented rights in favor of universal human rights and affirmed that under the new goal, "the law-governed state," the protection of individual rights are to be not the means but the end of government;

• repudiated, by 1990, the principles of the CPSU's political monopoly and Lenin's teaching on its vanguard role in a mobilized society;[54]

• rejected the priority of economic over political rights and affirmed their interdependence, thereby agreeing with Henry Shue (see chapter 21);

• slowly and reluctantly abandoned the subordination of ethnic-group self-determination to "socialist internationalism";

• abandoned the principle of the international competition of social systems and clashing concepts of human rights (see also chapter 8).

Except for some areas still living in the past, the populace expressed their rejection of old thinking and of communism by restoring precommunist place names and toppling statues of Lenin and other Bolsheviks. All three standards for democracy—participation, access, and control—set by Article 21 of the Universal Declaration of Human Rights (UDHR) began the long journey toward realization in the former USSR.

Part 1 of Article 21 of the UDHR reads: "Everyone has the right to take part in the government of his country, directly or through chosen representatives." All the nondemocratic elements of the communist approach to citizens' rights which negated Article 21–1 of the UDHR had changed significantly by the 1990s. These changes brought the apparent irreversible end of communist absolutism.[55] But difficulties for democracy loomed, first in the central government's loss of authority, its dissolution, and its replacement on September 5, 1991, by a weak Supreme Soviet, president, and State Council; and, second, in the tendency to dictatorship in some former republics of the southern tier and to executive dominance and ethnic conflict in virtually all of them.

Article 21 continues: "Everyone has the right of equal access to public service in his country." Progress in this measure was evident in the partial opening up of government posts to noncommunist, non-*nomenklatura* candidates. Their political inexperience, however, prompted dependence on the services of bureaucrats of the old *nomenklatura*. In parliament and local soviets sit conservatives of the old power group; a new political class of moderate and radical reformers who have never before served in democratically elected or executive posts but are now city mayors, members of high executive councils, and deputies to local and central legislatures; and persons of various professions who were once political prisoners or exiles because of their dissident views—such as the late Andrei Sakharov, USSR People's Deputy from 1989 until his death, and Sergei Kovalev, deputy of the Russian Republic Supreme Soviet and chairman of its Human Rights Committee.

Article 21 concludes: "The will of the people shall be the basis of the authority of government; this shall be expressed in periodic and genuine elections which shall be by secret vote or by equivalent free voting procedures." Article 21–3 sets the hardest conditions of all for democracy: government by consent, elected in genuinely free, competitive elections.

Stage one of democratization—still within the framework of the one-party socialist system—brought "socialist pluralism," the freedom for diverse views, inaugurated by then-General Secretary Gorbachev's disclaimer to a monopoly on truth.[56]

The 1989 elections under the system of socialist pluralism favored conservatives. Although many CPSU officials were defeated, the elections were not equal; some local party committees headed off competition, and one third of the deputies, seven hundred fifty of them, were chosen not by direct election but from within officially recognized, old-line social organizations such as the CPSU (a hundred deputies, including Gorbachev), the youth organization Komsomol, and the official trade unions. In response, the Academy of Science rebelled and sent liberal delegates, including Andrei Sakharov.

The president was given extensive paper powers in March 1990 and later that year, but he never was directly elected, either to his first office as president of the

Supreme Soviet, to which he was elected by the Congress, or to his second office as president of the USSR.

Socialist pluralism changed to infant multiparty pluralism in 1990. President Gorbachev assented to this in February. In March 1990, at the same time the USSR Congress elected him to the new post of president, it voted to replace Article 6 of the USSR Constitution, which legalized Communist party absolutism through monopoly power as the "leading and guiding force of Soviet society," with a new article legalizing the de facto existing multiparty system.

In principle, absolutism's dismantling now was complete. The rulers' monopoly of both power and truth had ended. The country had gone legally from socialist pluralism to pluralized democracy. But as Vitalii Korotich has said, it is easier to organize demonstrations than political parties. Absent effective presidential authority and the means of aggregating the "people's will," there would be a "vacuum of power."

The shutters had opened onto the public square where determined demonstrators —in some places, violent mobs—replaced yesteryear's courageous little knots of dissidents and the obedient marching masses. The society had become "civil" to the extent that it had become autonomous and politically active. It remained uncivil to the extent that it carried on the absolutist legacy of intolerance or pent-up frustration. Editors of *Soviet Justice* feared that the creative "stirring of the masses" had made it "impossible to tame the violent disturbance of spontaneity," which "will triumph over reason. Then the energy of the millions may be differently channeled and be transformed into a blind, terrible, destructive force."[57]

On the other hand, spontaneity actually may be the very soul of reason and defender of democracy, as was demonstrated during the coup attempt and failure of the State Committee on the State of Emergency (the coup committee of August 19 to 21, 1991).

Absolutism's end brought two great changes: large gains for human rights in politics and laws, and loss of the authority of those laws as well as the government that had made them. Power and the decisive forces for human rights shifted to the former Union republics and their internal subdivisions. But after the August coup as before it, much of former Soviet society teetered "between democracy and anarchism,"[58] a situation noted by Elena Lukasheva in the next chapter.

Political Rights of the Civil Society

The end of Soviet communist absolutism almost eliminated such long-standing issues in USSR-western relations as political trials, political prisoners, and limits on emigration.[59] After the collapse of the Union, the responsibility for political imprisonment fell completely on individual successor states. Issues of psychiatric abuse and prison reform also shifted to the republics. The KGB had retained great power[60] but, already subject to public criticism, even exposure,[61] it was decentralized and shorn of its armed troops after the August coup. By then, some (mainly dead) victims of repression had been rehabilitated.

As a result of the battle for rights to freedom of expression and information which was waged inside and outside parliament from 1989 to 1990 by a coalition of former dissidents, reform lawyers, and deputies, criminalization of expression was narrowed to the advocation of violent overthrow, pornography, propaganda of war, incitement to ethnic hatred, and the revelation of state secrets.[62]

The 1990 press and media law recognizing independent publication was formalized through the registration of periodicals. Gorbachev tried to bring back censorship—in fact, succeeded for a while in radio and television—in the face of media criticism over the armed takeovers, with fatalities, of various facilities in Vilnius, Lithuania, and Riga, Latvia, in January 1991.[63] But after the August 1991 coup, Russian broadcasting became among the most outspoken anywhere.

Growing religious freedom received formal support in a 1990 law on the freedom of conscience. It endorsed the hitherto criminal activity of organized religious instruction but left unresolved issues of church ownership (as between, say, the Orthodox church in the Ukraine and the Uniate [Eastern-rite Catholic] church whose buildings it took over when Stalin outlawed the Uniates in 1946).

A law on associations continued the limitations on purpose (the bans against goals of violent overthrow, inciting racial hatred, disseminating pornography or propaganda of war, etc.) and, like the other two laws, contained requirements of registration with local authorities, although refusals could be appealed in court. Such new laws on rights became subject to a range of interpretations in the successor states, whose legislations on civil liberties are far from uniform or complete, and whose new constitutions would take time to develop.

Gorbachev's liberalism had other limits, which were connected to his sensitivity to criticism. After the first mass protest against the government on May Day, 1990, he pushed through a decree providing punishment of up to six years' confinement for "public insults or slander of the President."[64] The law opened the way for some prosecutions and provided a bad example for any local tyrants in the republics.

The *possibility* of freely assembling and demonstrating had gone from zero to wide tolerance by the 1990s, but USSR law allowed authorities to deny permission to assemble or demonstrate without appeal, a useful option for conservative local rulers. A consequence of *glasnost'* and activism, coupled with discontent, had been growing unrest. Repressive governmental responses to demonstrations occurred regularly, without any public protest from Gorbachev, from almost the start of *perestroika*.

Rights of personal security are the most complex and intractable sphere of political rights. They rely on the active, professional cooperation of law enforcement and justice officials in protecting people's rights in prison (where conditions remain in violation of human rights throughout much of the former USSR).[65] The seriously defective law and practice of the former Soviet criminal process still belies the formal rights to be presumed innocent until proven guilty, to an effective defense,[66] to impartial justice by independent judges, and to privacy and freedom of movement.

Optimists about the rule of law pin their hopes on the first signs of progress toward it. They assume the existence of a relatively unified lgal profession with a "strong inclination to put these reforms into practice." They also tend not to look beneath the surface of the laws, at the directives and practices which vitiate them.[67] The legal profession contains some brilliant and dedicated individual reformers and trial attorneys. But they are stretched thin and lack a strong professional bar association. I join with the more cautious observers, Russian legal scholars among them, who note the legal profession's divisions of interest, their limited status and resources, inadequate training, and precarious judicial independence.[68] The rule of law is still far off.

For the full realization of the 1991 USSR Declaration on Rights and Freedoms of the Individual (the last act of the USSR Congress of People's Deputies on September 5, 1991), constitutional courts will be an essential part of any guarantees of human rights. A constitutional court should provide the individual and private groups with a remedy for violation of constitutional rights, even to the point of voiding legislation.[69]

The Constitutional Review Committee (CRC), a fourth branch of the former Soviet government, was set up in 1989 to monitor the constitutionality of governmental acts (laws and other legislative acts) and acts of public organizations, and their compliance with international human rights norms.[70] CRC's chair, S.S. Alekseev, characterized it to the old USSR Supreme Soviet on August 26, 1991, as a "watered down constitutional court without any real powers" which should be replaced by a real constitutional court. One is beginning to operate in Russia. At the Union level this may be a long way off. Central government had little enough legitimacy before the August putsch, and in Bonner's words, "no legitimate authority" after it.[71] This leaves urgent need for constitutional courts in each successor republic and some sort of international mechanism, as Elena Lukasheva suggests in chapter 5, for protecting human rights, including economic rights.

Economic Rights and the Freedom of Choice

> A person both hungry and free is a worse combination than a person hungry and unfree. Previously there was no such combination. In the first place, we werenot hungry. In the second place, we were not free. Now we have them both.
>
> (Pavel Bunich)[73]

On May Day, 1964, five months before Khrushchev's party comrades ousted him as First Secretary, this writer crossed Palace Square, Leningrad, with the other marchers. They cheered when they heard the names of their organizations called out from the reviewing stand: "Long live the Mikoian Fish Combine!"

"Long live the Communist Youth League!" But after the cry "Long live communism!" complete silence reigned save for the shuffle of thousands of feet. Communism was dead for the marchers, some told this writer then, because it had not delivered on Khrushchev's bright promises to catch up with and overtake the west in living standards.

There followed an era of false security and minimal comfort under Brezhnev, secured by foreign food purchases and the cannibalization of the Soviet economy. The regime based its legitimacy on its people's social and economic benefits. Brezhnev left to his successors an obsolete, wasteful, and militarized economy created by the administrative-command system built up under Lenin and Stalin.

The status of economic and social rights showed the government's misplaced priorities in three ways. First, the realization of most economic and social rights (other than job security) somehow had got more and more lost. Second, ideological priority over political rights actually hampered the fulfillment of the latter. The denial of real political rights prevented the public accountability of a bumbling ruling elite for their disastrous economic, environmental, and social management. Third, the denial of virtually all private property in the means of production contributed not only to the loss of incentives and the absence of a market economy, but also to the weakness and vulnerability of Soviet society and its politically paralyzing dependence on the state for its legal means of subsistence (save mainly small-scale private farming on garden plots).

As a result, ironically, the most serious deterioration in fulfillment of human rights today lies in the sphere of social and economic rights—rights to what Article 25 of the Universal Declaration of Human Rights describes as "a standard of living adequate for the health and well-being of himself and of his family, including food, clothing, housing and medical care and necessary social services, and the right to security in the event of unemployment, sickness, disability, widowhood, old age, or other lack of livelihood in circumstances beyond his control."[73]

Such deprivation discredited the Communist party and its brand of state socialism. Noting this, the writer Chingiz Aitmatov told the first meeting of the USSR Congress of People's Deputies:

> While we were surmising, judging, and laying down the law as to what socialism must and cannot be, other people already have it, have built it, and are enjoying its fruits. . . . I have in mind such prosperous, law based societies as Sweden, Austria, Finland, Norway, the Netherlands, and finally Spain, Canada across the sea, not to mention Switzerland, which is a model. . . . We can only dream about the social security and level of prosperity enjoyed by the workers in those countries. . . .[74]

The deprivations in Soviet life mean a poverty-stricken, ill-housed, and relatively short-lived society. They mean also hungry, malnourished people spending long hours and flagging energy in queues that seem endless. The country faces the shock of transition to a market economy. That in turn threatens the republics with the possibility of further coup attempts.

Governments at all levels and in most parts of the former USSR face two hurdles in rethinking about rights. One is public distrust and fear of private entrepreneurial property and activity—a leveling mentality. The other is public fear of and opposition to what a market economy may do to their valued security of jobs and wages.[75] "The masses," said Gavriil Popov, mayor of Moscow, "long for fairness and economic equality. And the further the process of transformation goes, the more acute and the more glaring will be the gap between those aspirations and the economic realities"; and the more evident will be the contradictions between the policies leading to denationalization, privatization, and economic inequality on the one hand and, on the other, the populist character of the forces that were set in motion in order to achieve those aims.[76]

The study of public attitudes and the leadership patterns of decision suggests that the growing gap "between those aspirations and economic realities" plus government indecisiveness over plans for marketization—rather than the substance of any particular economic plan for a market economy—is the main obstacle to public trust and government legitimacy, hence to compliance with existing laws governing citizens' economic rights. Yurii Levada of the Public Opinion Center linked the deep "credibility crisis" with leadership's "indecisiveness." Central authority, he said, has been undermined by the "inconsistency of measures and the traditional secrecy of those responsible for decision making, the fluctuations of the 'line.' " This "seriously augments the growing mistrust in the leadership. And not simply mistrust in yet another promise or act of the authorities but in the legitimacy of the authority as such."[77]

The paradox of private property is as real in the former USSR as it is everywhere else. Property concentrated in government hands destroys not only economic freedom but also the basis of political autonomy and a civil society. But the unregulated concentration of property in the hands of private owners or management opens the door to new forms of corruption and social injustice. Small wonder that in a human rights dialogue this writer co-organized in New York in 1991 ("Market Economies with a Human Face: Economic, Social and Cultural Rights"), the Russian reformers shared with U.S. conservatives a concern over freeing up a functioning market, while conservatives shared with U.S. liberals a concern that the market not trample on people's rights to social protection! A mistaken reliance on an ill-prepared and unregulated market could bring further disaster.

Nationality Rights: The Disappearing "Soviet People"

> All peoples have the rights of self-determination. By virtue of that right they freely determine their political status and freely pursue their economic, social and cultural development.
>
> (U.N. Covenants of 1966)[78]

Until 1988, repression preserved the cohesion of the USSR. It covered up a diversity of identities and interests under slogans of proletarian or socialist internationalism and the 1977 Constitution's formulations of a socialist society "in which on the basis of the rapprochement of all classes and social strata, of the juridical and actual equality of all nations and nationalities, and their brotherly cooperation there has formed a new historical community of people—the Soviet people." To the extent that one "Soviet people" ever existed from Kharkov to Khabarovsk, it has disappeared in the breakup brought about by economic collapse,[79] the lifting of the old communist constraints, disillusionment with the old Union, distrust of the center, and long-repressed as well as new national enmities. As "common fear of the camps . . . vanished, the Soviet people's main sort of community collapsed. The Soviet people dissolved with inconceivable ease into nations, strata, and groups which turn into mobs at the first opportunity."[80] That exaggerates the extent of disorder, but not by far.

A message from the USSR Supreme Soviet Presidium "to the Peoples of Lithuania, Latvia and Estonia" in 1990 appealed to the people of those independence-seeking republics to stay in the Soviet Union, to help in combining "free development of the nationalities with the advantages of participation in a Union of sovereign socialist states, the path to which is opened by the imminent conclusion of a new treaty of the Union."[81] A year and a month later—on the eve of the scheduled signing of a treaty of the Union to replace the centralist treaty engineered on December 30, 1922—came the August coup.

After the coup failed, independence, not a Union treaty, was "imminent." To some republics, "free development" seemed incompatible with a union that would be anywhere near its previous centralized form. For others, such as the independent Baltic republics, union was already out of the question.

Under Gorbachev, the Union government had perpetrated its share of human rights violations in the border republics. It seems that officials in Moscow, in league with local conservatives, sometimes helped to stir up local trouble. I heard some testimony to this effect from a former KGB officer at a Helsinki Watch seminar in Moscow on September 13, 1991. The central government's response was sometimes unjustifiably repressive. At other times, the response seemed one-sided and therefore inflammatory. Excessive use of force ranged from the brutal crackdown in Alma-Ata, Kazakhstan, in December 1986[82] to the killing of twenty peaceful demonstrators and injury to hundreds of others in Tbilisi on April 9, 1989 (a small scale Tiananmen massacre),[83] to unjustified violence against Azerbaijan popular-front activists in Baku in January 1990, and to the killings of nonviolent protesters against Soviet takeovers of facilities in Vilnius and Riga in 1991, as well as to bloody attacks on customs posts in Lithuania and Latvia.

At the same time, the Union government remained slow to react to conflict and to pogroms against minorities such as the Armenians in Azerbaijan, some of the victims of which this writer interviewed in Erevan in September 1991.

Whether reading former Soviet sources or out in the field, one could not but be struck by the failure of Soviet forces and the Soviet government in general to act effectively against such threats to peace and rights as the blockade of road and rail traffic into Armenia from Azerbaijan and its Nakhichevan Autonomous Republic, and from Georgia, and the deportations or flight of Azeris from Armenia and Armenians from their villages in Azerbaijan.[84]

Within each successor state, ethnic minorities, both indigenous and nonindigenous (there are about sixty-fiv million people in nonindigenous ethnic minorities), now confront their republics' governments and other nationalities with Maare Grossman's message at Festival Field, Tallinn, on June 17, 1988: We refuse to be less equal.

Even while seeking partial or total separation from Moscow, the republics' governments face similar demands for self-determination (as autonomy or even full separation) from within; for example, Abkhazians and Ossetians feel (and are) threatened in Georgia, as are Armenians and Azeris in Azerbaijan, Gagauz (Christian Turks) and Slavs in Moldova, and Russian speakers in the various states. Whatever the outcomes and causes, the brekdown of mutual tolerance into interethnic conflict has cost hundreds of lives and uprooted at least 600,000 refugees—some sources give figures of a million and a half.[85]

By late 1990, all but one Union republic, Kirgizia, had followed the lead of Estonia's 1988 proclamation of sovereignty.[86] After August 1991 all republics followed Lithuania's March 1990 lead and declared independence. Within the successor states, independence left unresolved similar issues of equal rights and self-determination. The damage done to interethnic relations by Moscow's slow, sometimes repressive reacions to the changes it originally unleashed[87] will not be repaired with anything short of equality and some form of self-determination for minorities.

On the cost of indecision, we have the perspective of the thirteen economists who formulated the "500-day program," which was originally endorsed by Gorbachev and approved by the Russian parliament. (The program was subsequently rejected, in October 1990, by Gorbachev, initially in favor of a compromise with the later ousted premier's, Nikolai Ryzhkov's, more gradual and centrist version.) The economists wrote of "irreparable losses" due to delays in launching reform. These losses are not only economic but political and they include precious lost opportunities for accord with the republics at an earlier stage in August 1990. "Lack of agreement on an action plan increases many times over the likelihood of a paralysis of power. Energy is expended not on construction but on confrontation."[88] Genuine cooperation and coalition between the center and the republics on the basis of mutual interest seemed to many Soviet public opinion leaders to be the only possible way to peaceful reform.[89] Gorbachev was unable or unwilling to follow this course until the coup left him with little choice but to reach out to Yeltsin and the other republics' leaders for whatever cooperation they saw fit to negotiate with the center. By then it was too late to save the Union.

Minorities Outside their Homelands

About sixty-five million Soviet citizens live outside their homeland areas. The tide of refugees and Russians moving out of Central Asia swells the total. Measures in pursuit of self-determination violate the international human rights of the republics' minorities if they infringe on individual rights to life, liberty, personal inviolability, equality under the law regardless of nationality, or the cultural rights of individual members of minority groups (Article 2–2 of the Universal Declaration of Human Rights; Article 26 of the International Covenant on Civil and Political Rights; Article 12 of the UDHR; and Article 27 of the Covenant on Civil and Political Rights, respectively).

Some expatriates, such as the Slavic migrants, claim that their individual human rights are threatened by new local laws on citizenship, language, education, property, voting, and the like in the republics where they reside. As of the spring of 1992, equal rights to citizenship for all ethnic groups existed in the laws of Russia, Ukraine, Moldova, Kazakhstan, Lithuania, Belarus, and Tajikistan. Law in Estonia and a Latvian draft law discriminated against most immigrants, in an effort to preserve the survival of the Estonian and Latvian ethnic groups. Legislation on citizenship continues to unfold in the successor states.[90] Interviews with representatives of minority groups and with representatives of various views among titular nationalities in the Baltic republics during September and October 1991 confirmed for this writer the depth and complexity of such conflicts between claims to equal rights and claims to rights of self-determination and ethnic survival.

Still-displaced nationalities, such as the Volga Germans and Crimean Tatars, have sought to return to Soviet homelands from which Stalin brutally exiled them in World War II.[91] Issues such as these also will take time and a great deal of determination to resolve.

Soviet Jews are one of the nationalities without a real homeland in the former USSR (discounting Stalin's creation, the Birobizhan Autonomous Republic). They have recently gained cultural and religious freedom, in fact and in law. Anti-Zionist campaigns from above have abated under a government which does less than its predecessors to make Jews feel unwanted in their land of birth. But residual discrimination, bigotry from below, and the beckoning of kin and a possible better life abroad, plus liberalized emigration, are causing Jews to emigrate in record numbers—at peak, some quarter of a million a year. Gorbachev's acknowledgment and condemnation of anti-Semitism in October 1991, was welcome, but perhaps too little and too late to stop Jewish emigration.

Elena Bonner puts anti-Semitism in the larger context of "increasing aggressiveness against people of other nationalities" in the former USSR. Pogroms have hit in the Caucasus and Central Asia, but not against Jews, as she has pointed out.[92] Nevertheless, memories of the holocaust haunt Jews as they do the once-again pogrom victims, the Armenians. As do Armenians in Azerbaijan (and as a result, Azerbaijanis in Armenia) so Jews sense that their rights to dignity, equality, security, and freedoms are jeopardized by discrimination and bias. Most Jews are aware of the sinister, Nazi-like threats and virulent outpourings from small nationalist hate groups like Pamiat, Fatherland, and Patriot. Various observers see a potential for these small national socialist hate groups to stir up violent disturbances and mass movements. This they could do by scapegoating and playing on the anti-Semitism apparent in a portion of the population of Russia, Ukraine, and some other parts of the former USSR.[93]

Then there is the belief, supported by disturbing reports of fact, that racists have the support of conservative officials.[94] Certainly, opponents of economic reform and the dismantling of the huge party-government apparatus could gain comfort from diatribes like that of writer Alexander Romanenko. He told a meeting of the Patriot organization in Leningrad (since renamed St. Petersburg), that "Marxist Leninist Science mounts a struggle against Zionism because Zionism is the ideology and policy of the Jewish bourgeoisie: the struggle against Zionism is the struggle against the class enemy."[95] By depicting Jews not only as racial enemies of pure Russian culture, but also as class enemies, the ultranationalists join the fray against reform.

Conclusions: Between Might and Rights

Our discussion has looked back to the self-destructive rigidity of absolutism and forward to the beginnings of democratic alternatives to it. We have traced the conversion of rights from ends to means under communism, when only the regime was free, and back again to ends, at least in theory.

Might made rights throughout much of Russia's more than five centuries of independence and imperial growth. Reforms mitigating absolutism were habitually followed by retreats from rights in the various spheres. Once before, from 1905 to 1917, absolutism snapped because of its own rigidity, only to be replaced in late 1917 by a revitalized form of absolutism, Bolshevism. Now again, a renewed movement for individual rights is threatened by a multiple crisis of political delegitimation, economic breakdown, and ethnic and regional disunion.

Communism's economic failings led Gorbachev to launch *perestroika* and brought freedom and new thinking on human rights more easily than it did bread. Barely had the Union government framed de facto freedoms with laws on individual rights in a civil society—rights to freedoms and personal inviolability— than it slid down the road to collapse due to the slow reordering of misplaced priorities of economic and social rights, the divisive issues of nationality rights, and the distrust of the center.

The 1980s opened with the illegal exile to Gorky of Andrei Sakharov and his co-champion of human rights, Dr. Elena Bonner. Twelve years earlier, Andrei Sakharov had proposed that the USSR enter into deeper international concord, join in an antihunger struggle, promote a "law on geohygiene," pass a law on free press and information, abrogate laws violating human rights, grant amnesty to political prisoners, permit a conclusive exposure of Stalin, and undertake deep economic reform.[96] None of my Soviet or western colleagues foresaw that five years after Sakharov's exile, a new Soviet leader would launch a *perestroika* which would eventually embody Sakharov's vision; or that on December 16, 1986, Gorbachev would telephone Sakharov to invite him and Bonner back from exile, unconditionally.

How could one foresee that Sakharov, like some other former dissidents, would become a people's deputy before the great loss of his death on December 14, 1989? Nor did anyone, save conservative foes of *perestroika*, foresee the uncontrolled breakthrough of activism beyond *perestroika* that would both enhance and imperil the struggle to realize human rights in the USSR.

As the Soviet peoples moved through and beyond *perestroika*, the *content* of rights issues changed and broadened. Both violations of rights and responsibilities for upholding them shifted from the central government toward the new political forces outside of it, and into the republics. The human rights issues and conflicts have not gone away in the 1990s; they have become more complex, more difficult to monitor and resolve.

When Sakharov died on December 14, 1989, progress had already turned Russia upside down. After staying outside a universal movement toward human rights, Soviet Russia had joined it, unleashing a tide of unrest.

Five differences since 1917 bring slight hope.

1. Despite some interstate hostilities in the former USSR, the region as a whole has broken a historic pattern by being neither aligned nor mobilized any longer against the outside world.

2. The international climate is more favorable for reform. Western Europe is a community, not a battlefield.

3. More far-reaching democratic mechanisms function. Russia's historic thread of absolutism has snapped, possibly beyond permanent repair. The words of former liberal leader Paul Miliukov in 1922 ring truer today: "We are witnessing the birth of Russian democracy, in the midst of the ruins of the past, which will never return."[97]

4. An international human rights movement has arisen to advocate new standards of human rights in global and regional settings.

5. High literacy and a developed mass media, including television, serve to educate and involve the public in the issues confronting their infant democracy and could be enlisted in the human rights education advocated in this dialogue by Charles Henry and Riane Eisler.

Formidable obstacles remain until new thinking produces real guarantees of human rights throughout the former USSR. The guarantee of human rights depends on economic recovery and regional cooperation toward it, the resolution of ethnic conflict by the resolution of the sensitive issues of individual and group rights, the development of legal systems complete with authoritative constitutional courts that protect inviolable personal rights and assure due process of law; on reforms in legal education to return the legal profession to the standards of the prerevolutionary bar, an ever stronger network of nongovernmental human rights organizations, and real personal and ethnic group self-determination with a respect for the rights of others. To the extent that these conditions come about, and economic recovery begins, the rest of the world may breathe a little easier. For it has high stakes in post-Soviet democracy, human rights, and peace.

Notes

1. Alexis de Tocqueville, *Democracy in America* 1848, trans. George Lawrence, ed. J.P. Mayer, 12th ed. (New York: Doubleday Anchor Books, 1969), 239.

2. Andrei Sakharov, "Memorandum," March 5, 1971, and "Progress, Coexistence and Intellectual Freedom," June 1968, in Andrei D. Sakharov, *Sakharov Speaks* (New York: Vintage Books, 1974), 135–58. Andrei Sakharov, "Memoirs," *Time*, (May 14, 1990), 42.

3. "Legal Reforms in the Soviet Union: Prospects for Human rights and Economic Transformation," Conference held in New York, NY, November 14–15, 1990. On the durability of despotism, see Bertram Wolfe, *Three Who Made a Revolution* (New York: Delta, 1964), 11–38. For a latter-day Slavophile rejection of western values, see, e.g., Aleksandr I. Solzhenitsyn, *Letter to the Soviet Leaders* (New York: Harper & Row, 1974); "Address at Harvard Commencement," *The New York Times* (June 9, 1978); on Russian collectivism, see, e.g., Edward L. Keenan, "Human Rights in Soviet Political Culture," in *The Moral Imperatives of Human Rights*, ed. Kenneth W. Thompson (Washington, DC: University Press of America, 1990), 69–80.

4. On democratization, denationalization, and voluntary union of independent states, see Gavriil Popov, "Vkus vlasti," *Izvestiia* (June 28, 1990).

5. Alan Riding, "Eastern Leaders at Summit Warn of New Divisions in Europe," *The New York Times* (November 21, 1990).

6. *Perestroika* has brought with "activism . . . a large element of unpredictability." "Perestroika, Lenin, sotsializm," *Sovetskaia iustitsiia* 8 (April 1990): 2, 4.

7. Bertram Wolfe, 29.

8. Marquis de Custine, *The Empire of the Czar: A Journey Through Eternal Russia* (New York: Doubleday Anchor Books, 1989), 139.

9. Bertram Wolfe, 23.

10. Marquis de Custine, 183.

11. Michael Karpovich, *Imperial Russia, 1801–1917* (New York: Holt, Rinehart and Winston, 1932), 13.

12. The interest of Catherine the Great (1762–96) in the Enlightenment vanished with the coming of the French Revolution. Alexander I (1801–1825) turned away from a limited rule of law proposed by the great jurist Michael Speranskii (1772–1839).

13. Thomas Riha, ed., *Readings in Russian Civilization*, vol. II, rev. ed. (Chicago: University of Chicago Press, 1969), 303–314.

14. Nicholas V. Riasanovsky, *A History of Russia*, 4th ed. (New York: Oxford University Press, 1964), 377.

15. Franco Venturi, *Roots of Revolution: A History of Populist and Socialist Movements in Nineteenth Century Russia* (London: Weidenfeld and Nicholson, 1960); Avrahm Yarmolinsky, *Road to Revolution: A Century of Russian Radicalism* (New York: Collier Books, 1962).

16. Nicolas Berdyaev, *The Origin of Russian Communism* 1948, 2nd ed. (Ann Arbor, MI: The University of Michigan Press, 1960), 37, 41.

17. John D. Klier, "The Concept of 'Jewish Emancipation' in a Russian Context," in *Civil Rights in Imperial Russia*, eds. Olga Crisp and Linda Edmondson (Oxford, England: Clarendon Press, 1989), 140. The Basic Law (Constitution) of 1906, together with the judicial reforms of 1864, recognized in principle an impressive list of rights to freedom and due process. The government violated its own laws; no effective appeal against its violations existed. William E. Butler, "Civil Rights in Russia: Legal Standards in Gestation," Crisp and Edmondson, 1–12; Richard E. Wortman, *The Development of Russian Legal Consciousness* (Chicago: University of Chicago Press, 1976). On the half-free press under censorship, see Caspar Ferenczi, "Freedom of the Press under the Old Regime, 1905–1914," Crisp and Edmondson, 191–214.

18. Quoted in Linda Edmondson, "Was There a Movement for Civil Rights in Russia in 1905?" Crisp and Edmondson, 267–268.

19. Richard Thornburgh, "The Soviet Union and the Rule of Law," *Foreign Affairs* 69: 2 (Spring 1990), 14.

20. W. Bruce Lincoln, *The Great Reforms: Autocracy, Bureaucracy, and the Politics of Change in Imperial Russia* (Dekalb, IL: Northern Illinois University Press, 1990).

21. Susan Eva Heuman, "Socialist Conception of Human Rights: A Model from Pre-revolutionary Russia," in *Human Rights: Cultural and Historical Perspectives*, eds. Adamantia Pollis and Peter Schwab (New York: Praeger, 1978), 44–59.

22. Crisp and Edmondson, vi–vii.

23. Donald W. Treadgold, *Twentieth Century Russia*, 6th ed. (Boulder, CO: Westview Press, 1987), 105–198.

24. Marc Raeff, *Understanding Imperial Russia* (New York: Columbia University Press, 1984), 218.

25. S. A. Smith, "Workers and Civil Rights in Tsarist Russia," Crisp and Edmondson, 164.

26. Robert Paul Browder and Alexander F. Kerensky, eds., *The Provisional Government 1917. Documents*, 3 vols. (Stanford, CA: Hoover Institution, 1961), vol. I, 191–242 ("Justice and Law Enforcement"); Peter Juviler, *Revolutionary Law and Order: Politics and Social Change in the USSR* (New York: Free Press, 1976), 4–12.

27. He continues, "We, however, do not understand our own history. We have forgotten to celebrate the centennial of the abolition of serfdom and the great reforms following, especially judicial reform. Arkady Vaksberg, "Kakim dolzhno byt' pravovoye gosudarstvo?" *Literaturnaia gazeta* (June 8, 1988).

28. H.J. White, "Civil Rights and the Provisional Government," Crisp and Edmondson; 287–312; S.A. Smith, "Workers and Civil Rights in Tsarist Russia, 1899–1917," Ibid.; 145–170.

29. Meisel and Kozera, *Materials for the Study of the Soviet System* (Ann Arbor, MI: George Wahr), 22.

30. Konstantin Pobedonostsev, *Reflections of a Russian Statesman* (London, England: Grant Richards, 1898), excerpted in *Riha*: 391.

31. V. I. Lenin, *Proletarian Revolution and the Renegade Kautsky*, excerpted in *The Lenin Anthology*, ed. Robert C. Tucker, 2nd ed. (New York: W.W. Norton, 1975). 465, 469.

32. Nicolas Berdyaev, *The Origin of Russian Communism* (Ann Arbor, MI: The University of Michigan Press, 1960), 113, 144.

33. Oliver Radkey, *Elections to the Russian Constituent Assembly of 1917* (Cambridge, MA: Harvard University Press, 1950), 13–22.

34. Treadgold, 108–141.

35. Moshe Lewin, *Lenin's Last Struggle* (New York: Pantheon, 1968).

36. Aryeh L. Unger, *Constitutional Development in the USSR: A Guide to Soviet Constitutions* (New York: Pica Press, 1982).

37. Article 125, 126: 1936 Constitution.

38. Meisel and Kozera, passim; Juviler, 15–38; Treadgold, 126–195; John N. Hazard, *Settling Disputes in Soviet Society* (New York: Columbia University Press, 1960).

39. On early Soviet nationality policy, see Richard Pipes, *The Formation of the Soviet Union* (Cambridge, MA: Harvard University Press, 1954).

40. J.V. Stalin, "The Tasks of Business Executives" (1931), *Works*, vol. 13 (Moscow, 1955), 43 ("capture" not "storm" in text).

41. A. Tsipko, "The Roots of Stalinism," 22.

42. W.H. Chamberlin, *Russia's Iron Age* (London: Gerald Duckworth, 1935).

43. Peter H. Juviler, "Forward," to Yuri I. Luryi, *Soviet Family Law* (Buffalo, NY: William S. Hein & Co., 1980), i–vi; H. Kent Geiger, *The Family in Soviet Russia* (Cambridge, MA: Harvard University Press, 1968).

44. Peter H. Juviler, "The Soviet Family in Post-Stalin Perspective," in *The Soviet Union Since Stalin*, eds. Stephen Cohen, et al. (Bloomington, IN: Indiana University Press, 1980), 229–230.

45. *Pravda* (November 3, 1987).

46. Anatoly Marchenko, *My Testimony*, trans. Max Hayward (New York: Dutton, 1969), xvii, 3, passim.

47. The enhanced mention of the Party's leading role, moved up to Article 6, even though placed "within the framework of the constitution," meant further sanction of the political will over higher law. Individual rights carried even more qualifiers as to their purposes of strengthening the socialist system and building communism than they had in the 1936 Constitution.

48. Tatyana Mamonova, *Zhenshchina i Rossiia: Al'manakh* (1979), translated as *Women and Russia: Feminist Writings from the Soviet Union* (Boston: Beacon Press, 1984); Peter H. Juviler, "Soviet Marxism and Family Law," *Columbia Journal of Transnational Law* 23: 2 (1985), 385–400.

49. Peter H. Juviler, "The Urban Family and the Soviet State: Emerging Contours of a Demographic Policy," in *The Contemporary Soviet City*, eds. Henry W. Morton and Robert C. Stuart (Armonk, NY: M.E. Sharpe, 1984), 84–112.

50. Bill Keller, "Soviets Adopt Emergency Plan to Center Power in Gorbachev and Leaders of the Republics," *New York Times* (November 18, 1990).

51. Seweryn Bialer, *The Soviet Paradox: External Expansion, Internal Decline* (New York: Alfred A. Knopf, 1986).

52. Peter H. Juviler, "Law and Individual Rights: The Shifting Political Ground," in *The Impact of Perestroika on Soviet Law*, ed. A. J. Schmidt (Boston: Martin Nijhoff, 1990), 108–113.

53. V. O. Mushinskii, "Pravovoe gosudarstvo i pravoponimanie," *Sovetskoe gosudarstvo i pravo* 2 (1990), 21–27.

54. A. Tsipko, "The Roots of Stalinism," *Nauka i zhizn'* 1 (January 1989), abstr. in *CDSP (The Current Digest of the Soviet Press)* XLI: 12, 21, 22.

55. Anatolii Denisov (USSR People's Deputy and professor), "Mezhdu diktatury i anarkhiei," *Nedelia* 25, (June 18–24, 1990), 3.

56. *Pravda* (July 15, 1987).

57. "Perestroika . . . ," 4. "Hatred," said Anatoly Rybakov, "has become an integral part of our deformed conscience, eating into society's every cell, dehumanizing it and awakening the most reprehensible instincts in people's hearts." Interview with Olga Martynenko, "Children of the Arbat in 1937," *Moscow News* 35 (September 9–16, 1990),

16. See also, A.N. Yakovlev, interviewed in " 'Sindrom vraga': anatomiia sotsial'noi bolezni," *Literaturnaia gazeta* 7 (February 14, 1990), 10.

58. See note 55 above.

59. Emigration procedures eased (on the Soviet side) in 1988 directives and 1990 law. The release of political prisoners lowered their number from a known 750 in 1986 to a known 50 in mid-1990. International Helsinki Federation, *Human Rights Concerns in Selected Helsinki Signatory Countries. Prepared for the CSCE Human Rights Meeting Paris, May–June 1989*, 16; "List of Political Prisoners in the USSR as of October 30, 1990, ed. Cronid Lubarsky, *USSR News Brief: Human Rights* 10 (1990). Allowing for unverified cases, actual numbers are higher.

60. Deputy Yurii Vlasov's speech of May 31, *Izvestiia* (June 2, 1989); Viktor Yasman, "The KGB and the Party Congress," *RL (Radio Liberty Report on the USSR)* II: 32 (1990), 12–14.

61. Peter H. Juviler, "Guaranteeing Human Rights in the Soviet Context," *Columbia Journal of Transnational Law* 28: 1 (1990), 151.

62. Juviler, "Guaranteeing Human Rights," 149.

63. Press law of June 12, 1990, in *Ved. SSSR (Vedomosti S'ezda narodnykh deputatov SSSR i verkhovnogo soveta SSSR)* 26, item 492 (June 12, 1990). Yuri Baturin, Vladimir Entin and Mikhail Fedotov "*Glasnost'* Struggles: An Insider's Account," *Meeting Report* (Kennan Institute for Advanced Russian Studies, June 11, 1990). Beyond the reach of the law, press freedoms ran into difficulties over paper supply and printing. On this and Baltic censorship, see Peter Juviler, "Human Rights after Perestroika: Progress and Perils," *The Harriman Institute Forum* IV: 6 (June 1991), 6.

64. *Ved. SSSR* 22, items 391–392 (May 21, 1990).

65. Helsinki Watch, *Overview: Prisons and Jails in the Helsinki Countries*, prepared for the Moscow Conference on the Human Dimension (September 1991); *Perestroika i prava cheloveka*, special supplement to *Novoe vremia* (December 1988); *Amnesty International Report* (1985, 1986, 1987, 1988); D. J. Peterson, "The Zone, 1989: The Soviet Penal System under Perestroika," *RL* I: 37 (1989), 1–6; the article on the imprisonment, mistreatment, prison writings, and death in December 1986 of Anatolii Marchenko, in "Iz istorii sovremennosti: 'Zhivi kak vse,' " *Ogonek* 40 (1989), 16–19.

66. On investigative abuses: Andrei Mikhlin, "Zapret pytok: pravo osuzhdennykh k lisheniiu svobody na gumannoe obrashchenie," *Novoe vremia* supplement (December 1988), 16–17. The uneven contest between defense and prosecution, say reformers, must give way to a truly adversarial process (*sostiazatel'nost*). The presumption of innocence has received legislative recognition. Even with improved access to counsel, physical and procedural abuses reported in the past can go on until counsel's rights of participation in the investigation are strengthened and abuses of the new law on rights of defense ended. See, e.g., Viktor Kogan in *Sovetskaia iustitsiia* (1988) 3, 12–13; 7, 26–27; 19, 21–22. The handling of prosecutions of alleged coup plotters after the August 1991 putsch appears to leave a whole lot to be desired, from a human rights viewpoint.

67. John Quigley, "Law Reform and the Courts," *Columbia Journal of Transnational Law* 28: 1 (1990), 59–75.

68. Eugene Huskey, "Between Citizen and State: The Soviet Bar (Advokatura) Under Gorbachev," Ibid., 95–116; Peter Juviler,"Secret Justice and Personal Rights," has appeared in *The Soviet Sobranie of Laws*, eds. Richard M. Buxbaum and Kathryn Hendley, (Berkeley, CA: University of California, Institute of International and Area Studies, 1991), 156–172.

69. This goes beyond the Soviet right of complaint in court against illegal acts of officials violating citizens' rights. That received legislative backing in a 1987 complaint law which was so weak as to be stillborn. A 1989 replacement only slightly improved on

the 1987 law. *Ved. SSSR* 22 (1989), item 416, law of November 2, 1989.

70. Law on constitutional supervision in the USSR, *Ved. SSSR* 29 (1989), item 572, December 23, 1989, article 21, part 3.

71. Speaking in New York, October 22, 1991. See also, e.g., Peter Reddaway's depiction of central authority as disintegrating "into at least fifteen different countries." *The New York Review of Books* 7 (November 1991), 53.

72. USSR People's Deputy and economist, Pavel Bunich, interviewed in *Ogonek* 18 (April 1990), 1.

73. Marat Baglai, "Sotsial'no-ekonomicheskie prava: oslabliaiutsia garantii?" *Novoe vremia* supplement (December 12, 1988).

74. *Izvestiia* (June 3, 1989).

75. A. Chubais and A. Levinson, quoted in "Obshchestvennyi vybor," *Kommunist* 12 (1989), 31–32. Prevent price-gouging not by restrictive controls but by increasing supplies of food and raw materials, argues the head of the USSR Union of Cooperatives, the economist and People's Deputy V. Tikhonov in "Sut moei kontseptsii," *Literaturnaia gazeta* (August 9, 1989), 10.

76. Popov, 27.

77. Yuri Levada, "Credibility Crisis: Perestroika's Main Problem," *Moscow News* 21, (1990), 8.

78. Article 1 of United Nations 1966 Covenant on Economic, Social and Cultural Rights and 1966 Covenant on Civil and Political Rights, ratified by the USSR in 1973.

79. Deterioration of the general quality of life fed local separatism. USSR Supreme Soviet appeal to the parliaments of the Union and autonomous republics, June 14, 1990, *Ved. SSSR* 25, item 466, (1990).

80. Vladimir Sokolov, "K rynku—pod prikrytiem armii?" *Literaturnaia gazeta* 37 (September 12, 1990), 11.

81. Appeal of the Presidium of the USSR Supreme Soviet, July 20, 1990, *Ved. SSSR* 30 item 552 (1990).

82. See, e.g., Jeri Laber's account of the December 1986 riots in Alma-Ata, Kazakhstan, after the removal of the First Secretary, the Kazakh Kunaev and his replacement with a Russian, Kolbin, from outside the republic, in "Stalin's Dumping Ground," *The New York Review of Books* (October 11, 1990), 50–53.

83. On the Tbilisi massacre of April , 1989: talk by Dr. Jennifer Leaning, Physicians for Human Rights, Helsinki Watch Committee, June 7, 1989; PHR press release, May 25, 1989; Celestine Bohlen, "Military Gas Used in Soviet Georgia," *New York Times* (May 25, 1989).

84. On tardy and inadequate protection for Armenians, see Elena Bonner, "The Shame of Armenia," *The New York Review of Books* (October 11, 1990), 39–40. On deportations and brutalization of Armenians, see, e.g., "Report of the Delegation of the First International Andrei D. Sakharov Congress of the Visit to the Shaumian District, 5 September 1991."

85. Margot Jacobs, "USSR Faces Mounting Refugee Problem," *RL* II: 38 (1990), 14; Elena Bonner talked of 1.5 million refugees, New York, October 22, 1991. This writer interviewed victims of "ring" operations against villages in the Shaumian District of Azerbaijan near the Azerbaijan border in September 1991, and refugees stranded by the Azeri blockade of Stepanakert airport, that same month.

86. On declarations of sovereignty and power of legislative veto over Moscow laws, see, e.g., Estonian declaration and Law of November 16, 1988, *Sovetskaia Estoniia* (November 18, 1988); center's negative response in *Pravda* (November 28, 1988); Joel Aav, "Estonian Parliament Does Not Shrink Back," *Supplement to the Estonian Kodumaa Weekly* (December 14, 1988); declaration of state sovereignty of the Byelorussian SSR,

July 27, 1990; *Argumenty i fakty* 31, (August 4–10, 1990), 1–2; interview with Armenian President Ter-Petrossian, trans. from *Berliner Zeitung* (August 28, 1990) in FBIS–SOV–90–170, 55–56.

87. For self-criticism of the procrastination in tending to the rights and needs of the Armenian population of Nagorno-Karabakh, see *Ved. SSSR* 29, item 464, 1988; Gorbachev spoke about past underestimation of the nationality crisis at the 28th CPSU Congress. *Pravda* (July 3, 1990).

88. S. Shatalin, et al. "Message," *Komsomolskaia pravda* (November 4, 1990), trans. in FBIS–SOV–90–214, 56–58.

89. Yurii Korolev, "Five Aspects of Our Crisis," *Moscow News* 27 (1990), 5. RSFSR People's Deputy and member of the Constitutional Drafting Commission of the RSFSR Viktor Sheinis, "Eskalatsiia konflikta i rasstanovka sil," unpublished note, copy given by him to this writer, October 1990.

90. Helsinki Watch, *New Citizenship laws in the Republics of the Former USSR* (New York, April 15, 1992).

91. The government has recognized the Crimean Tatars' right of return to the Crimea; conflict has ensued with local non-Tatars and authorities over land, housing. "Soobshchaet komissiia," *Izvestiia* (August 11, 1990).

92. Interview with Elena Bonner by Sergei Zaitsev, trans. from *Vienna Wochenpresse* (September 6, 1990), 26–27 in FBIS-SOV–90–174, 33–35.

93. Ibid.; Gennadii Denisovskii, Polina Kozyreva, and Mikhail Matsovskii, "Anti-Semitism Among Russians. How Prevalent Is It?" *Moscow News* 22 (June 10–17, 1990), 5: reported acceptance of Jews' equal rights and right to emigrate by vast majority of those polled by U.S.-Soviet team in the Moscow region; but over a quarter of respondents (two percent Jewish) manifested moderate to extreme anti-Semitism and 71 percent saw it as "obvious fact of life today." See also Nina Tumarkin, "Russians against Jews," *The Atlantic* (October 1990), 32–45; Ilya Smirnov, "Playing with Cheats the Scientific Way," *Moscow News* 30 (August 5–12, 1990), 8.

94. Andrei Makarov, the "social prosecutor" hired by the April writers' group, attacked by the mob led by Otashvili-Smirnov into the Writers' House January 18, 1990, obtained a sentence of two years on Otashvili (later found hanging in his cell) for inciting to racial hatred and violence. Makarov at Helsinki Watch, New York, (October 31, 1990).

95. "Daidzest reportera. Miting obshchestvenno-patriotisheskoi organizatsii 'Patriot.' Leningrad, Manezhnaia ploshchad', 26.04.89," 2, acquired form the recorder, Gennadii Vinogradov.

96. Sakharov, "Progress, Coexistence and Intellectual Freedom," 86–89.

97. Paul N. Miliukov, *Russia Today and Tomorrow* (New York: The Macmillan Company, 1922), viii.

5

Human Rights:
A Time for Hard Decisions

Elena Lukasheva

The failure of the socialism our society tried to create is evidenced by the economic collapse, the disintegration of the federation, the acute interethnic conflicts, and the absence of even a brief period in our history which one could describe as favorable for the fulfillment of human rights. Yet the human rights situation is a measure of the quality of a social system and the democracy or totalitarianism of its politics.

Disregard for human rights was not the consequence of an accidental turn in society's evolution: from the very start it was part and parcel of the doctrine and practice of state and legal development. The essence of democratic statehood is the recognition of the primacy of human rights as natural and inviolable. These rights are a prerequisite for the rule of law which limits state power. The state must recognize the autonomy of the individual; its structures must serve the goal of ensuring individual liberty rather than of suppressing the individual.

Marxist-Leninist doctrine stressed the all-decisive social environment and the priority of class and collective interests, ignoring the individuality of the human being. State ideology played down the responsibility of the individual, pointed to external rather than internal reference points for the individual, and emphasized the omnipotence of the state and its superior role. The state's omnipotence in the property, social, and even private spheres suppressed individual creativity, fostered servile, blind obedience, and deprived the individual of freedom of choice and opinion. Individuals were subjected to *totalitarian socialization*. They did not understand their position was that of slaves; on the contrary, massive propaganda made people feel "the masters of their own lives."

Marxist-Leninist doctrine rigidly classified people by their class origins. There was the ruling class of workers, there was peasantry that had to be "tolerated," there were classes that were to be wiped out. The class approach rendered completely irrelevant the issue of the rights of a human as an autonomous individual with his/her interests and aspirations. Nicholas Berdyaev pointed to

Marxism's most vulnerable aspect: it refuses to see the individuals behind class, it seeks to see a class with its class interests behind each idea and judgment.[1]

The priority of class interests found its expression in the idea of proletarian dictatorship as a form of government that was restrained by no laws, restricted by no rules, and dependent on coercion.[2] Proletarian dictatorship is essentially incompatible with human rights and individual freedom; it is the antipode of the law-ruled state. Proletarian dictatorship rejects the universality of human rights and recognizes them only for the working class. However, even the idea of rights for the working class is false. The ruling elite came into power under the slogan of democracy for the people, but it did not trust this people. The peasantry's voting rights were abridged, the rights of the working class were illusory, while any semblance of opposition to the new government was ruthlessly stamped out. It was great historical deceit. For more than seventy years under the Soviet regime, society was denied free, contested elections and the freedoms of opinion, belief, conscience, and the press; the right to life and the inviolability of the person were trampled upon. The totalitarian state made the individual toe the line by destroying any freedom of choice and self-determination, thereby turning the political and individual rights of the citizen into a fiction.

There is no denying that after the chaos and economic dislocation following World War I and the Civil War, the state, drawing on administrative-command methods, set up economic structures which created conditions for combating unemployment and ensuring minimal social guarantees for the individual. Today, one often hears or reads that equality in poverty turned the individual into a drifter sponging off the state. Certainly, living standards were low. But the allegation, which seems to have become quite common today, that the entire nation degenerated into a society of spongers, appears completely out of place. For decades, people worked for a mere pittance of wages and salaries and were exploited by the state which appropriated the lion's share of the surplus product. "Free labor zones" existed in the USSR where peasants toiled just for entries in accountants' books "to be paid later on." The perplexity people feel now is not a loafer's syndrome but a result of the psychological discomfort and pressures stemming from habituation to the *diktat* of the state that left people no choice and ruled out any alternative forms of life.

Looking back at the history of our society, one can recall the attempts to ease repressions at one stage or another, such as the "Thaw"; but the most important fact is that citizens in our country have never enjoyed genuine rights which make the individual's life meaningful. The individual has been totally dependent on the state and motivated mainly by fear. One of the fundamental ideas of universal human thinking—the idea of the priority role of the natural rights of man which limit the powers of the state—was just brushed aside. The state acted as an authority that was limited by nothing whatsoever, granting rights to its citizens or taking them away at its discretion, turning its citizens into unthinking "cogs" obediently following orders and instructions—all this against the background of massive propaganda for "a new superior type of democracy," "true power of the people," and "unprecedented historic accomplishments in the human rights sphere."

That the partocratic state power did succeed in fooling the people is the most paradoxical thing in this historical situation. There were people who were completely taken in by propaganda. Others (and they were the majority) understood the illusory nature of our life but were unable to grasp the entirety of the regime's ruthlessness and falseness due to the lack of transparency of government, the lack of information, and the imposed ideological stereotypes. Only a handful of people joined the human rights movement and vigorously opposed human rights violations, risking their freedom and sometimes their lives.

Such was our human rights legacy as the country entered the period in its development which subsequently came to be called *perestroika*. The slogans of *glasnost'*, freedom, and pluralism of opinion were a godsend to a society gripped with skepticism, despair, and apathy. They helped people to get over their indifference and social lethargy and helped to turn conformists into citizens. The society was seized by mass euphoria: people believed that democratic changes would soon bear fruit and transform their entire fossilized way of life. Hardly anyone could have foreseen at that time all the hardships and misfortunes society would have to go through as it advanced along the new road, the immense price it would have to pay for breaking away from totalitarianism, the administrative-command system, and pseudodemocracy.

Today we are standing on the ruins of the old system. So far, we have failed to create anything essentially new. Undoubtedly there have been spectacular changes, fragile as they are, bringing advances toward democracy in the last few years. From a legal viewpoint, these shifts were consolidated in the Law on the Press and Other Mass Media, the Law on Public Associations, the Law on Freedom of Consciousness and Religious Organizations, and the Declaration of Human Rights and Freedoms, as well as in other legislation. However, democratic development is hampered by the inconsistencies of authorities, by resistance from the vestiges of the administrative-command system, and by the impoverishment of the people.

Have we brought about a decisive shift toward guaranteeing human rights? (This which must be the principal criterion in assessing changes in social development.) Unfortunately, we have not. The reasons for this sad conclusion will become clear if some questions are answered first.

Can Democracy Be Effective without Moral Foundations?

We stepped into democracy right from slavery, we injected into it the tenacious spirit of despotism with its lack of moral restraints. The logic of such consciousness leads from total obedience and subordination to the *despotism of democracy* which knows no values-motivated limits. While earlier one had to eulogize "leaders," now one must lash at those in high places; while earlier people were expected to approve unanimously any action of the state, now all actions of government must be denounced. Yesterday, all were to follow blindly anything they were told by authorities; today, disobedience and anarchy rank among the supreme civic virtues. State autocracy is being ousted by people's autocracy in its most disgusting form, ochlocracy—mob rule.

Such somersaults in social consciousness are inevitable during a transition from totalitarianism to democracy, especially in a society which has never known democratic traditions. Was not the socialist regime so enduring in this country just because Russia had not completed the stage of capitalist development and thus had failed to form bourgeois-liberal traditions with their fundamental idea of the universality of human rights? Revolutionaries developed a negative attitude to bourgeois democracy and subsequently rejected liberal ways of thinking, as Peter Juviler discusses in chapter 4.

After 1917, prerevolutionary authoritarian-patriarchal mentality came to be replaced by totalitarian social consciousness whose central element is unconditional subordination to authorities and unanimous approval of all their actions. Therefore, at the present stage of our society's evolution, one cannot rely on that segment of public consciousness which holds to the genuine universal human values of justice, dignity, and respect for the interest of one's compatriots.

Current populist trends are bringing anarchic authoritarianism, poor political culture, and the degeneration of common sense. Endless rallies, pickets, and hunger strikes are often accompanied by downright immoral slogans and ideas, self-righteously peremptory statements, complete disregard for any arguments of opponents, and the apparent belief that by fair means or foul one's aim must be reached. All these are traits of ochlocratic thinking, a kind of despotism of the people which is obvious in the streets and, what is more, quite often manifests itself in parliaments.

The prerevolutionary legal theorist Bogdan Kistiakovskii wrote that, due to its inner necessity, any police state quite naturally must wind up in anarchy.[3] It happens this way because law and order in totalitarian society depend on state bodies rather than on the legal consciousness of the people. Therefore when totalitarianism is destroyed, legal culture initially lacks the properties needed to serve as the basis of public order. They take time to nurture. Berdyaev observed that "the currents of Russian democracy were inherited from our slavery and they must be rectified by the practice of self-government."[4]

We must admit that the "despotism of democracy" stage is an inevitable result of our long experience with absolutism. Russian democracy as it exists today lacks moral foundation, and moral foundation depends upon individual self-discipline. Without such a foundation, moves toward democracy and human rights lead to chaos, anarchy, and unpredictable social consequences. Thus, one should not really be overenthusiastic about the progress made in our democratization.

We should concern ourselves with the *quality* of democracy, which is determined by the level of individual consciousness, moral standards, and culture—the prerequisites of genuine democracy. The will of the people cannot be recognized formally without regard for its content simply because it is asserted or simply because it is the will of a majority to dominate in any sphere, to wish anything whatsoever, or to give or take away anything whatsoever.[5]

Berdyaev saw democracy as a spiritual phenomenon, linked with spiritual values and aims, with a striving for the perfection of the individual. He exposed the vices of abstract democratic ideology which lift responsibility from the individual, from the human spirit, thereby depriving the individual of autonomy and inviolable rights and shifting all responsibility and all freedom to "the quantitative mechanics of the masses," whereby personal strivings for perfection, molding of the character, and inner spiritual effort are ignored. "Democratic metaphysics of this kind attaches great significance to the agitation and instigation of the masses, to external action, while neglecting the essential inner evolution of society's human material. This is the way democracy degrades morally."[6]

Have we entered this path? Have we not talked up freedom, while passing over responsibility in silence? It seems we view freedom in a totalitarian way: we remember only too well V. I. Lenin's oft-repeated proposition that one cannot live in society and be free from society.[7] This proposition is irrefutable; to reject it only because it is Lenin's is just as wrong as it was to take anything Lenin said for gospel. After all, this idea is not at all Lenin's revelation, it dates back to much earlier times. Hegel stressed that liberty is not arbitrariness or freedom to engage in some extraordinary activities. "When we hear that freedom consists in general *in opportunities to do whatever one wishes* we can regard this view as completely devoid of any culture of thought; this view does not contain even a hint of understanding of what free will is in itself and for itself, as well as of what law, morality, etc. are."[8]

We always shy from one extreme to the other. The totalitarian system stressed responsibility; today we focus on freedom, forgetting that "only the responsible is free and only the free is responsible."[9] Thus, a bias toward self-centeredness, irresponsibility, and the application of tough pressures on authority structures, even on courts, is obvious in our society. Society is unable to keep within a civilized framework if criteria of what is permissible are missing. Legal boundaries of freedom must exist. If those boundaries are violated, the country will plunge into the abyss of anarchic mob rule.

Authorities are inert out of a fear that they will be accused of authoritarian practices. Hence, they do not respond with appropriate measures to the actions of those who break legal and moral norms; their inaction breeds chaos. Respect for public law and order and common human moral values is going, and the atmosphere of an absolute power vacuum and irresponsibility is setting in. Discipline is plummeting, as is production; the crime rate is zooming. The anarchy is pushing to the forefront politicians who exploit the base instincts of the public, their discontent and nationalism. These developments, if not reversed, may end in a grim new dictatorship.

In the present chaotic situation, the government inevitably has to take unpopular economic steps. Certainly, such issues cannot be decided by rallies, no matter how frequent and large. Of course, such steps would have been more effective and less unpopular four or five years ago, but it is a tradition in our society that it is always the people who pay for leaders' blunders, and pay dearly.

The state of our post-totalitarian society prompts us to predict that if a legal and moral foundation is not created for democracy to rest upon, society may revert to chaos and civil strife. An emphasis on individual responsibility and respect for the rights and interests of others in a democracy are indispensable prerequisites for society's health and its civilized exercise of rights and freedoms.

For the purpose of maintaining normal order in society, both international instruments and national legislation of modern states contain provisions which impose limitations on the exercise of rights. Article 29 of the Universal Declaration of Human Rights provides for limitations which "are determined by law solely for the purpose of securing due recognition and respect for the rights and freedoms of others and of meeting the just requirements of morality, public order and the general welfare in a democratic society."[10]

What has just been said must not be taken as a call for abridging democracy. Not at all! We mean here self-discipline of the individual, respect for the rights and interests of others, that is, the *moral criteria of democracy*. Immanuel Kant wrote about man's self-restraint in his free choice of actions. For Kant, freedom was inseparable from morality: in the final analysis he equated the concept of morality to the idea of freedom.[11] Genuine freedom, according to Kant, requires that we *always treat mankind in our own person as well as in the person of any other as the end and never only as the means*.[12] Lack of respect for society, other individuals—for their freedom, honor, dignity, and security—is an unfavorable background for democracy and human rights; it weakens individuals' potential and alters their humanistic nature.

We have yet to define the principles underlying our democracy and placing limits on it, or our path toward mature participation in it. It is time we scrapped the ludicrous myth that each kitchen hand is able to run the state. Only individuals who will not push the nation to the brink of an abyss should play a part in government. They will not allow to triumph principles like "grab everything and divide equally" or "plunder what was plundered by others," so dear to Bulgakov's Sharikov; they will not deprive people of the natural incentives that keep life going; and they will repudiate the macabre maxim that the end justifies the means.

The challenge for us in these decisive times it to develop a *quality* of democracy based upon respect for the individual, for his/her rights and potential for self-government. "Democracy," Berdyaev wrote, "musters the potential of human nature, their talent for self-government, for wielding power. . . . Only one who is able to wield power over oneself is able to wield power at all. Loss of personal and national self-control and stirring up chaos do not pave the way for democracy, on the contrary, democracy becomes impossible—it is then always the course toward despotism."[13]

Self-discipline and individual morality are incompatible with the vicious instincts of an angry mob demanding to lynch partocrats, democrats, or all those who belong to other ethnic groups or religions; they are as incompatible with attempts at dividing society into "we" and "they," as they are with nationalism and chauvinism.

Does the New Government Guarantee Human Rights?

First and foremost, it should be made clear exactly what government we mean. The Soviet state has ceased to exist. Independent sovereign states whose regimes range from democratic to national autocratic have been formed. Each government, regardless of the regime, stresses its commitment to democracy and human rights, although these rights are abused practically everywhere. Here again one must point to the legacy of totalitarian rule and its disregard for human rights and the individual. The legacy lingers, even though totalitarian rule may have been replaced by democratic government.

Democracy within our new government is burdened with the same traits as is the public: intolerance, vanity, populism, and intransigence toward any opposition. It is understandable, since those in power now were molded by the totalitarian system, and the task of remolding the personality and breaking away from totalitarian thinking patterns is formidable. Do we not remember congresses of people's deputies of the USSR and the triumph of the "aggressive-obedient majority" and their bitter opposition to the new thinking represented by Andrei Sakharov? The process of democratic evolution of the Russian Parliament is not smooth either.

Old all-Union structures that were to safeguard human rights have been scrapped. In any case, they were extremely ineffective. The judicial protection of citizens' rights had been making agonizingly slow progress. Constitutional and procurators' review also failed. The unmanageable administrative-legal mechanisms of humans rights protection served to protect bureaucrats from complaints rather than to safeguard citizens' rights.

The goal now is to set up new human rights mechanisms in the independent sovereign states. So far, former republics and their leaders have been busy asserting their sovereignty. Their human rights pledges look more like incantations than real work aimed at creating human rights safeguards. An important development in this respect, however, has been the creation of the Constitutional Court of Russia, with the protection of human rights as one of its priority functions.

New states prove truly democratic to the extent that they create mechanisms for protecting citizens' rights. In the absence of such mechanisms, the individual, just as before, can only be reduced to the pathetic role of a beggar asking the state for favors. It is important to study the experiences of time-tested, effective foreign mechanisms of safeguarding human rights, such as constitutional courts, ombudsmen (people's advocates), judicial systems, and administrative justice.

In the meantime, as old mechanisms are crumbling while new ones have not been created, individuals have found themselves unprotected and dependent on bureaucratic arbitrariness. Citizens have no faith in state support or help, so if in trouble they appeal to newspapers, radio and TV networks, academic institutions, or private individuals; they go on hunger strikes or picket on the steps of government buildings—this is becoming a tradition with us. A state that sets the goal of becoming *a state under the rule of law* must realize that its first priority is human rights protection in all spheres. Its ability to safeguard these rights is the criterion of how civilized the state is; for these rights, apart from being the source of state power, restrict such power as well.

The Soviet state had always solved its problems and reached its goals at the expense of the individual. Its leaders' only means of implementing utopian programs of socialist and communist construction was the ruthless exploitation of the people, of their patience and enthusiasm. "Great transformations" crushed millions upon millions of lives, scattered GULAGs all over the country and reduced the "emancipated" peasantry to fear-crippled serfs.

Perestroika appeared at first to be a huge step toward the spiritual emancipation of people; it resurrected hopes for a decent life. But people had been deceived by the party and by the state for so long and so shamelessly that it was the last hope. New authorities gave assurances that the goals of "transformation," "acceleration," and "renovation" would not be attained at the expense of the people. Now, again, people are urged to "have patience," for periods ranging from five to six months (yet another Utopia!) to ten years—truly a long-suffering people, every day sinking more deeply into misery with no relief in sight and hope evaporating! The people keep on paying the horrible price for the inane social experiment they were thrown into more than seventy years ago.

The return of the Soviet successor states to the path of civilization is hard and excruciating, but the most disconcerting thing is that the brunt of this comeback again must be shouldered by the people. Had not years been wasted before the quite obvious (but long ignored) decision to switch over to a market economy was taken, the fate of peoples would not have been so appalling. And the indecision, slackness, or, perhaps, unwillingness of authorities is again paid for by the people.

During the long overdue transition to a market economy, minimal but tangible guarantees that had protected the individual from hunger and poverty have disappeared. The USSR was a pioneer in recognizing economic, social, and cultural rights alongside the traditional political and civil rights. Neither that country nor its successors have been able to guarantee its citizens the right to work, to health care, to rest, or to living standards worthy of human beings.

Had a well-substantiated and balanced strategic plan of economic reforms been drafted at the initial stage of *perestroika* (and political leaders should have realized that an administrative-command economy can be transformed only by radical reforms, not by refurbishing), the individual would not have landed in such a dire situation. Even the new government of Russia is unable to predict with sufficient certainty the impact of privatization or liberalization of prices on the population. Indeed, could one seriously have believed the promise that the economy would be stabilized sometime in September or October 1992, given the current rate of production?

Realistic comprehensive programs of social guarantees must be worked out. All the policy turnabouts, the uncertainty, such controversial steps as the privatization of housing and scheduling of reforms have driven the people to despair. Their patience is wearing thin because it is always the ordinary person who is hostage to leaders' errors and differences of opinions. Our leaders and MPs would do well to remember that.

At this juncture we have neither clear legal mechanisms to protect human rights nor even minimal social guarantees. Unfortunately, these issues have not figured high enough on the agenda of parliaments and governments.

Effective human rights mechanisms must be created *now*, both within independent sovereign states and at the interstate level. Such structures are absolutely indispensable to protect the individual from bureaucratic arbitrariness, social vulnerability, and the consequences of the tense inter-nationality relations which took shape in the territories of the former USSR.

How Can Human Rights Be Safeguarded in the Former USSR?

The defeat of the August 1991 coup led to a rapid and uncontrollable collapse of the federation, which triggered off negative processes in the economic, political, and cultural spheres with a most disastrous impact on human rights.

"The centrifugal rush" and the inevitable sovereignization tore apart economic ties and brought about a further slump in production, making the prospect of closing down become very real for quite a few industrial enterprises. In their turn, these developments affected living standards, whipped up inflation, and led to even more acute shortages of goods. A number of republics announced plans to issue their own currencies, banned all exports, and set up customs checkpoints, all of which added to the gravity of the situation. As the common economic space crumbled, moreover, so did the common legal and humanitarian space that bound millions of people by millions of historical ties; these ties should have been severed gradually and in a reasonable way.

In some regions, the process of republics' gaining of independence has been accompanied by outbursts of nationalism; this inevitably results in abuses of the human rights of nonindigenous populations and in encroachments on the interests of ethnic minorities. Hundreds of thousands of people have become refugees. To protect their dignity and often their lives, they have had to flee from places where they were born or have lived for years. Their individual rights to the inviolability of their homes, to freedom of conscience, to free choice of their place of residence, as well as the security of their persons, were left unprotected. Some independent republics, such as the Baltic states, took steps which abridged the rights of their nonindigenous populations, making citizenship acquisition procedures more complex, for example.

The uncontrolled disintegration of the former USSR threatens grave consequences in all spheres including the sphere of human rights. In these circumstances the creation of the Commonwealth of Independent States (CIS) was a positive development. It would be naive, however, to assume that the continuation of this process is going to be easy.

The Alma-Ata Declaration, signed on December 21, 1991, by heads of eleven states (all former Soviet republics except Georgia and the Baltic states), established the basic principles of the Commonwealth. One of the fundamental provisions of the Declaration emphasizes respect for human rights and freedoms, including the rights of ethnic minorities.[14] However, the creation of the CIS cannot automatically safeguard human rights on the territories of the former Union. Outbreaks of nationalism cannot be overcome overnight. Emotions that had been held back for decades—the desire to get rid of imperial domination— were transformed into national self-assertion, which sometimes manifests itself in extreme forms.

Berdyaev wrote that "self-assertion may take the forms of nationalism, i.e. seclusion, exclusiveness, hostility toward other nationalities.... [N]ationalism has much more to do with hostility toward others than with love of one's own."[15] In our context, nationalism is aggravated by economic collapse, poverty, and chaos, which in turn lead to inter-nationality conflicts, each people claiming that it was robbed by others. Peoples cannot acquire freedom traveling this road. The tragedy of Yugoslavia and the unceasing armed clashes in Nagorno-Karabakh, in the Dniester area (Moldova), and in other parts of the country prove it beyond any doubt. Nationalism may unleash a civil war in this country.

The conflict between democratic and conservative forces in republics may prove another contributing factor. Our fragile democracy, torn apart by inner contradictions, cannot be a guarantee against all these disasters, nor could the CIS as launched in December 1991.

There is one more danger. Should human rights be abused in any of the CIS states, that state may bar other states from the process of restoring these rights, referring to its sovereignty and therefore the inadmissibility of any outside interference into its internal affairs. Such a situation would ignore the universally recognized principle of international law which holds that abuse of human rights by a state is not exclusively its internal matter but a concern of the entire international community.

All these developments—the rise of nationalism, the possible emergence of authoritarian postcommunist regimes on the territories of the former USSR, and the collision of sovereignty and human rights—leave no room for optimistic prognoses for reliable protection of human rights in the independent states. These developments are aggravated further by decades of governmental disrespect for the individual, the low legal culture, and legal nihilism.

All the more urgent, then, is the creation of a legal mechanism for protecting human rights on the territory of the Commonwealth. This does not mean that internal state structures will cease to concern themselves with human rights. On the contrary, as was pointed out earlier, reliable domestic legal mechanisms must be set up to protect human rights and freedoms. They must be reinforced, however, by interstate human rights structures which address the issue of human rights throughout the territory of the CIS, with a focus on the rights of minorities and citizens' associations as well.

The world has accumulated rich experiences of regional cooperation in the field of human rights. The most successful example is the cooperation among member states of the Council of Europe which adopted the European Convention for the Protection of Human Rights and Fundamental Freedoms and the European Social Charter and set up the European Commission and Court of Human Rights. If cooperation in this sphere is deemed expedient and useful among states with stable democratic traditions and law, it is no less relevant among the member states of the CIS, where the situation may be stabilized and human rights ensured only by concerted efforts.

The CIS should create a *common humanitarian space*. Its member states should adopt a convention on human rights and freedoms (or a Euro-Asian Convention on Human Rights) to serve as its legal foundation. The convention would contain a catalogue of principles in the field of international human rights cooperation which would set out fundamental rights and freedoms (political, individual, economic, social, and cultural). Ratification by CIS member states' parliaments would obligate members to observe its provisions and give the convention the status of law directly applicable and binding on each state.

The convention should also provide for the creation of implementing mechanisms: an interstate commission and a Euro-Asian court of human rights. The commission would be authorized to consider petitions about abuses of human rights from both individuals and groups of citizens; one state would be able to complain about human rights violations by another state. Individual petitions would be addressed to the commission after all domestic remedies have been exhausted.

An interstate (Euro-Asian) court of human rights would take up cases after they had been considered by the commission when the latter was unable to arrive at a decision, due to some reason or another. The decision of the court must be final.

To be objective and impartial, these organs must include a representative of each state. In cases of mass human rights violations threatening law and order, the commission and court may bring the issue before the CIS council and the heads of states. Developments have indicated that such conflicts will occur. Therefore there must be an effective mechanism for resolving them.

One more thing must be taken into account. The independent states either do not recognize legislation of the former USSR or recognize only those parts of it which do not collide with their domestic legislation. As a result, the legal system of the new states will be riddled with lacunae. Undesirable in any sphere of law, this abnormality may have especially dire consequences in the sphere regulating people's lives and activities. The legal status of the individual must not be vague. The convention should render the legal status of the individual clear and unambiguous and enable her or him to appeal to state organs, particularly to a court of law. The rights of individuals, including ethnic minorities, to petition interstate organs if their grievances are not settled in a satisfactory way would strengthen individual and collective rights.

The Alma-Ata Declaration emphasizes the desire of the CIS members to create democratic states under the rule of law. This objective may be reached, first and foremost, through the creation of effective national and interstate systems safeguarding human rights and freedoms, and through the humanization of our entire life. Together these systems would provide norms for guiding public life in the independent states.

The situation as it is today stems from our totalitarian past. Frankly, though, a lot of aggravating factors have been added in the last few years. The idea of the priority of human rights is lacking in our new political thinking. The tradition of disregard for the individual and her or his rights is a hallmark of Soviet legal thinking which has always given the pride of place to "the religion of totalitarian collectivism" and never to individual rights and interest; this tradition accounts for the slackness and go-slow tactics of authorities in creating state protections for human rights. Clearly, the state today is unable to provide economic security for the individual. This challenges the successor states simultaneously to carry out more effective reforms, to nurture a democratic political culture, to gather experience with democracy, resolve interethnic disputes, and set up legal guarantees for human rights. If this challenge is not cause for hopelessness, it is hardly one for naive optimism either.

Notes

1. N. Berdyaev, *Sud'ba Rossii*, 1990, 299.
2. V.I. Lenin, *Polnoe sobranie sochinenii*, vol. 41, 381.

3. B. Kistiakovskii, *Gosudarstvo pravovoe i sotsialisticheskoe*, 25.
4. Berdyaev, 215.
5. Ibid., 211.
6. Ibid., 213.
7. Lenin, vol. 12, 104.
8. Hegel, *Collected Works*, 1935, 444.
9. Berdyaev, 212.
10. *Prava cheloveka. Sbornik mezhdunarodnykh dokumentov*, 1986, 29.
11. I. Kant, *Collected Works*, vol. 4, 1965, 292.
12. Kant, 270.
13. Berdyaev, 214.
14. *Izvestiia*, December 23, 1991.
15. Berdyaev, 314–315, 316–317.

6

Individual Rights Before October 1917: A Russian Perspective

Evgenii Skripilev

> Without the history of a subject there can be no theory about the subject.
> (N.G. Chernyshevskii)

The Estate System and Individual Rights

The so-called estate system characterized the Russian autocracy and its social relations throughout the eighteenth and nineteenth centuries, during the slow evolution into "bourgeois" (constitutional) monarchy. The estates (*sosloviia*) were categories of persons, each with its own specific "rights" and duties. Distinctions among estates rested on occupation (clergy, merchant, guild master, peasant, nobility), the character of duty to the state ("poll-tax-paying estates"— peasants and petit-bourgeoisie—and "non–poll-tax-paying estates") and real or imaginary high-born descent and ancestral services (hereditary nobility).

The peculiarities of the estates' roles and functions in public life, their rights and obligations, were prescribed by numerous legal norms contained in the Collected Laws of the Russian Empire, in effect until the October Revolution. The nobility enjoyed the greatest rights. Their rights and privileges, including preferential access to administrative power, to land, and to the ear of the tsar, date back to the reign of Catherine the Great in the late eighteenth century.[1]

The peasants, on the other hand, had the fewest rights. For centuries, as serfs, they were the property of the landowners. Serfdom was as widespread as it was

---

Editor's note. This chapter contributes to theories on the significance of prerevolutionary tradition, rights, and reform. It brings back for us the history of a half-century of the expansion of individual rights owing to changes both in government policy and in the nature of the opposition with its growing advocacy of legality (the subject of the following chapter by Susan Heuman) and growing popular involvement. All differences in approach aside, chapters 4, 6, and 7 remind us that the introduction of the idea of universal human rights and the struggle to realize them began not in 1986 but with the birth and development of ideas of rule of law and individual rights in pre-Bolshevik Russia.

disgraceful. A law of 1767 prescribed exile in penal servitude for any serf who dared to complain against his master. Article 1410 of the Statutes on Criminal Punishments and Corrections of 1845 established criminal punishment for selling a Russian subject into slavery with another national and Article 1411 did the same for trading in African Negroes;[2] but at the same time, Russian law did not forbid the sale of serfs. Other penalties and disabilities suffered by peasants included their subordination to the authority of special administrative agencies and people and the jurisdiction over them of a special county court which followed local customary law rather than general law.

In 1889, the position of land captains was established. These officials assumed both administrative and judicial functions for their districts, replacing the elected justices of the peace, and intensifying surveillance of all organs and officials of the peasant administration.

Criminal law and procedure involved particularly serious violations of individual rights, especially before the reforms of 1864. The violations included closed court hearings; great weight given to confessions and less weight given to the defensive testimony of the accused and to testimony of women, of non-nobles, of non-scholars, and of laymen (as distinct from clergy);[3] and widespread corporal punishment administered by canes, whips, *knuty* (clubs), and rods.[4] (The nobility, the clergy, and merchants of first and second guild were exempted from corporal punishment, and the branding of convicts and corporal punishment of women was banned.) The estate membership of a person was taken into account not only upon passing of sentence, but also in the decision as to how that sentence would be served. Curtailment of one's individual rights continued after one had served out his or her punishment. The statutes on criminal punishment and correction stipulated that certain punishments also entailed the loss of various rights and privileges associated with membership in a given estate, permanently or for a specified time.

Women had unequal rights. A husband had the right to demand that his wife live with him. The wife's place of residence was dependent on the husband's place of residence. Without his permission, a wife could not make certain agreements or take a job. Women were not allowed to become members of the bar, and they had no right to vote in elections to the State Duma (the parliament first elected in 1906).

Rights of Association and Expression

The activities of private organizations and associations are an important part of individual and social freedom at all times. The legislation of autocratic Russia, as that of other countries, divided associations into those that were legal—"permitted by law"—and those that were unlawful, illegal, "secret," and even "criminal." Between the first legal formulation in 1782 and the 1905 Revolution, no private organization could be formed and operate without recognition by the government.[5]

The government feared secret societies. Beginning in 1822, every official had to sign a pledge not to belong to any secret society. Even those organizations which passed muster as not being "somehow harmful for the state system or to public morality"[6] were under constant and vigilant patrol of the political police and appropriate ministries.[7] The same control operated over unregulated meetings of any groups.

A private association had to get the permission of the Department of the Police of the Ministry of the Interior, which approved the statutes of associations and clubs and gave permission for public lectures and readings, exhibitions and congresses. By the end of the 1890s, other ministries also received the right to permit this or that association to operate. As a rule, statutes indicated the purposes of the association and the means of achieving them, its ways of meeting expenses, its makeup, the rights and duties of its member, its administrative procedures and accountability, and the resolutions in the case of its closing or the liquidation of its affairs. During the 1890s, every statute had to state that membership in an association was closed to active-duty military personnel of the lower ranks and cadets, to most minors, and to persons who were subject to limitation of their rights by courts.

In general, private organizations and unions operated at the provincial (*guberniia*) level. The government frowned on the organization of local branches of associations because that would complicate surveillance and control over them. Despite this, a few organizations became all-Russian, with local branches or departments (the Russian Technical Society, the Russian Society for the Preservation of Public Health, and the Russian Society of the Red Cross).

Along with the tolerated and persecuted associations there also existed privileged associations. A few dozen associations were called "the Emperor's." They could appeal to the emperor, and they received substantial subsidies and enjoyed various other privileges. Some organizations were sponsored by a member of the royal family who was elected president or honorary president.[8]

Freedom of the press was not guaranteed in Russia. Russian literature suffocated for long years in the grip of governmental (secular, religious, military) censorship dating back to Peter I and Catherine II. The first censorship law of 1804 obliged censors "to ban books and works which are against morality, but to make available to society books which contributed to the truthful education of the mind and the formation of morals." The same idea appeared in subsequent censorship statutes.

The Model Regulation on the Press of 1865 gave the censorship committee the right to issue a warning and, after two warnings, to suspend or confiscate a publication and to fine and initiate a criminal prosecution of the publisher and editors. The Chief Administration on Affairs of the Press under the Minister of Internal Affairs controlled censorship and oversaw the book trade. The minister was empowered in 1873 to halt any edition that concerned matters of state importance and whose publicity or discussion "in the opinion of the higher government" was found to be inconvenient. Up to 1905, the Chief Administration on Affairs of the Press published 562 circulars which forbade the press from airing various matters of domestic and foreign policy.[9]

Seventy-eight Russian writers appealed to the government on January 8, 1895, to revise the press law. To their petition was attached a "note on revising press laws," in which it was shown that press legislation did not accord with the law. The petition had no effect.

Judicial Reform

The judicial reform of 1864 was a major event in the history of Russia. It enhanced the legal status of the individual. Previously, the court was not separate from the administration. The judicial statues of November 20, 1864, proclaimed: "Judicial authority is separated form executive, administrative, and legislative." The statutes established juries and the bar and provided for the election of justices of the peace. Irremovability of judges, open trials, and adversary procedures were introduced. The medieval theory of formal truth based on confession was replaced by a free assessment of evidence by the judges.

The establishment of jury trials and of the professional bar marked a big step forward in improving the procedural position of the accused (defendant). However, several years after the introduction of the judicial statutes, something occurred which liberal jurists called "the spoiling" of the statutes. In 1872 there was added to the Senate (the highest court) a "special session for the trying of cases of state crimes and illegal organizations."[10] Alongside the chairman and five senators sat the so-called estate representatives, nobles appointed from among the provincial officials by the tsar upon the recommendation of the Ministries of Internal Affairs and Justice. The special session applied the rules of the judicial statutes' criminal procedure to political cases; nevertheless, the majority of cases were tried behind closed doors or before a hand-picked public. Reports on a number of cases were published in abridged form. In 1878 the government transferred the hearing of political cases to the military district court,[11] whose procedures were simplified and closed. These courts often passed death sentences.

It must be noted that in tsarist Russia, in general, the pretext for curtailment of all kinds of individual freedom, even as punishment, often was not the commission of a particular crime but so-called political unreliability. Characteristic for Russia was the widespread, one may say pervasive, police surveillance carried out at first by the Third Department of the Imperial Chancellory and later by the Department of the Police.

From the early 1880s, the Committee of Ministers was authorized to declare "a state of emergency" in parts of Russia.[12] Lenin later called the law on the state of emergency "one of the most relied on, basic laws of the Russian Empire."[13] A state of emergency empowered the local authorities to curtail existing rights and expel various suspicious and "harmful" persons from the area by administrative procedure. People could also be sent into exile with the agreement of the Special Board of the Minister of Internal Affairs. In its extreme form of "extraordinary protection," the "state of emergency" gave full authority to the provincial governor or to a specially appointed local chief to whom the entire local, civil, and military apparatus were subordinate. Such officials could form special military police commands, transfer any case to the military court, dismiss subordinate officials, sequester real property, and confiscate movable property.

If that were not enough, by rules issued in June 18, 1882, there was established yet one more stage of the "exceptional state"—martial law, under which complete power was transferred to the military establishment and the civil authorities were put under military jurisdiction in many spheres. In 1901 more than a third of the Russian population lived under the so-called "state of emergency."

Constitutional Rights

As they attempted to liquidate absolute monarchy in Russia, a considerable part of the Russian intelligentsia—notably, such revolutionary populists as Piotr Lavrov, Mikhail Bakunin, and Piotr Tkachev—at the same time looked unfavorably on political contests and the establishment of a constitutional parliamentary system. They lost sight of the fact that bourgeois democracy, with its civil and political freedoms, meant an enormous step forward (see also chapter 4 on this).

The first Russian Marxist, Georgii Plekhanov, and the group he led, Emancipation of Labor (*Osvobozhdenie truda*, formed in 1883), served the cause of individual rights by including in their political programs demands for: a democratic constitution; universal franchise and pay for public representatives; universal, secular, free, and compulsory education; the guarantee of the inviolability of the person and the home; unlimited freedom of conscience, expression, the press, assembly and association, and movement and occupation; complete equality of all citizens regardless of their religious and ethnic origins; the replacement of a standing army with general conscription; the reform of all civil and criminal legislation; and the elimination of estate categories and of inhumane punishments. In addition to democratic reforms, Plekhanov's organization looked to measures specially in the interest of workers and peasants.[14] The first program of the Bolshevik party, issued in 1903, took up a number of demands from Plekhanov's draft aimed at eliminating the many survivals of the precapitalist economic, social, and political systems.[15]

Before the 1905 Revolution, problems of the rights and freedoms of Russian subjects were usually elaborated by various liberal law professors in their solid university courses and research work. Without fail, they analyzed the theories of western European and American authors on such subjects as individual freedoms, constitutionalism and parliamentarianism, and the separation of powers. Also analyzed was current legislative, administrative, and court practice, with more or less careful comparisons of western European and Russian political and legal systems. During the second half of the nineteenth and beginning of the twentieth century, some eminent Russian jurists devoted a major part of their work to the problem of civil and political rights—among these men were S.A. Muromtsev, L.I. Petrazhitskii, P.I. Novgorodtsev, and B.A. Kistiakovskii (see chapter 7). Some jurists connected individual rights with economic and social preconditions. Whatever their philosophical views, these and other scholars were united on the goal of a Russian society that must be, they said, the creation of a law-governed state which alone could guarantee the rights of the individual.

The 1905 Revolution brought significant changes in the character of Russian writing about social relations. Jurists published many newspaper articles and brochures in which they explained the meaning of the rights of man and citizen and of civil and political freedoms. They criticized the truncated character of the existing Russian legal norms, even including those that appeared in connection with the tsar's manifesto of October 17, 1905; and they exposed violations of legislation on freedoms proclaimed by this document. One cannot deny that this literature, to a certain extent, contributed to the political and legal education of the people.

Russian liberal jurists had worked the theory of the law-governed state and its Russian adaptation around the time of the 1905 Revolution. For them, one of the criteria of a law-governed state was the recognition that the citizen had a certain sum of rights which only the court could curtail.[16] Usually, citizens' freedoms were divided into three groups: (1) personal freedoms—the inviolability of the person and the home, the privacy of correspondence, the freedom of profession, and the freedom of movement; (2) social freedoms—of conscience (faith), thought, expression, press, and assembly and association; (3) economic or material freedom—of property, labor, industry, and trade. Liberal jurists usually look to the courts to protect the guarantees of these freedoms.

The 1905 Revolution was noteworthy for the formation of many political parties, each of which included in its platform its own understanding of individual rights and freedoms and its own ways of achieving and guaranteeing them. Thus, the Agrarian Socialist (Populist) party proclaimed the slogan, "There is nothing higher and dearer than the individual"; the program of the Labor (Popular Socialist) party was built around the theme of "the human individual" and stated: "Only through full employment can the rights of each human individual be guaranteed"; "the inalienable rights of the individual must be recognized"; "the state must guarantee not only legal but also other interests of the individual"; "labor must be made universal, productive, and useful. Only this way is it possible to provide every individual with the necessities of life. . . ."

The Marxist V.V. Vorovskii (assassinated in 1923 while on diplomatic assignment in Lausanne) reproduced all these slogans in his article "The Populist-Socialist Party and the Individual." He correctly reproached its authors in that they "do not know yet that the individual human beings do not still exist in this world; that they had long ago been replaced by the entrepreneur, the worker, the landowner and day laborer, the trader and peasant, the intellectual and the policeman. . . ."[17]

The 1905 Revolution resulted in reforms of the state and legal systems, including in rights and freedoms of citizens. On October 17, 1905, the tsar issued The Manifesto on the Reform of the State System, which mentioned the "obligation of the government" to carry out the tsar's will: "to give to the population an unshakable foundation of civil freedom on the basis of the real inviolability of the individual, freedom of conscience, expression, assembly and association." The manifesto also contained a promise of participation in the new State Duma for "those classes of the population hitherto disenfranchised." The concluding section of the manifesto contained the commitment "to establish, as an unshakable rule, that no law may be adopted, no law may enter into force, without the approval of the State Duma and that the elected representatives of the people receive the possibility of real participation in supervision over the legality of the actions of the authorities set up by us."[18]

All this was an important step forward. The four freedoms promised by the October manifesto received their legal affirmation in a number of acts, including the Fundamental Laws of the Russian Empire (in the version of April 23, 1906). The Fundamental Laws declared that nobody shall be prosecuted for a crime other than according to procedures established by law; nobody may be detained other than under circumstances defined by law; nobody may be convicted and punished except for criminal acts which are listed in the criminal laws in effect at the time the crime is committed.

The right of assembly, recognized by the Fundamental Laws, was regulated by the Temporary Rules of March 4, 1906, on meetings, associations, and leagues. These rules distinguished between public and nonpublic meetings. Nonpublic meetings were freely permitted; public meetings required permission for prior information of the authorities [a provision repeated in the legislation under Gorbachev more than eighty years later—Ed.]. No later than three days before the meeting, it was necessary to inform the head of the local police of the place, time, and subject of it, and to list its organizers (names and residences). A meeting was not allowed if it was "against the law or public morality" or if it was deemed to threaten "public peace or security." The governor or chief of the local police could assign an official to be present at a public meeting. The latter watched out for public order at the gathering and could, in some cases, close the meeting. Outdoor meetings required the permission of the governor or the head of the local police. The head of the police could refuse permission, letting the organizers know within one day before the proposed opening of the meeting and indicating the reason for his refusal [the similar Soviet decree required no statement of cause—Ed.].

Armed persons and students were not permitted at public meetings. Meetings were forbidden close to the residence or in the physical presence of the tsar, nearby to the place where the State Council or Duma were meeting, or nearby to other premises listed in the rules.

The rules proclaimed the right to form associations and leagues for purposes that did not violate the law and on condition of notifying the governor or the mayor. The activity of nonprofit organizations was regulated by the Temporary Rules of March 4, 1906, which also distinguished between associations and leagues—the combination of two or more associations was called a league.

Censorship was noticeably relaxed. The Temporary Rules of November 24, 1905, and an edict of March 18, 1906, abolished prior governmental censorship, the deposit required upon publication of a newspaper, and the administration's right to levy fines. The periodical presses began to answer only before the court. No special permission from the authorities was required to open a newspaper, a magazine, or a book publishing enterprise or book store. It was sufficient simply to notify the governor or mayor two weeks before publication. And an edict of April 26, 1906, abolished prior censorship of nonperiodical presses and the publishers of books and brochures.

The Fundamental Laws also established religious freedom for Russian subjects and stipulated that they may not suffer the curtailment of their rights regardless of their religion. The legislation of the period of the 1905 Revolution also proclaimed the rights to personal inviolability, the freedom of movement, and the privacy of correspondence. However, even while these rights were being proclaimed, the government authorities violated them, one way or another (through illegal searches or confiscations in people's homes, the inspection of letters, the passport system, the curtailments of freedom of movement, as examples). By 1906, the government had already begun to liquidate the democratic gains of 1905. On August 19, 1906, the Council of Ministers decreed the establishment of field courts-martial in instances of martial law and states of siege.[19] They heard cases behind closed doors in summary procedures lasting no more than two days.[20] The sentences went immediately into effect and were carried out within one day on the order of the officer who had summoned the courts-martial. The most frequent punishment meted out by the field courts-martial was death by hanging or shooting.

Dual Power

The February Bourgeois Democratic Revolution of 1917 marked a new stage in the development of rights and freedoms of the individual in Russia. By general admission, Russia became the freest country in the world. This had to do with a number of historical peculiarities. "Dual power" existed, that of the bourgeois Provisional Government and that of the soviets of workers' and soldiers' deputies. Each in its own way proclaimed a program of individual rights and freedoms and abolished curtailments which had existed under the autocracy.

The February Revolution greatly stimulated the lawmaking activity of the revolutionary organizations of the working people: soviets of workers' and soldiers' deputies, factory and local committees, land committees and other peasant organizations, and soldiers' committees. "Order No. 1" of the Petrograd Soviet of March 1, 1917, to the garrison of the Petrograd military district played a significant role in democratizing the army and affirming the civil liberties of off-duty soldiers and sailors. The order called for the immediate election of committees of representatives from the lower ranks in all military units and ships of the Navy to the soviet. Rudeness to the soldiers of any rank—in particular, addressing them with the familiar "ty" ("thou")—was forbidden. Officers' titles of address, such as "your excellency," were also abolished and replaced with such terms of address as "Mr. General" or "Mr. Colonel."

The Petrograd Soviet ordered the introduction of the eight-hour working day in industrial enterprises and established factory committees and other organs of workers' control. Elected soldiers' committees of companies and regiments oversaw the actions of the officer corps and the elections of military commanders. Factory committees took part in the management of enterprises and established workers' control over production. Freely formed trade unions played an important role in the struggle for collective bargaining, not only in Petrograd but also in the provinces.

Between March and May 1917, the peasants began to transfer landowners' properties to the control of rural district committees and to divide the land, to lower lease payments, and to seize farm inventory.

The Provisional Government issued a declaration on March 3, 1917, stating that it would be guided by the following principles: (1) full and immediate amnesty in all political and religious cases, including cases of terrorism, mutiny, and agrarian crimes, etc.; (2) the freedoms of expression, press, association, assembly, and strikes, and the extension of political freedoms to military personnel within limits permitted by military conditions; (3) the abolition of all estates (a measure that had failed in the Dumas of 1906 and 1907 and on which the Provisional Government took no action), and an end to discrimination based on religious belief or nationality.

The Provisional Government also carried out a number of reforms of criminal law and of the courts and prisons. In April 1917, it abolished exile and replaced it with jail terms. It abolished corporal punishment in prisons as well as punishment cells and fetters and dismissed part of the prison administration. Field courts-martial were abolished in the Petrograd military district and outside war zones. However, after demonstrators were fired upon during the July antigovernment demonstrations in Petrograd that led to the end of the period of dual power, the Provisional Government restored the death penalty at the front and the activity of the field courts-martial, now renamed Military-Revolutionary Courts to deceive the masses.

With relative ease, the Provisional Government did away with the institution of land captains (the local political chiefs set up during the reactionary period in

1889) and the institution of estate representatives in the courts and the special presence in the governing Senate, which also had included estate representatives. It planned for juries to sit not only in the district courts, as they did already, but also in the higher judicial chambers, as well as in the senate.[21]

When the Provisional Government dealt with the court system and procedures, and in general with pre-existing institutions, it tried not to break up those whose activity "did not contradict the new system." It declared among its goals to be the restoration of the judicial reform of 1864, which had been "spoiled by subsequent legislation."

On March 20, 1917, the Provisional Government abolished the old discriminations on the bases of religious belief and nationality. This meant the lifting of limits on an individual's place of residence, on movement, on acquisition of property, on engagements in crafts and trade, and on entry into educational institutions and state service. But limitations on the use of local languages were abolished only in the conduct of the business of private associations, in private schools, and in the keeping of trade accounts. The law of April 12, 1917, on meetings and unions, proclaimed the freedom of trade unions and their right of juridical person after registration with the courts. Prior to this, the courts had sometimes refused to register trade unions on the pretext of the absence of a law, or on the pretext of taking exception with one or another point of a trade union's statutes.

It cannot be denied that a number of legislative acts of the Provisional Government completely satisfied the criteria of a bourgeois democracy. The decree of April 15, 1917, on the conduct of elections for the city dumas and city district administrations, established universal, equal, direct, and secret suffrage. The act of September 1, 1917, which created the so-called directorate consisting of five persons headed by A.F. Kerenskii, declared Russia to be a republic.[22] When Kerenskii was asked why the act did not include the words "democratic" republic, he replied that there was no need for this, since the term "democratic" referred not to the particular form of state system (monarchy, republic, etc.) but only to the political relationship involved. However, the working people who had created the soviets no longer wanted to create the usual bourgeois parliamentary republic, even the most democratic. They were demanding a republic of soviets.

Individual rights appeared to play an important part in the thinking of the commission under Prof. N.I. Lazarevskii which began its work on a constitutional draft on October 11, 1917 (that is, two weeks before the Bolshevik takeover—Ed.). Of the nineteen sections of the draft constitution, five related to citizens' rights and freedoms: (1) a declaration of the rights of civil freedom; principles which could underlie the constitution (the monarchical principle, the principle of popular sovereignty, the principle of full self-determination of the populace); (2) guarantees of the rights of civil freedom; states of emergency; (3) principles of federalism, autonomy, self-determination, and state unity;

(4) status for state and local languages; (5) popular representation; bicameralism; immunity and maintenance of deputies; compatibility of office with state service, etc.

During the discussion of the declaration of the rights of civil freedom, it was decided to include in the Constitution of Russia not only the principles of "rights of freedom," but also the rights "of positive status," that is, the rights of citizens to specific services from the state. Here the commission introduced a qualifier, to the effect that "the affirmation of all rights of that kind might turn out to lack practical meaning." However, the question of listing basic obligations of citizens aroused no opposition.[23]

Conclusions

The problem of individual rights in prerevolutionary Russia was extremely complex and contradictory. For a long time, serfdom and the inequality of the estate system, as well as administrative and police abuse, had dominated the country. The absence of restraints on government power at all levels, the pervasive regulation and police supervision, the lack of openness, the officials' commission of all sorts of abuses with impunity—all this most severely limited the freedom of the individual. The process of liberation of the individual was lengthy and painful.

The capitalist development of Russia compelled the autocratic government to take steps in the direction of transforming the absolute monarchy into a bourgeois or constitutional monarchy. The repeal of serfdom in Russia in 1861 and the ensuing reforms of the 1860s and 1870s introduced some elements of bourgeois democracy. The court reform of 1864 was extremely important; it established new principles for the court system and judicial process.

Russian revolutionaries and liberals alike tried to achieve elementary civil and political rights and freedoms for the people; but of course one should not lose sight of the differences between them in principles and methods for achieving this goal, or in their hopes for such rights and freedoms. Both the revolutionaries and the liberals demanded that changes be made in the "way of government" by the creation of an organ of national representation to which the executive power would be responsible. But whereas liberals advocated only the limitation of the autocratic monarchy by replacing it with a constitutional monarchy, the revolutionaries insisted on the liquidation of absolutism and the establishment of a republic under which the rights of the individual could best be guaranteed.

The Russian Revolution of 1905 compelled the autocracy to make serious concessions to the people in order to preserve itself. The promised rights and freedoms contained in the manifesto of October 17, 1905, were affixed in a number of laws. Thanks to freedom of the press, established during the period of revolution, public opinion acquired a certain amount of influence over the activities of bureaucratic institutions and particular officials.

The everyday practice of the autocratic government, its limitation of the rights of parliament, the State Duma, and the coup of June 3, 1907 [imposing a new conservative, class-weighted electoral law—Ed.], did enormous harm to the freedoms of individuals. During the February Bourgeois Revolution of 1917, the rights and freedoms that had been violated under tsarism were restored and expanded. Russia became the freest of all belligerent countries in World War I. On the one hand, the revolutionary organizations of the workers—such as the soviets and the soldiers' and factory committees—declared as restored various rights and freedoms which had been negated or curtailed by autocracy. On the other hand, the bourgeois Provisional Government, through its legislation, formalized the freedoms which had been gained in fact by the people. It worked out generally democratic laws, for example, on elections to organs of local governments and to the Constituent Assembly. However, it did not decide on the formal abolition of the estate system.

When all is said and done, one must recognize that the sum total of rights and freedoms achieved by the people during the course of this long struggle, especially as a result of two Russian revolutions, signified the creation of a model of a law-governed state. However, far from all human rights, least of all social and economic, received real guarantees.

Notes

1. *Polnoe sobranie zakonov Rossiiskoi imperii (PSZ)* 22: 16187; 6: 3890.

2. *Ulozhenie o nakazaniiakh ugolovnykh i ispravitel'nykh.* Petrograd, 1916, 313–14.

3. *PSZ* 5: 3006; *Svod zakonov Rossiiskoi imperii, zakoni ugolovnye.* St. Petersburg, 1857, 335.

4. For prerevolutionary impressions of this, see courtroom speech of lawyer P.A. Aleksandrov at the trial of Vera Zasulich, 1879, in *Sudebnye rechi izvestnykh russkikh iuristov*, Moscow, 1956, 147; A.I. Gertsen, *Sobranie sochinenii v 30 tomakh*, vol. 8, 1956, 147.

5. *PSZ* 21: 15379.

6. *PSZ* 42: 44402.

7. In this spirit were the law of June 4, 1874, "On punishments for forming illegal associations and participating in them," the circular of the Minister of Internal Affairs, P.A. Balueva, in 1874, Articles 124–137 of the 1903 Criminal Code.

8. At least fifteen types of groups existed at the turn of the century: horse racing, hunting on horseback, mutual aid of present and former students, city and villager firefighters, poor relief, student mutual aid, consumers, agricultural, temperance, musical-choral, bicycle, mutual aid generally, mutual aid upon bereavement, mutual aid of persons getting married. A.D. Stepanskii, *Samoderzhavie i obshchestvennye organizatsii Rossii na rubezhe 19–20 vv.*, Moscow, 1980, 12.

9. M. Lemke, "V mire usmotreniia," *Vestnik prava* (September 1905), 100.

10. *2 PSZ* sec. I: 50956 (1872).

11. *2 PSZ* sec. II: 58778 (1878).

12. "Decree on measures for measures of the protection of state security and public order, August 14, 1881," *SZRI*, 14, 1892 append. I to p. I.

13. V.I. Lenin, *Poln. sobr. soch.*, 9, 331.

14. "Vtoroi proekt Programmy russkikh sotsial-demokratov," in G.V. Plekhanov, *Sochineniia*, vol. 2, 1922, 403.

15. These included gentry latifundia, autocracy, the estates, etc. The program called in addition for a range of individual political and socio-economic rights, elected judges, separation of church from state and school from church, replacement of a standing army with the people in arms, repeal of indirect taxes, and introduction of a progressive income tax.

16. A.K. Dzhivelegov, *Prava i obiazannosti grazhdan v pravovom gosudarstve*, Moscow, 1906, 5.

17. V.V. Vorovskii, *Izbrannye proizvedeniia o pervoi russkoi revoliutsii*, Moscow, 1955, 77–78.

18. *3 PSZ* 25: sec. I: 26803.

19. *3 PSZ* 26: sec. I: 28252.

20. Field courts-martial consisted of a chairman and four officers (army or navy). *Gosudarstvennyi duma. Vtoroi sozyv. Zakonodatel'nye materialy*, St. Petersburg, 1907, 265.

21. *Vestnik vremennogo pravitel'stva* 1 (March 5, 1917), 46.

22. *Vestnik vremennogo pravitel'stva* 182 (October 20, 1917), 228.

23. "Vremennoe pravitel'stvo i uchreditel'noe sobranie," *Krasnyi arkhiv* 3 (1928), 107 and ff.

7

Prerevolutionary New Thinking

Susan Heuman

Legal theorists in nineteenth- and early twentieth-century Russia struggled with the idea of setting up a rule-of-law state, *pravovoe gosudarstvo*—which is a translation of the German liberal concept of *Rechtstaat*. The term *Rechtstaat* is often used to mean a state based on law, but its definition varies depending on the theorist using the term. For liberal lawyers in Russia at the turn of the century, it was a state based on a constitution, but it did not necessarily mean that the constitution would protect civil liberties or that it would be based on popular sovereignty. For others, it indicated a democratic constitutional form based on popular sovereignty. The difficult discussions on the need for a legally based state took place in a Russian empire where law was an ambiguous concept and the attitude to it was ambivalent.

Decree versus Law

The interest in setting up a legally based state, a *Rechtstaat*, was complicated by several factors. There was no general theory of law (*pravo*) on which to build. The predominant solution to governmental problems was to pass regulations (*zakony*) to deal with immediate situations and not cope with the general problem of *pravo*. The *soslovie* system (the estate system) divided the population into four groups on the basis of "differences in rights"—the nobility, the clergy, the urban residents, and the rural residents[1]—and did not correspond to the newly emerging classes in the society. The estate system discouraged citizens from considering themselves individuals separate from the collective. In order for a democratic government to be created, the relationship between the individual and the state would have to become a partnership that would empower citizens to act independently of the state political monopoly. At the same time, the individuals would turn into citizens who had a consciousness of the law and the responsibilities connected with the exercise of broader political freedoms.

From the time of Peter the Great, the tsars established a governmental system designed to serve the will of the center.[2] Law was identified with the head of state rather than with legal precepts. As Professor Richard Wortman explains in his seminal work, *The Development of Russian Legal Consciousness*:

> The image of a patriarchal tsar dispensing a personal justice maintained its hold in the eighteenth and early nineteenth century and fed a distrust of formal institutions that might dilute the monarchs' power to extend personal grace, benefits, and privilege. Personal connections, access to high individuals close to the tsar, gave the Russian nobility a way to avoid submitting themselves to the demeaning rule of petty officials. [3]

Although the failure to codify the law was recognized as a problem during each reign, the tsars drew back from permitting the establishment of an overarching theory of law. Having refused to build a codified law based on a general theory of law, the autocracy resorted to the solution of issuing regulations (*zakony*) to deal with every problem. Thus, Marc Raeff has described the Russian Empire as a *Reglamentstaat*, with a multitude of separate written regulations.[4]

The autocracy's situation was complicated in the first half of the nineteenth century with the growth in numbers of bureaucrats and the growth of legal education; officials trained in law gradually started to replace the noblemen who had controlled the legal system.[5] Their consciousness of law was based on the idea of creating a *Rechtstaat*, a state that would run in an orderly fashion through institutions, regular procedures, and according to regulations—a concept that contradicted the idea of the personal rule of the tsar. The conflict between the tsarist idea of personal rule and the idea of the rule of law led to political conflict and a fundamental ambivalence toward law. It was that conflict and ambivalence which ultimately undermined the great legal reforms of the 1860s.

Introduced under Alexander II just after the emancipation of the serfs, the legal reforms of 1864 created an independent judiciary, jury trials, and a bar (*advokatura*). By the turn of the century, judges were appointed for life and conducted public jury trials; there were substantial rights of appeal and greater attention to procedural rights for defendants. Judges upheld the independent role of law, even abrogating executive administrative orders which they deemed illegal.

Had legal institutions been successfully established throughout the empire during the reform period, a more powerful and resilient legal culture might have developed. As it happened, however, the government intervened whenever it felt threatened by the independence of judges and juries.[6] For example, the courts had considerable autonomy in the area of political crimes until the Vera Zasulich case in 1878. Zasulich shot and wounded the St. Petersburg governor general as a retaliatory gesture for his having beaten a revolutionary prisoner named Bogoliubov. When Zasulich was acquitted to cheers in the courtroom, the regime intervened by taking many political trials out of the public realm of jury trials and remanding them to military courts-martial. During the trials of the People's Will party (*Narodnaia volia*) in the 1880s, forty-two of the seventy-three cases were heard by military courts and seven by special Senate session. Only the least significant were heard in public jury trials.

Military courts were formed when a governor general or a person of equal stature requested them for areas of the empire that were under martial law. Field courts-martial were to be used when a civilian criminal action was "so obvious" that investigation was unnecessary.[7] Clearly, the distinction between civil and political crimes was difficult to ascertain at a time of revolution. However, the Imperial Russian government considered revolutionary unrest and common street crime interwoven and equally destructive to the government and civilian population.[8] In 1906, about a thousand political prisoners had been executed during field courts-martial in one year. In a 1906 report by the Military Justice Administration, an official rationale was given for the upsurge in military judicial actions.

> The significant increase in the criminal actions of the revolutionary organizations directed to overthrowing the existing state order and the principles of society has been marked by a whole series of terrorist acts and an extraordinary increase of the most terrible crimes, directed not only against the government power but the lives, health, freedom and property of the peaceable population. In the struggle with these extremely dangerous phenomena . . . swift and correspondingly stern judicial repression has the greatest significance.[9]

Estate and Class: The Reforms of 1864

The legal system set up under the reforms of 1864 applied to only a small part of the population—about ten to fifteen percent. The great majority of the people were peasants emancipated from serfdom in 1861 who lived in traditional village communes, under the jurisdiction of local custom. The land redemption payments and taxes imposed upon the communes as a condition for emancipation made the actual freedom of the peasants impossible (they could not leave the commune) until their debts were erased by official decree during the Stolypin era (1906–11). The commune was finally eliminated by Stolypin's program to turn the peasantry into freeholders. Beginning in 1906, Stolypin created the conditions for this transformation by issuing a series of laws that paved the way for peasants to be relieved of the burdens of redemption payments and to own their own land. Although these measures, intended to stem the tide of revolution, were successful in creating peasant smallholders, it was too late to prevent the end of the tsarist regime.

Although the peasants did have some access to the courts under the 1864 legal reforms, the large majority were segregated into a separate estate within the realm where they were allowed to live according to their specific customary law (*obychnoe pravo*) or popular law (*narodnoe pravo*).[10] These unwritten rules were not always compatible with the realm of written laws—laws for the upper classes, town dwellers, and educated society. Much like other developing societies, the Russian Empire in the postreform era was a dual society. The peasants were freed from the landlords' control, but they were separated from the rest of society by their own laws and courts as well as by communal land tenure and the world of the commune. In modern terms, peasant Russia was a vast South African-style "homeland." This patriarchal, legal apartheid was justified by the separate world of peasant laws.[11]

The legal status of persons was determined by their position as it was classified according to the legal estates of the *soslovie* system. The first estate was the nobility, the second was the clergy, and there were separate estates for town dwellers, peasants, and others in society. Each of the estates had its own legally defined rights and obligations.[12] Though class relations were changing, the state reacted to the increase in social and political unrest by trying to reinforce the status quo.[13] But new class groups such as workers, professionals, and the intelligentsia had no place in the antiquated *soslovie* system. The state recognized only an amorphous category called the *raznochintsy* (people of various origins who no longer belonged to a traditional group). Because the *soslovie* system was arbitrarily defined by the state, it became difficult to decipher in legal or social terms. This dependence on the state and the bureaucratic structure made the Russian estate system less autonomous than the sort of estate that had existed in France before the French Revolution.

By the beginning of this century, the social classifications of legal status were so ill-defined that there were actually two distinct worlds in Russia. One comprised the heritage of the collective *soslovie* system of the arbitrary autocracy, the landowning nobility, and the rural world; the "other world represented an underdeveloped but emerging civil society of classes, defended by a reformist bureaucracy willing to face a modern world that traditional Russia preferred to ignore."[14]

A clear opposition to the *soslovie* system was articulated during debates in the first and second Dumas, in 1906 and 1907. On the day before the Stolypin *coup d'etat* of June 3, 1907, a proposal for the abolition of the soslovie system stated:

> For the full development of the principle of legal equality and individual freedom in the state, it is necessary to abolish the *soslovie* system, that is, the division of the population into groups solely according to the principle of common origin, as a result of which members of *soslovie* corporations possess political and other rights (established by law and transmitted by heredity), which are unequal for various groups.[15]

Formulating a legal system that would fully encompass the multifaceted worlds of the prerevolutionary Russian Empire was an awesome, if not impossible, task. The disparate elements of the complex society had to be revealed and defined, and then integrated into one legal order that would make civil society cohesive.

This was complicated by the fact that the society was an incongruous mixture of impressive capital cities and a growing number of industrial complexes set against the vast backdrop of the overwhelming majority—the peasantry—and a growing working class.

The people were subjects who were granted certain rights and privileges based on their social and economic status. The tsar was the "autocratic [*samoderzhavnyi*] and unlimited [*neogranichennyi*] monarch,"[16] and he did not make any concessions that resembled contractual rights, mutually binding agreements between the sovereign and the people. The transformation of the legal and political system in the Russian Empire necessitated a change in the relationship between the individual and the state.

The Prerevolutionary Quest
for Constitutionalism

The American and French concepts of constitutionalism did indeed make an impact on movements for reform of the Russian style of government. A.D. Radishchev saw a hopeful model in the United States Constitution; the Decembrists wrote a constitution as a part of their program, and there was talk that Tsar Alexander I would adopt parts of the proposal for a constitutional monarchy formulated by M.M. Speranskii (1809) and later by N.N. Novosil'tsev (1820). Furthermore, there was a tradition of legal education in the late eighteenth and the nineteenth century that provided the foundation for a legally conscious part of the civil service.[17]

The courts that had been established by the 1864 reforms were opened in 1866 and functioned until they were closed in December 1917 by the decree of the People's Commissar of Justice; the decree also closed all the judiciary institutions and abolished the bar. Although there were many barriers to the effective practice of the law in the context of the tsarist autocracy, there did exist among lawyers a commitment to developing constitutional guarantees, the protection of individual rights, and the separation of state powers. For liberal opponents to the autocracy, these elements were considered central to the stabilization and gradual change of the society. After their establishment, the courts represented a standard of legal ethics and practice comparable with the courts in France, Germany, Britain, and the United States.[18]

However, the individual was far from the center of the legal system in the Russian Empire. The law was essentially a body of norms protected by the power of the state. It was the failure to create a stable society based on a popularly accepted legal system that prompted responsible advocates of civil rights to attack the existing order.

In 1909 the controversial volume *Vekhi* (*Landmarks*) appeared. It was a collection of articles by leading members of the intelligentsia who lamented the failure of the liberals and radicals to take an effective stance against the autocracy and become part of the governing process. It was an attack on the existing order as well as on the revolutionary tactics of certain of its opponents. Bogdan Kistiakovskii (1868–1920), a lawyer and sociologist, wrote a critical essay, "In Defense of Law, The Russian Intelligentsia and Legal Consciousness," which sparked a nationwide debate on the question of legal consciousness. It was one of the best introductions to Russian "legal nihilism," an insightful historical review of the failure of the Russian intelligentsia to acquire a respect for legal institutions.[19] Political concerns in the Russian Empire had always taken precedence over the proper functioning of the judiciary. Kistiakovskii considered illusory the widespread notion that the Russian people would instinctively develop a type of social organization that would be superior to one constructed on the values of a legal order. This view, he argued, was only a justification for Russian suspicions of the west. Indeed, the existing *soslovie* system reinforced the Slavophile ideal of a *Gemeinschaft* (community), or an organic, communal-familial collective approach to society and law. It was western-oriented liberals like Kistiakovskii who supported the idea of a *Gesellschaft* (society), or an approach to law based on the protection of the inviolable rights of the individual.[20]

Legal reformers were faced with the lack of legal consciousness among the population. As subjects, the people had servile souls and waited to be directed by their tsar father. Thus Petrazhitskii wrote in his *Theory of State and Law* (1909) that ideally the law

> communicates the firmness and the confidence, the energy and initiative essential for life. A child brought up in an atmosphere of arbitrary caprice (however benificient and gracious), with no definite assignment to him of a particular sphere of rights (although of a modest and childish character), will not be trained to construct and carry out the plans of life with assurance. In the economic field, particularly, he will be deficient in confidence, boldness, and initiative: he will be apathetic, act at random, and procrastinate in the hope of favourable "chances," help from another, alms, gifts, and the like.[21]

The individual had to become an active citizen who wanted to live in a society guided by and based on law.

A fundamental disrespect for the law complicated attempts to establish a rule-of-law state. Aleksandr Herzen explained that the Russian people had lost any sense of respect for the law because of the corrupt ways of the government; that, in fact, the Russian people tried to break the law any time it was possible, for, after all, the government did this too.[22]

Reviving Severed Roots: Prerevolutionary Traditions in a Contemporary Setting

During the Gorbachev years, historians and legal scholars in the Soviet Union started examining prerevolutionary ideas about a constitutional system based on the rights of the individual.[23] The numerous references to *pravovoe gosudarstvo* —a law-governed state—indicated their belief that a multiparty system must rest on a constitution and that individual rights could be exercised and protected only in a legally based order.

In the present world of the mass media—television and journalism—the concept of a law-based state has taken on a magical, even mystical, quality. The new uncensored world of journals in the era of *glasnost'* generated the catchword and slogans which characterize the type of system that should replace the existing decaying remains of the old order. But these slogans are impressionistic symbols rather than terms describing new political, social, and economic realities. As Roland Barthes described in his *Mythologies*, an overused political concept can indeed become a myth that no longer has the same political and ideological content and hence is depoliticized speech.[24] The idea of a *pravovoe gosudarstvo*, a law-based state, and a market economy have become slogans indicating a way of being saved from communism—sometimes resembling the path to being "saved" after sinning in a Christian fundamentalist's world view. As Sergei Kovalev, the people's deputy of the Russian Republic who is also a co-chairman of the Memorial Society, stated at a recent talk in New York just after the unsuccessful coup of August 1991, *pravovoe gosudarstvo* had become a chant— a demand used to bring down the corrupt regime. And now, he points out, it is time to make the slogan a reality; a law-based state must actually be built.[25]

Citizens of the Russian Empire in the nineteenth and early twentieth centuries struggled to escape their authoritarian tsarist roots by establishing a democratic constitutional system with a multiparty system, but they had to look to other societies for their models. They understood that law delimits interests or creates compromises among them; there can be law only where there is freedom for the individual. In this sense, the legal order is a system of relationships in which all persons in a society possess the greatest possible freedom of activity and self-determination. The question remained, how capable was the intelligentsia of participating in the legal reorganization of the state, the conversion of state power *from a power of force* into a *power of law*. Law needed to gain in stature and be basic to the rights of the individual and the society, rather than being dependent on political considerations and secondary to ethical ones. In present-day Russia, there is a need for education in the principles of law and such legal processes as elections so they can be effective. The mass media can today speed the educational process if it plays a serious and positive role.

In the era following the failed coup and the hopes of establishing a government based on the principles of human rights, there are a series of new challenges. The issue of national rights as an integral part of human rights is part and parcel of the move for national self-determination. The type of social contract that will be viable for the complicated mixes of nationalities coexisting within many of the republics remains to be seen.

There was a burgeoning movement to establish national rights as fundamental human rights before the 1917 Revolution. Only recently has interest grown in understanding the prerevolutionary heritage in the struggle for constitutionalism, federalism, and national rights. The Ukrainian born M.P. Dragomanov (1841–95) and his ideas on constitutionalism and minority national rights were the subject of an international conference in Kiev which was sponsored by the Ukrainian Academy of Sciences in September 1990. In honor of the 150th anniversary of his birth, Dragomanov's nationalist and federalist ideas were honored at the conference; he is being regarded now as a new national hero for the Ukrainians. His previously neglected works have been republished, and scholars who attacked him for "bourgeois nationalist" ideas were publicly exposed for their ideological blinders in the past. Dragomanov was one of a series of nineteenth-century Ukrainian activists who struggled to establish the national identity of the Ukrainian people. His opposition to the Great Russian dominance over the Ukrainian people was a major focal point in his work.

Educated Russian society had only a few voices that articulated the plight of the non-Russian nationalities. In the wake of the Polish Revolution of 1830 to 1831 and the romantic nationalist movements of the 1840s in western Europe, the westernizing revolutionary Herzen had called for a liberal revolution and a constitution which would guarantee the civil rights of speech, conscience, and creed and end the oppression of minority nationalities by the Great Russians. At approximately the same time that the secret Ukrainian society—the Brotherhood of Cyril and Methodius—voiced its national demands and was silenced, Herzen left for London. There, in 1847, he founded the journal *Kolokol* (*The Bell*) and contributed articles to *Poliarnaia zvezda* (*The Polar Star*) to continue propagating his ideas for the decentralizing and dismantling of the tsarist government. In 1851 he wrote:

> Centralization is contrary to the Slav genius; federalism, on the other hand, is its natural form of expression. Once the Slav world has become unified, and knit together into an association of free autonomous peoples, it will at last be able to enter on its true historical existence. . . . The majority of the Slav peoples have never been subjugated by a conquering race. For them submission has, on the whole, been confined to the recognition of an overlord and to the payment of some form of tribute. Such, for instance, was the Mongol rule in Russia. As a result, the Slavs have managed to preserve for some hundreds of years their nationality, their way of life and their language.[26]

In the 1859–60 series of articles entitled "Rossiia i Pol'sha" that Herzen published in *The Bell*, he openly demanded self-determination for the Ukraine. He wrote, "Now tell me, what kind of heirs to the Congress of Vienna are we if we assign where a strip of land should belong without asking the people who live there what they want. . . . In my opinion the question is answered simply: The Ukraine should be recognized as a free and independent country. . . ."[27] Herzen's call for Ukrainian independence was predicated on the idea that the Ukrainian people should become a part of a Slavic federation only if they elected to do so. In that way, the Ukrainian people would be self-determining. Herzen passionately proclaimed:

> Untie their hands, unleash their tongues; Let their speech flow completely freely, and then let them speak their mind on whether they will join us (Russia) ... or you (Poland), ... or if they are clever, to extend both of their hands to a brotherly union and remain independent of both powers. That is why I value federalism so highly. In such a system, federal parts are connected by a common goal and no one part belongs to another—not Geneva to Berne, nor Berne to Geneva. [28]

In 1860, the Ukrainian historian N.I. Kostomarov, one of the founders of the Brotherhood of Cyril and Methodius, responded to Herzen's comments on the Ukrainian question in a letter to Herzen.[29] Herzen was sufficiently impressed by the letter to publish it in full; moreover, he announced that Kostomarov's letter would represent *Kolokol*'s position on the Ukrainian national problem.[30] Kostomarov's letter articulated a nonseparatist Ukrainian nationalist position; that is, Ukrainian national autonomy did not require that the Ukraine sever all relations with the rest of the Slavic peoples.

> The solution to the problem is simple: the disputed lands do not belong to this or that land—they belong to the people who have always inhabited it, inhabit it now and cultivate it. ... We do not demand for ourselves anything which is independent of the general desires of all of Russia. No one of us thinks of tearing Southern Russia from connections with the rest of Russia. On the contrary, we would wish that all other Slavs would join into one union with us even under the sceptre of the Russian government, if this government is made up of free peoples.[31]

In keeping with this democratic tradition, M.P. Dragomanov made a case for Ukrainian autonomy and federalism without demanding separatism, much as Kostomarov had. (Kostomarov and Dragomanov were colleagues in the Brotherhood of Cyril and Methodius.) In Dragomanov's view, the Ukrainian people were not in a position to protect themselves from the imperialist designs of the Great Russians or the tendencies toward annexation he felt were developing among the Poles. Dragomanov was wary of the Polish nationalists even after the 1863 uprising against Russian rule had been crushed. He feared Polish nationalism at the same time he supported the rights of the Poles to self-determination, because he was aware of their dream of re-establishing an independent Poland within the boundaries of 1772—which included Ukrainian territory in the Russian Empire as well as territories lost to Austria and Prussia.

Dragomanov militantly demanded the end to the subjugation of minority nationalities in an 1892 article: "Observing the history of all civilized nations, we must come to the conclusion that the system of compulsory nationality is the same universal phenomenon of social life as the system of compulsory religion."[32]

The traditions started in the prerevolutionary era are being revived in reprinted political and legal works such as M. P. Dragomanov's *Sobranie sochinenie*, published in 1991; *Vlast' i pravo, iz istorii russkoi pravovoi mysli*, published in 1990, which reprints the works of B.N. Chicherin, V.S. Soloviev, B.A. Kistiakovskii, P.I. Novgorodtsev, S.N. Bulgakov, and N.A. Berdyaev.[33] There are republications of *Vekhi* as well as numerous articles on prerevolutionary life and culture in the journal *Nashe Nasledie (Our Heritage)* and numerous scholarly journals. These newly republished works open the previously closed world of what the Soviet regime termed bourgeois legal thought to the public.

The problem of implementing human rights in societies facing extreme economic difficulties makes the goal of establishing a government based on human rights appear to be an awesome task. It remains to be seen if the societies of the former Soviet Union will refrain from using authoritarian tactics such as the military courts-martial of the early part of the this century in dealing with those involved in treason, or if the desire to create a real constitutionally based society will prevail and open, fair trials will be held. Will the population be empowered with real human rights (including national rights) or is that an impossibility in the face of the impending economic crises? Can people exercise human rights if they are hungry? Or will those rights only be nominal political rights that the hungry are too weak to exercise?

The task of creating an awareness of law and human rights that responds to the needs of the societies growing out of the crumbled Soviet system is the issue of the day. We can only hope that the lessons that can be drawn from the rich traditions of prerevolutionary legal thought can find their proper place in the continuing evolution of legal culture.

Notes

1. Gregory Freeze, "The Soslovie (Estate) Paradigm and Russian Social History," *American Historical Review* 96, 1:12.

2. Marc Raeff, *The Well-Ordered Police State* (New Haven, CT: Yale University Press, 1983), 216.

3. Richard Wortman, *The Development of a Russian Legal Consciousness* (Chicago: University of Chicago Press, 1976), 285; Andrzej Walicki, *Legal Philosophies of Russian Liberalism* (London: Oxford University Press, 1987), 21.

4. Marc Raeff, "The Bureaucratic Phenomenon of Imperial Russia," *American Historical Review* 84, 2: 403 (1979).

5. Richard Wortman, *The Development of a Russian Legal Consciousness* (Chicago: University of Chicago Press, 1976).

6. The Russian judiciary was not considered much inferior to the European judicial systems, though there was interference with the system on the part of the state. See Walicki, 102–103; A.A. Goldenweiser, *V zashchitu prava* (New York: Chekhov Press, 1952), 211–12. See Samuel Kucherov, *Courts Lawyers and Trials under the Last Three*

Tsars (Westport, CT: Greenwood Press, 1953); John Hazard, "The Courts and the Legal System," in *The Transformation of Russian Society*, ed. Cyril E. Black (Cambridge, MA: Harvard University Press, 1960), 148–50; A.F. Koni, *Sobranie sochinenii* (Moscow, 1966), vol. 2, 171–73,180–81; Richard Wortman, *The Development of a Russian Legal Consciousness* 282–83; and N.A. Troitskii, *"Narodnaia Volia" pered tsarskim sudom, 1880–1891 gg.* (Saratov, 1971), 24–25.

7. William F. Fuller, *Civil-Military Conflict in Imperial Russia* (Princeton, NJ: Princeton University Press, 1986), 174.

8. Ibid., 172–91.

9. TsGVIA, f. 1, op. 1, d. 70270 (Military Justice Administration otchet data for 1906), l. 17, as cited by Fuller, p. 173.

10. Moshe Lewin, "Customary Law and Rural Society in the Post-reform Era," in *The Making of the Soviet System* (New York: Pantheon Books, 1985), 72–74; David Macey, *Government and Peasant in Russia, 1861–1906* (DeKalb, IL: Northern Illinois University Press, 1987), 15–19.

11. Leonard Schapiro, "The Pre-Revolutionary Intelligentsia and the Legal Order," in *Russian Studies*, ed. Ellen Dahrendorf (New York: Penguin Books, 1987), 58–60.

12. For a full discussion of the complex system of sosloviia see Gregory Freeze, "The Soslovie (Estate) Paradigm and Russian Social History," Macey, 339.

13. Freeze, 27.

14. Frank Wcislo, "Soslovie or Class? Bureaucratic Reformers and Provincial Gentry in Conflict,1906–1908," *The Russian Review*, vol. 47, (1988), 23. See also Leopold Haimson, "Conclusion: Observations on the Politics of the Russian Countryside (1905–1914)," in *The Politics of Rural Russia* (Bloomington, IN: Indiana University Press, 1979), 261–300, Leopold Haimson, "The Parties and the State: The Evolution of Political Attitudes," in *The Transformation of Russian Society*, ed. Cyril E. Black (Cambridge, MA: Harvard University Press, 1969); Roberta Manning, *The Crisis of the Old Order* (Princeton, NJ: Princeton University Press, 1982), ch. 14; V.S. D'iakin, *Samoderzhavie, Burzhuaziia i dvorlanstvo v 1907–1911 gg.* (Leningrad, 1978).

15. "Gosudarstvennaia duma, vtoroi sozyv," *Zakonodatel'nye materialy* (St. Petersburg, 1907), 265.

16. Marc Raeff, *Understanding Imperial Russia, State and Society in the Old Regime* (New York: Columbia University, 1984), 22.

17. Richard Wortman, *The Development of a Russian Legal Consciousness*; W.E. Butler, "Civil Rights in Russia: Legal Standards in Gestation," in *Civil Rights in Imperial Russia*, ed. Olga Crisp and Linda Edmondson (Oxford: Oxford University Press, 1989), 1–12.

18. A.A. Goldenweiser, *V zashchitu prava*, 211–12; W. Lednicki, *Pamiatniki*, (London: 1963), vol. I, 309. Most recently, see Sergei Kazantsev, *Sud prisiazhnykh v rossii, 1864–1917*, (Leningrad: Lenizdat, 1990); Susan Heuman, "A Socialist Conception of Human Rights, A Model From Prerevolutionary Russia," in *Human Rights: Cultural and Ideological Perspectives*, ed. A. Pollis, P. Schwab (New York: Praeger Press, 1979).

19. B.A. Kistiakovskii, "V zashchitu prava: Intelligentsia i pravosoznanie" in *Vekhi, sbornik statei o russkoi intelligenstii* (Moscow, 1909), 125–55; Walicki, 348.

20. See Andrzej Walicki, "Personality and Society in the ideology of Russian Slavophilism: A Study in the Sociology of Knowledge," *California Slavic Studies* 2: 7–8 (1963).

21. L.I. Petrazhitskii, *Teoriia gosudarstva i prava* (Moscow, 1909), 151.

22. Aleksandr Herzen, "Du developpement des idees revolutionaires en Russia," *Sobranie sochinenii*, (Moscow, 1956), VII, 121.

23. See A.A. Goltsblat, "Pravovoe gosudarstvo ili diktatura, k voprosu o meste teorii

pravovogo gosudartsvo v politicheskoi praktike Rossii," in *Konstitutsionnyi vestnik* 4 (Moscow, 1990), 25–39; O.F. Skakun, "Teoriia pravovogo gosudarstva v dorevoliutsionnoi Rossii," in *Sovetskoe gosudarstvo i pravo* 2 (1990); V.V. Sonin, V.P. Fedorov, "Pravoponimanie v dorevoliutsionnyi nemarksistkoi iuridicheskoi mysli Rossii," in *Gosudarstvennyi stroi i politiko-pravovye idei Rossii vtoroi poloviny XIX stoletiia,* ed. M.G. Korotkikh, V.V. Iachevskii (Voronezh, 1987); and E.V. Kuznetsov, *Filosofiia prava v Rossii* (Moscow, 1989).

24. Roland Barthes, *Mythologies* (New York: The Noonday Press, 1990), 144–46.

25. Sergei Kovalev, "The Quest for Human Rights in the Soviet Union: A Report from the Front Lines," a speech given at the Association of the Bar of the City of New York on August 27, 1991.

26. Alexander Herzen, "An Open Letter to Jules Michelet," *From the Other Shore* (New York: George Braziller, Inc., 1956), 175–76.

27. Herzen, "Rossiia i Pol'sha," in *Kolokol,* as quoted in Kistiakovskii, "Gertsen i Ukraina," 24.

28. Ibid., 25.

29. Kostomarov signed the letter *Ukrainets,* a pseudonym that Kistiakovskii later adopted to avoid reprisals. Kistiakovskii, "Gertsen i Ukraina," 24.

30. Ibid., 29.

31. Ibid., 27.

32. M.P. Dragomanov, "K voprosu o natsional'nostiakh v Rossii," in *Sobranie politicheskikh sochinenii M.P. Dragomanova,* 2 vols., ed. B.A. Kistiakovskii (Paris: Societe Nouvelle de Librairie et D'edition, 1905) I, 864–70; M.P. Dragomanov, *Istoricheskaia Pol'sha i velikorusskaia demokratia* (Geneva: H. Georg, 1882), later published as vol. I of the collected works of Dragomanov edited by Kistiakovskii (cited above). Georg von Rauch, 132–33.

33. *Vlast' i pravo,* ed. A.V. Poliakov and I.Iu. Kozlikhin (Leningrad: Lenizdat, 1990).

8

Postcommunist New Thinking on Human Rights

Vladimir Kudriavtsev and Elena Lukasheva

Our country's preoccupation with human rights reflects the influence both of a growing global movement for them and of our own new political thinking. This rejection of totalitarian ideology associates a civilized way of life and progress with the individual's genuine participation in the making of political, economic, social, and cultural decisions. The role of human rights is to guarantee that participation, to transform the human being from a passive witness into an active participant in all world events.

The human rights idea traces back into the distant past over a long and tortuous road. It has been closely linked with democratic traditions. The concept of human rights turned into a political platform in the course of bourgeois revolutions; it gained a new resonance in our time when we became urgently aware of problems of survival, of preserving the human race and life on earth, of mutual cooperation, and of affirming universal humanitarian ideas and shared moral values. Human rights take an ever more regular place in the vocabulary of the most diverse political activists and thinkers and among the slogans of mass social movements in many countries. They received a new resonance in our society during the stormy, urgent years of *perestroika*, or restructuring.

From Old to New Thinking

Rethinking our life requires that we look soberly at the actual situation of human rights and freedoms in Russian society. This requires, in turn, that we assess also the ideological and psychological legacy in that sphere, which we have inherited from the first revolutionary years, the period of Stalinist dictatorship, and the years of stagnation under the Brezhnev administration.

Is this the time to set ourselves such a task? After all, a mass of complicated problems confronts the country; we are living through serious economic, political, and spiritual crises. Is it appropriate to take up questions of rights and freedoms, of mechanisms and guarantees for their protection and fulfillment, when the customary social ties are being destroyed, when discipline is falling, when public order is breaking down? Cannot humanitarian reforms be postponed until better times?

We think that they cannot. Nothing is more appropriate than a concern for human rights. Beyond this, we are convinced that the crisis wracking our society cannot be overcome without the liberation of human beings, without the creation of conditions for their real, active participation in all spheres of social life. Without the protection of their independence and freedom. Evidently, in our plans for the renewing of our society, we flagrantly underestimated the importance of the rights dimension for *perestroika*.

For decades, the prevalent views in the USSR, which assumed complete social protection of the individual under socialism, a high level of citizen political activity, and an absence of nationality problems, were based in stereotypical thinking. Great harm was done to our protection of human rights and our social development by the bitter ideological struggle around problems of human rights which dictated its own rules of the game: unqualified denial of one's own shortcomings, self-satisfied declarations about our indisputable advantages, and accusations against western countries of using the human rights struggle as a pretext to interfere in our internal affairs. This also damaged our international standing; it complicated even more an already complex situation of human rights protection that was characteristic of the period of stagnation but has much deeper historical and ideological roots, going back to the Revolution and the beginnings of the subsequent totalitarianism regime.

We are trying to create a humane, law-based society in which there will be different economic relations and new social structures and political systems, and in which the role and place of the individual in society will grow; individuals will be free, fully entitled members of the human collective, masters of their fates, and not cogs of the state machine. All these changes should be helped by a total rejection of the dogma still lingering in the sphere of human rights. We turn now to the question of how we should be thinking about economic, class, and individual political rights.

Economic Rights

We vastly oversimplified our approach to the economic foundation of human rights, considering that socialist property automatically creates all conditions for their complete fulfillment. Historical experience has shown, however, that the socialization of property should not be reduced to its complete takeover by the state in disregard of the principles of commodity production and exchange of equivalents based on the action of the law of value. Our state not only took over property, but swallowed the entire civil society as well. This inevitably led to the undermining of freedom and the alienation of the individual, not only from property but also from authority.

Private enterprise and the market are important not only in a purely economic sense, a utilitarian sense, but also because under market conditions there is freedom of choice; and because participants in the exchange act as equal partners in a social intercourse, feeling a real dependence between their labor and its results. Without economic freedom, it is difficult to obtain political freedom; in fact, the state takeover of property signifies the ruination of civil society and its institutions. In such a situation, human rights lose their meaning as natural and inalienable and end up being completely at the discretion of the state, which does as it pleases as far a giving these rights to the people, limiting them, or completely disregarding them. Human rights must grow naturally out of a healthy economic base, in which the citizen acts, not as an executor of commands and orders, alienated from property and bound by limitations and bans, but as master, realizing his interests and needs in a free interaction with other participants in the economic process. This is an essential condition, not only for guaranteeing human rights, but also for forming a law-based state.

The demonopolization of state property is becoming a reality of our development, laying the foundation for real freedom and human equality. At the same time, it is extremely important that we preserve and strengthen the social protection of the individual from the economic expansion of other property-holders, be they state or societal organizations or private persons whose entrepreneurial activities are now permitted. Protection of this sort requires taxation, pension, and unemployment legislation as well as other measures directed toward the guarantee of social justice.

From Class Dogma to Universal Values

We must rethink the relationship of *class interests* to individual interests and rights. To assert unconditionally the priorities of class interests inevitably pushes the interests of the individual into the background, transforming the individual into a means for obtaining the ends of the class or of the society as a whole. As ideas take hold that the present generation may be sacrificed in the name of a bright future, the uniqueness and the value of each human life is ignored and the understanding of the inviolability of the world of each individual is lost.

The priority of class interests may be explained and to a certain extent justified during the time of a revolutionary takeover of society. But once it reaches beyond the bounds of an extreme revolutionary situation into periods of normal social life, it inevitably leads to a deformation of relations between human being, the social group, and society.

In a normally developing civilized society, every person must have equal access to political and social life regardless of their social class. Human rights are a fundamental value inherent in people as members of the human race and a standard for progressive development of society. They must become the guidelines for the development of our life today.

We are part of human civilization and, as part of it, recognize the universality of human rights. In this context, rights lose their restrictive association with a given social system; they become universal criteria for a person's freedom and well-being and, in the final analysis, are an indicator of the effectiveness of the political and social system. International standards of human rights embody humanistic and democratic traditions and collective wisdom. They define the minimal "floor" below which a civilized state may not go. The fallacy of our conceptual approach to human rights lay in its cultural and political isolationism, in ignoring the humanistic world experience, in attempting to assert "our own" priorities, and in the alleged superiority of our judicial protections of rights when there already existed a powerful array of legal and moral values which had been created as a result of a difficult quest.

Individual Autonomy

Thinking on human rights today must give first place to the freedom, the autonomy, of individuals. The idea of subordinating individuals and their rights to the interests of the collective held sway for a long time in our doctrine and practice. Collectivism, interpreted in accordance with the ideals of barracks socialism and in the spirit of the administrative-command system, reduced human diversity to the lowest common denominator; it eliminated any forms of dissent and sowed hypocrisy and dual morality. In such a form, collectivism resembled the herd instinct more than anything else. Collectivism demanded a uniform positive reaction to any act of the state. It automatically excluded freedom and pluralism of opinion, without which political life is distorted and becomes one-sided and bereft of alternatives. Hegel wrote of Kant, the humanism of whose teaching about freedom he greatly valued: "He took a big step forward in asserting the principle that freedom is the pivotal point of human existence, the highest peak from which in no circumstance must one look up from down below, so that the human being recognizes no authority and nothing in which his freedom is not esteemed."[1] The purpose of the law-based, humane society is to guarantee such freedom of individuals, so as to assure their self-determination and their purposeful political participation in self-government.

The logic of the totalitarian view on the relationship of freedom and coercion is clearly that command, the suppression of freedom, and the forbidding of thought and action supposedly facilitate the solution of political and economic problems; that they help to strengthen discipline and order, and that they protect society from social upheaval and instability. But historical experience shows the total illusory nature of these dogmas: the temporary stability that may be obtained by command methods turns into years of decline, stagnation, and apathy. Unless citizens have a feeling of involvement in the social, political, and economic processes, it is impossible to assure the healthy functioning of society or its movement along the road of progress and freedom toward the strengthening of its political, economic, and intellectual potential.

Our society is experiencing enormous political and emotional overload as individuals gain their freedom. Views and positions were bottled up inside us for many years; they produced positive and constructive beginnings for democracy, but they acquired sometimes distorted forms. Different groups and associations use anarcho-syndicalist, monarchical, or nationalist slogans; conflicts over the content and purpose of the movement for change have run out of control in a number of cases. Today, the question of the relationship between freedom and responsibility is the red thread that connects an otherwise fragmented political pluralism.

A sense of responsibility cannot, however, be instilled by coercive means: this is a dead end. We now hold to the principle that people may not be held criminally responsible for their opinions, unless they be connected with real actions harming the state and social system, public health and morality, or the interests of other persons. Obviously, in a society long gripped in the vise of official unanimity, far from all views and positions will be usual or attractive. However, the society must learn tolerance, must live through its maladies and through the political process and the persuasive power of real positive results. Calls for the use of strong-arm methods and the nostalgia for "the strong hand" are survivals of the command-administrative system which can bring grave consequences for society.

In these times, we must firmly confront all manifestations of anarchy, opportunism, and the destructive willfulness that leave one unrestrained by conscience and morality—not with criminal punishment, but with humanistic ideals of reason and freedom. This is an inseparable part of the protection and the guarantee of human rights.

Rule of Law

Humanity has long struggled for idea of the primacy of law—of the subordination to law of all political and economic structures without exception—against lawlessness and authoritarianism. Totalitarian theories nurtured lawlessness instead of the rule of law, rejecting the legal principles and mechanisms without which any concept of democracy and human rights is meaningless. Today, we turn to the idea of the law-governed state, whose main purpose is to guarantee individual rights and freedoms, to regulate social relations, to mediate conflict, and, on the basis of the separation of powers, to create a barrier against the usurpation of public authority.

The concept of law-governed states used to be subjected to vicious attacks in our political theory, which accused it of antidemocratic content and a reactionary political basis. Thus we rejected proven instruments for the normalization of relations between public authority and the citizens, for the protection of their rights and interests. The contemporary recognition of the idea of the law-governed state and the institutional measures directed toward its affirmation (increasing the role of representative organs, raising the prestige of the court, establishing constitutional supervision) are important steps along the way to overcoming the underestimation of the inalienability of human rights and the empty, paternalistic intoning of those rights for decades.

Democracy and human rights can make steady progress only within the framework of the law-governed state. However, the establishment of the law-based state is a quite complicated process. It is difficult to overcome the loss of prestige of the law and law enforcement organs and the contempt for law and individual interests which was nurtured during the decades of nihilism in theory and lawlessness in practice. The state and the citizens continue to be unequal partners in the social interchange; the citizens continue to take the role of petitioners, even in matters of protecting their lawful rights and freedoms. To raise the citizen to the level of equal partner in the government and to affirm his or her dignity and honor is possible only through a far-reaching program of reform and re-education. Otherwise there will be no law-governed state to act as an instrument for the protection of inherent, inalienable human rights.

The importance of judicial protection of citizens' rights from abuse and violation by officials should be emphasized. Such a defense must comprise all constitutional rights of citizens without exception or limitations. The court procedure for the protection of citizens' rights is the most democratic and effective. It must occupy a firm place in the practice of the law-governed state.

It is impossible to guarantee human rights outside the context of democratic procedural principles: the presumption of innocence, the nonretroactivity of law (which would increase penalties), and the principle that "all is permitted which is not forbidden." The administrative-command system nurtured the opposite of the last principle: "all is forbidden which is not permitted." As well, it excluded pluralism of opinion and freedom of discussion; it transformed the right to freedom of opinion and conscience into an empty declaration. The principle we uphold, "everything is permitted which is not forbidden" implies guarantees of individual freedoms in law-governed states. It was already formulated in the French Declaration of the Rights of Man and Citizen of 1789. Carrying out that principle makes it possible to eliminate the rigid regulation of all human activity which had been asserted for decades.

We have not yet destroyed the authoritarian-bureaucratic system. It resists, it attempts to repress or to limit human freedoms; it enmeshes them in a tangle of prohibitions. This is especially noticeable wherever local officials in various republics seek to preserve the lack of free choice in elections and to squelch independent economic initiatives, to persecute criticism and ways of thinking, and to ignore the laws that have been recently passed to protect the individual.

The unfree person, gripped in the vise of prohibitions and limitations, will never become an active participant in the revolutionary renewal of our society.

For that reason, the preservation of command and prohibitory methods repressing the individual serves the purpose only of those who try to preserve the outmoded, obsolete order of things. The consistent implementation of the principle of "all is permitted which is not forbidden" is a most important part of the process of democratization, of the transformation of the individual into a co-holder of political authority and property—the precondition for people's realization of their rights and legitimate interests.

A Bill of Rights for the Future

New approaches to human rights must start with the recognition of a common civilization where human rights and freedom are universal values. Only the guarantee of the entire complex of their human rights will end the estrangement of individuals from power, the economy, and the means of distributing social benefits. In this context, the Declaration of Rights and Freedoms of the Individual was passed on September 5, 1991.

The Declaration got mixed reviews. Some acknowledged the document's importance. Others sharply criticized it, saying that it repeated the 1977 Constitution, added nothing to the rights proclaimed in it, listed unattainable rights, and came at the wrong time.

Let us try to respond to these assertions. First of all, does the Declaration expand on the rights listed in the Constitution? Undoubtedly. None of these rights, proclaimed in the Declaration, was in the 1977 Constitution: the right to life; the rights to freedom of opinion and conviction; the rights to ideological, religious, and cultural freedom; the rights to information, to equal access to professional training in accordance with one's capabilities, and to hold any public office; the rights to freedom of movement, to choice of domicile, and to leave the country and return to it; a ban on deprivation of citizenship and exile abroad; the right to defend one's good name; and the right to strike. There were, as well, a number of others not previously included in our Constitution.

The Declaration contains a number of principles of special importance for our society as it endeavors to free itself from totalitarianism: a rejection of any state-imposed ideology; the protection of the rights, freedoms, and reputations of those making up opposition minorities; the barring of privileges for any particular social groups or strata. The Declaration can be said to accord with international standards of human rights.

Again the question, are these rights real, can they be guaranteed in a time of civil discord, when the accustomed social ties have ruptured, the economy is devastated, and unemployment is mounting? The situation is indeed very difficult. But does the difficulty of realizing these rights justify excluding them? We think not. Unless social development is directed toward human rights goals, it inevitably will be doomed to degradation. The array of rights contained in the Declaration must be implemented by the legislation of the former Union republics; otherwise, we will slide into chaos and open the way to massive violations of human rights.

That is why we should strive to create the legal basis for a common humanitarian space over the territory of the fragmented Union. That is the answer to the question about the timeliness of passing this declaration. The problem now is to activate the Declaration, and not leave it on the dusty shelves of legal offices. This brings us to the matter of its legal force.

The Declaration was originally drafted to be part of the Constitution of a federated USSR. That Union disintegrated before the Declaration's passage as an independent document in the last act of the old USSR Congress of People's Deputies. The independent states which emerged at this stage of mounting centrifugal forces, and their quest for absolute sovereignty, may ignore certain principles of the Declaration. Threats of human rights violations, especially threats against the rights of nonindigenous residents in the newly independent states, arise from outbursts of nationalist egoism and the formation of authoritarian regimes in some former Union republics.

One can anticipate complex legal issues with the new international relations. The first stage of this process inevitably will bring a turn toward isolationism, a preference for the rights of "our own" citizens, a rejection of a number of universal standards contained in the Declaration. Problems have already arisen over the qualifications for citizenship, rights to health care, education, and social security, as well as other issues.

Millions of people, the nonindigenous population in particular, whose rights are already being violated in a number of former Union republics, are becoming hostages to extreme separatism. If these negative processes are to be stopped and the Declaration's standards to be observed universally, there must be a mechanism for doing so.

The Declaration has become an international as well as an internal document. It must be opened to signing by independent states which have expressed a desire to join a new union, and it could be signed at the same time as a new union treaty is signed. By such a process, the states that are parties to the Declaration undertake to embody its norms in their constitutions and laws, all the way from rights of free expression and movement to rights of citizenship and conscientious objection to military service. The Republic of Moldavia adhered to the Declaration, although it did not express a wish to join a new union. Other former Union republics may wish to do this, so that the Declaration's signers might include nonmembers of the new union. A protocol to the Declaration could state the principles by which member states would cooperate on issues of human rights. Among them must certainly be the now internationally recognized proposition that human rights are not simply a state's internal affair.

A set of agencies will be needed to guarantee human rights for the new union in a common legal and humanitarian space: a human rights commission under the union's state council, and human rights ombudspeople—those attached to the parliaments of the republics and others to the local government councils at all levels.

A constitutional court must play a big part in protecting human rights, with legal provision for individual complaints, as has worked well in a number of foreign countries. A special interrepublic human rights court could be established as part of the system of conflict resolution.

As we all know, the constitution that was to include both a union treaty and the Declaration did not appear. Nevertheless, the Declaration has meaning as a basic law of the land. One of the roles of the central authority must be to protect the rights of all citizens living on the territory of the former Union. All such citizens should be able to invoke the Declaration—a right of particular importance for the many of them subjected to blatant discrimination in their regions. And one more thing: the Declaration is direct-acting; its provisions must hold even in the absence of laws elaborating on it. This means that citizens have the right to invoke the Declaration under any circumstances.

Only through such arrangements can new thinking on human rights be fittingly adapted to the challenges of their protection and advancement despite the breakup of the USSR.

Note

1. W. F. Gegel' (Hegel), *Sochineniia*, vol. 11 (1935), 444.

9

The Legal Status of Foreign
Employees in Russia

Paula Garb

Far more is understood about the difficulties citizens of the former Soviet Union experience in leaving the country than about the complications faced by foreigners who want to stay there, either temporarily or permanently. Perhaps one reason is that until fairly recently the notion of outsiders choosing to live in Russia seemed absurd. This study calls attention to the little-known community of foreigners and their problems historically in the former Soviet Union and currently in Russia.

Although the focus here is on foreign employees (or "foreign specialists," as they were referred to in Soviet laws), all foreigners living in Russia share similar problems due to inadequate legislation[1] and those problems will be viewed from the perspective of foreign employees. I have singled out the category of foreign employees because these people tend to be the kind of foreigner who settles permanently in the country. Yet these individuals are the least protected by legislation which does not provide incentives or reliable mechanisms to enable them to become permanent residents or citizens of the country.

The information and opinions presented here are based on personal experiences working as a translator for several Soviet publishing agencies, observations of the experiences of other such employees, and research on the history of U.S. and Canadian workers in the USSR.[2]

It is particularly important to raise these issues now that the economic and political reforms in Russia are attracting to the country large numbers of foreigners who are professionals and skilled workers. Such foreign employees at Russian enterprises and in joint and foreign business ventures are important to economic reform because advanced technology as well as work and management skills shared in the workplace could spare the country decades of "reinventing the wheel." Furthermore, a country that is serious about democratic reforms should be concerned about its laws on foreigners: an open society can be gauged by how it treats not only its own citizens but also the foreigners who want to live there. While significant advances in emigration have been seen in recent years, few changes have occurred in the policies on foreigners entering and staying.

Before Russian enterprises, joint ventures, and foreign businesses can reasonably employ more foreigners, fundamental revisions will have to be made in the laws concerning such individuals. In rewriting those laws it is important to study the history of foreign migrants in the former USSR, and particularly the current problems they face as a result of inadequate legislation that opens the door to arbitrary decisions, Russian xenophobia, the residues of Stalinist spy mania, and entrenched bureaucracy.

In the early 1920s, immigration practices were geared to attract foreigners to participate as equals in the country's industrial and agricultural development. Tens of thousands came, mainly from the United States but also from Western Europe.[3] In most cases they were motivated by the desire to contribute to the socialist experiment. Not only could people with foreign passports join trade unions and the Communist party, they could also hold public office, for example as deputies in local governing bodies (soviets), if they worked for a Soviet organization. In some cases foreigners were placed in management positions, including middle and top levels.[4]

This situation changed dramatically in the Stalin period. During the purges of the late 1930s, foreigners who had been made to feel quite at home just a decade earlier were suddenly most unwelcome, deprived of the basic rights to life, employment, and housing. Foreigners who did not have Soviet passports[5] were expelled from the country. If they were married to a Soviet citizen they were often given the option to take Soviet citizenship in order to remain. If they refused, they had to leave without their spouse. Foreign-born Soviet citizens who were party functionaries or held managerial positions were dismissed from their jobs and in most cases were also arrested and executed, accused of being spies or saboteurs.

Beginning with the Khrushchev thaw in the late 1950s, but especially in the 1960s and 1970s, foreigners were once again welcome in the USSR, although never to the same extent as in the 1920s. Increasingly they came to the Soviet Union as tourists, exchange students, diplomatic personnel, journalists, and employees of western companies doing business with the Soviet Union. However, the motivation of the migrants was different from that of the earlier wave. These people initially came to the country on a temporary basis, usually with no intention of settling, but ended up wanting to stay whether because they married a Soviet citizen or simply discovered that they liked living there.

If a person decided to remain in the country indefinitely, the only way to do so was to find some form of employment that provided a visa which could be extended periodically by the employer, either in the foreign economy (a foreign business) or in the Soviet economy (a Soviet organization). Theoretically a foreigner could apply for Soviet citizenship or permanent residency, but these options were rarely pursued; if they were, permission was seldom granted. Between

1975 and 1992, I personally knew only one American who applied for Soviet citizenship, and he was denied. I knew eight people with permanent residency, but most of them had obtained this status through a long and arduous process—a process that required them to apply from their home country and wait for permission for as long as a year.[6]

Foreigners who could not secure jobs in the foreign economy could move into the Soviet economy *only* if they had acceptable skills as translators into their native languages, were willing to live in Moscow, and were cleared through a two-month security check showing no ties with any foreign intelligence agency. In this case these foreigners could count on a job at one of the few institutions[7] that had government approval to hire foreign translators on a contract basis; only then could visas and housing be arranged.

The terms of the contracts stipulated the same pay rates earned by Soviet employees doing the same work, the same social benefits, which included paid sick leave, vacations, free health care, free education, minimal-cost child care, housing comparable to that of ordinary Soviets, a free round-trip ticket to their home country in between contracts (every two or three years), and a portion of the salary in hard currency. Overall it was a fair and attractive package, and secure as long as work performance was adequate.

By the 1980s several hundred citizens from every continent were working for Moscow publishing agencies that were oriented to audiences abroad. Along with the members of their families these foreign nationals constituted a substantial international community scattered throughout the capital. They lived in ordinary apartment houses among Soviet neighbors and worked together with Soviet colleagues, and their children attended local Soviet schools.

What was and still is the legal status of such foreign nationals, most commonly referred to by their employers as *inospetsialisty* (foreign specialists)? Article 37 of the Constitution of the Russian Federation, which is a slightly revised version of the Soviet constitution of the Russian Federation, states the following: "Individuals who are not citizens of the Russian Federation and who are on its territory legally, have the same rights and freedoms and obligations as citizens of the Russian Federation with exceptions provided for by the Constitution, laws and international treaties of the Russian Federation. . ."[8] This article indicates that foreign citizens have equal rights. However, their protection is guarded. The statement lacks the direct reference in the old Soviet constitution that foreigners were guaranteed due process of law to protect their rights of person, property, family, and other rights.[9] The law on foreigners and government regulations that were intended to specify foreigners' rights and obligations[10] (which has remained in effect)[11] at best make the legal status of foreigners less clear, and at worst essentially negate the equitable thrust of the constitution.

The main problem is that the category of "foreign specialist" is totally absent from these regulations and legislation, which leaves these foreigners vulnerable to arbitrary bureaucratic measures and human rights violations. The law specifies regulations only for "temporary" foreign visitors (tourists, invited guests, foreign correspondents, foreign business representatives) and for "permanent residents" (people with a *vid na zhitel'stvo* or the rough equivalent of a green card in the United States). While most foreign specialists have lived in the country as long as ten to twenty years (and until very recently planned to remain there indefinitely), they are technically regarded as "temporary" foreigners. The absence of a clear legal status allows the bureaucracy to make arbitrary decisions, regarding these foreign specialists sometimes as "temporary" residents and at other times as "permanent." This leaves the foreign specialists without the advantages of either status, only the disadvantages of each.

To be sure, native-born citizens suffer immensely from these types of shortcomings in their legislation and legal system, especially under conditions of deepening economic and political crisis and chaos. However, the current troubles of foreign specialists are different and certainly warrant attention as well. When Russian citizens lose their jobs, they still have an apartment that the state cannot take away, and are not in danger of being deported. This is not the case with foreign specialists. When Russian citizens retire or are retired they get a pension. Foreigners do not. When the children of Russian citizens reach adulthood they can stay with their parents in the same country, in Russia. This is not true for the children of foreigners. Let us examine these problems one by one.

In the current economic crisis whole publishing houses have closed down or have drastically cut their staffs, and so large numbers of foreign translators have lost their jobs. Many of them have spent their entire careers working in the Soviet Union, and worry that they cannot successfully start their lives all over again in their home country. Since their jobs have provided them with a visa and housing, if they want to remain living in the country, they must find other jobs that also can provide a visa and housing. Those who are unsuccessful in their quest are left in limbo and at risk of eviction and deportation.

For instance, several Indian families who have lived for years in Moscow have been told by their former employer, a major publishing house, that their visas and permits to live in their apartments have expired, and that they must leave the country. So far, the only leverage these families have to remain is the last contract they signed, which ensures that their employer will pay their airfare home.[12] Their employer does not have the hard currency to pay for their tickets now;[13] but when the money does become available the families will be forced to leave, whether they want to or not. This was confirmed to me by the publishing house's official who is directly responsible for all foreign employees.[14]

Foreign specialists who are still living in the housing provided by their employers and want to remain there have tried to determine whether they can privatize the apartments, like their Russian neighbors. This is in the hope that having secured a permanent residence they will be able to apply for a permanent visa. One of the major roadblocks is that they cannot get anyone to show them the administrative orders that would shed light on the current "ownership" of the apartments—whether they belong to the publishing houses, the city soviet, or other agencies. So they do not even know how to begin procedures for privatization.

Another problem of major concern to long-term foreign residents who have no plans to leave is the question of retirement. Will they be allowed to remain in the country after they are no longer able to work, assuming they have accumulated enough seniority as stipulated by law? Permanent residents can be sure of this, but not people whose visas are dependent upon their jobs at Russian organizations. There have been many cases of foreign employees, no longer able-bodied, having put in more than twenty years of work at a Russian publishing house, losing their visas and being sent back to a country in which they had no pension fund accumulated, and unable to count on a Soviet pension being sent to that country in the local currency. Even if the foreigner remains in the country it is unlikely that a pension would be paid by the government.

Other difficulties involve adult children who have grown up with their foreign parents in Moscow. If they are unable to continue their education after secondary school and if they cannot find a job that can qualify them for a visa, the visas they had from their parents' employers are canceled. They must either return to the country of their parents' origin or a third country where they may not know the language, have no living experience, and not have relatives to help them adapt. Such situations can lead to heartrending family dramas.

The 1981 legislation on foreigners further complicated an already tenuous status for the children of foreign specialists and their Soviet spouses. Before 1981 the law stated that such children, if born to a foreign parent and a Soviet citizen residing at the time of birth in the USSR, *may be* Soviet citizens. This left the choice up to the parents, who could either apply for a Soviet birth certificate or not. Since 1981, the law reads that such children *are* Soviet citizens. Sometimes these children have found themselves on different sides of a national border running right through the middle of their parents' precarious households. Now the visa bureau (UVIR) will not recognize the foreign passports of such children when the foreign parent wants to take them out of the country. Instead, such parents have to go to their embassies to fill out an invitation to the children to visit their own country, take that invitation to the local militia station that processes exit permits for Soviet citizens, stand in enormously long lines just to submit the various papers, and wait up to two months for the exit permit. Even in an emergency this procedure could take at least a couple of weeks at the local militia, whereas, at UVIR, exit visas for foreign specialists can be ready the same day.

What is interesting about this particular problem is that only UVIR seems to be interpreting the 1981 law in this way. The Ministry of Foreign Affairs, which handles entry/exit visas for foreign correspondents, business representatives, and diplomats, recognizes the foreign passports of children of foreign and Soviet parents.

In 1987 foreign specialists formed an ad hoc committee, with representatives from each of the Soviet enterprises in Moscow that employs large numbers of foreigners. The main action they took was to write letters explaining their problems, first to their respective managements and then, after no satisfactory response, to President Mikhail Gorbachev at the USSR Supreme Soviet and Prime Minister Nikolai Ryzhkov at the Council of Ministers. Letters were submitted in June 1988. The only indirect reply came through UVIR, in response to the letter to the USSR Supreme Soviet. The foreign specialists who signed the letter were invited in April 1990 to a discussion with an UVIR official who essentially explained the status quo and offered no time frame for changes.

In the autumn of 1988 employers explained to foreign specialists that a high-level commission was to be set up to discuss just what legal status they should be granted and what concrete changes in the law were required to resolve these problems. It was promised that as soon as such a commission met, the foreign specialists could send a representative to participate in the deliberations. If such a commission ever met, it was without the knowledge of the foreign specialists.

Gradually the foreign specialists stopped taking group actions, seeing that they were eliciting no meaningful response. Today they are fighting individually and privately, trying to accomplish something for themselves and their families any way that works. For instance, one employee I know returned to his home country with his wife, while his adult son (who did not want to leave because he had known no other home, had a Russian wife and child, and a job with a foreign firm) arranged to remain in his parents' apartment by paying hard currency monthly as rent to one of the officials of the father's former employer. In a bureaucracy that makes decisions arbitrarily, often the most effective solution is bribery.

These problems are not being tackled for various reasons. One has to do with the long-standing cultural attitude toward foreigners. A complex and contradictory mixture of admiration, jealousy, and fear makes Russians both welcoming and unwelcoming, often at the same time. Even today, decades after the Stalin period, when borders are being opened, the legacy of suspicion of foreigners remains to be fully challenged. As recently as December 1992, for the first time in all the years I lived in the Soviet Union, an official openly told me he thought I might be collecting information for the CIA. In fact I was doing field work in the Urals for a University of California research project, studying social mobilization around environmental issues.

The old Soviet organizations that have traditionally been the only ones allowed to hire foreigners are still running lengthy security checks on prospective employees. The manager of the English language translators at a major publishing house in Moscow told me in December 1992 that he has so far been unsuccessful in having the security check waived so that he can hire qualified translators and put them to work immediately, without waiting several weeks. Supposedly this is a policy set by the KGB, not by the publishing house. Any loosening of the old controls that would enable ordinary former state enterprises to employ qualified foreigners does not seem feasible in the near future.

At best the apparent lack of concern for opening up the Russian economy to foreigners or solving the problems of foreigners is a consequence of bureaucratic inertia and the attitude on the part of officials and lawmakers that new legislation on foreigners can wait; after all, the foreign community is small and its problems minute in the context of issues being raised throughout the country. The foreigners, however, argue that the revisions required in this law should not demand a great deal of the lawmakers' time, precisely because the problems are so minute relative to the bigger issues and because the solutions are so obvious if guided by a commitment to the constitution and universal human rights, including the right to social security or the rights of families as stipulated in international agreements[15] signed by the former Soviet Union.

Officials used to urge the foreigners not to worry: each person's problems could be resolved to the benefit of the individual. They used to maintain that they understood the predicament of foreign specialists and would not do anything to hurt them. In the harsher conditions today, when these same officials' lives are unraveling at the seams, they tend to take a tougher, less humane stance, like the official who expressed no sympathy for the Indian families he will evict forcefully, if necessary, just as soon as his organization has enough money for their airfare back to India. Arbitrary approaches, so dependent on the individual dispositions of people in authority, can no longer be tolerated in a society striving to be governed by the rule of law. Foreign citizens, like Russian citizens, want to know their legal rights and restrictions clearly. And if a bureaucrat violates them, foreign nationals need to be ensured legal protection by lawyers guided by clearly defined laws, not by confusing regulations and administrative orders kept under lock and key.

Perhaps this discussion of Russian policies on foreigners will facilitate the accommodation of foreign nationals in Russia generally, as well as in the context of efforts by the United States and other countries to assist Russia in creating a viable market economy. It is also hoped that it will prompt greater interest in improving world standards for the legal rights of international migrants; to be sure, Russia is not the only country that needs to improve its approach to "outsiders."

Notes

1. For instance, foreigners with permanent residency have the same problems as foreign specialists when it comes to leaving the country with their Russian children. They also have the added inconvenience of waiting up to two months for an exit permit for themselves from UVIR (visa bureau). Foreigners on temporary visas who are not in the category of "foreign specialist" have the same disadvantages as all other foreigners in the restrictions on purchasing certain goods and services in rubles. However, in this respect there are differences between temporary foreigners and foreign specialists. Accredited foreign journalists and diplomats who are on temporary visas are allowed to buy all their

airline tickets and hotel accommodations in rubles even though their incomes are entirely in hard currency, while foreign specialists, exclusively earning rubles, cannot buy these services in rubles. Unfortunately an article on the diversity of problems faced by each category of foreigner would require much greater length than permitted here. It is hoped that this article will provide an illustration of characteristic problems in Russian legislation on foreigners and the need to seek solutions.

2. See Paula Garb, *They Came to Stay: North Americans in the USSR* (Moscow: "Progress" Publishers, 1987); Paula Garb, "Culture Learning and Cultural Adaptation among North Americans in the USSR," Dissertation, USSR Academy of Sciences, 1990.

3. G.Ia. Tarle, *Druzia strany sovetov* (Friends of the Land of the Soviets) (Moscow: "Nauka" Publishers, 1968).

4. See Anna Louise Strong, *I Change Worlds: The Remaking of an American* (New York: Garden City Publishing, 1937); Tracy B. Strong and Helene Keyssar, *Right in Her Soul: The Life of Anna Louise Strong* (New York: Random House, 1983); Robert Robinson, *Black on Red: My 44 Years Inside the Soviet Union* (Washington, DC: Acropolis Books, 1987).

5. It was common in those days for foreigners to take Soviet citizenship while maintaining their foreign passport.

6. When applicants are in their native country waiting for permission to return as a permanent resident, they risk losing their temporary status and perhaps may never receive permanent residency. Another obstacle is that a Russian citizen who is a close relative must make the invitation for this status. Exceptions have been made to these rules, which is why they are all the more frustrating. When officials create rules as they go along the outcome is never predictable.

7. These institutions are Progress Publishers, Mir Publishers, Raduga Publishers, Radio Moscow, Novosti Press Agency, the weeklies *Moscow News* and *New Times*. They are all located in Moscow.

8. "Konstitutsiia (osnovnoi zakon) Rossiiskoi Federatsii—Rossii," *Izdanie Verkhovnogo Soveta Rossiiskoi Federatsii*, 1992 (Constitution [Fundamental Law] of the Russian Federation—Russia, Publication of the Supreme Soviet of the Russian Federation, 1992).

9. *Constitution (Fundamental Law) of the Union of Soviet Socialist Republics* (Adopted on October 7, 1977) (Moscow: Novosti Press Agency Publishing House, 1977).

10. See *Zakon SSSR "O Pravovom polozhenii inostrannykh grazhdan v SSSR,"* 1981 (USSR Law On the Legal Status of Foreign Citizens in the USSR); *"Pravila prebyvaniia inostrannykh grazhdan v SSSR" ot 10.05.84* (Regulations on Foreign Citizens in the USSR, May 10, 1984); *Postanovleniie Soveta Ministrov SSSR ot 28.08.86* (Resolution of the USSR Council of Ministers, August 28, 1986).

11. The most recent contract offered by Progress Publishers in December 1992 cites these regulations as the legal basis for policies on foreign employees.

12. Contracts no longer have this clause.

13. Russian organizations can pay the airfare of their Russian employees in rubles, but must come up with hard currency for their foreign employees.

14. This information is based on conversations with the employees and an official in December 1992. I have chosen not to name the publishing house or the official in order not to exacerbate the predicament of these families.

15. Articles 9 and 10 of the International Covenant on Economic, Social and Cultural Rights; and Section 1(b) of the Final Act of the Conference on Security and Cooperation in Europe, Helsinki, 1975.

Part 2

The USA:
Progress and Regress

10

The Human Rights Paradox

Bertram Gross

We should recognize, as Hawthorne did, the innocence as well as the evil in our natures.   (Michael Kammen)[1]

My country right and wrong—when right to be kept right, when wrong to be set right.   (Carl Schurz)[2]

In 1939 Winston Churchill portrayed Russia as "a riddle wrapped in a mystery inside an enigma." Today, whatever one may say about the former Soviet Union, the United States is indeed a riddle.

For more than a century after the 1776 Declaration of Independence and the 1791 Bill of Rights, Arnold Toynbee once wrote, U.S. ideals of the rights of man were an inspiration to "the depressed majority of mankind." But recently, he lamented, the United States has become "a champion of an affluent minority's vested interests" and consequently the world's "arch-conservative power."[3]

This contradiction is more puzzling now than it appeared to Toynbee. On the one hand, for many a million in the United States, the "rights of man," as then defined, have been largely fulfilled. ("Fulfilled" signifies whatever realization in real life is implied by the more traditional "enforced" and "implemented," except that the latter terms connote external compulsion or executive domination with too little emphasis on internalization of human rights norms.) More recently, Americans have transcended the ancient rights of man through activism in various human rights movements. Women, members of ethnic minorities (Native American, African-American, Latino- and Asian-American), working people, consumers, and many brands of civil libertarians have stoutly assaulted archaic bastions of arch-conservative privilege. Victorious or not, their example in trying to defend or extend human rights has been an inspiring example to millions throughout the world. This helps explain why oppressed people in other parts of the world continue, as in the distant past, to see the United States as a haven of refuge or a beacon in the darkness.

On the other hand, most of the founding fathers who signed the Declaration of Independence or voted for the Bill of Rights championed the vested interests of an affluent minority and opposed the extension of elite rights to such lesser folk as unpropertied white men, women, slaves, or Native Americans. And in both past and recent years, extremists of "arch-conservative power" have cruelly and continually undermined the basic rights of millions of people within the United States and abroad.

This dialectical combination of forward steps "to be kept right" and wrongs "to be set right" is nothing new.[4] In much of human history, new rights and moral advance have appeared side by side with new wrongs and moral degradation; and higher standards of living, with destitution and hunger. A little more democracy at home has often coexisted with a lot more violent expansionism abroad. The extension of rights from a few to a few more and particularly to many more has usually frightened the original few, provoking passive resistance or active opposition. With progress in education, literacy, science, technology, and with higher levels of material living, however, "we evaluate ourselves and our performance by more and more demanding criteria."[5] This leads to an escalation of claims for the legitimation of new rights. Yet every recent decade has seen increasing destruction of the natural environment upon which human life and all rights—old or new—depend. Although these apparent contradictions abound in *all* countries, they are particularly confusing in the United States.

The United States in a Topsy-Turvy World

This study has been written while major historical shifts—some sudden, many slow—have been turning old ideas and power structures upside down. As U.S.–USSR relations gradually improve, old hopes for mutual security are being revived. New hopes—and new threats—are being born.

Yet any mind adjusted to an apparently endless cold war and an accelerating exploitation of natural resources could understandingly be slow, as Seneca put it in reflecting on the decline of the Roman republic, "in unlearning what it has been long in learning."[6] The diverse people in any power structure, including reformers, cannot easily convert to new ways of combining government responsibilities with competitive markets or to the environmentally sound civilian growth needed to replace military activities. Many people find it difficult to live without *the* enemy—whether that enemy be communism, anticommunism, or capitalism.

With the internationalization of private and public capital, the partial growth of a world culture, and the increasing interdependence of all nations, there is no longer any truly national economy, power structure, or culture. Nor is there much meaning left in the now obsolete distinctions between West and East, North and South, and the so-called first, second, and third worlds. Many things learned as right during rapid industrial growth—an escalating arms race and the tacit acceptance of unlimited national sovereignty (and even self-determination or autonomy)—now seem wrong. In both private and public life much "wrong that was" seems surprisingly right. Neither young nor old is entirely sure about the differences between right and wrong. On these, as on other matters, the Left seems bereft, the Middle muddled, and the Right not always right—or wrong.

As steps are being taken toward fulfilling old rights, old wrongs come to the surface. New wrongs, with both old and new roots, such as Iraq's takeover of Kuwait, burst upon the world stage. In response, the U.S. president promptly projected powerful military forces into Saudi Arabia and the Persian Gulf and soon obtained international support and assistance through the U.N. Security Council. Some saw this action as U.S. leadership with the help of the Soviet Union toward building a new, post–cold war world order: If the Gulf crisis could be successfully handled, perhaps the United Nations would be able to assume the responsibilities for peacekeeping that were given it by the 1945 charter but which were impaired by more than forty-five years of cold war confrontation. But some aspects of the U.S. action reflected the "American Century" thought and action,* which was embodied in old-style gunboat diplomacy and the more recent unilateral strikes against Lebanon, Grenada, Libya, and Panama. Some may even have seen the United States as responding to the decline of Soviet power (and compensating for its own economic decline) by reappearing on the world stage as *the* military superpower.

Glorious Triumphs

Recognizing past progress—even when partial and much less than glorious—helps to demonstrate that, no matter how formidable the obstacles, victories can be had. It also identifies those rights that are "to be kept right" at home and are still an inspiration to people in other countries. The American dream of freedom has never been American only. It has been a vision cherished around the globe. The first European settlements in North America inspired hope among all classes for a new Golden Age in a New World. The British colonies offered freedom from religious oppression, military conscription, and the pauperization triggered by the breakdown of feudalism. In the Declaration of Independence, the colonists proclaimed the highest ideals of the European Enlightenment. Its ringing affirmation of "certain unalienable rights ... life, liberty and the pursuit of happiness," became an inspirational world classic. From George Washington and

---

*Under the label "Manifest Destiny," (and later "Pax Americana" or the "World's Policeman") this concept goes back to the Spanish-American War at the end of the nineteenth century and the subsequent emergence of the United States as the decisive power in ending World Wars I and II. The term itself first came into widespread use in an article by Henry Luce after World War II had started in Europe: "The world of the 20th Century, if it is to come to life in any nobility of health and vigor, must be to a significant degree an American Century." ("The American Century," *Fortune*, February 1941.)

Thomas Jefferson onward, the cultural heroes of the United States have become, in the euphoric words of the Brazilian Marxist Darcy Ribeiro, the "heroes of all humanity."[7]

Honor should also be given to hundreds of others—from John Paul Zenger and Thomas Paine to Sojourner Truth, Frederick Douglass, Elizabeth Cady Stanton, Chief Sitting Bull, and Eugene Debs; from Henry Thoreau to Martin Luther King, Jr., and Cesar Chavez. This author honors still more the thousands of unknown heroines and heroes who have struggled daily for basic human rights in the face of brutal discrimination or the current desolation of urban ghettos, reservations, and rural slums.

A Living Constitution

> The government they [the founding fathers] devised was defective from the start. . . . Let us quietly commemorate the suffering, struggle and sacrifice that has triumphed over much of what was wrong with the original document.
> (Thurgood Marshall, Associate Justice of U.S. Supreme Court)[8]

In the original draft of the Constitution, the framers invented a unique form of tripartite federalism. As proposed in 1787,* the Constitution's first three articles established a system of "checks and balances" to prevent the concentration of too much power in the federal executive. The first three articles did this by dispersing federal authority among three intertwined branches: a bicameral congress (the House of Representatives and the Senate), an executive branch headed by a president, and the judiciary.

The members of the House of Representatives were to be elected in accordance with the population of each state. The Senate was to consist of two members from each state who would be chosen by the state legislatures; it was thus supposed to be a check on the "popular" House. Congress was given many detailed legislative powers, including taxing, spending, borrowing, coining money, protecting the rights of authors and inventors, conducting a national census every ten years, establishing armed forces, and declaring war. Certain rights were reserved for the House, others for the Senate. Certain powers were forbidden to Congress (and also the states), among them the levying of any tax or duties on "articles exported from any state."

Like senators, the president was to be chosen by electors from each state, rather than by popular vote. He was to have a limited role in legislation, to "take care that the laws be faithfully executed," to initiate treaties and make certain appointments "with the advice and consent of the Senate," and to be commander-in-chief of the armed forces (a vital requirement of constitutional

---

*The delegates from the thirteen states were formally authorized by the Second Continental Congress only to amend the loose Articles of Confederation. In proposing the Constitution, they knowingly exceeded the formal authority given them.

democracy). After being nominated by the president and confirmed by the Senate, federal judges were to "hold their offices during good behavior."

Among other matters, the fourth article dealt with the states, guaranteeing to each "a Republican Form of Government." The fifth provided an amending process. The sixth designated the Constitution, all federal laws, and all treaties as "the supreme law of the land," binding on all federal and state officials. It also sustained the rights of all parties to "debts contracted and engagements entered into" before the Constitution. But before the new Constitution could be ratified, amendments were proposed to limit the federal government's authority. In fact, the new tripartite government "almost didn't happen. . . . In 1787 a group of concerned citizens wanted to see the proposed constitution go down to defeat. They viewed it as a plot to install a tyrannical government, not unlike that of the despised British colonial system. . . . Thomas Jefferson wrote James Madison from Paris expressing his concern about 'the omission of a bill of rights . . . providing clearly . . . for freedom of religion, freedom of the press, protection against standing armies, and restriction against monopolies."[9] Jefferson and Madison both argued that ratification should be made conditional upon a bill of rights similar to the 1776 Virginia Bill of Rights[10] and to Madison's famous Bill 82 in the Virginia House of Delegates.[11] With Jefferson's help, Madison drafted a set of amendments. In opposition, Alexander Hamilton argued that "the proposed constitution, if adopted, will be the bill of rights of the union." Any additional rights "are not only unnecessary . . . but would be even dangerous." Besides, he asked rhetorically, "what is the liberty of the press? Who can give it any definition which would not leave the utmost latitude for evasion?"[12]

Hamilton did not have his way. Ratification was delayed until a firm commitment was made to adopt amendments that would limit the powers of the federal government. Based on this commitment, the Constitution was ratified, coming into effect in 1789. And on December 15, 1791, the U.S. Bill of Rights, "the great American charter of personal liberty and human dignity," came into effect as the first ten amendments.

The famous First Amendment went far beyond earlier ideas of religious tolerance. It prohibits any law "respecting the establishment of religion or prohibiting the free exercise thereof." It also protects the freedom of speech and of the press, and "the right of the people peaceably to assemble, and to petition the government for a redress of grievances." The Second Amendment, still controversial, deals with the "right of the people to keep and bear arms." The Third, a relic of the colonial era, protects people from having to take soldiers into their houses. The Fourth protects "the right of the people to be secure . . . against unreasonable searches and seizures." The Fifth prohibits double jeopardy and the forcing of an accused person "to be a witness against himself." A less well known part of the Fifth Amendment prohibits taking private property for public use "without just compensation." According to the Sixth Amendment, the accused person in all criminal prosecution "shall enjoy the right to a speedy and public trial" and other protections, including "the assistance of counsel for his defense." The Seventh Amendment recognizes the right to trial by jury. The Eighth prohibits excessive bail or fines and the inflicting of "cruel and unusual punishment" (at that time, public flogging and hanging were considered neither cruel nor unusual). The Ninth and Tenth Amendments hold that other rights, not specified, were to be retained by the states or the people. Only in the Sixth Amendment was a right explicitly *created*. The other rights, presumed already to exist, were to be *protected*.

There are also some deeply grounded traditions not mentioned in the Constitution. The first was the creation of political parties, something that the founders had argued against strongly. Yet under the circumstances of coping with conflicting views, they soon reversed themselves. As amendments were being acted on, the Hamiltonians organized as the Federalist party and the Jeffersonians as the Democratic Republican party (later called the Democratic party). In this way, the various interests identified by James Madison—landed, manufacturing, mercantile, moneyed, and the many lesser interests—could do something more than articulate specific interests through pressure and persuasion on the officers of government. They could support political parties that would aggregate diverse interests, nominate candidates for public office, and try to get their candidates elected.[13] By 1800, as the first parties fought for the presidency, they had their representatives in the electoral college vote for the party candidates rather than allow them to exercise their own judgment. This undid the earlier effort to keep the president from being elected by popular vote. A ruling party could now elect its candidates for both president and the Congress. Thus, while the tripartite federal structure dispersed responsibility and accountability, a dominant party might be held responsible by the voters. (The difficulties in holding political parties responsible for governmental action are discussed in the final section of this chapter.)

Second, without authorization in the Constitution, the Supreme Court established its authority (and that of other federal courts) to declare federal statutes unconstitutional. In *Marbury v. Madison* (1803), the Court overruled an act of Congress on a minor matter; no serious objection was raised. By 1857, when the Court overruled the Missouri Compromise (*Dred Scott v. Sanford*) and held that no slave could be a citizen, the court's authority of judicial review was taken for granted. It took a civil war (and the constitutional amendments ratified after the Union's victory) to overturn the Dred Scott decision.

Third, even before the Declaration of Independence, the founders did something that is rarely recognized in the history books. They broke with the British tradition of exclusive executive prerogative in initiating bills. Individual members of colonial state legislatures started to introduce their own bills at a time when all governors were representatives of the British crown. They continued doing this in the sessions of the Continental Congress which set up the Articles of Confederation in 1774 and continued to meet after the British forces were defeated in 1781. Under the 1787 draft of the Constitution, it was clear that no president or department head could introduce any bill in Congress. That right was reserved exclusively for members of the Senate and the House of Representatives, with the latter having the exclusive right to propose revenue measures. While many members have introduced bills at the request of the president or an agency head, many of the most important statutes in American history originated with the Congress without initial executive support. In no other country is there such a record of major laws bearing the names of individual members.*

Taken together, the Constitution, the Bill of Rights, and the various traditions constituted a landmark in the history of human efforts to create the machinery of representative government, constitutional federalism, and, eventually, democracy.

Crawling Toward Democracy

> When the Constitution was framed, no respectable person called himself or herself a democrat. (Charles and Mary Beard)[14]

Although the word "democracy" never appears in the Constitution, the first words of its preamble, "We the People," had a faintly democratic ring to them. Yet only a tiny portion of the adult population had anything to do with the framing of the Constitution. The fifty-five well-to-do men who proposed it were selected by state legislators who themselves had been elected by about 120,000 out of a population of four million. "The vote on ratification," writes Richard Kluger, "was cast by not more than one-sixth of the adult population." Kluger points out that "there was no talk at Philadelphia about such ideas as universal suffrage, the rights of labor, the equality of women, free public education—concepts that would have been as alien to the delegates as wireless telegraphy and the internal-combustion engine." [15] The antimonarchist leaders of that era wanted a nondemocratic republic. They felt that the extension of suffrage beyond propertied white males could lead to all the horrors of democracy: anarchy, despoliation of the rich by the poor, control of affairs by illiterate, untrustworthy people, and so on. The only democratic aspect of the Constitution's formulation was that the discussions among the elitist formulators and the ratifiers—albeit behind closed doors—were conducted among gentlemen who treated each other as equals. What they wrought was democracy for a few: for "men of property."

---

*Some of the acts known by the names of their congressional sponsors: Adamson, Carey, Dawes, Elkins, Esch-Cummins, Clayton, Frazier-Lemke, Hatch (1887 and 1939), Humphrey-Hawkins, Johnson, La Follette, Landrum-Griffin, McNary-Haugen, Mann-Elkins, Norris-LaGuardia, Pendleton, Sherman, Taft-Hartley, Volstead, and Wagner. Some of these have may been informally inspired by executive officials. Generally, however, these laws won executive support only after support was mobilized by nongovernmental lobbyists and/or executive officials acting on their own. The Taft-Hartley Act, however, was enacted over a veto by President Truman.

Pierce Butler summed up their views by stating that the real value of the new union was that "it was instituted principally for the protection of property and which was itself to be supported by property."[16]

The most controversial forms of property were slaves, who made up almost a fifth of the population. Hot debates took place—and compromises were fashioned—on three aspects of protecting the property rights of slave owners. On whether slaves should be counted in apportioning seats in the House of Representatives, the Constitution gave the slave-owning states more representation by counting every slave as three fifths of a person (Article 1, Section 2). It also deferred until 1808 any moves toward the abolition of slavery (Article 1, Section 9) and required that slaves who ran away to "free states" be returned to their owners.

The entry of new states into the Union triggered a balancing act in which the number of slave states and "free states" represented in the Senate was equally balanced: eight to eight in 1800, twelve to twelve after the Missouri Compromise of 1820 (allowing slavery in some states and abolishing it in others), and fifteen to fifteen by 1848. A more complicated compromise, including a toughened fugitive-slave act, was worked out when California entered in 1850. A few years later in Kansas, a state of near civil war emerged between slavery and antislavery forces, and the compromise tottered. It broke down completely in 1857, when a slave by the name of Dred Scott sued for his freedom on the grounds that he had lived for five years in Missouri, where slavery was forbidden. Denying his petition, the Supreme Court also declared the Missouri Compromise unconstitutional on the grounds that it interfered with the property rights of slave owners. "The distinguished men who framed the Declaration of Independence," wrote Justice Roger Taney, "perfectly understood the meaning of the language they used . . . it would not . . . be supposed to include [Negroes] so far inferior that they had no rights which the white man was bound to respect."[17]

By the following year, when Abraham Lincoln declared that "this government cannot endure permanently half slave and half free," [18] the possibility of civil war between north and south loomed on the horizon. Even before Lincoln took office as president in 1861, southern states started to secede from the Union. By April, when Lincoln sought to preserve the Union by denying states' rights to self-determination and secession, the Civil War was in full swing.[19] Despite the north's superiority in manpower and industrial might, Lincoln's war to save the Union dragged out. After months of complex maneuvering, Lincoln issued his famous Emancipation Proclamation freeing all slaves in the Confederacy, at that time not under federal jurisdiction. This encouraged more slaves to escape their masters and join the Union forces. By May 1865, after vast devastation and about a million casualties, the Union was saved and a more powerful central government emerged.

To consolidate the Union victory, three constitutional amendments were ratified: the Thirteenth (1865), which forbids slavery; the Fourteenth (1868), which gives the Congress authority to enforce the Bill of Rights in the states and provides that no state shall deprive any person of life, liberty, or property without due process of law; and the Fifteenth (1870), providing that a citizen's right to vote "shall not be denied or abridged . . . on account of race, color or previous condition of servitude." A freedman's bureau, a civil rights act, and various reconstruction reforms nourished temporary illusions that genuine freedom was around the corner. "Hello, Massa," a former slave allegedly said upon seeing his former owner among a group of Confederate prisoners he was guarding, "bottom rail on top this time!"[20]

In the face of organized southern violence against former slaves and massive racism in the so-called free states of the north, most of these laws became prime examples of dead law. The laws that lived were the anti-Black laws enacted by state legislatures. "Most of the Black men of the South, within a few years of their emancipation, had been reduced to a state of helpless peonage."[21] By the end of the century, Supreme Court decisions "nullified nearly every vestige of the federal protection that had been cast like a comforting cloak over the Negro upon his release from bondage."[22] In both south and north, "bottom rail" stayed at or close to the bottom.

In contrast, the Supreme Court brought to life a "sleeper" that, having no direct connection with the fate of former slaves, had been purposely hidden in the wording of the Fourteenth Amendment. As Charles and Mary Beard revealed in 1927, two members of the committee that drafted the amendment, Representatives John Bingham and Roscoe Conkling, a prominent Republican and successful railroad lawyer, explained that they had added the word "person" (in addition to "citizen"), not to help former slaves, but to help protect "joint stock companies" from the oppression of state or local regulation, expropriation, and "invidious and discriminating" taxes.[23] Under a flood of judicial decisions, the fictive personality of state-chartered corporations became one of the fundaments under the towering structure of corporate law. Every corporation was thereby entitled to all the rights, including due process, at all levels of government that the Constitution granted to mortals. Despite occasional dissents, these rights have long been upheld.[24]

With this due process protection against state government regulation, and with massive government aid to corporate collectivities through land grants, protective tariffs and other subsidies, northern industry expanded rapidly and the United States began to emerge as a potential great power. All this took place under the ideological umbrella of a weak central government. For decades, the Supreme Court declared unconstitutional many laws that limited the rights of large corporations or, as Arthur Schlesinger puts it, "countered the aggressions of local majorities on the rights of minorities and individuals."[25]

Nonetheless, much progress was made. Decades before the Thirteenth, Fourteenth and Fifteenth Amendments, the Jacksonian democrats started the long process of asserting white people's rights to public land and public education.

They also succeeded in gradually diluting the property qualifications on the voting rights of white males. In 1848, Elizabeth Cady Stanton and Lucretia Mott organized the first public gathering ever held for women's rights. In their Declaration of Sentiments and Resolutions, * they paraphrased the attack in the Declaration of Independence on King George by cataloging the "repeated injuries and usurpations on the part of man toward women."[26] Twenty years later, with the help of Frederick Douglass, the early feminists called for a women's suffrage amendment to the Constitution, a measure finally ratified in 1920. A few years earlier, the passage of the Sixteenth and Seventeenth Amendments authorized the collection of income taxes (previously declared unconstitutional by the Supreme Court) and the direct election of Senators. Later amendments allowed District of Columbia residents to vote in presidential elections (the Twenty-third Amendment, 1961), eliminated poll taxes or any other tax as a requirement for voting in national elections (the Twenty-fourth Amendment, 1964), and reduced the voting age from twenty-one to eighteen (the Twenty-sixth Amendment, 1971). More recently, voting rights have been extended further by legislation providing more protection for minority voters and by campaigns to remove barriers to voting registration. Supreme Court decisions on apportionment have gone far to formally establish the principle of "one person, one vote," the basic premise of voter sovereignty. Under this premise, the government might reign but the people are supposed to rule.

The biggest changes came with the New Deal of President Franklin D. Roosevelt. During its first years, the Roosevelt administration succeeded in pushing through Congress a whole series of laws to help save American capitalism by strengthening the role of the federal government. Mostly, they aimed at helping people who were trapped by the horrors of the Great Depression to receive the larger incomes that would help to stabilize the markets for goods produced by private business. Yet these measures infringed somewhat on corporate and managerial rights. Outraged by restrictions on their traditional power, old-time executives and stockholders protested and fought back. The outcries were amplified by trade associations, a business-dominated press, and business spokespeople in legislatures and political parties. From 1934 to 1936, a conservative Supreme Court struck down one New Deal law after another. A majority of the nine members ruled that such measures allowed unconstitutional regulation of business, invaded the reserved powers of the states, or induced the states to exceed their powers.[27]

Facing a constitutional crisis, Roosevelt launched a campaign to reform the Court by expanding its size so that he could pack it with justices who favored the New Deal. While he lost this battle, he won the war. Under the pressure of deep-seated public support for New Deal measures as testified to by Roosevelt's

---

*The document's "Resolutions" section might be regarded as the U.S.'s second Bill of Rights.

massive election victory in 1936, the Court's majority shifted. By expanding the interpretation of the Constitution's interstate commerce clause, beginning in early 1937, it rejected all appeals against New Deal measures, thereby permitting new waves of progress.

Resisting Fascist and Communist Empires

The Second World War [against the fascist Axis] revealed the American system of liberal capitalism at its best. . . .

(Howard Zinn)[28]

At no time since 1917 has anti-communism failed to occupy a major, even a central, place in the politics and policies of the capitalist world.

(Ralph Miliband and Marcel Liebman, 1984)[29]

Workers of the world, we apologize.

(Banner in Moscow march, 1989)

From 1917 to 1989, Karl Marx's dream of a heaven on earth spread across the world in many versions. Revolutionary socialists proclaimed that the abolition of private property rights would end exploitation. Representing all workers and peasants and their allies, a temporary communist dictatorship would guarantee the economic rights of all (except the surviving remnants of capitalism). The immense productive forces of technology would be freed from the fetters imposed by capitalism. Humankind could then gradually pass from scarcity to abundance. Under the banner "to each according to his needs," the human race would enter full communism. In place of poverty, unemployment, and the business cycle: unending prosperity. In place of colonies: independence. In place of war: eternal peace. Thus, with the prelude to true civilization brought to a close, the history of human freedom would begin.[30]

For many in the capitalist world, this dream of economic justice was a nightmare. A few revolutionaries (Rosa Luxemburg and Emma Goldman among them) predicted that a Communist party dictatorship could no longer represent the working classes. Evolutionary socialists, a much larger group, warned that the use of violence would destroy all human rights. The specter of expropriation haunted corporate board rooms.

Some time after the Bolsheviks' *coup d'etat*, the United States, Britain France and other allies supported White Russian counterrevolutionaries in a bloody civil war—first by direct intervention, then by military aid. When the Civil War ended, the capitalist intervention continued at a lower level. The Red Army then tried to seize Poland. Failing there, it took control of other republics that had won independence from the former tsarist empire: Georgia, Armenia, and Azerbaijan. Elsewhere, they used communist parties in other countries to foment revolution or to support Soviet foreign policy.

Within the major capitalist states, anticommunism was traditionally divided into two camps: reactionaries and reformers. The reactionaries came right to the point with an insistence that all communist groups be suppressed. They also went on to demand resistance to, or even suppression of, all socialist reformers on the ground that many of the socialists were communists in disguise and that in any case well-intentioned socialist reforms would inevitably lead to thoroughgoing nationalization or even communist revolution. Communists, socialists, anarchists, trade union organizers, and even pacifists were portrayed as bomb-throwing wild men panting to pour across the world, burn churches, and "nationalize" women. In the United States during the early 1920s, "red scares" became the excuse for hard-to-justify deportations and for police violence against reformers, trade unions, and isolated socialist or communist sects. By the end of the 1920s, this form of anticommunism, dedicated to maintaining or restoring the "old order," prevailed in eastern Europe—particularly Poland, Bulgaria, Yugoslavia, and Rumania.

Reformers, meanwhile, often held that the best protection against communism was a more enlightened capitalism, after which some form of socialism could come gradually. A little suppression might be necessary, but only as part of a positive program of improving the conditions of the lower classes, raising mass purchasing power, and mollifying class conflicts. Toward this objective, socialists and the larger, more far-sighted finance capitalists must work together against the reactionaries. In Great Britain, the Scandinavian countries, France, and Germany under the Weimar Republic, this approach became very powerful, with the socialists often entering capitalist governments or even assuming full responsibility for governance in a capitalist society.

Reactionaries and reformers had something in common. They both tried to reveal the full facts about mass murders and repression in the USSR. Much of the detailed work was done by former members of communist parties and by socialists or former socialists.[31] They often managed to break through the Bolsheviks' propagandistic and ideological screens and get their facts straight about the mass murder of peasants during the first Five Year Plan and the murdering of Stalin's opponents in the Soviet Communist party.

In turn, members of communist parties and other Marxist parties in many countries often closed their eyes to unpleasant facts. A major tendency was to emphasize the "humanistic" intentions of the Soviet communists and the historic achievements that presumably counterbalanced the defects in the first workers' society. Another tendency was just to leave the Communist party. In the USSR, those who opened their eyes to the realities of Leninism and Stalinism (both of which continued long after the Lenin's and Stalin's deaths) became "closet dissidents," conforming in public and sublimating their disagreements. A few exceptional people expressed their hidden convictions indirectly through art, literature, and music.

The tensions created by anticommunism diminished in the United States with the 1933 recognition of the USSR by the new president, Franklin D. Roosevelt. The Soviet Union was also widely recognized as having conquered the capitalist business cycle at a time when the United States, like other capitalist countries, was mired in the depths of a catastrophic depression.

Early in the same year, the nature of these tensions changed as a new leader of anticommunism, Adolf Hitler, came to power in Germany. Building on the example of Mussolini in the 1920s, Hitler's German National Socialists (Nazis) forged a creative synthesis between reactionary and reformist anticommunism. Offering a dynamic alternative to both capitalism and socialism, they joined with Italy and Japan in championing a new fascist order that would put an end to Bolshevism.

While fascism had some open or covert supporters (and financial backers) in the United States, France, and Britain, the aggressions perpetrated by the fascists gave anticommunism a bad name. Some of the most fervent anticommunists sounded suspiciously like Hitler, Mussolini, and the Japanese warlords. In the underground movements of all three countries, most communists (except those who converted to fascism) leaped into the forefront of antifascism. The USSR called futilely for collective security against fascist aggression in Manchuria, China, Ethiopia, the Saarland, the Rhineland, and Austria. In 1935, even before Hitler's bloodless takeover in the Saarland and Rhineland, Stalin called on all communist parties to drop revolutionary activities temporarily and work in various united fronts or popular fronts against the fascist threats.

For a few years, communism got a big boost by the USSR's antifascist stance and its success in "abolishing unemployment." Thousands of idealists— including hundreds of well-known authors, actors, artists, and intellectuals— joined the Communist party or supported communist causes. One of those causes was to work with John L. Lewis and other critics of the American Federation of Labor in the organization of industrial unions in basic industries. Another was to work through the American Negro Congress and other groups for an end to discrimination against African Americans. Eleanor Roosevelt openly cooperated with the American Youth Congress, despite its ties with the Communist party. The communists, in turn, supported President Roosevelt in most aspects of his New Deal reform program and in his futile efforts to "quarantine the aggressors." When Roosevelt refused to support the elected Spanish government against the 1937 rebellion backed by Hitler and Mussolini, many U.S. communists went to Spain to fight fascism as members of the Abraham Lincoln Brigade.

With the Hitler–Stalin pact of 1939 and the outbreak of World War II, the USSR and communist parties temporarily lost face. But when Hitler's troops suddenly moved into Russia, Roosevelt and Churchill came to Stalin's support. Communists throughout the world promptly joined the anti-Axis coalition. Roosevelt moved gingerly to educate people on the horrors of additional Axis victories. Full domestic support came only after the Japanese attack on Pearl Harbor on December 7, 1941. In place of Dr. New Deal, Roosevelt's Dr. Win-the-War took over and by war spending achieved the New Deal's goal of putting the jobless to work.

The use of military resources was strategically planned on a global scale. Complex and heated bargaining took place among the Big Three (Roosevelt, Stalin, and Churchill), the American–British Combined Boards, the competing military bureaucracies, and the theater commanders. Out of this process emerged the operations that scored a stream of victories against fascist empires: the 1942 defeat of the Germans at Stalingrad, the overthrow of Mussolini in 1943, the opening of the Second Front in 1944, and in 1945 the fall of Hitler and the Japanese militarists. All these operations were backed up by a military-industrial-scientific complex far superior to that of the fascist Axis. The resulting improvements in weapons systems guaranteed eventual victory—even without the atom bomb. The dropping of atom bombs on Hiroshima and Nagasaki foreshadowed American supremacy in the postwar world.

But even during this era of good feeling, "persistent mutual suspicion was accompanied by the bickering over relative contributions that seems to be a part of 'grand alliances.' "[32] U.S. suspicions grew in March 1945, first when the USSR violated the Yalta agreement by forcibly installing a communist government in Romania, and then when it threatened northwestern Iran. Soviet suspicions intensified when the atom bombs dropped on Hiroshima and Nagasaki forestalled Stalin's entry into Japan (earlier urged on him by the Truman administration). They became stronger when Truman suddenly cut off lend-lease aid to the Soviet Union. Later, in order to get congressional support for a large loan to bankrupt England, he broke off negotiations with Stalin for a postwar loan that was to have taken the place of the cut-off lend-lease aid.

Wartime comity had already broken down by February 1946 when Stalin revived his earlier doctrine of inevitable conflict between communism and capitalism. From the U.S. embassy in Moscow, George Kennan sent home a long cable bewailing Soviet expansion and urging some form of containment. In March 1946, Churchill surprised Truman with his famous Iron Curtain speech in Fulton, Missouri. Truman tried to balance the scales by inviting Stalin to visit the United States and make a public address. Stalin responded by consolidating Russian control wherever the Red Army had forces in eastern Europe and making threatening efforts against Greece and Turkey. Truman responded, first with aid to Greece and Turkey, and then with the Marshall Plan to help reconstruct the war-devastated countries of western Europe.

Relations became more tense as the Chinese communists (initially with Soviet backing) took over mainland China and encouraged anticolonial liberation movements in other areas of the world. The United States opposed both the Soviet Union and China through the United Nations (which it then dominated completely), NATO, and other military alliances that also bypassed the U.N. The cold war became red hot when in 1950 North Korea invaded South Korea and Truman responded by coming to the defense of the latter under the auspices of the United Nations.

By this time, anticommunism had become a powerful force in domestic politics. By the end of World War II, the House Un-American Activities Committee, which had been inquiring into alleged radicals in government before the war, renewed its investigations. In the Senate, Senators Joseph McCarthy, Pat McCarran, and Richard Nixon were developing a "broad brush" anticommunism that attacked radicals and liberals alike; and major officials of the Truman administration were blamed for "losing China." Forestalling more stringent congressional action, President Truman initiated security checks on government employees. In 1947, the liberals and socialists in the Congress of Industrial Organizations (CIO), conceding the correctness of many of the right-wing charges, started a campaign to decommunize the CIO. By the mid-1950s the communists had been reduced to marginal status in the unions. (Domestic anticommunism is also discussed in "Setbacks on Civil Liberties" in the last section of this chapter.)

After the United States withdrew from Korea, U.S. anticommunism became more portentous in the international arena. While still useful in attacking domestic reformers, it also justified strong attacks on communist repression (as supported by most domestic reformers) and the continuation of U.S. expansionism. From 1953 to 1980, including most of the Carter administration's years, the U.S. government actively supported nondemocratic regimes that were actually or nominally anticommunist. This support involved covert U.S. actions to overthrow elected regimes in Iran (1953), Guatemala (1954), British Guinea (1953–64), Indonesia (1957), Ecuador (1960–63), the Dominican Republic (1965), Costa Rica (in the 1950s and 1970s), and Chile (1970–73).[33]

Before the end of the 1950s, the Eisenhower doctrine of using armed force to aid Middle Eastern countries threatened by communist aggression was openly applied by landing U.S. troops in Lebanon. After Castro's successful takeover in Cuba, John F. Kennedy campaigned against Vice President Nixon by being more anticommunist than either Eisenhower or Nixon. In his 1961 inaugural address, he raised cold-war rhetoric to a high level of eloquence: "Now the trumpet summons us again.... We shall pay any price, bear any burden, meet any hardship, support any friend, oppose any foe to assure the survival and success of liberty."[34]

After failing to overthrow the Castro government in Cuba through the covert Bay of Pigs invasion, the Kennedy administration displayed its willingness to "pay any price" by coming close to the brink of nuclear war in forcing the withdrawal of the USSR's nuclear missiles from Cuba. The Johnson administration went still further, forcing thousands of Americans and millions of Vietnamese to bear the burden of injury or death in a ghastly war against the so-called "Moscow-Peiping axis," the term used by Kennedy's secretary of state. During the détente initiated by Richard Nixon and Leonid Brezhnev in 1972, the USSR increased its military spending and its expansionist commitments in the third world while the United States slowed down its military expenditures. After the Soviet invasion of Afghanistan, the Carter administration dropped détente and started a new arms buildup.

The Reagan administration accelerated the arms buildup and went further in promoting "freedom fighters" against Marxist-Leninist governments in Nicaragua, Afghanistan, Angola, Mozambique, and Cambodia. It also bombed Libya, ousted the government of Grenada, and sent a large part of the U.S. fleet into the Persian Gulf. Reagan made U.S.–Soviet relations more intense by reviving "rollback" (an idea previously put forward by Dwight Eisenhower's secretary of state, John Foster Dulles, but not supported by Eisenhower himself) and publicly denouncing the Soviet Union as an "evil empire." With the help of the AFL-CIO, Soviet bloc emigres, many human rights organizations, and the CIA, his administration supported most dissident movements in the Soviet bloc and most nationality groups seeking freedom from the Soviet Union's empire.

Having established even hardier anticommunist credentials than Nixon, Reagan then outdid Nixon in going far beyond earlier concepts of détente. He staked his reputation on the perception that Mikhail Gorbachev was truly different from his predecessors, and that the newly declared openness (*glasnost*) and restructuring (*perestroika*) should be taken seriously. A slow process of unprecedented U.S.–USSR agreements got under way. The continuation of these policies in the first two years of the Bush administration coincided with the peaceful overthrow of communist regimes in Poland, Hungary, Czechoslovakia, Bulgaria, and, with the dramatic breaching of the Berlin Wall, East Germany.

Neither Mass Depression nor World War III

> What is it that converted capitalism from the cataclysmic failure which it appeared to be in the 1930s into the great engine of prosperity of the postwar Western world?
>   (Andrew Shonfield)[35]

As World War II got under way in Europe, adult Americans saw that it was the war, far more than the New Deal, that was conquering the Great Depression. "What happens when the war is won?" they asked fearfully. "Will we return to mass unemployment? or another war?"

Even before Pearl Harbor, President Roosevelt addressed these fears, unfurling the banner of a postwar "world founded upon four essential human freedoms [of speech and religion, from fear and want] . . . everywhere in the world."[36] In the Atlantic Charter, Roosevelt and Churchill linked freedom from fear and want with the disarmament of the Axis powers and the creation of "a wider and permanent system of general security."[37] In January 1944, Roosevelt presented Congress with an economic bill of rights. "In our days these economic truths have become self-evident. We have accepted so to speak a second Bill of Rights under which a new basis of security and prosperity can be established for all—regardless of station, rank or creed."[38] Among these rights are:

- the right to a useful and remunerative job in the industries or shops or farms or mines of the nation;
- the right to earn enough to provide adequate food and clothing and recreation;
- the right of every farmer to raise and sell his products at a return which will give him and his family a decent living;
- the right of every businessman, large and small, to trade in an atmosphere of freedom from unfair competition and domination by monopolies at home and abroad;
- the right of every family to a decent home;
- the right to adequate medical care and the opportunity to achieve and enjoy good health;
- the right to adequate protection from the economic fears of old age, sickness, accident, and unemployment;
- the right to a good education.

"All these rights," Roosevelt proclaimed, "spell security." He also challenged the conservative belief that security for all would require the sacrifice of freedom. And he added this: "Unless there is security here at home there cannot be lasting peace in the world. One of the great American industrialists of our day— a man who rendered yeoman service to his country in this crisis—recently emphasized the grave dangers of 'rightist reaction' in this Nation. All clear thinking businessmen share his concern." Roosevelt then asserted that failing to recognize that "necessitous men are not free" could lead to "rightist reaction" and "the spirit of fascism here at home."[39] Lofting promises of "jobs for all" into the 1944 presidential campaign and subtly implying that opponents were supporting the spirit of fascism, he pushed the Republican opposition into crying "me too" on behalf of postwar jobs for all. This helped set the tone for the November election, in which he accomplished the unprecedented feat of winning a fourth term in the White House.

A few weeks after the election, Senator James Murray and Senator (also Vice-President-Elect) Harry Truman issued a report asserting that transitional measures to liquidate war production were not enough. To provide a postwar "economic substitute for war production," they proposed a full employment bill to give government more "responsibility for the expansion of our peacetime economy so that it will be capable of assuring full employment." Their draft aimed at assuring the "right to a useful and remunerative job" through a full employment economy with enough revenues to finance other economic rights. With Roosevelt's encouragement, the bill was formally introduced in both houses of Congress just a few weeks before his death. "Into the murk," as Robert A. Donovan put it," flashed a beacon that lifted the long-range hopes of liberals, Democrats and labor in particular . . .the Full Employment Bill of 1945."[40]

Recognizing the need for a sustained postwar demand, a middle-of-the road group of corporate executives supported the bill "in principle," but suggested instead a law to promote coordinated policy-making aimed at "high employment" without any emphasis on rights. The final outcome of a hectic legislative struggle was the Employment Act of 1946, which dropped the *right* to employment opportunities. This rejection, in turn, led to eliminating any responsibility to assure or guarantee full employment. Rather, the new law did something a little different. It articulated *acceptance by the federal government of responsibility for preventing another mass depression rather than for actually attaining and maintaining full employment.*

Successful U.S. reconversion, of course, derived from much more than the Employment Act of 1946. Its immediate predecessors included tax measures allowing corporations to pile up reconversion reserves, the Contract Settlement and Surplus Property acts, the work of the Office of War Mobilization and Reconversion (OWMR), and subsidized college education for veterans through the G.I. Bill. Then came low-interest mortgages (particularly for veterans) and huge road, sewage, and hospital construction programs that subsidized the enormous expansion of suburban areas. And right from the beginning, as Richard W. Fisher has pointed out, American economic might and policy leadership "shaped the trading and monetary systems as masters of a smooth-running, free trade economy, as custodians of a well-managed currency and as financiers of the world."[41]

American economic might did not exist independently from military might. As Fisher partially recognized, the military wherewithal supplied by American cold-war policies was decisive in repelling socialist and communist threats and building the multicontinental markets of the "free world." With the Korean War, the huge expansion of U.S. military spending stimulated growth in Japan as well as in Europe and the United States. While this growth slowed somewhat during the Eisenhower years (1953–60), it picked up under President Kennedy and zoomed higher with President Johnson's intervention in Vietnam. During this period (1961–68) Kennedy and then Johnson resorted to deficit spending both as an economic stimulus and as a way of converting from a wartime to a peacetime economy, but this was followed by a partial return to huge military spending. Kennedy cut taxes. Johnson used debt instead of taxes to finance the combination of military expansion and the welfare state programs of the Great Society.

During the eight years of the two Reagan administrations, the process of military expansion went still further. But not in the sense of going back to old-time forms of military power. The Reagan administrations built up military forces based on enormous amounts of atomic overkill and of the more expensive, ultratechnical and unconventional electronic battlefield forces (often mislabeled "conventional" instead of merely "non-nuclear") scattered around the world. In part, this was done by cutbacks in so-called social expenditures and increases in consumer and business debt. In larger part, it was done through the military Keynesianism (labeled "supply-side economics") that provided war contractors with an abundant supply of profitable contracts, millions of people with jobs, and the nation with the greatest peacetime federal deficits in history. These deficits helped develop the amalgam of policies that helped keep the "great engine of prosperity" running.

Since then, that engine has never stopped running. Despite predictions of inevitable capitalist collapse, no nation in the western world has been even close to another cataclysmic failure. A journalist had to invent the word "recession" to describe the moderate downturns of a tamed business cycle.[42] And every recession has thus far been followed by an upturn. This record is as striking as the fact that while World War I was followed by another world war in twenty-one years, more than forty-five years have passed without global warfare.

Progress on Civil Liberties and Rights

> The good news is that in 1984 Americans, far more than most peoples, on the whole enjoy rights: the liberty to express oneself, to guard one's privacy, and to receive fair and equal treatment in the hands of government as a matter of law and not at the whim and sufferance of officials high or low.
>
> (Norman Dorsen)[43]

Norman Dorsen's good news is real. Jumping off from constitutional provisions, hundreds of federal and state and local laws and thousands of judicial decisions have extended the Bill of Rights much further. *Under certain conditions,* all people, it has been held, may expect fulfillment of rights to privacy; to information on what the government does at home and abroad, what goods and services people buy, and what danger they may face in work places; to organization and collective bargaining; to adequate legal services; to foreign travel; to access to communication media; to protections from the cruel and inhuman punishment of death sentences; to control of their own bodies; to various benefits under Social Security, Disability and Workmen's Compensation laws; and to appeal against arbitrary decisions by administrative agencies. They have been promised various rights to fair wages; to freedom from discrimination based on religion, color, ethnic origin, sex, or sexual preferences; to affirmative action to redress the effects of past discrimination; to fair housing; to adequate medical services; to healthy working conditions; and to protection against monopoly pricing, consumer fraud, and environmental pollution.

Much action has also been taken to affirm, extend, or protect the rights of weaker groups: employees; women; racial, ethnic, or national minorities; juveniles and older people; gays and lesbians; teachers; scientists and inventors; artists; students; civil and criminal defendants; prisoners, both before and after trial; crime victims; military personnel; disabled people; retarded people and mental patients; refugees, resident aliens, and undocumented aliens.

Some of these rights have aimed at setting limits on government power (although usually with the result of expanding some arms of government in an effort to limit others). Many rights have directly expanded public government power in an effort to limit the powers of private corporate governments. None of these rights have come into being as gifts or favors from on high. They have come, rather, as the result of organized struggles through the labyrinthine channels of legislative, administrative, judicial, and electoral action.

Some of these struggles have helped democratize the various branches of government. Since World War II, the legislative process has been democratized through more staffing for the members and committees of Congress, more requirements for members' recorded votes and public reports on their outside income, curtailments of the authority of the House Rules Committee, and the elimination of secrecy by Senate–House conference committees (where the final version of a law is usually written). Congressional committees have often done outstanding work in investigating misfeasance or malfeasance by executive agencies or organizations receiving federal funds. The investigations of the Watergate and Iran-Contra scandals, despite their weaknesses, went far beyond what might have been possible in most other democracies. The Senate has often taken its advise and consent authority seriously in reviewing the qualifications of presidential nominees to executive or judicial positions. The role of the comptroller general and his or her General Accounting Office has been broadened from checking on the legality of executive actions to investigating efficiency and desirability as well. Administrative lawmaking has been made more public, as well as more subject to judicial review. The Supreme Court has changed its decisions under the weight of appointments, appeals by plaintiffs, and public opinion or pressure. Major obstacles to voting have been removed. Political parties have moved somewhat toward giving the electorate a genuine choice.

Recent elections around the country revealed things that would have been impossible a half-century earlier: thousands of African-Americans and women were elected to public office or appointed to official positions, while others were being hired into occupations or positions previously closed to these groups. In *Time* Magazine, Richard Lacayo reported, "Millions of black Americans marched quietly into the mainstream, creating a vibrant middle class with incomes, educations and life-styles rivaling those of its white counterpart."[44] Something similar, together with important qualifications, might be said about Asian-Americans and Hispanics.

Many of these struggles have been won only after demonstrations, strikes, and other forms of mass confrontation. Often, the drama of these struggles and victories has resounded around the world. This happened when labor won the right to organize during the 1930s (and later in many parts of public employment), and with the civil rights and antiwar movements of the 1960s and 1970s. The ongoing women's and environmental movements have set examples for people in many other countries. Some of the best examples are provided by those who have used First Amendment rights to uncover past and present sins.

Investigative reporters for a few major newspapers and a host of progressive magazines have done wonders in uncovering denials of human rights by corporations, government agencies, political parties, and even the White House itself. From the muckrakers of the early twentieth century to Rachel Carson's *The Silent Spring* and David Halberstam's *The Best and the Brightest*, to Jonathan Kwitny's *Endless Enemies* and Noam Chomsky's *Turning the Tide: U.S. Intervention in Central America and the Struggle for Peace* and Kenneth O'Reilly's *"Racial Matters": The FBI's Secret File on Black America*, well-documented books of revelation have exposed a plethora of wrongs to be righted. A collection of all the books and articles exposing illegal or unconstitutional acts of the FBI and CIA fill a ten-foot library shelf. Some of the factual material in these documents was first unearthed by congressional investigative committees, whose hearings and reports could scarcely be contained in a thirty-foot shelf. *At no other time in human history and probably in no other country have so many critics of the status quo succeeded in publishing their views.* Although these views have rarely been given much coverage in the major media, they have unquestionably contributed to the remarkable progress already outlined.

Communist criticism from abroad has also been a contributing factor. As the cold war developed after World War II, communist leaders in the Soviet Union levied fierce attacks on racial discrimination in the United States. As explained by William E. Leuchtenberg, President Harry Truman "put the cold war to advantage by stepping up the pace of desegregation of the armed forces."[45] Communist attacks also helped him overcome domestic opposition to other actions: setting up the Fair Employment Practices Commission, appointing the first African-American to the federal bench, and strengthening the Justice Department's civil rights division. Truman also backed up his attorney general's filing of *amici curiae* briefs in support of endeavors by the National Association for the Advancement of Colored People to wipe out judicial enforcement of restrictive covenants (which the Supreme Court did in 1948) and declare racial segregation in the schools unconstitutional (which was done in *Brown v. Board of Education*, 1954). This latter decision, according to Richard Kluger, "restored to the American people a measure of the humanity that had been drained away in their climb to worldwide supremacy."[46]

Tragedies "Too Deep for Tears"

> There are words like *Liberty*
> That almost make me cry.
> If you had known what I knew,
> You would know why.   (Langston Hughes, "Refugee in America")

Since violations of human rights have usually been interwoven with obvious accomplishments in human rights, it is natural to accentuate the positive and forget the negative. Victims of imperial violence, poverty, prejudice, crime, and civil-liberty setbacks can be swept out of conscience and consciousness and dropped down a giant "memory hole."[47] According to a study of amnesia, "the ruin of factual memory halts any further development of interpretative memory. A person can no longer have insights into his [or her] own experience."[48] This lack of insight also occurs when people never have a chance to learn, let alone forget, unpleasant facts about their country's or family's past.[49]

Current injuries can also be ignored. They can be dismissed as minor defects, easily glossed over by comparisons with countries where human rights violations are worse. Official statistics usually underestimate the damage. Official policy is often based on myths that blame the victim or give an exaggerated impression that wrongs are really being righted. Those who see behind the myths can subdue their consciences through the cynicism that whispers that nothing can really be done about it, or by charitable actions that have the effect of pacifying the victims while helping the givers look or feel good.

For the victims, denials of human rights have always aroused feelings which, as Langston Hughes affirms, could almost make one cry. They can lead to thoughts which, in Wordsworth's words, "lie too deep for tears." These feelings and thoughts are most poignant for victims who are tragically viewed as stereotypes and whose individuality is denied as a result of being treated solely as a member of an allegedly inferior ethnic group or class. This invidious classification of people is compounded by the reverse stereotyping that glorifies victims or demonizes all members of empowered groups. It is unwittingly continued by well-intentioned studies that deal separately with one portion of the broad poverty-opulence spectrum with too little perspective on the spectrum by which each portion is defined. It is preserved by approaches that conceal the conflicting interests at work within every person, group, community, power structure, population, and nation[50] or blur those deeper interests that adversaries may have in common.

Imperial Violence

> The invaders . . . massacred women and children and had no reservations about starving a hostile people into submission.
>
> (Stanley Katz)[51]

> The commercial empire of the Republic! That is the great fact of the future. Ah! as our commerce spreads, the flag of liberty will circle the globe, and the highways . . . of all mankind will be guarded by the guns of the Republic.
>
> (Albert J. Beveridge)[52]

Neither displaced Native Americans nor imported Africans equaled the European settlers—better called conquerors—in fire power or the power to decide where and how to live. To win control of the North American continent,[53] the leaders of the thirteen small states on the Atlantic coast had to displace not only the French, Spanish, and Dutch empires but also the natives who had been there for thousands of years. Some tracts of land could be bought from the Native Americans with money, gifts, or treaties. Still larger claims on native lands were bought from the rulers of France and Russia. But none of this could have been done without "the guns of the Republic."

And the guns could not be made or used without a lot more people. The Hudson Bay Company, as well as the Massachusetts, Ohio, Virginia, and Mississippi companies, suffered from a desperate labor shortage. They needed more people to fight their adversaries in moving west, south, and north to expand agriculture, transportation, industry, and commerce. In addition to skilled artisans, lawyers, and soldiers, they needed obedient workers who would endure hard labor and dangerous conditions and not return to their previous ways of life.

The colonists soon learned that the millions of Native Americans who inhabited the "uninhabited" wilderness did not fit these requirements. Few Native Americans could be captured and held very long as slaves. "The only good Indian," ran a motto going back more than 200 years, "is a dead Indian," and the settlers sought that goodness by slaughtering tens of thousands. The Native Americans who survived were crowded into "reservations" or pushed farther to the west. Most of those who were captured knew the land so well that they were able to run away, elude their captors, and seek refuge with tribes that were still intact. Others were infected by Old World diseases which they had never before encountered and against which they had developed no immunity. "The most lethal of all aspects of interracial contacts was the impact of European diseases, especially small pox, which struck heavily among the native population. Most of the tribes encountered by white men during the first century and a half of colonization either succumbed to disease or retreated inland."[54] Stories abound of colonizers taking the infected clothes of a white person who had died of smallpox and giving them as gifts to unsuspecting natives.

For a while, the colonizers imported poor working men (very few women) from England as indentured servants. (Indentured servants contracted to work virtually as slaves for a given number of years, after which their work would win their freedom.) But many of these escaped or won their freedom legally and soon began having families, the "dangerous undeserving landless rabble" who had long been regarded as a horror by upper-class Englishmen. By preventing their servants from winning freedom, the landowners found temporary solutions. But they soon found a better way to preserve their King-endorsed and God-given right: vastly expanding the importation of Africans to serve as slaves. Thus, as Edmund S. Morgan has explained, "The rights of Englishmen were preserved by destroying the rights of Africans."[55]

On the ships that carried them to the British colonies, the captured Africans were kept chained and huddled together under disastrously unhealthy conditions. Yet the survivors were much more productive than Indians were: back home in Africa they had developed some immunity to European diseases. Besides, as Morgan also points out, "traders imported women in a much higher ratio to men than was the case among English servants. . . . They could be kept unarmed and unorganized. . . subjected to savage punishments by their owners without fear of legal reprisals, and since their color disclosed their probable status, the rest of society could keep close watch on them."[56]

Living conditions on the plantation were better than on the slave ships. Like livestock, slaves were too valuable to be allowed to waste away or to die prematurely. Besides, the large supply of women made it possible to accumulate capital through breeding, while also providing the masters with opportunities to satisfy their own sexual desires at little or no cost. For the slaves, even those assigned to work in the masters' houses rather than in the fields, life was one continuous series of humiliations, debasements, and ever-present threats of violence. Despite occasional revolts—which were brutally suppressed—these conditions created what has been graphically described as "the enforced feeling of personal inferiority, the calling of another Master, the standing with hat in hand . . . the defenselessness of family life."[57]

Naturally, most of the slave-owners saw it differently. As one of them put it:

> The nature of our climate and the flat, swampy situation of our country obliges us to cultivate our lands with negroes, and without them S. Carolina would soon be a desert waste.[58]

For the thirteen colonies as a whole, even those without slaves, slavery became the "hard working and indispensable base of a lavish society"[59] and the basis for "the introduction in 1619 of representative government—important to Englishmen who contemplated migration to the New World."[60] Later, under the slogan "freedom of the seas," Edmund S. Morgan asserts, slave labor produced the tobacco crop that helped win the assistance of other countries, especially France. "To a very large degree it may be said that Americans bought their independence with slave labor."[61]

During this period, Thomas Jefferson stoutly advocated decentralization in opposition to Hamilton's strong centralism. Upon becoming president, he outdid Hamilton in his display of central executive energy. Stretching the Constitution to its outer limits, Jefferson spent fifteen million dollars on the purchase from Napoleon of the vast territory between the Mississippi and the Rocky Mountains (the Louisiana Purchase). Later presidents wrested or bought the Oregon territory from Canada, Florida from France, and Alaska from Russia. "They snatched from Mexico, by war and chicanery," as Darcy Ribeiro put it, "another belt equal to triple the original thirteen colonies and to half of the Mexican land area."[62] With pioneering encouraged under the slogans "Westward Ho" and "Go West, young man," the federal government established control over all the lands between the Atlantic and the Pacific and between Canada and Mexico.

Expansion did not stop at these borders. In the Monroe Doctrine of 1823, the government declared that the western hemisphere must be free from any further colonization by European powers. This doctrine soon evolved into the concept of Manifest Destiny. After Latin American colonies had won their independence from Spain, the United States liberated the remaining Spanish colonies (the Philippines, Guam, Puerto Rico, and Cuba) and annexed the first three of these along with Hawaii and part of Samoa. The continental vision expanded to encircle the globe.

But the doctrine of Manifest Destiny, which started the twentieth century with the 1900 re-election of William McKinley, included economic penetration more than territorial incorporation or old-style colonialism. Even before the Civil War, Americans attained the goal of Columbus: reaching the east by sailing west. To obtain markets and raw materials, private companies crossed the Pacific to both Japan and China. They also moved north and south, winning economic dominance in Canada and most countries of South America, Central America, and the Caribbean. In all cases they were helped by the government's dollar diplomacy or gunboat diplomacy and in some cases—as with Cuba, Puerto Rico, the Philippines, Haiti, Nicaragua, and other countries of Central America—by military intervention.

As people in the United States were recovering from the open horrors of the Korean War, covert intervention took its place. The U.S. government gave military and economic support to various military dictators who used anticommunism as an excuse for tyranny. Among these were Duvalier in Haiti, Trujillo in Santo Domino, Somoza in Nicaragua, and Marcos in the Philippines. Mainly by using the CIA, U.S. presidents sponsored successful overthrows of the governments of Guatemala, Iran, Indonesia, Brazil, and Chile. In Cuba, they failed. In Angola and Afghanistan, they helped arm guerrilla fighters against allegedly Marxist regimes.*

After the greater horrors of the Vietnam War, public opposition to direct military intervention—an opposition disparagingly called the "Vietnam syndrome" —became still deeper, and the U.S. government began to give indirect help. In some parts of the world, indirect help was provided for anticommunists who had no desire for violence—such as the Solidarity movement in Poland, the dissidents in eastern Europe, and many of the independence movements among the USSR's republics. Throughout Latin America, and particularly in Central America, communist-inspired wars of liberation provided a justification for supporting death squads organized by local military establishments.

Enjoying widespread popularity, however, President Reagan made the overthrow of Nicaragua's Sandinista government a high priority. His support of the CIA's covert operations in Nicaragua became so open that many observers pre-

---

*Friedrich Engels once remarked that "some terrible rubbish is published in the name of Marxism." In the same spirit one may wonder how many twentieth-century leaders of "Marxist" regimes understood Marx's writings or would have had Marx's approval.

dicted a direct U.S. invasion. As it later turned out, the Sandinistas were overthrown by majority vote in what was the most closely observed—and perhaps the most democratic—election in Latin America. The Reagan administration's use of U.S. troops was limited to situations in which serious armed opposition was unlikely, such as the military actions in Lebanon, the Persian Gulf, and Grenada. President George Bush continued this tradition with the U.S. invasion of Panama through "Operation Just Cause" to capture Manuel Noriega, a former CIA employee. Reports on U.S. and Panamanian casualties and the devastation of an entire neighborhood of poor people in Panama City (barely mentioned in the major media) inflicted no damage on the president's popularity in opinion polls.

The Poverty-Opulence Spectrum

The law, in its majestic equality, forbids all men to sleep under bridges, to bed in the streets, and to steal bread—the rich as well as the poor.

(Anatole France)[63]

The two most striking economic groups of 1989 represented a stark contradiction: billionaires—and the homeless.

(Kevin Phillips)[64]

With a majestic sense of equality, the U.S. Supreme Court has denied the right of anyone to sleep in the park across from the White House. But elsewhere in the nation's capital and throughout the "New Calcuttas" of the urban United States,[65] people enjoy the right to "bed in the streets" and parks or under bridges. They also enjoy this right with more protection from the weather in airports, bus stations, libraries, church basements, railroad cars, tar-paper shacks, automobiles, and subways. Some can be seen near the homes or offices of the well-to-do; others do not want to see or to be seen. "You don't want to go to town, " a homeless woman whose family had lost a 280-acre farm in Iowa told a reporter. "You don't want to see people."[66]

Although estimates range from 350,000 to 3.5 million, nobody really knows the number of homeless people in the United States.[67] This ignorance has created misery among states that might lose federal aid or congressional seats based on Census Bureau statistics.[68] It afflicts any local officials trying to plan enough shelters to get the homeless off the streets and out of sight.[69] But a few things *are* known. There is no typical homeless person. One survey reports these overlapping categories: 75 percent unemployed, 35 percent substance abusers, 25 percent mentally ill, 20–25 percent with prison records.[70] Some were previously employed in factories now closed or farms now abandoned. That displacement itself has sometimes led to substance abuse or mental illness. A large proportion are children.

Yet all the homeless have something in common: their poverty. The un-poor (whether rich or middle income) are not known to have used their right to bed in the streets. The poor, in turn, are far more numerous than the homeless. How numerous? For decades, the federal government has had an official answer. In 1987, for example, official data showed that there were *only* 33 million poor people: 13.5 percent of a total population of 244 million. This figure was based on a subsistence "poverty line," an annual income below which, in Adam Smith's words, people could not get commodities that "the custom of the country render it indecent for creditable people, even of the lowest order, to be without."[71] The line was drawn in the mid-1960s by Mollie Orshansky "at three times a [1955] Department of Agriculture's low-cost budget for food, adjusted for family composition and rural-urban differences."[72]

Since then, contrary to Orshansky's intentions, it has been used in deciding which people deserve government aid and in celebrating an overall decline in officially measured poverty since the 1960s. In 1990, Patricia Ruggles of the Urban Institute made a long-delayed adjustment of "minimally adequate consumption" to more recent standards, including the huge increases in housing costs. Her findings raised official eyebrows by showing that by any serious definition, actual poverty rose substantially in the 1980s. She also offered a set of alternative concepts. The most convincing one raised the overall percentage of the population living in poverty from 13.5 to 24.1. As if wary of shocking too many people, she used percentages only, without revealing that the overall rate of 24.1 percent amounted to 58.8 million people.[73] Going behind the overall rate, she also showed that the poverty rate for elderly people (contrary to official data) had risen and that the rates for children and female-headed households, respectively, had soared to 32.6 and 49.8 percent.

Other studies have revealed additional facts about the U.S. poor.[74] Contrary to some widely accepted myths, well-documented studies show that most poor people

• are jobless,* employed irregularly, or, if working for pay, receive substandard wages;

• are more susceptible than others to localized or general recessions;

• are less equal than others in their access to adequate health service, libraries, parks, playgrounds, and other publicly provided facilities;

• exhibit lower rates of life expectancy than others, along with higher rates of morbidity, disability, and death;

• live in environmentally dangerous neighborhoods and, when not homeless, in overcrowded or substandard housing;

• are more the victims than the perpetrators of crime;

• have few, if any, assets (net worth) and are often head over heels in debt, even when there are two wage-earners in the family;

---

*The terms "jobless" includes many more millions than those covered by official data on the "unemployed," a concept that excludes millions of people "outside the labor force."

• take less part than others in community affairs, labor unions, lobbying, and voting;

• are white, although the proportion of poor people is higher among African-Americans, Hispanics, Native Americans, and some other ethnic minorities.

In earlier decades, political leaders responded to problems of joblessness, low wages, and recession by eloquently asserting various versions of the right to a job at decent wages and public assistance rights for those unable to work for pay.* These two rights were backed up by high-minded proposals for general fiscal and monetary policies aimed at "full" or "high" employment, for creative public action in housing, health, education, training, public works, and conservation, and for more participation by poor people in decisions affecting themselves and others. In recent discussions of poverty, however, these approaches seem to have been abandoned. Public discussion has centered, rather, around

• a "culture of poverty" that traps people in "an outlook and style of life which is radically present-oriented" and attaches "no value . . . to service, to the family, friends or community";[75]

• welfare rights, (public assistance, food stamps, housing subsidies, etc.) which help to pacify, or even humiliate, aid recipients;

• job training or "workfare" that employs a few people in temporary, low-paid, or dead-end jobs and does not address the declining supply of good jobs;

• affirmative action (or equal opportunity) policies that result in the hiring of more women and minorities (usually at lower wages than enjoyed by white men) and in pitting various minority groups against each other.

Reverberating debates over these matters seem to have obliterated from memory the U.S. Catholic bishops' call for a "new American experiment" on behalf of economic rights, full employment, and improved welfare programs.[76] By focusing on the poor, they have also distracted attention from the rich.

Adam Smith was frank on these matters. "Wherever there is great property," he wrote in 1776, "there is great inequality. For one very rich man, there must be at least five hundred poor, and the affluence of the few supposes the indigence of the many." In 1990, Kevin Phillips, a former assistant to Richard Nixon, broke the conservative taboo on the subject of inequality by documenting the huge upsurge of riches during the years of the Reagan administration, "a heyday for [such] unearned income as rents, dividends, capital gains and interest." He highlighted nonpartisan data on the decline of the after-tax income among lower- and middle-income families in contrast with major increases among the wealthiest twenty, ten, five, and one percents. More important, he dealt with the concentra-

---

*With many variations, these rights were set forth in President Roosevelt's Economic Bill of Rights (1944), the U.N.'s Universal Declaration of Human Rights (1948), the Hawkins-Humphrey Full Employment and Balanced Growth Act of 1978, and in the "Quality of Life Action" bills (early 1980s) of Representatives Augustus Hawkins and Charles Hayes.

tion of wealth, as measured by net worth (total assets controlled or used minus liabilities). He distinguishes between four classes of rich people: simple millionaires (those reporting at least a million dollars in net worth), whose numbers, adjusted for inflation, "doubled between the late seventies and the late eighties" to one and a half million people; decamillionaires (reporting ten million dollars, net worth), whose numbers almost tripled, to reach 100,000; centimillionaires (reporting $100 million net worth), whose numbers did triple; and billionaires, whose numbers rose from a handful in 1980 to fifty-one or fifty-two by 1988.[77]

"Let me tell you about the very rich," Scott Fitzgerald once wrote. "They are different from you and me." They are also different from each other. When you have seen one rich person, you have not seen them all. The billionaires, centimillionaires, and decamillionaires are more equal than others. They employ mere millionaires to use all the complex methods needed to get, hide, or justify their amassed wealth and the power it provides. It may be noted, by the way, that Adam Smith's ratio of 500 poor people to one man of "great property" is astonishingly close to Ruggles' estimate of fifty million poor people and Phillips' data on 100,000 centimillionaires. One may add that for every good study of the rich, there are probably 500 studies of the poor by "poverty professionals."

However the ultrarich are counted, it is clear that many of them interpret the free market in terms of the old principle that might (or money) makes rights. "Today's Neo-Darwinists," write Susan and Martin Tolchin, "carry out their legacy in a variety of imaginative ways, creating in effect a new set of rights to be used for their own purposes. One of these new rights could be called the right to pollute," and, they add later in the same book, "the right to sell products abroad that have been banned in this country."[78]

While the "great engine of prosperity" has kept on running without any *general* depression, mass depression has not been prevented. It has merely been contained. In the 1960s and 1970s it was limited mainly to African-American and Hispanic ghettos and Native American reservations. In the 1980s, new islands of mass depression were added: the urban and rural areas hit by plant closings, declining basic industries, and farm failures. Throughout this mass depression archipelago, official unemployment has ranged as high as twenty to twenty-five percent—much like the national averages during the Great Depression. Moreover, for African-Americans, Hispanics, and Native Americans—and for all teenagers—official unemployment rates were steadily at least twice as high as for other parts of the population. Even during general upturns, employment in "smokestack industries" has been slowing down or declining while the largest proportion of new jobs are low-wage, part-time, or irregular. Even with more two-income families, many middle-class people have reason to feel insecure. Lower-income working people have been losing real income. Millions are jobless—many more than officially reported. For some people, the "trickle down" approach to income has really worked; they have received a shower of tax cuts and government subsidies. For others, it has been a drizzle. For at least a third of the population, it has been an intermittent drip.

As single issues, many economic rights have enjoyed a half life. Rights to fair wages, housing, health care, a clean environment, Social Security, and welfare have been pursued separately. Enough small legislative victories have been won to suggest the possibility of proper financing if the economy were operating at a higher levels of employment with more protection against inflation. But the rights of low- and middle-income people are still often regarded as too costly, inflationary, or utopian, if not even subversive. These impairments of economic rights have had many consequences. The reformers' high ground of "human rights and fundamental freedoms for all"[79] has been replaced by free-market rhetoric as a facade for government subsidies to some banking and nonbanking corporations.

Workers' Rights at Bay

> You can't strike a multinational conglomerate.
>
> (Union maxim)

> Gone are the not-so-good days of blackjack and machine guns. . . . Enter the slick smiling lawyer, armed with the latest strategies to subvert workers' legal rights to collective bargaining.
>
> (Nancy Stiefel)[80]

Historically, organized labor has been the most powerful force in support of human rights. Without the gains made in union organizing after the rights to organize and bargain collectively were established in the Labor Relations Act of 1935, the remarkable progress referred to earlier in this chapter would have been inconceivable. This helps explain the attention to labor unions and union members in the 1970 report of the American Civil Liberties Union (ACLU).[81]

But in the 1980s, as specialized groups arose to defend human rights abroad, they developed a "rightspeak" that excluded labor's rights as a part of human rights. In 1984, as U.S. labor's rights were under sharp attack, the next ACLU report, *Our Endangered Rights*, failed to include the rights of labor unions and union members. As of 1989, plans for the next decennial report (after the year 2000), according to Norman Dorsen, would include attention to employee rights only. Whether the right to organize and bargain collectively will return to the agenda remains to be seen. While this shift of attention by the ACLU may be inexplicable, the declining membership of the U.S. labor movement helps explain many of labor's setbacks in civil liberties.

Any explanation of declining union membership, in turn, requires a look at many factors. After World War II, the growth of conglomerates and transnational corporations has undermined the bargaining power of all unions that operate in one economic sphere or in one country. Many unions have made strides in overcoming past racism, sexism, and corruption, and even in escaping bureaucratic traditions of over-tight home office management. But no U.S. union has yet found a way to represent the employees of a transnational conglomerate operating across the boundaries of countries, languages, and cultures.

Under the new conditions of transnational capital, major business organizations look at the world labor market as a whole. Often, they transfer their operations to countries where subsidiaries may operate in a union-free environment and without government controls over health, safety, or environmental pollution. In operations at home, they have sought somewhat similar conditions. With considerable support from the federal government and consulting firms, they have launched powerful drives to cut down the legal protections of labor, stop organizing campaigns, and reduce the effectiveness of existing labor unions by "double breasting" (cutting operations into two parts, one organized and the other unorganized). The result has been an absolute reduction in the number of union members, a sharp decline in the proportion of employees who are union members, and a still sharper decline in the percentage of union activists.

Under these conditions, labor unions have been forced into a series of defensive positions in collective bargaining and a withdrawal from previous initiatives on overall macroeconomic policy. In its latest statements on the national economy, the AFL-CIO has dropped the "dangerous" idea of full employment and responsible growth without inflation and has suggested merely that "Congress must be willing to step in quickly with appropriate antirecession actions, including adequate support for the unemployed."[82] Despite the fact that joblessness and recession are two of the major factors in undermining labor's rights, defeatism has gone so far that the AFL-CIO has adopted a narrower agenda rather than enter the fray to cope with macroeconomic policy.

Setbacks on Civil Liberties and Rights

Endangered rights well sums up the current situation.

(Norman Dorsen)[83]

Dorsen's words can also be used to sum up most of U.S. history. Within a few years after the first Bill of Rights, the Federalists passed the Alien and Sedition Acts and sent Jeffersonian editors to jail—despite the First Amendment's assurance of press freedom—for criticizing the administration too vigorously. A little later, the Jeffersonians, now in power, did some of the same with Federalist press critics. During the War of 1812, mob violence was used to destroy the presses of an antiwar paper. And in every war thereafter, "military necessity," "national security," and "vital interest" have been used as a defense for breaking the promises in the Bill of Rights and other fundamental laws of the land.

Sometimes and to some extent, as with Abraham Lincoln's suspension of some civil liberties during the Civil War, these violations had a serious justification. In many others, however, they were based on wildly exaggerated fears. This happened during the "red scares" after World War I. It resumed during the period of New Deal reforms. The House Un-American Activities Committee (with the backing of a special un-American activities group of the U.S. Chamber of Commerce) attacked New Deal liberals as socialists, pinkos, fellow travelers of the Communist party, crypto-communists, or communists in disguise.[84] Although a few were indeed members of a socialist or communist sect, most were sincerely trying to save U.S. capitalism from the debacle of the Great Depression.

As World War II started in Europe, the Roosevelt administration initiated an attorney general's list of subversive organizations and a new system of loyalty checks. After the war, as U.S.–USSR confrontations became more and more bitter, the House Un-American Activities Committee expanded its efforts. Its members once again blurred distinctions among liberals, U.S.-based radicals, a small number of whom belonged to or sympathized with the U.S. Communist party, and those who simply sought a reduction of the cold war. There developed a tendency, as reported by Theodore Draper, to see in any moderation at all not merely a sin of timidity but an act of treason.[85] With this kind of witch- hunting and red-baiting getting wide coverage in the media, many people—even moderate Republicans—had to go out of their way to develop anticommunist credentials.

During the witch-hunting of the so-called McCarthy era, which in fact antedated Senator Joseph McCarthy's election to the Senate, a few thousand people were hounded out of their positions in government, academia, and the media. Hundreds of thousands more were forced to suppress or change their views on domestic and foreign issues.[86] (Even President Truman's secretary of state was accused of being a tool of world communism.) As Director of the FBI, J. Edgar Hoover collected derogatory information on many of America's leading intellectuals, journalists, and celebrities. His "hit list" also included public figures whom he might later want to attack or blackmail. The long list of his suspects would come to include Martin Luther King, Jr., presidential candidate Adlai Stevenson, President John F. Kennedy, and many members of Congress. Later, the FBI and the CIA engaged in illegal, and indeed unconstitutional, hounding of dissenters during the Vietnam War. Still later, in 1988, Republican candidate George Bush attacked the American Civil Liberties Union as though there was something sinister in the ACLU's traditional role of defending the U.S. Constitution (while the Democratic candidate seemed unable to articulate why he was a "dues-paying member" of the ACLU).

Civil liberties and civil rights groups have brought to light many of the most dangerous assaults on human rights. Some of these have already been referred to earlier in this chapter. In his 1984 book, *Our Endangered Rights*, Norman Dorsen shows how the good news on the economy was accompanied by the bad news of an assault on civil liberties during the first years of the Reagan administration. The essays Richard O. Curry has brought together in the book *Freedom at Risk: Secrecy, Censorship and Repression in the 1980s* carries this analysis up to more recent days.[87] From such publications one can learn that

• *First Amendment* freedoms are being attacked by private pressure groups and executive, legislative, and judicial initiatives that go surprisingly far toward censoring newspapers and magazines, stifling criticism through irresponsible libel suits, purging libraries, shrouding government actions in secrecy, and thrusting religion into the public schools;

• the *Second Amendment* has been misconstrued as endowing people with an unqualified right "to keep and bear arms" without reference to the necessity of a "well-regulated militia";

• *Fourth Amendment* rights of people "to be secure . . . against unreasonable searches and seizures" have been weakened by new technologies of surveillance, police entries into homes without warrants, and President Reagan's pardon of two FBI agents who had knowingly authorized such entries;

• *Fifth* and *Sixth Amendment* protections of accused persons have been eroded by police and prison abuses that deny due process and by judicial decisions that weaken the prohibition against compulsory self-incrimination. A long tradition of personal attacks on those who "take the Fifth" has been capped by right-wing demands to abolish the Fifth Amendment;

• *Sixth* and *Seventh Amendment* guarantees of jury trials have been sidetracked in criminal cases by plea-bargaining and in civil cases by a new system of using retired judges (the "rent-a-judge system"), as well as a recent Court of Appeals decision that an antitrust case is too complicated for a jury. The right of accused persons to a "speedy" trial has been undermined by the overcrowding the dockets and the undermanning of the courts; the right to "assistance of counsel" is more fully enjoyed by those rich enough to hire high-class assistance;

• *Eighth Amendment* prohibitions are violated by excessive and discriminatory bails and/or fines and the imposition of "cruel and unusual punishments";

• the *Ninth* and *Tenth Amendments*, on rights retained by or reserved to the people, are threatened by extremist legislation to regulate personal behavior or by right-wing judicial activism that intrudes upon personal privacy in general.

In recent decades, moreover, the Supreme Court has narrowed concepts of equality under the law. Randall Kennedy points out that to obtain relief under the "equal protection of the law" provisions of the Fourteenth Amendment, one must now prove that "public authorities *intentionally* set out to hurt plaintiffs on account of race."[88] Perhaps unintentionally, this posture by the Court has coincided with elaborate private and public subterfuges that have invalidated the 1954 Court decision which held that "separate educational facilities are inherently unequal." In some areas, particularly in the northeast, Kennedy observes, "the degree of racial separation in the schools is greater than in 1954." In *Bowers v. Hardwick* (1986) the Court's majority (in a five-to-four vote) openly denied personal privacy or equal protection under the law to gays and lesbians. In a dissent, Associate Justice Stevens argued that any denial of rights should be based on "something more substantial than a habitual dislike for, or ignorance about, the disfavored group."

A horrifying example of regress because of insufficient progress is provided by dislike of, and ignorance about, new immigrants. One wave after another of Germans, Scandinavians, Irish, southern Europeans, eastern Europeans, and Jews had to face discrimination at the hands of earlier settlers. "Ever since we got here," many a first-generation American has proclaimed, "my family has been against those immigrants." Many of these prejudices were written into the Immigration Control Act of 1924, embodied in the internment of Japanese Americans during World War II, and, after the war, in denying admission to Jewish survivors of the Nazi concentration camps. Similar prejudices are expressed in the hostility—sometimes brutally violent—toward the more recent waves of Asian, Latin, and Caribbean immigrants.

As publicly recognized standards of human conduct have risen, open discrimination has ebbed. In its place one can find subtle sexism, respectable racism, amiable anti-Semitism, and hidden homophobia practiced by holier-than-thou bigots who, without even being aware of what they are doing, do what they instinctively feel is necessary to keep "inferiors" in their "proper" place And as always, dissenters face both antipathy from the ignorant and repression from the state. Many active opponents of U.S. foreign policy, as the Center for Constitutional Rights has documented, have faced such violations of human rights as these: "intimidating visits by the Federal Bureau of Investigation to persons who have traveled to Nicaragua or Cuba; the theft of documents and mailing lists from the files of religious, solidarity, political, and other activist organizations under the cloak of a common robbery; the opening of correspondence, the tampering with or the loss of the luggage of politically active persons returning from Central America; the auditing by the Internal Revenue Service of the financial records of organizations critical of the U.S. government; and the planting of paid informers in churches and other organizations, all in the name of 'national security.' "[89] Nobody can possibly tell what effect such actions have had on people who, although not directly affected, censored themselves instead of speaking their minds openly.

As well, the growing concentration of mass media power has overshadowed the progress made by those who have spoken out boldly in the articles and books of revelation. "Five media corporations," reports Ben H. Bagdikian, former dean of the School of Journalism at the University of California at Berkeley, "dominate the fight for the hundreds of millions of minds. . . ." By the 1990s, they "will control most of the world's important newspapers, magazines, books, broadcast stations, movies, recordings and videocassettes." Already, "they control the public image of national leaders who, as a result, fear and favor the media magnates' political agendas; and they control the information and entertainment that help establish the social, political and cultural attitudes of increasingly larger populations." As a result, Bagdikian argues, the great freedom in the United States to read, watch, or listen to anything available is counterbalanced by the declining diversity of what is available to most people and the declining access to the mass media by "idiosyncratic outsiders and ideas."[90]

Money Rights versus Voting Rights

> To the extent that a citizen's right to vote is debased, he is that much less a citizen.
>
> (Chief Justice Earl Warren)[91]

> America is becoming a special interest nation where money is displacing votes.
>
> (Brooks Jackson)[92]

In recent decades, voting rights for minorities have been somewhat better protected than in the past. Registration campaigns have become more effective. It even seems that the two major parties may agree on moving toward some form of universal automatic registration.[93]

Yet the enormous inflation of campaign spending has debased ever citizen's right to vote, to use the words of a Supreme Court decision on apportionment by state legislators. A fund of $500,000 for a local election campaign, raised from, let us say, a hundred or so big contributors, may have more power than 500,000 voters. Candidates for the Senate have to raise many millions either to run or, if their fundraising is successful, to scare possible opponents out of running. Many incumbents have to spend more time in raising funds to pay off the debts incurred in their last campaign or to prepare for the next campaign than they devote to their duties in office. The money goes to purchasing media time or advertisements, hiring professional campaign managers who know how to arrange events that will win free media time, financing many forms of opinion research, arranging for telephone banks and the professionalized organization of campaign workers and volunteers, and, above all, for creating a packaged image that may have little connection with the record or character of the candidate.

Enormous contributions to incumbents have increased the number of "safe seats" in legislative bodies. Under these financial pressures, the Democratic party has been pressured to trim its sails to the financial winds and assure the "fatcats" and political action committees (PACs) that their interests will be protected. Thus, there is a very real sense in which dollars buy voters both at the polls and in the legislative bodies. There is some unpleasant truth in the charge that, during the 1980s, "to preserve and extend their freedom of action, the banks began buying politicians—Democratic and Republican, progressive and reactionary—with campaign contributions and personal loans."[94]

In 1988, before the national electios, Democrats offered to remedy the situation through federal financing of congressional elections and stronger efforts to control private campaign contributions. However, the Democrats themselves backtracked on other major remedies, such as free television time for candidates and shorter campaigns, and, ultimately, "led by Robert Dole, the Republicans successfully filibustered the bill eight times."[95] The major media cooperated by an almost complete blackout on this undemocratic method of killing a relatively mild reform measure.

Although voters may be kept in the dark on such details, they are not completely fooled. Increasingly disillusioned, they stay away from the polls in droves. Presidents are usually elected by "majorities" consisting of less than a third of the voting-age population. In local elections, the participation is usually still lower. Millions of people believe, with some good reason, that their votes do not count.

Notes

1. Michael Kammen, *People of Paradox* (New York: Vintage, 1973), 298. Kammen also quotes Erik H. Erikson: "Whatever one may come to consider a truly American trait can be shown to have its equally characteristic opposite." (*Childhood and Society*, 1950.) Neither Kammen nor Erikson implied that the contradictory nature of human nature was uniquely American. Kammen, in fact, compared the early Americans with the paradoxical people of England, France, and Spain. My effort might be seen as an updating on the United States—with a special focus on human rights—of Kammen's *People of Paradox*.

2. Carl Schurz, Speech, U.S. Senate, 1872. This was probably in response to an earlier statement of a different nature by Stephen Decatur: "Our country! In her intercourse with foreign nations, may she always be in the right; but our country right or wrong" (1816) (A.S. Mackenzie, *Life of Decatur*). A more recent restatement of Schurz's motto appears in Dwight Bombach (with William Bohmbach), *What's Right With America: A Handbook for Americans* (New York: Bantam, 1986.) In place of "America—Love It or Leave It," a 1976 bumper sticker, he ends his review of "what is to be kept right" with a "love it and change it" admonition to "get your hands busy, even dirty, improving things here."

3. Arnold Toynbee, *America and the World Revolution* (New York: Oxford University Press, 1962), 92 et seq.

4. According to Immanuel Kant in "An Odd Question Raised Again," Part II of "The Strife of the Faculties," in *On History*, Lewis W. Beck, ed. (New York: Bobbs Merrill, 1983), the march of "progress" (however it may be defined) has been accompanied or followed by three processes: retrogression, stagnation, and oscillation.

5. Gabriel Almond, Martin Chodorow and Roy Harvey Pearce, *Progress and Its Discontent* (Berkeley, CA: University of California Press, 1977), 14.

6. Seneca, *Troades I*, 633.

7. Darcy Ribeiro, "The Anglo-Americans," in *The Americas and Civilization* (New York: Dutton, 1971), 361.

8. Thurgood Marshall, informal remarks to the National Bar Association, *New York Times*, (August 11, 1988).

9. Philip Morris Companies, Inc. "The Story of a Government That Almost Didn't Happen," public service advertisement, November 1989.

10. The Virginia Bill of Rights and similar provisions in other state constitutions were built on such precedents as the Magna Carta of 1215 and the British Bill of Rights of 1689. See "Constitution of Virginia," in *Sources of Our Liberties*, Richard L. Perry and John C. Cooper, eds. (American Bar Foundation, 1959), 301–13.

11. William Lee Miller, *The First Liberty* (New York: Knopf, 1982).

12. Alexander Hamilton and John Jay, "The Federalist Number 84," in *The Human Rights Reader*, Walter Laqueur and Barry Rubin, eds. (New York: NAL/Dutton, 1990).

13. The distinction between associations (sometimes called pressure or interest

groups) that *articulate* interests and political parties that *aggregate* interests has been sharply set forth in *The Politics of Developing Countries*, Gabriel Almond and James Coleman, eds. (Princeton NJ: Princeton University Press, 1960).

14. Charles and Mary Beard, *America at Midpassage* (1930). More specifically, as Stanley Katz has observed, "the framers never intended that we should be a democracy. They were republicans, and horrified by the thought of democracy." Letter to the author, May 18, 1989.

15. Richard Kluger, *Simple Justice* (New York: Vintage, 1977), 30–31.

16. Ibid.

17. Dred Scott v. Sanford, 19 Howard 393 (1857).

18. Lincoln, Speech at Republican State Convention, Springfield, Illinois, June 16, 1858.

19. All states entered the Union willingly, it should be noted, and the U.S. Constitution made no provision for secession. In the USSR, in contrast, many republics entered under compulsion, while the Soviet constitution has always recognized the right to secede.

20. James M. MacPherson, *Battle Cry of Freedom* (New York: Oxford University Press, 1988), 862.

21. Kluger, 53.

22. Ibid, 83.

23. Charles and Mary Beard, *The Rise of American Civilization* (New York: Macmillan, 1st ed. in 1927; rev. 1-vol. ed. 1934), 111–14.

24. In 1938, Associate Justice Hugo Black brought these facts to light in a thunderous dissent (in *Connecticut General Life Insurance Co. v. California*, 1938) that led to a *New York Times* headline: "Black is Only Justice Ever to Hold Corporation Is Not A Person Under The Due Process Clause." (Gerald T. Dunne, *Hugo Black and the Judicial Revolution* [New York: Simon & Schuster, 1975, 178].) In subsequent dissents, Associate Justices Douglass and Goldberg joined in this view. Thus, as pointed out by Ralph Nader and Carl J. Mayer, corporations have invoked (a) First Amendment rights to justify expenditures for cigarette advertising and election campaign expenditures and revoke disclosure requirements on stock offerings and corporate takeovers; (b) Fourth Amendment rights against unreasonable searches to impede health and safety investigations; and (c) Fifth Amendment rights against self-incrimination to bar a trial in a criminal antitrust suit. In 1986, "corporations received the most sweeping enlargement of their free speech rights in a 5–3 decision" in which the Supreme Court overturned a California law requiring public utilities to give consumers certain information. In an unusual proconsumer dissent, Justice William Rehnquist argued that to "ascribe to such artificial entities an 'intellect' or 'mind' [for constitutional purposes] is to confuse metaphor with reality." Ralph Nader and Carl J. Mayer, "Corporations Are Not Persons," The *New York Times*, Op-Ed (April 9, 1988). "Too frequently," the authors argue, "the extension of corporate constitutional rights is a zero-sum game that diminishes the rights powers of real individuals." They therefore propose "a constitutional amendment that declares that corporations are not persons and that they are only entitled to statutory protections conferred by legislatures and through referendums."

25. Arthur Schlesinger, *The Cycles of American History* (New York: Houghton Mifflin, 1986), 242.

26. Nancy E. McGlen, *Women's Right: The Struggle for Equality in the 19th and 20th Centuries* (New York: Praeger), 1983.

27. In the case of the *Schechter Poultry Corp. v. United States*, for example, the Court in May 1935 invalidated the compulsory code system drawn up by the National Recovery Administration as called for in the National Industrial Recovery Act of 1933.

28. Howard Zinn, *Postwar America: 1947–1971* (New York: Bobbs-Merrill, 1973), xvii.

29. Ralph Miliband and Marcel Liebman, "Reflections on Anti-communism," in *Socialist Register, 1984: The Uses of Anti-Communism*, Miliband and Liebman, eds. (Merlin Press, 1984), 1

30. In his *A Short History Of Ethics* (New York: Macmillan, 1966), 211, Alistair MacIntyre points out Marx's concern with human freedom. "Freedom is so much the essence of man that even its opponents realize it," Marx had written. "No man fights freedom; he fights at most the freedom of others." According to MacIntyre, Marx envisioned freedom "in terms of the overcoming of the limitations and constraints of one social order by bringing another, less limited social order into being."

31. Even Karl Popper, author of *The Open Society and Its Enemies*, had been a socialist in his early years in Vienna. Popper's attack on Marxism, one should note, is prefaced by a vivid recognition of the humane aspects of Marx's work and its enormous appeal to anyone concerned with justice in the world.

32. John A. Garraty, "The Cold War," in *The Columbia History of the World* (New York: Harper & Row, 1972).

33. Stephen Van Evera, "Wars of Intervention: Why They Shouldn't Have a Future, Why They Do," *Defense and Disarmament Alternatives* (Institute for Defense and Disarmament Alternatives, March 1990).

34. Inaugural address, January 1961

35. Andrew Shonfield, *Modern Capitalism: The Changing Balance of Public and Private Power* (New York: Oxford University Press, 1965), 3.

36. Franklin D. Roosevelt, State of the Union Message, January 6, 1941.

37. Franklin D. Roosevelt and Winston Churchill, The Atlantic Charter, August 14, 1941.

38. Franklin D. Roosevelt, State of the Union Message, January, 1944.

39. State of the Union Message, January 11, 1944. The reference to "the spirit of fascism" was one of the first articulations of the possibility of a new form of fascism in the United States. This germ of an idea later sprouted in "Friendly Fascism: A Model for America," *Social Policy* (November–December 1970), and *Friendly Fascism: The New Face of Power in America* (New York: Evans, 1980).

40. Robert A. Donovan, *Conflict and Crisis: The Presidency of Harry S. Truman, 1945–1946* (New York: Norton, 1977), 112.

41. Richard W. Fisher, "America Has Lost Its way," *The New York Times*, Op-Ed (July 4, 1987).

42. This was Murray Rossant of *The New York Times*, later of the Twentieth Century Fund.

43. Norman Dorsen, Introduction, in *Our Endangered Rights*, Norman Dorsen, ed. (New York: Pantheon, 1984), ix.

44. Richard Lacayo, "Between Two Worlds," *Time* (March 13, 1989).

45. William E. Leuchtenberg, *A Troubled Feast: American Society Since 1945* (New York: Little Brown, 1983), 20–21.

46. Kluger, *Simple Justice* (New York: Vintage, 1975), 10.

47. "Memory hole" is George Orwell's term, in his novel *1984*.

48. Edmund Bolles, *Remembering and Forgetting: An Inquiry into the Nature of Memory*" (New York: Walker and Co., 1988), 208. In rejecting the old idea of memory as a storehouse of information (now more effectively stored in print and computer files), Bolles regards remembering as a creative, constructive process. History, one may add, is the same. In some ways, however, as William Faulkner once observed,

"The past is always with us. In fact, it is not even past."

49. In the USSR, the largest human rights group is Memorial, an organization trying to unearth all the well-buried facts of Stalinist and neo-Stalinist repression. This mode of accountability is not a matter of punishing those held responsible for past sins. As Aryeh Neier explains, it is more a means of "recognizing the moral responsibilities that arise from the past." "What Should Be Done about the Guilty?" *The New York Review of Books* (February 1, 1990). Neier distinguishes between getting the truth about terrible crimes out into the open (or even acknowledged by governments) and, on the other hand, "punishing those responsible."

50. Karen Horney was one of the first to develop the inner-conflict approach to the human psyche or personality. See *Our Inner Conflicts* (New York: Norton, 1945). This idea may be carried a little further by metaphorically describing the human soul as a legislature in which many conflicting interests struggle for influence over attitudes and behavior. This concept may also be applied to families, small communities, informal groups, formal organizations, nations, blocs, and any structure of power. The dynamics of these groupings can rarely be understood without at least an identification of their internal conflicts.

51. Stanley Katz, Introduction to Nicholas Canny, "The Ideology of English Colonization: From Ireland to America," in *Colonial America: Essays in Politics and Social Development*, Stanley Katz, ed. (New York: Knopf, 1983), 72.

52. Speech by Albert J. Beveridge of Indiana during his successful campaign for election to the Senate. More of this speech appears in James Oliver Robertson, *American Myth, American Reality* (New York: Hill and Wang, 1980), 272.

53. The British settlers refused to believe that distant islands governed by King George should rule a vast continent. They wanted a continent of their own. In 1774 they called their first assembly the Continental Congress. Later, during the war with Britain, they issued new paper money and called it *continental*.

54. Alden T. Vaughan, in *Columbia History of the World*, 675. William H. McNeil adds to this well-documented story by reporting that in 1616–17, as a result of French settlement in Nova Scotia, a great pestilence of some sort swept through the Massachusetts Bay area. "Thus God prepared the way . . . for the arrival of the Pilgrims three years later." A subsequent outbreak of small pox "convinced the colonists (if they needed convincing) that Divine Providence was indeed on their side in conflicts with the Indians." William H. McNeil, *Plagues and Peoples* (New York: Anchor Press/Doubleday, 1976), 186.

55. Edmund S. Morgan, "Slavery and Freedom: The American Paradox," in *Colonial America: Essays in Politics and Social Development*, Stanley Katz, ed. (New York: Knopf, 1983), 572–96.

56. Ibid.

57. W.E.B. DuBois, *Black Reconstruction in America, 1860–1880*, (World Publishing, 1935), 9.

58. Charles Cotesworth Pinckney, *Columbia History of the World*, 397.

59. Robertson, *American Myths, American Reality*, 99.

60. Pinckney, 665.

61. Morgan, 574.

62. Ribeiro, 366.

63. Anatole France, *Crainquebille*.

64. Kevin Phillips, *The Politics of Rich and Poor* (New York: Random House, 1990), 3.

65. "New Calcutta: At Least Help the Homeless off the Street," *The New York Times* Editorial, (December 25, 1982).

66. Isabel Wilkerson, "As Farms Falter, Rural Homelessness Grows," *The New York Times* (May 2, 1989).

67. On September 6, 1988, a high HUD official reported success in getting a conference of home-builders to "lower the estimate of the maximum homeless population to one million from three million." Joe Davidson, "As Homeless Suffer, a Federal Aid Council Focuses on Politics: Keeping the Estimates Down," *The Wall Street Journal* (March 15, 1989).

68. In 1990, the Census Bureau tried to carry out its constitutional obligation of "enumeration" by traditional methods. It sent forms through the mail and then sent enumerators around to ring door bells. The homeless, they soon learned, have no mail boxes or door bells. They then sent some secial squads to track the homeless down. Where they cannot be tracked down, the bureau used estimates based on sample surveys.

69. In 1982, President Reagan said that the homeless "make it their own choice for staying out there." Where the choice was entering a dangerous shelter or "staying out there," Reagan's observation was well-based. Some of the homeless felt safer in a library, bus station, street, or park than in the so-called shelters.

70. According to the U.S. Conference of Mayors and the Urban Institute, as reported by S. Robert Lichter, "Media's Typical Homeless Are Anything But," *The Wall Street Journal* (December 14, 1989).

71. Adam Smith in volume 1 of *The Wealth of Nations*.

72. Michael B. Katz, *The Undeserving Poor* (New York: Pantheon, 1989), 115.

73. Patricia Ruggles, *Drawing the Line: Alternative Poverty Measures and Their Implications for Public Policy* (Washington, DC: The Urban Institute Press, 1990).

74. Many of these are summarized in Katz, *The Undeserving Poor*.

75. The quoted words are from Edward C. Banfield's enormously influential *Heavenly City Revisited* (Boston: Little Brown, 1974), 281. The vast literature on the culture of poverty is rather well summarized in Katz, *The Undeserving Poor*.

76. Pastoral Letter, *Economic Justice For All*, (November 1986).

77. Kevin Phillips, *The Politics of Rich and Poor* (New York: Random House, 1990). Explains the inherent tendency toward underestimates in reported wealth.

78. Susan J. Tolchin and Martin Tolchin, *Dismantling America: The Rush To Deregulate* (New York: Oxford University Press, 1983).

79. Article 55 of the U.N. Charter.

80. Quoted by James Farmer, "The Hired Guns of De-Unionization," *The New Republic* (August 25, 1979).

81. Clyde W. Summers, "The Rights of Unions and Union Members," in *The Rights of Americans: What They Are—What They Should Be*, Norman Dorsen, ed.

82. Bar Harbour, Florida, February 15–19, 1988.

83. Dorsen, Introduction, in *Our Endangered Rights*, Norman Dorsen, ed, ix.

84. Walter Goodman, *The Committee* (New York: Farrar Straus Giroux, 1968).

85. Draper, *A Present of Things Past* (New York: Hill and Wang, 1990).

86. See Bertram Gross, "Purges and Conversions," *Friendly Fascism*, 89–94.

87. Richard Curry, *Freedom at Risk: Secrecy, Censorship and Repression in the 1980s* (Philadelphia, PA: Temple University Press, 1988).

88. Randall Kennedy, "*Brown* Plus 35," *The Nation* (May 29, 1989).

89. William L. Wipfler, "United States Achievements and Shortcomings Since Signing the Universal Declaration of Human Rights," *Breakthrough* (July 1989).

90. Ben Bagdikian, "The Lords of the Global Village: Conquering Hearts and Minds," *The Nation* (June 12, 1989).

91. Reynolds v. Sims, 337 U.S. 533 (1964).

92. Brooks Jackson, *Honest Graft: Big Money and the Political Process*, rev. ed. (New York: Knopf, 1990), 320.

93. The National Voter Registration Act of 1989, already introduced in both houses of Congress, seems to have powerful bipartisan support. "Bill to Ease Registration of Voters Makes Gains," *The New York Times* (May 7, 1989).

94. Editorial, *The Nation* (May 7, 1990).

95. David Corn and Jefferson Morley, "Beltway Bandits," *The Nation* (May 29, 1989).

11

A Russian View of U.S. Principles and Practice

Irina Lediakh and Oleg Vorobiev

To express our views and understanding of the human rights situation in the United States is not the easiest of tasks, for the present book is intended for both American and Russian readers. Naturally, we are aware that our American readers know better than do we the human rights situation in their own country, although Russians like to say that you see more from a distance. We are fully aware of the complexities but nevertheless have taken on the huge task of analyzing the way in which the American legal system guarantees and defends human rights.

We try to emphasize the positive aspects of this system, to discern its relevance to the formation of a democratic, law-based state in our own country. We pay attention also to the violation and curtailment of rights. We are taking as our point of departure America's own principles, laws, and concepts. This, in short, is the logic of our approach.

In the aftermath of many years of ideological confrontation, when human rights were used for mutual accusations and to increase international tensions, we have tried to be as objective as possible, in order to contribute to mutual understanding and cooperation in this sphere. How far we have succeeded, we'll leave to the reader to decide.

American Federalism and the Protection of Rights and Freedoms

The radical renewal of the Russian Federation is the most complicated and urgent task before our country. Therefore, we begin with federalism, a distinctive trait of the U.S. system of government, and one of the most important constitutional principles directly linked with the system of human rights. Our topics are such leading issues as the division of jurisdiction between the federation and the states for legislation about rights and freedoms; which mechanisms serve to resolve conflicts between the center and the states; and what principles underlie the interaction that guarantees human rights and freedoms. These questions were of vital significance in the history of the establishment of the American federation, from the moment of the adoption of the Constitution in 1787 and the Bill of Rights in 1791, and in the subsequent development of each.

For a long time, practical problems of constitutional law consisted of issues that federalism's founders—Thomas Jefferson, for example—interpreted as principles of the interaction of the center and the states in a democracy, of popular sovereignty, and of freedom. The path of the federation was strewn more with thorns than with roses. Tragic periods, such as the Civil War, could not be avoided.

Throughout American federalism's contradictory history, the dominant principle was that of a jurisdictional division between the federation and the states, first of all in the sphere of legislation. Having acknowledged the states as autonomous sovereign formations, the founders of the United States, in the Tenth Amendment to the federal Constitution (part of the Bill of Rights), noted that powers not delegated to the United States government—that is, to the federal government—by the Constitution, nor prohibited by it to the states, are reserved to the states or to the people. This principle acknowledged the historical primacy of the state constitutions, where from the earliest era the protection of rights and freedoms was recognized as a leading task of state government. In contrast, the Bill of Rights is incorporated in the national constitution in the form of amendments to the basic text.

The bills of rights of some states endorsed the principle of equality of rights and, in some cases, "equal protection" of the law. State courts interpreted the principle of equality as a natural, inalienable right of the person. The text of the Bill of Rights of the State of Virginia prohibits compensation or privilege except for compensation for the performance of public functions.[1] In 1814 the Supreme Court of Massachusetts found, in the case of *Holden v. James*, that any individual enjoying privileges and advantages denied to other persons who are in the same circumstances flagrantly contradicts the principles of civil freedom and natural justice and the spirit of the Constitution. In this same vein, if anyone be subjected to requisitions, confiscations, suits, or other actions which all others are spared, the principle of equality is violated.[2] Principles of equality served in some states as a basis for condemning slavery, demanding its abolition, and, in certain cases, for the legislative prohibition of slavery and segregation.

The states' bills of rights contained principles identical with and often adopted directly from the federal Bill of Rights; yet many of these principles have no expression in federal law. For example, federal law does not include the right of migrant agricultural workers to form trade unions and to conclude collective agreements; but this right is recognized in the constitutions of the states of New York, Florida, Missouri, and New Jersey, as well as in Puerto Rico.

Federal-state collisions occur in the applications of the laws. For example, the guarantee of free expression in forty-two state constitutions contains a number of additional guarantees, including citizens' responsibility for an abuse of that freedom. Recently, this discrepancy served as a cause for a case in the U.S. Supreme Court, *State of Texas v. Johnson* (1989). During the 1984 Republican National Convention in Dallas, outside of the hall, a citizen publicly burned a U.S. flag as a sign of protest against the government policy. He was sentenced to one year in jail and fined $2,000 under a Texas law which made it a crime to desecrate the flag. The appellate court of the State of Texas reviewed the sentence, finding this state law to be unconstitutional under the First Amendment. The act of burning the flag, if not accompanied by a disturbance of public order and violence, was held to be an exercise of free expression and protest in accordance with the First Amendment, based on the well-known position of Judge Robert Jackson, stated more than forty years ago in the case of *Board of Education of West Virginia v. Barnett* (1943): "Those who begin with the coercive elimination of disagreement soon show up among those who eliminate those who disagree with themselves. The unification of opinion by force may lead only to the unanimity of the grave."[3] The U.S. Supreme Court upheld the appellate opinion by a five-to-four decision. That is, this opinion found the law of the state in conflict with the First Amendment of the federal Constitution. The court noted in particular that its decision, which is a constitutional defense of insults to the flag, is an affirmation of the principle of freedom which is embodied in the flag.

The legal battle over the prerogative to protect the flag did not end with this Supreme Court decision. That same year, 1989, Congress passed a federal law on protecting the flag which established punishment for flag-burning in the form of a fine or imprisonment of up to one year, or both. In response, there followed new flag-burnings as protest, and new criminal cases. Citing the Johnson case, the federal courts found the federal law to be unconstitutional and acquitted the defendants; and the U.S. government appealed this decision to the Supreme Court. In the summer of 1990, the Supreme Court, by a six-to-three decision, upheld the verdict of the lower courts. It found federal and state laws had the same fundamental flaw; that is, they infringed on the rights guaranteed under the First Amendment of the U.S. Constitution. The court, once again, proclaimed that the state had no right to forbid the expression of any idea simply because society found it to be offensive or unacceptable.[4]

Professor of Law A.E. (Dick) Howard, of the University of Virginia, concludes that federal-state relations grow out of the following principle: If acts of Congress are in accordance with the principles and norms of the federal Constitution, then acts of states contradicting Congress must be found to be illegal.[5]

The states differ among themselves on the question of whether constitutional rights may be exercised directly without the implementation of laws. Thus, the courts found the right to form trade unions and conclude trade agreements that is affixed to the constitution of the State of New Jersey to be directly self-executing. But the state courts of Florida and Missouri were not prepared to directly apply the equivalent principles of their state constitutions in a defense of that right. In our opinion, an instance of the failure of state courts to directly apply the individual rights affirmed in their state constitutions represents an inadequacy of judicial guarantees of individual rights at the state level.

The unique combination of a system of common law with a precisely written constitution is generally considered to be a distinguishing characteristic of American constitutionalism. The combination works in the context of a federal-state division of jurisdiction over questions of rights and freedoms. The necessary flexibility of political and legislative maneuvering under such circumstances is attained through the use of such effective mechanisms as the principle of precedent, checks and balances, rule of law, judge-made law, and the absolute and complete independence of the judges.

This interaction lends the character of a living constitution to the basic law of the country and the procedures for changing it, which were purposefully complicated according to former Supreme Court Chief Justice Warren Burger. In effect, the courts have the right of free interpretation of the norms of law and the Constitution. American judges are inclined to examine legal questions in a broad political, ethical, and social context.[6] How the members of the Supreme Court weigh context, precedent, and "original intentions of the framers" differs from Court to Court as the history of recent decades shows. The principle prevails, however, that decisions of the U.S. Supreme Court based on federal and state constitutions must be respected by all the courts in the country at every level. Thus, decisions of the Supreme Court define the correct meaning of the state constitutions.

The federal and state courts are guided by the principle articulated in Article VI of the federal Constitution: "This Constitution and the laws of the United States which shall be made in pursuance thereof; and all treaties made, or which shall be made, under the authority of the United States, shall be the supreme law of the land," and shall prevail in collisions with state law. Moreover, whereas decisions of the federal courts, particularly those of the Supreme Court, may expand the scope of citizens' rights protected in state courts, the decisions of state courts are not binding on the federal courts and do not, of themselves, expand the scope or raise the "floor" of the rights that are protected by the federal courts.

Two approaches distinguished the Supreme Court's rulings of the last fifty years. Beginning in 1937, the Court acted mainly in the spirit of the so-called doctrine of national supremacy, which expressed the principle of the unlimited freedom of the federal government within the limits of the authority given it by the U.S. Constitution. Guided by this doctrine, the Court supported government regulation of a very wide range of matters involved in the working of the national economy.[7] The constitutional authority of Congress to regulate international and interstate commerce became an effective instrument for extending federal police powers into such traditionally intrastate spheres of activity as criminal prosecution.[8] The Supreme Court recognized also the right of Congress to establish general rules in such areas as family and civil law.[9] Its decision in *Roe v. Wade* (1973) legalizing abortions in effect repealed the legislation of approximately forty states which had regulated that matter.[10] Thus, even in those spheres in which the basic responsibility for formulating and applying legal norms lay with the state, the latter, to an increasing degree, were obligated to act in accordance with rules mandated by the federal government.

In 1969, under Chief Justice Warren Burger (1969–86), the Supreme Court began to act in the spirit of the concept worked out by the court itself, so-called balanced federalism. In the case of *National League of Cities v. Usery* (1976), the Supreme Court found in favor of states' rights for the first time in fifty years when it overruled the 1975 amendments to a federal law on fair labor standards which had established a federal wage scale for the states, because their purpose was to deprive the states of the freedom of regulation which fell within their traditional jurisdiction.

The States' Growing Role

In recent years in the United States, there has been a noticeable revival of the states' role in the regulation of rights and freedoms. In our view, this is above all connected with the enormous federal deficit. Under these conditions, the economic and social rights proclaimed in many state constitutions, above all, the rights to education, health care, and a clean environment, are protected more at the state level.

State courts are sufficiently independent that, while they observe the principle of federal law, they still may develop their own constitutional doctrines. Here is an example of this legal situation. At a time when the Supreme Court refused to invoke the Fourteenth Amendment (affirming equality and equal protection under the law) as the basis for the equal distribution of assets between rich and poor public schoo's, the courts in several states (in 1989, three states) obligated the appropriate agencies to carry out the financial reform of the schools, basing their actions on their own constitutions.

In the opinion of many American researchers, including Professor Howard, the renaissance of the role and importance of state constitutions is an indicator of the health of the federation.[11] Experiments in the states can be educational, for both other state governments and the federal government. States may become laboratories of new social and economic experiments, without risk to the whole nation, as Supreme Court Justice Louis Brandeis correctly suggested.[12] In fact, many federal innovations—from unemployment benefits to zero-based budgeting— received their stimulus from successful experiments in the states.

However, in assessing this complicated, often contradictory, process, we must take note that in the early 1980s the Reagan administration's new movement for states' rights had as its goal the weakening of federal standards and legal protections in the sphere of racial discrimination, and returning discretion in this sphere to the states, a circumstance which had given rise to the existence of the problem in the first place. A revival of the states' role in protecting the rights of all

American citizens highlights real problems in contemporary America. At the same time, we must not forget that, by its very nature, federalism serves as a kind of barrier against conformism and imposed uniformity.

The Lowly Status of Social and Economic Rights in Law and Practice

This category of human rights in the United States suffers a number of peculiarities which, in our view, follow from two basic circumstances. First, there is the point of view among many western, and especially American, jurists that social and economic rights have a status different from political rights—that they are secondary in importance, derivative, dependent on circumstances, and, in comparison with political and civil rights, relative. Second, the legal protection of these rights is in fact limited by comparison with the protections enjoyed by political rights and civil freedoms. The wave of neoconservatism in the United States in the 1970s and 1980s reinforced this view.

Economic and systemic crises in the late 1960s and the early 1970s shook conceptions of the "welfare state" to their foundations and prompted a widespread shift to neoconservative and libertarian ideologies. The neoconservatives' points of departure were the rejection of state interference in the economy and a demand to return to the principles of laissez-faire and the "minimal state," as well as to the practice of the "state as night-watchman." The neoconservatives declared that the economic and social impact of the welfare state was the root of all evils—inflation, unemployment, and falling living standards. Likewise, they asserted that the recognition and strengthening of social-economic rights had compelled the federal government's intervention into the economy, thus hampering the market economy and threatening freedom of enterprise and private initiative. Calling for the "defense of the eternal values" of capitalism, the neoconservatives sometimes go so far as to deny completely the importance and necessity of this category of rights.

Ideologues of neoconservatism consider that social programs of the state weaken the stimulus to work, encourage parasitism, and reduce people's economic ability and entrepreneurial impulse while increasing their dependence on the government and its officials, thereby undercutting individual freedom.[13] One American neoconservative, George Gilder, targeted the welfare state by rejecting programs to alleviate poverty, unemployment, and job discrimination, and writing that the social programs of the federal government bar the way to the psychological, moral, and metaphysical resources of productivity and progress.[14]

This trend of thought finds its most consistent expression in the works of such analysts as Robert Nozick, Friedrich Hayek, Daniel Bell, Robert Nisbet, and Milton Friedman. Social and economic rights cannot be considered fully established rights in the United States. Many American theorists state that it is much more important that rights be realized in practice than that they be proclaimed yet not realized. From our point of view, denying the legal force of social and economic rights undermines both the social and legal protections of working people.

The U.S. political and legal system is distinctive for the special role of the courts, not only in the application of laws, but in the process of lawmaking. This special role applies also to the sphere of social and economic rights. At the beginning of this century, the Supreme Court found that the Fourteenth Amendment's guarantee of due process of law was violated by the legislation of the ten-hour maximum working day in New York (*Lochner v. New York* [1905]). The Court evaluated that state law was a dubious intervention into the rights of the individual to work as much as they wished. Influenced by the socially activist New Deal program of President Franklin Roosevelt, the courts changed their position on these rights. Principles of judicial discretion and precedence, and the flexibility of legal ideology, permit the courts to decide cases on the basis of the situation, adapting current legal practice to the pragmatic relationships between state and citizen.

According to the testimony of many American jurists, U.S. court practice in general (and especially practice of the Supreme Court) more often and more willingly affirms negative guarantees of human rights—that is, guarantees of rights to protection from the action of the state—than it does positive guarantees of human rights—that is, rights that require the direct action of the state, for instance in the form of direct social intervention. Thus, the Court cannot reliably guarantee the social protection of citizens or make provisions for their social and economic needs.

A graphic illustration of the predominantly formal character of Supreme Court decisions is provided by the famous decision in *Brown v. Board of Education* (1954). The Court's recognition of the anticonstitutionality of racial segregation in public schools had enormous importance as an affirmation of the constitutional principle of citizens' equality under the law in the sphere of education. In practice, however, during the fifteen years after the adoption of this decision, sixty-one percent of white pupils and fifty-six percent of blacks attended segregated schools.[15]

Despite the Court's general reluctance to affirm positive social and economic rights, the Supreme Court under Chief Justice Earl Warren (1953–69) marked an era of "advancing egalitarianism," remarkable for the broad application of the constitutional principle of equal protection under the law—the protection of citizens against discrimination in education, housing, and hotel accommodations, and the protection of indigents in the criminal process.

The egalitarian Warren Court stood out in contrast to the approach taken by the Court after the four new appointments by Richard Nixon, who became president in 1969. Under its new chief justice, Warren Burger, the Supreme Court reduced to a minimum the egalitarian orientation of its predecessor. In *Lindsey v. Normet* (1972), the Court declared that the Constitution does not guarantee legal defense to indigent citizens. Further, despite a 1954 decision in which the right to education was recognized as fundamental, in *San Antonio Independent School District v. Rodriguez* (1973), the Supreme Court refused to recognize a constitutionally guaranteed right to education. It wrote that insofar as a right to education is neither directly stipulated in the federal Constitution nor indirectly a fundamental right, local school districts' funding of part of the expense of education by means of local property taxes (which of course favors the wealthier districts) does not deny any fundamental constitutional right by denying in effect the right to an equal education to those who live in poorer school districts. According to the Court's decision, the plaintiff, Rodriguez, incorrectly cited the Fourteenth Amendment as a guarantee of a minimal protection in the sphere of education.[16]

The realization of economic and social rights depends on the government carrying out social programs. Of course, the government's economic role must have its limits. Extensive federal ownership and centralization of the economy and politics inevitably leads to a greater dependence by citizens on the government and, correspondingly, limits citizens' rights and freedoms. Clear confirmation of this is the experience of socialist states during the domination of the command-administrative system, with the absolute preponderance of state property in the economy. From this viewpoint, there must be limits also to the judicial protection of economic and social rights in the United States. The realization of such rights depends directly on the state of the economy and may be blocked by crises, depressions, inflation, and other occurrences which from time to time strike the market economy. In this regard, American jurists justly point to the problem of enforcing Court decisions: Does the Court have the necessary authority to ensure the realization of citizens' lawful claims?

In the 1980s, the doctrine of neoconservatives was losing its dominant position. Influenced by resolutions in the U.N. General Assembly on the equal validity of all categories of human rights, by the increasingly rooted recognition of the status of social and economic rights as universal rights, and by an ever-wider recognition of the international covenants on human rights, the U.S. courts increased their implementation in national law, legislation, and court practice. A number of works have appeared in the United States on theories of law in which these rights are recognized as equal and real, and their rejection as inevitably bringing on the loss of civil and political rights.[17] Thus the ideological confrontation over the status of social and economic rights intertwines with the more general question of the necessity for social activity of the government and its responsibility to its citizens. The latter, in its turn, is a measure of the state's social nature and degree of democracy.

Social Inequality and the Practice of Discrimination— Realities of Contemporary America

As already shown, in comparison with other industrially developed western countries, the United States is distinctive in its rather low level of protection of social and economic rights. Many American researchers acknowledge this. Robert Goldstein comes to the conclusion that the United States is "the most socially unjust among these countries."[18] The United States is one of the richest countries in the west, indeed, in the whole world, in terms of per capita national income and many other indicators. Yet strikingly enough, poverty in the United States is greater than in any other developed capitalist country.

The key to this seeming paradox is in the first place that wealth and well-being in American society are distributed extremely unjustly, and social programs are not so generous as in other developed countries. In 1987, thirteen percent of the population lived below the poverty line in the United States, seven and a half percent did in Great Britain, and five percent did in Sweden and Germany.[19] The gap between rich and poor keeps on widening. In 1963, one percent of the wealthiest families held twenty-five percent of the country's wealth; in the mid-1980s, thirty-five percent.[20] America in the 1980s followed the path of reducing both social programs and taxes. In 1981, the family whose annual income was less than $10,000 began to pay twenty dollars a year less in income taxes, but at the same time suffered a $400-per-year curtailment in social programs.[21] Meanwhile, various loopholes in the federal tax laws in 1982 permitted 250 Americans with annual incomes of more than $200,000 to pay not a cent in income taxes; 130 companies, in at least one of the years from 1981 to 1985, paid no income taxes, and together saved $73 billion in taxes.[22]

Homelessness

The continued growth of officially documented inequality in America shows up especially clearly in the increasing number of homeless people. How are we to explain the well-known fact that in the United States about three million people live on the streets and in shelters? The most common explanation of this phenomenon, even on the official level, tends to point to mental disturbances and a syndrome of vagrancy. When he answered a question about this in the student auditorium of Moscow University in the summer of 1988, then-President Reagan explained that it is a purely American understanding of freedom: I live where I want to live. Evidently such explanations are unconvincing, especially as regards such a mass phenomenon as homelessness.

Special research on the homeless was conducted by the Washington, D.C. Department of Housing Construction and Urban Development and the private Robert Wood Johnson Fund in 1988 and 1989. The department ascertained that no more than one-third of the homeless suffer from mental disturbances. The data of Professor Wright of Tulane University shows that of 83,000 homeless applying for help at the clinic of the Robert Wood Johnson Fund, less than five percent had been patients of psychiatric clinics immediately before they became homeless.

One of the obvious reasons for the increase in homelessness is the shortage of inexpensive housing; according to data cited by National League of Cities President John Jacob in his report, "The State of Black America in 1989," the number of poor families had grown by twenty-five percent over the previous decade, while in the same period the number of low-rent apartments and houses had decreased by twenty percent. His report also shows that in the 1980s the proportion of income spent by low-income families devoted to housing sharply increased: the overwhelming majority of poor families spends more than half of their monthly budgets on housing; two out of five families pay out seventy percent of their wages for the same purpose. During those same years, the construction of cheap housing fell eight percent. The construction of apartments subsidized by the Department of Housing and Urban Development was also curtailed. In 1981, 144,000 subsidized apartments were built; but in 1986, only 17,000. Such dramatic changes are explained by the fact that during the period from 1981 through 1986, funds budgeted to the Department of Housing and Urban Development for housing construction diminished by two-thirds, from $30.2 billion to $10 billion.

Moreover, families with high incomes "take away" housing from indigent families. The budget of New York City, for several years now, has been short by several billion dollars because the federal government established a regime of tax abatement for those who built new housing or bought inexpensive housing on which they made capital repairs. As a result of this tax-abatement program for housing renovations, about one million inexpensive apartments disappeared from the housing market since 1970, which is one of the chief reasons for homelessness today.

Awareness of the urgency of the problem led evidently to the passage of the 1988 Aid to the Homeless Bill (the McKinney Act), intended to assist hundreds of thousands of people who lacked their own home. A special interagency committee, consisting of the official heads of fifteen federal departments and agencies, was formed and allotted special funds. In 1988, the committee received $950,000; however, with the curtailment of resources for building cheap housing, the activity of the committee could provide no more than a drop in the bucket. Assessing the work of the interagency committee in March 1989, members of Congress and representatives of private organizations to help the homeless subjected it to the sharpest criticism. They stated that the committee was unable to carry out the law on aid to the homeless. In its report, the National Coalition for the Homeless concluded that the committee "ignored its obligations, and spent for nothing the funds assigned to it."

Later, the Bush administration announced a three-year program of housing construction costing $4 billion. It would seem that the first step to solving the housing problem must be to make apartments available to Americans who live below the poverty line.

Problems of the American Woman Today

In any modern state, the position of women is an indicator of democracy, the standard of living, and the well-being of society as a whole. What, in this regard, is the position of the American woman? Does she run up against any problems in America today? This is not an idle question. It is a matter of record that throughout the nineteenth century American women had limited legal rights in many spheres of their lives, including those whose parameters were defined by the federal and state constitutions.

The real and personal property of a married woman was, as a rule, under the control of her husband. She had no right to conclude contracts, to make agreements, to draw up her own will, or to bring a suit in court without the agreement of her husband. Women were deprived of voting rights, of the right to hold government office, and of the rights to act as witnesses in court and to perform jury duty. So deeply rooted in tradition were these limits that they were rarely contested as unconstitutional in the courts. Thus, in 1874, the U.S. Supreme Court found to be constitutional a Missouri state law which denied women voting rights; in two other decisions made at the same time, the Court found to be constitutional state legislation which forbade women from engaging in legal practice (in re *Lockwood*, 1884). In the twentieth century, the Supreme Court continued to maintain its position of limiting the legal status of women. In a 1948 decision, it found to be valid a Michigan law forbidding women to work as bartenders, except for the wife or daughter of the bar owner.[23] In a 1961 decision, the Court found to be constitutional a limitation of women's service on juries.[24]

Beginning only in the mid-1960s, the unequal legal status of women in the United States was revised, through judicial interpretation of the constitutional principle of equal protection under the law and through legislation against discrimination in employment on the basis of gender. A 1963 law forbade government employers from a departure from the principle of equal work for equal pay; additional provisions passed in 1972 and 1974 extended this prohibition to employers in the private sector. Those who violated the law were liable for up to two years' back pay, and if they were found to have intentionally violated the law, the back-pay liability was for three years. In certain cases, employers could be sentenced to prison for up to six months. Moreover, the Civil Rights Act of 1964, Executive Order 11478 of 1969, and the Equal Employment Opportunity Act of 1972 expanded the requirements for equality in the private sector workplace. An exception is made for enterprises employing fewer than fifteen workers.

The Civil Rights Act of 1964 bans discrimination in the hiring and firing practices of employers on the basis of gender. Title Seven of the law and Executive Order 11246 directly forbid employers from discrimination in wages on the basis of race, gender, religion, or national origin. But enforcement has been lax. On the average, women receive thirty-two percent less than do men; and sexual segregation of the work force occurs all over the country.[25] A finding by the government's Commission on Equal Employment Opportunity, issued on July 17, 1985, similarly found that federal legislation does not require employers to pay men and women equally when they are carrying out different jobs, although the jobs may be of equal worth.

On May 19, 1984, in its survey of labor relations practice, the *San Francisco Examiner* reported that forty-nine million American women are subject to systematic pay discrimination. A week's pay for a woman equals, on average, sixty percent of the average man's pay, while the pay of a black or Latino-American woman is only a little more than one-half that received by a man. African- and Latino-American women experience a burden of dual discrimination, both as women and as people of color. A former federal judge, George Edwards, wrote in 1983 that the country "would need a long time before women would be recognized as 'persons' and 'citizens' in the constitutional and legal sense. In the practice of the Supreme Court this recognition is even less significant than as regards blacks of the male gender."[26] What American writers have come to call the feminization of poverty reflects not only discrimination at work, but also the fact that the majority of women are employed in occupations that are segregated by sex and relatively low-paying—such as secretarial positions, secondary school education, and nursing.[27]

Women's economic well-being and independence is further threatened by their dual role as mother and worker. A 1978 law forbids employers to refuse pregnant women those benefits which other workers enjoy; however, it does not oblige employers to give maternity leave. Sheila Kammerman, a researcher at Columbia University, found that among 118 countries, the United States is the only country whose legislation (with the exception of certain state laws) does not provide for giving mothers paid maternity leave or leave to care for a sick child.[28] It is up to the discretion of the employer whether the woman will receive child-care leave. At this writing, only five states require paid maternity leave, and only nine states guarantee that a woman who has taken time off to give birth will be allowed to keep her job.

The question of the right to abortion directly concerns the quality of life for women and such rights and freedoms as the right to privacy, the right to free choice and self-determination, and the right to life. This problem has important moral and social aspects; women's real situation in society depends to a great extent on how it is resolved.

In 1973, in its decision in *Roe v. Wade*, the Supreme Court recognized women's constitutionally guaranteed right to legal abortions during the first three months of pregnancy. It thus obliged all fifty states to recognize the right to abortion. However, in recent years these decisions have been criticized and contested in the courts many times, and many states have adopted restrictive abortion laws. Finally, in 1989, the Court heard the case of *Webster v. Reproductive Health Services of Missouri*, the central issue of which was the constitutionality of a 1986 Missouri law which forbade abortions in clinics financed by the state. The decision marked the end of the Supreme Court's recognition of the right to free reproductive choice through abortion as a fundamental constitutional right and opened the door to test cases of much more restrictive laws that were being considered in other states; in fact, it has led to the possible overthrow of *Roe v. Wade*, which would leave the reproductive rights in the hands of each individual state.

In general, the U.S. courts are moving away from the emphasis on the constitutionality of the right to abortion and toward an emphasis on the fetus's right to life—at the expense, of course, of free choice and self-determination for women. American analysts suggest that the selective restriction of rights to abortion has a negative effect, above all on the position of indigent and young women. It thus touches an enormous number of women, especially in view of the fact that one-third of all pregnant women generally have abortions. Today, the fight to maintain the legalization of abortions at the federal and state levels has been taken up by various feminist organizations and women's movements.

Racial and Ethnic Minorities and Problems of Discrimination

The United States is home to members of a vast number of racial and ethnic groups from all over the world. Today, racial conflicts remain an urgent political problem, despite the fact that in the 1960s and early 1970s laws were passed which made African-Americans and whites equal citizens and banned many forms of discrimination: the Civil Rights Act of 1964, the Voting Rights Act of 1965, the Fair Housing Act of 1968. Many people consider these laws to be the most important for civil rights in the history of the United States. Drew S. Days III, now head of the human rights program at Yale University Law School, has written: "America advanced in race relations during the period from the *Brown* decision in 1954 to the end of the 1960's farther than it had in the preceding hundred years. In less than a generation a society that had created and maintained a racial caste system became a place where racial discrimination and segregation constituted offenses to public policy."[29]

However, getting the law to work has required considerable effort. In both the south and the north many employers, in order to protect the status quo, have resorted to various procedures in hiring which, although not overtly discriminatory, considerably reduced opportunities for members of national and ethnic minorities. Many enterprises and organizations began to arbitrarily require psychological tests, aptitude tests, greater educational qualifications, and certain experience, so that under the best of circumstances nonwhite job applicants could expect to receive only second-rate and low-paid jobs. This practice flagrantly contradicted the requirements and goals of Title Seven of the Civil Rights Act of 1964. Testimony to this has been the growing number of lawsuits over hiring practices.

A step forward in fulfilling the Civil Rights Act was taken by the decision of the U.S. Supreme Court in the case of *Griggs v. Duke Power Company* (1971).

The Court found that all requirements for hiring are discriminatory and racist in nature and contradict Title Seven unless it can be shown that they are essential for the performance of the job in question. The Supreme Court decided also that the Civil Rights Law not only bans open discrimination, but also any practice which, although just in form, in reality is discriminatory. Affirmative action continues to be a leading rights issue in the interplay of Congress, the President, and the Supreme Court.

It has proven no less difficult to fulfill the spirit of the voting and housing acts. Minorities have run up against a variety of discriminatory practices in these spheres—for example, "gerrymandering" an electoral district settled by predominantly African- or Latino-Americans so as to split it into separate electoral districts in which they are no longer the majority population. Some progress has been made on this. In 1985, 6,000 African-Americans were elected to office at all levels of government, including the mayoralities of Los Angeles, Detroit, Chicago, and Philadelphia. By 1989, African-Americans had been elected to the offices of governor of the state of Virginia and mayor of New York City. This picture sharply contrasts with that of 1963, when no more than 500 blacks were elected to government office at any level.

Though discrimination on the basis of race and nationality is forbidden by law, it continues to be almost open in character when it comes to the sale and renting of housing. About a third of poor African-Americans live in homes of the "low standard" category, in districts with a predominantly dark-skinned population. Sometimes court recognition of this takes the form of reverse discrimination. The number of African-American students in colleges for the ten years from 1972 to 1982 grew from three to ten percent; the proportion of African-Americans among professionals (such as lawyers, doctors, and engineers) increased during those years from 2.3 percent to 4.3 percent.[30]

Still discrimination continues in various other forms. For example, in many southern states African-Americans know that there are bars and restaurants in which they will not be served, motels which will refuse them a room, and sports or golf clubs where they may not play.[31]

Looking back on the 1980s we see that discrimination in employment has been the most widespread and harmful of all. For example, in 1983 an African-American worker with a college education earned as much as a white worker who had a high school education. Unemployment figures show similar differences, with African-American unemployment rates two to three times higher than those for European-Americans. We must not forget that these official statistics do not take into account a mass of ghetto dwellers who have lost all hope of finding work, are isolated from the outside world, don't register with any official agencies, and therefore have fallen out of sight of the official statistics. Estimates have it that in the first half of the 1980s only fifty-four percent of able-bodied African-American males in the United States were actually counted as part of the country's work force.[32]

While the specific data may change somewhat from year to year, they consistently show that in every sphere African-Americans fare worse than European-Americans do, be it in life expectancy, in rates of violent deaths, in rates of illness with cancer, heart disease and diabetes, and in rates of infant mortality.[33] There are more African-American youths in prison than there are in colleges, quite probably as a result of social inequality, relatively high unemployment, and the surviving racial prejudice in certain segments of American society.[34]

Amnesty International reports on racial discrimination in the justice system. It becomes most evident in the use of the death penalty against African-Americans, especially in southern states. In Virginia from 1908 until 1962 only African-Americans were sentenced to death for rape (they made up fifty-five percent of those convicted of rape).[35] In Georgia, eleven times as many persons are sentenced to death for the murder of whites as for the murder of African-Americans. Similar data pour in from many quarters.[36]

The Rights of American Indians

Most Soviet experts on America approached the question of Native Americans by stating dramatically that the indigenous peoples of America were on the edge of extinction at the end of the twentieth century. They usually cited high unemployment, infant mortality, the growth of crime, and the short lifespan of indigenous people to back this up. This information comes from American sources and is accurate, but our purpose here is to shed light on the legal status of these indigenous peoples, in particular the discrimination against them. It contradicts many of the principles of human rights that are fixed in the American Constitution and its amendments.

Indians living on reservations have the legally protected, inalienable right to regulate their internal affairs independently in a system of self-government. However, this system operates within the framework of a so-called federal tutelage, which significantly limits their autonomy and self-government. This paternalism infused the Court's language in an 1886 decision: "Indian tribes are under the guardianship of the nation. This community is dependent on the United States, mainly in the sense of receiving its daily bread, dependent to the extent of the realization of their political rights. They are not joined by union relations with the states and they do not receive from them any protection. . . . The obligation of the federal government to protect them follows from their weakness and their helplessness."[37]

The legal authority of the tribes is inalienable and created neither by the Congress nor by the federal Constitution. Nevertheless, Native Americans have a special legal status characterized by limited constitutional protection and by great subordination to tribal law. Though born in the United States and considered to be U.S. citizens,[38] Native Americans and their tribes do not come under the jurisdiction of the federal Constitution, except as certain provisions directly concern them or apply to them as a result of a treaty or a legislative act.[39] Courts generally consider that, since the tribes are not federal institutions, their members do not have the guarantees of the Fifth Amendment on due process of law.[40] Since the tribes and reservations are not states, the provisions and guarantees of the Fourteenth Amendment also do not apply to them.[41] Hence arbitrariness, especially of police power. Indigenous Americans are subject to arrest three times more often than African-Americans and ten times more often than whites. This doubtlessly contradicts the constitutional guarantees of the Fourteenth Amendment which forbids deprivation of life, liberty, or property without due process of law and guarantees to all equal protection under the law. In the late 1970s, the U.S. Supreme Court issued a number of decisions sanctioning criminal prosecution of Native Americans at the federal level for crimes for which their tribal courts had already passed sentence. The Court did not see in that a violation of the constitutional ban on double jeopardy for the reason that the federal government and the Native tribes are different sovereigns.[42]

In the State of Arizona, 15,000 Native Americans—largely Navajo and Hopi—were forcibly resettled; Minnesota tribes had nearly 7,500 acres of land taken from them and the Mohicans of New York state lost 18,000 acres of arable land. According to data of the American Indian Movement (AIM), all 370 land treaties have been violated by the federal government. Further, the courts' favorable rulings on some Native land claims does not settle the problem of ownership of Native Americans' primordial lands for many indigenous tribes. A considerable number of American experts say that federal laws still overtly allow the seizure of indigenous peoples' lands without compensation and without legal land-seizure procedures.

The federal government retains enormous power over Native Americans and their lands, based not on the Constitution but on the role of guardian that the government has taken on. Before colonization, twelve million indigenous peoples lived on the territory of the present-day United States; today, the number is about 1.9 million (in the 1990 census). Dozens of tribes have disappeared. Native Americans have relatively short life spans, higher unemployment, and wide incidence of malnutrition.

Should we finish our necessarily short and therefore quite incomplete survey of the complex of discrimination in contemporary America on such a gloomy note? We think not. Of course, overcoming racial and gender barriers to achieve real equality remains an urgent problem in the United States. At the same time, favorable conditions are emerging for achieving this in the contemporary world. The radical, revolutionary transformation of the Soviet Union and the countries of eastern Europe, the improvement of relations between east and west and, above all, the improved relations between the former USSR and the United States exert the most direct and positive influence on the course of events in the whole world. The reduction of arms and military expenditures to reasonable levels of sufficiency permits the freeing of resources which may be used to address many social problems that have been awaiting their solution in many countries of the world, not excluding the United States.

Notes

1. *Texas Law Review*, vol. 63 (1985), 1200.
2. R. Williams, "Equality Guarantees in State Constitutional Law," Ibid., 1201.
3. In this case also the Supreme Court found the law of Virginia contravening the freedom-of-religion provision of the First Amendment by requiring students to salute the American flag. David O'Brien, *Storm Center: The Supreme Court in American Politics* (New York-London, 1986), 245.
4. U.S. Lexis 3087 (1990), 6.
5. A.E. Dick Howard, "Federalism," Seminar on the Rule of Law, Moscow and Leningrad, March 19–23, 1990, 11.
6. *Sovetskoe gosudarstvo i pravo*, no. 10 (1990), 108.
7. National Labor Relations Board v. Jones & Laughlin Steel Corporation 301 U.S. I (1937); United States v. Darby, 312 U.S. (1941).
8. The Court upheld the congressional right to establish federal jurisdiction over kidnapping (crossing state lines) (Sooch v. United States [1936]), to aid giving testimony in a criminal case (Herman v. United States [1947]), to export or import firearms or to transfer them to persons under criminal investigation or guilty of a crime (Tot. v. United States [1943]; Bartlett, v. United States 432 U.S. 12 [1976]).
9. It supported the federal regulation of such matters as alimony (Orr v. Orr [1979]), maternity leave (Cleveland Board of Ed. v. La Fleur [1974]), disability payments to pregnant women (Geduldig v. Aiello [1973]).
10. Roe v. Wade, 410 U.S. 113 (1972).
11. Howard, 14.
12. Ibid.,15.
13. M. Friedman and R. Friedman, *Free to Choose: A Personal Statement* (New York, 1980), 27.
14. George Gilder, *Wealth and Poverty* (New York, 1981), 24–28.
15. *Judicial Policy Making in America* (New York, 1977), 248.
16. Harvard Law Review, vol. 95, 1452 ff.
17. A. Gewirth, *Human Rights: Assays in Justification and Application* (Chicago, 1982), 64; R.S. Downey, "Social Equality," in *The Philosophy of Human Rights: International Perspectives* (Westport, 1980), 127–35; L. Lomasky, *Persons, Rights and the Moral Community* (New York, 1987), 4–133.
18. Robert Goldstein, *United States: 1987*, 436.
19. L. Thurow, "A Surge in Inequality," *Scientific American* (May 1987).
20. "The Leverage of Our Wealthiest 400," *The New York Times* (October 11, 1984).
21. Nicholas Lemann, "Culture of Poverty," *The Atlantic* (September 1984).
22. "It's Time to Put Fairness in Taxes," *Detroit Free Press* (September 5, 1985); "Keep the Bite on Corporations," *The New York Times*, (March 17, 1986).
23. Goeseart v. Cleary, 335 U.S. 464 (1948).
24. Hoyt v. Florida, 368 U.S. 57 (1961).
25. W. Newman, L. Newell, A. Kiskman, "Pay Me What It's Worth," *Human Rights*, vol. 12, no. 1, 46.

26. J. Edwards, "Women and the Law: From Abigal to Sandka," *University of Cincinnati Law Review 52*, no. 474.

27. Helsinki Watch, *Human Rights in the United States: A Status Report* (New York-Washington, 1985), 14–16.

28. Sheila Kammerman, *Maternity and Parental Benefits and Leaves* (New York: Columbia University Center for the Social Sciences, 1980).

29. Quoted from Norman Dorsen, ed., *Our Endangered Rights. The ACLU Report on Civil Liberties Today* (New York, 1984), 75.

30. "King's Legacy," The *Michigan News* (January 20, 1986); "With Gain in South Carolina, Blacks Are on Ten States' High Courts," *The New York Times* (September 1, 1985); and "Minority Enrollment in Colleges Is Declining," Ibid. (October 27, 1985).

31. "Across the Rural South, Segregation As Usual," *The New York Times* (April 27, 1985).

32. "Behind Poverty Data," *The New York Times* (August 29, 1985); "Blacks Losing Ground, Urban League Asserts," ibid. (January 23, 1986); "America's Underclass," *The Economist* (March 15, 1986).

33. *The Philadelphia Inquirer* (March 16, 1989).

34. Helsinki Watch, 10, 14.

35. Amnesty International, *United States of America: The Death Penalty* (New York, 1987).

36. *U.S. News and World Report* (October 20, 1986).

37. United States v. Kagama, 118 U.S. 375 (1886).

38. 8 U.S.C. 1411 Supp. 11 (1978).

39. Groundhog v. Keeler, 442 F2d 674 (1971).

40. Santa Clara Pueblo v Martinez, 436 U.S. 49 (1978).

41. Talton v. Mayes, 163 U.S. 376 (1896).

42. United States v. Wheller, 435 U.S. 313 (1978).

43. R. Barsh, "The Red Man in the American Wanderland," *Human Rights*, vol. 11 (1984), 37.

12

Civil Liberties in the United States: Nature And Limits

Norman Dorsen

This chapter describes the varied doctrines that make up the system of civil liberties in the United States and the ways in which these liberties are enforced. The discussion also briefly reviews historical sources of civil liberties as well as some current problems.

Blackstone, the eighteenth-century English jurist, defined civil liberty in his *Commentaries* as "the great end of all human society and government . . . that state in which each individual has the power to pursue his own happiness according to his own views of his interest, and the dictates of his conscience, unrestrained, except by equal, just, and impartial laws." From a practical perspective, civil liberties are usually claims of right that a citizen may assert against the state. Thus, in the United States the term "civil liberties" refers to freedom of speech, freedom of the press, freedom of assembly and association, the right to vote, religious liberty, and the right to due process of law and to other limitations on the power of the state to restrict individual freedom of action. Civil liberties increasingly also encompass rights to equality since these permit participation in society without regard to race, religion, sex, or other characteristic unrelated to individual capacity.

Civil liberties are a logical corollary to the concepts of limited government and rule of law. When government acts arbitrarily, it infringes civil liberty; the rule of law combats and confines such abuse of power. The maxim, "government of laws, not of men," reflects this idea.

Civil liberties in the United States are conceived differently from the concept of human rights as reflected in such documents as the United Nations Charter and the Universal Declaration of Human Rights. While there is overlap, human rights theory has a foundation in mutual human and social obligation as well as

---

This chapter is a modified and updated version of the author's essay "Civil Liberties," in the *Encyclopedia of the American Constitution* 263 (L. Levy, K. Karst and D. Mahoney eds., 1986).

in the protection of individuals against government excess. Accordingly, human rights encompass some social and economic rights that are not within the American civil liberties tradition.

Although civil liberties are usually associated in practice with democratic forms of government, liberty and democracy are distinct concepts. An authoritarian structure of government may recognize certain limits on the capacity of the state to interfere with individual autonomy. Correspondingly, the notion that the individual may assert certain rights against the expressed will of the majority is at least superficially counterdemocratic. Thus, "civil liberties" does not refer to a particular form of political system, but to the relationship between the individual and the state, however the state may be organized.

Though lacking the univeralism and breadth of international human rights, civil liberties in the United States are based on the integrity and dignity of the individual. The spirit of both was expressed by George C. Marshall, who was chief of staff of the American Army in World War II and later served as secretary of state: "We believe that human beings have. . . rights that may not be given or taken away. They include the right of every individual to develop his mind and his soul in the ways of his own choice, free of fear and coercion— provided only that he does not interfere with the rights of others." An ongoing theoretical task for civil libertarians is determining when constraints on individuals are needed to assure that the rights of others are not infringed.

There are two principal justifications for preferring individual liberties to the interests of the general community—justice and self-interest. Justice requires norms by which persons in authority should treat persons within their power; self-interest invites the recognition that, if principle is to govern, our own rights are secure only if the rights of others are protected.

Because these justifications are abstractions to most people, civil liberties are often subordinated in practice to more immediate concerns of the state or prevailing opinion. In the United States, even administrations relatively friendly to civil liberty perpetrated serious violations. The administration of Franklin D. Roosevelt interned Japanese-Americans during World War II.[1] Abraham Lincoln suspended the right of *habeas corpus*.[2] And Thomas Jefferson was far more of a libertarian as a private citizen than as president when he countenanced internment camps for political suspects, censored books, and authorized unlawful search and seizure of private property.[3]

A Long Tradition

The roots of American civil liberties can be traced to ancient times. The first recorded use of the word "freedom" apparently appeared in the twenty-fourth century B.C., when a monarch of Sumeria "established the freedom" of his subjects by purging tax collectors, protecting widows and orphans from the injustice of "men of power," and ending the high priest's practice of enslaving temple servants.

The city-state of Athens made a lasting contribution to civil liberty. In the sixth century B.C., the magistrate Solon produced a constitution which, while falling short of full-blown democracy, gave the poor the right to vote and to call public officials to account. Solon is also credited with first expressing the idea of the rule of law. But Athens countenanced slavery and knew no limits on the power of the majority to adopt any law it chose; there was apparently no concept of individual rights against the state. The Stoic philosophers introduced the idea of "natural law" and the derivative concept of equality; all Athenian citizens were equal because all possessed reason and owed a common duty to natural law.

The Romans also contributed to civil liberties, first through a rudimentary separation of governmental powers and later by the elaboration of natural law. Justinian's *Institutes* recites, "Justice is the fixed and constant purpose that gives every man his due." Nevertheless, the Roman emperors were autocratic in practice; there were no enforceable rights; and censorship, restrictions on travel, and coerced religion existed.

In the Middle Ages there was little concrete manifestation of civil liberties. But the idea of a pure natural law was carried forward in Augustine's *City of God* and especially in Thomas Aquinas's *Summa Theologica*. On the secular side, the contract between feudal lords and their vassals established reciprocal rights and responsibilities whose interpretation was, in some places, decided by a body of the vassal's peers.

To a great extent, American law sprung from England, which exercised sovereignty until the Revolutionary War that began in 1775. Among English antecedents of civil liberties, the starting point is the Magna Carta of 1215, the first written instrument in world history which exacted from a monarch a promise to obey certain rules. This document was violated by some English kings and was certainly not intended as a manifesto of popular rights. Nevertheless, basic liberties are derivable from it—among them, the security of private property and of the person, the right to judgment by one's peers, the right to seek redress of grievances from the sovereign, and the critical concept of due process of law. Above all, as Winston Churchill said, the Magna Carta "justifies the respect in which men have held it" because it tells us "there is a law above the king."[4]

The second great charter of English liberty was the 1628 Petition of Right, a statute that asserted the freedom of the people from unconsented taxation and arbitrary imprisonment. The third major document of English liberty was the Bill of Rights, enacted in 1689. It declared that elections to Parliament ought to be free and that members ought not be punished for their speeches in debate, and it condemned perversions of criminal justice by the last Stuart Kings, including excessive bail and cruel and unusual punishments.

The American colonies also contributed to the development of civil liberties. The first colonial charter, Virginia's in 1606, reserved to the inhabitants "all liberties, Franchises and Immunities . . . as if they had been abiding and born, within this our Realm of England." The Massachusetts Body of Liberties of 1641 expressed in detail a range of fundamental rights, many of which were adopted in the American Bill of Rights; other colonial charters, notably Pennsylvania's, were also influential in protecting individual rights. In addition, a New York jury's acquittal in 1735 of the publisher Peter Zenger on a charge of seditious libel (defamation of the government) was a milestone in securing the freedom of the press.

Constitutional Protections

The American Constitution of 1787 is devoted almost entirely to structure and the allocation of powers within the national government, but it contains some explicit safeguards for civil liberty. It provides that the "privilege of habeas corpus," which requires a judge to release an imprisoned person unless he has been convicted of a crime or should be held to stand trial, may not be "suspended." The Ex Post Facto and Bill of Attainder clauses require Congress to act prospectively and prohibit retroactive legislation. Article III guarantees a jury trial in all criminal cases and defines treason narrowly and imposes strict evidentiary requirements to assure that the most political of crimes will not be lightly charged. And the Contract Clause was designed to assure a measure of security to economic interests.

Apart from the omission of a bill of rights, which was to be shortly rectified, the Constitution's principal deficiency from a civil liberties standpoint was its acceptance of slavery. Without mentioning the term, in three clauses it recognized the legality of that pernicious institution. The Dred Scott decision of the United States Supreme Court[5] cemented the legally inferior status of blacks and led to civil war by ruling that slaves or the descendants of slaves could not become American citizens. The Emancipation Proclamation (1863) and the Thirteenth Amendment to the Constitution (1865) freed the slaves, but the reaction that occurred after the end of Reconstruction in 1877, and decisions such as the *Civil Rights Cases*[6] and *Plessy v. Ferguson*[7] undercut the movement to racial parity, which did not regain momentum until the middle of the twentieth century.

The civil liberties of Americans are embodied primarily in the Bill of Rights, the first ten amendments to the Constitution (1791). James Madison proposed the amendments after the debates on ratification of the Constitution a few years earlier revealed wide public demand for additional protection of individual rights. The First Amendment guarantees the freedom of speech, press, assembly, petition, and religious exercise, as well as the separation of church and state. The Fourth Amendment protects the privacy and security of home, person, and belongings, and prohibits unreasonable searches and seizures. The Fifth, Sixth, and Eighth Amendments extended constitutional protection to those accused of crimes, including the right to due process of law, trial by jury, confrontation of hostile witnesses, assistance of legal counsel, and protection against coerced self-incrimination, double jeopardy, and cruel and unusual punishment. The Tenth Amendment reserves to the states and to the people powers not delegated to the federal government.

Although the Bill of Rights was originally applicable only to the federal government, most of its provisions were applied to the states during the 1960s through the due process clause of the Fourteenth Amendment, which was ratified after the Civil War in 1868. This amendment also provides a generalized guarantee of "equal protection of the laws" as well as a virtually unenforced right to unspecified "privileges and immunities."

A practical understanding of civil liberties in the United States may be aided by a discussion of three main dimensions of the subject: freedom of speech, due process, and equal protection.

The First Amendment provides that "Congress shall make no law . . . abridging the freedom of speech, or of the press." The almost universal primacy given free speech rests on several important values: the importance of speech for self-government in a functioning democracy, its utility in probing for truth, its use in exposing and thus checking government violations of law, and its capacity to permit personal fulfillment of those who would express and receive ideas and feelings, especially unpopular ones, without fear of reprisal.

Consistent with the First Amendment, even revolutionary speech is immunized from government control if it is not "directed to inciting or producing imminent lawless action and is likely to incite or produce such action."[8] Because advocacy of ideas is enhanced by membership in groups, the Supreme Court has ruled that the First Amendment also protects freedom of association, absent a compelling justification for governmental interference.[9] In the United States, perhaps more than anywhere else, the impulse to connect with others has been a dominant feature of society. This was true in the nineteenth century, according to the French observer Alexis de Tocqueville, who wrote, "In no country in the world has the principle of association been more successfully used or applied to a greater multitude of objects than in America." And in 1956 a prominent scholar noted the "extraordinary multiplicity of interest groups in the United States . . . the American passion for being a joiner." This "passion" to join permits individuals to satisfy their needs and desires through associations of every kind, and at the same provides a buffer zone that protects individuals against the power of the state.

The freedom of speech is not absolute. Obscenity[10] and fighting words uttered directly to an individual that are likely to provoke physical attacks[11] are unprotected under the First Amendment; and all forms of speech are subject to reasonable restrictions as to the time, place, and manner in which the speech may occur. More recently, the Supreme Court has ruled that the freedom of expression of individuals working in programs funded by the government can be curtailed as a condition of receiving the funds.[12]

The First Amendment provides especially strong protection against prior restraints—injunctions or other means of preventing speech from ever being uttered or published.[13] On the other hand, the amendment affords a lesser degree of protection to commercial speech,[14] to highly offensive speech of a sexual character,[15] and to defamations of private individuals.[16]

The concept of fair procedure, embodied in the due process clauses of the Fifth and Fourteenth Amendments, has been viewed as an element of civil liberties at least since Magna Carta, when the king was limited by "the law of the land." As Justice Brandeis wrote, "[I]n the development of our liberty insistence upon procedural regularity has been a large factor."[17]

Violations of due process cover a wide range of official misconduct in criminal cases, including lynchings, coerced confessions, criminal convictions of lawyerless defendants, and interrogations of suspects without cautionary warnings. In addition, due process principles have been applied to protect juveniles accused of delinquency,[18] employees dismissed from their jobs,[19] and individuals whose government benefits have been terminated.[20] Although each context may involve different procedural requirements, the civil liberty principle requires that individual interests of liberty and property may not be sacrificed without a process that determines facts and legal liability at hearings which are fairly established and conducted.

The equal protection clause forbids government, and in some situations private entities, to discriminate among persons on arbitrary grounds. The central purpose of the provision was to restore the recently freed black slaves to equality after the Civil War; and leading judicial decisions[21] and legislative enactments such as the Civil Rights Acts of 1866 and 1964 were particularly addressed to the condition of racial minorities. The constitutional guarantee of equality has been extended, although in each instance with important exceptions, to other discrete and insular minorities—ethnic and religious groups,[22] women,[23] aliens,[24] and children of unwed parents[25]—that the Supreme Court has deemed are incapable of adequately protecting their own interests through the political process. The Supreme Court has also expressed the equality ideal in declaring unconstitutional systems of legislative districting that accord votes in some districts significantly greater weight than votes in others.[26] Although the Court in recent years has rejected attempts to broaden the category of specially protected groups to include homosexuals,[27] it has assisted the mentally disabled[28] and, through enforcement of statutes, older persons[29] who have been the victims of discrimination.

A vexing equality issue is whether classifications designed to benefit racial minorities or women are consistent with civil liberty if such classifications accord preference to groups that historically were, and often still are, discriminated against. Against the background of slavery and legally enforced segregation, the Supreme Court has approved some types of affirmative action programs that favor blacks for employment and university admissions[30] on the grounds that a wholly "color blind" system would render illusory the promise of a racially just society. It has also upheld some forms of preference for women.[31] There is deep division in the Supreme Court and among members of the public over these programs, and it is often charged that they are themselves an obnoxious use of racial or sexual classifications. Justice Harry Blackmun responded to these contentions by stating: "In order to get beyond racism, we must first take account of race . . . . We cannot—dare not—let the Equal Protection Clause perpetuate racial supremacy."[32] Despite such views, there appears to be waning support for affirmative action and it is uncertain to what degree the current Supreme Court will approve its varied manifestations.

Constitutional Flexibility

Some liberties in the United States are traceable to the natural law tradition, described above, which long antedated the Constitution. For example, the Virginia Declaration of Rights asserted that "all men are by nature equally free and independent, and have certain inherent rights . . . namely, the enjoyment of life and liberty, with the means of acquiring and possessing property." This sentiment was reflected in the Declaration of Independence of 1776, which spoke of "inalienable rights," and implicitly in the Constitution itself. In 1798, Justice Samuel Chase wrote that natural rights "form the very nature of our free Republican governments,"[33] and over the years the Supreme Court has enforced a number of rights not explicitly grounded in the constitutional text, including, for a period, freedom of contract[34] and, in recent years, the right to travel[35] and freedom of association.[36] The Court's most celebrated recent decisions of this kind have recognized a series of rights that reflect values of personal privacy and autonomy. These include the right to marry,[37] the right to birth control,[38] the right to family relationships,[39] and the controversial right to an abortion.[40] These liberties, in the words of David Richards, are "fundamental conditions of the integrity and competence of a person in mastering his life and expressing this mastery to others."[41]

However, as indicated above, the Court has refused to include consensual homosexuality in the constitutional right to privacy,[42] and it recently has begun to consider whether, and in what form, there is a protected privacy interest in refusing medical treatment when that refusal can lead to death.[43]

The Supreme Court's decisions enunciating some of these rights have been challenged as inconsistent with the original intent of the Constitution. But apart from the difficulty (some would say the impossibility) of ascertaining original intent, some of the country's most illustrious judges have understood that the Constitution was not frozen in time. Chief Justice Marshall wrote for a unanimous Court in 1819 that it is an instrument "intended to endure for ages to come and, consequently, to be adapted to the various crises of human affairs."[44] Justice Benjamin Cardozo agreed: "The great generalities of the Constitution have a content and a significance that vary from age to age."[45] Further, the structure of the Constitution and the premises of a free society imply certain liberties which are not spelled out textually. Thus, the Ninth Amendment suggests quite clearly that the provisions of the Bill of Rights were not meant to be exhaustive: "The enumeration in the Constitution, of certain rights, shall not be construed to deny or disparage others retained by the people."

The frequent uncertainty and possible illogic of Supreme Court decisions protecting certain groups and rights—why nonmarital children and not homosexuals, why a right to travel and not a right to housing?—has led to scholarly and public criticism. In particular, there has been much dispute over the failure to recognize as civil liberties the rights to work, to a minimally adequate standard of living, and to health care, all of which are basic to human dignity. These interests are recognized under international human rights standards, to a degree by European democracies, and, at home, in the rhetoric of President Franklin Roosevelt, who included "freedom from want" among the Four Freedoms. The difficulty is not in the enunciation of these rights as a matter of principle but in their implementation when courts are powerless or loath to intervene so fundamentally in a market economy. In addition, whatever their standing as aspirations for a just society, until the time when these economic rights can be realistically considered as possible of achievement, their broad proclamation could encourage cynicism that would weaken the structure of individual liberty, as it has in some other countries.

In any event, there are inevitably disagreements and inconsistencies in the boundaries of civil liberties and the proper judicial role in their implementation. Filling in the "majestic generalities"[46] of the Constitution has always been a long-term and uncertain task.

An example of the difficulty is capital punishment—the right not to be executed even for a heinous crime. This liberty is widely accepted throughout the world, but the United States Supreme Court has not recognized it. Instead, the Court allows states to impose death for murder, subject to due process limitations, and has even permitted the death penalty to be imposed on the mentally retarded and on young people of sixteen or seventeen years of age. Many consider capital punishment an inherent violation of civil liberties because of the randomness in its application, its finality in the face of inevitable trial errors, its possible bias against racial minorities, and its dehumanizing effect on government and the people. The struggle over this and other claims of civil liberty continues in public opinion and the courts.

Another source of American civil liberties is the doctrine of separation of governmental powers, which was expressed most notably in the eighteenth century, by the French *philosophe* Montesquieu. Anticipating Lord Acton's famous statement, that power corrupts and absolute power corrupts absolutely, the Supreme Court ruled in 1874 that the "theory of our governments, State and National, is opposed to the deposit of unlimited power anywhere. The executive, the legislative, and the judicial branches . . . are all of limited and defined powers."[47]

The Supreme Court has enforced the principle of separation of powers in diverse circumstances. In the *Steel Seizure* case, it denied the president the power during the Korean War to seize private companies without legislative authorization.[48] During the Vietnam War, three justices rested on the separation of powers doctrine in the *Pentagon Papers* case by holding that under all but extraordinary circumstances the courts lack inherent power to enjoin news organizations from publishing classified information.[49] More recently, the Court invalidated statutes that authorized one house of Congress to veto action by the executive branch[50] and assigned to an official under congressional control certain budgetary functions required to be performed by the president or his aides.[51] The justices who rendered these decisions were seeking to enhance civil liberty by dispersing governmental authority and thus "preclud[ing] the exercise of arbitrary power."[52]

Neither the original Constitution nor the Bill of Rights guaranteed the right to vote, a cornerstone of democratic government as well as a civil liberty, and slaves, women, and those without property were wholly disfranchised. During the early nineteenth century, states gradually rescinded property qualifications; the Fifteenth Amendment (1870) barred voting discrimination by race or color; and the Nineteenth Amendment (1920) outlawed voting discrimination on the grounds of sex. Nonwhites were widely prevented from voting until the Voting Rights Act of 1965 and the invalidation at about the same time of taxes on voting (poll taxes) which some states levied. Subsequently, the Twenty-sixth Amendment (1971) extended the franchise to all citizens eighteen years of age and older.

Limits and Stresses on Civil Liberties

A controversial question is presented by the relationship between the right to property and civil liberties. As the Supreme Court stated in 1956, "Providing equal justice for poor and rich, weak and powerful alike is an age-old problem."[53] Although some would reject any link between economics and liberty, a prominent author of the Constitution, Alexander Hamilton, stated in *The Federalist Papers* that "a power over a man's subsistence amounts to a power over will." More recently, Professor Paul Freund, recognizing that economic independence provides a margin of safety in risk or protest, concluded in his book *The Supreme Court of the United States* that the effective exercise of liberty may require "a degree of command over material resources."

To a limited extent, the Supreme Court has concurred. It has prohibited discrimination against the poor in cases involving voting rights[54] and access to the courts,[55] and it has afforded procedural protection before government can discharge an employee[56] or terminate welfare benefits.[57] On the other hand, the Court has refused to recognize a general constitutional right to economic security. Thus, the Court has permitted reduction of welfare benefits below a standard of minimum need,[58] has permitted courtroom filing fees to keep indigents from obtaining judicial discharge of debts,[59] and has refused to recognize a constitutional right to equalized resources for spending on public education.[60] In 1970, the Court said, "In the area of economics and social welfare, a State does not violate [equal protection] merely because the classifications made by its laws are imperfect."[61] The idea that civil liberties imply a degree of economic independence is not yet a principle of constitutional law in the United States.

Invasions of liberty are usually committed by government, and civil liberties normally are claims that are asserted against the state. But it is well known that individuals also may be victimized by private power. The authority of medieval lords over their vassals was not merely economic, but extended to control over their liberty as well. Today, large institutions such as corporations, labor unions, and universities may seek to limit the speech or privacy of individuals who are subject to their authority. For this reason, Congress and some states have enacted laws to bar racial discrimination and other forms of arbitrary exclusion in the hiring, promotion, and firing of employees of private companies, in the sale and rental of private housing, in admission to private academic institutions, and in membership in certain private clubs.

It is important to recognize that civil liberties can never be entirely secure, for government and powerful private institutions, backed by popular will, often seek to achieve their goals without scrupulous concern for the legality of their actions. In the eighteenth century, the English statesman Edmund Burke wrote, "Of this I am certain, that in a democracy the majority of citizens is capable of exercising the most cruel oppression upon the minority." More recently, Professor Charles Reich observed that civil liberties are an "unnatural state for man or for society because in a short-range way they are essentially contrary to the self-interest of the majority. They require the majority to restrain itself, to say 'no' to its immediate impulses, and to allow things to go on that threaten it."[62] In the words of the Spanish writer Ortega y Gassett, "[Freedom] is the right which the majority concedes to minorities and hence it is the noblest cry that has ever resounded in this planet." The legal rights of minorities and the weak thus need special protection, particularly under conditions of stress.

The first such condition is economic stringency. Mass unemployment and high inflation tend to inflame ethnic rivalries and induce discrimination, and at times these conditions are offered to justify the repression of vocal dissent. The victims of such behavior include the dependent poor (often racial minorities) whose jobs and government benefits are among the first casualties of economic recession.

International tension also strains the Bill of Rights, for a nation threatened from without is rarely the best guardian of civil liberties within. As noted above, President Abraham Lincoln suspended *habeas corpus* during the Civil War and President Franklin D. Roosevelt approved the internment of Japanese-Americans during World War II. In addition, President Woodrow Wilson presided over massive invasions of free speech during World War I; McCarthyism, the virulent repression of dissent, was a product of the cold war of the late 1940s and early 1950s; and President Lyndon B. Johnson authorized prosecution of peaceful protesters during the Vietnam War. During the 1980s, until Soviet–American relations improved at the end of the decade, the United States government interfered with peaceful demonstrations, imposed widespread surveillance of Americans, banned travel and denied visas for political reasons, and imposed speech restrictions on former government officials.

A third perennial source of trouble for civil liberties in the United States has been misplaced religious zeal. Anti-Catholic and anti-Semitic nativism paralleled slavery during the nineteenth and twentieth centuries. The notorious Scopes trial of the 1920s, in which a public school teacher was convicted of teaching Darwinian evolution, reflected fundamentalist excesses.[63] We should recall that some religious groups have buttressed civil liberties by, for example, supporting the extension of civil rights to racial minorities and endorsing the claims of conscientious objectors to conscription in the armed services. But zealous extremists, who live under the delusion that a god has revealed the Truth to them, threaten civil liberties when they seek government support to impose their parochial views on everyone else. This problem has taken many forms, including attempts to introduce organized prayer in public schools, to outlaw birth control and abortion, to persecute homosexuals, and to use public tax revenues to finance religious schools. Such zealotry is a serious problem for civil liberties in the United States.

Judicial Review

Legislators and executive branch officials working under direction of the president (or state governors or mayors of cities) have power to advance fundamental rights in many ways. Yet such representatives are often pressed hard to act for the assumed interests of the public in ways that can hurt minorities or dissenters. The vulnerability of politically accountable officials to popular pressure teaches that freedom is most secure when protected by life-tenured judges insulated from electoral retribution. The doctrine of judicial review, announced by Chief Justice Marshall for a unanimous Supreme Court in 1803,[64] reposed in courts the final authority to define constitutional rights and to invalidate legislation or executive action that conflicts with the Constitution. The concept of judicial review is perhaps the most important contribution of the American political system to the development of civil liberty worldwide.

But there has always been tension between the checking authority of judicial review and the nation's democratic commitment to majority rule, despite the fact that the democratic political process needs civil liberties in order to function— the rights to vote, to speak, and to be able to hear the views of others. Periodic challenges to the legitimacy of judicial review have evoked impressive responses based on the structure of the Constitution, the pragmatic need for national uniformity, and history. Thus, the long-time dean of Harvard Law School, Roscoe Pound, after full examination of the evidence, concluded that judicial review is validated by the "clear understanding of American lawyers before the Revolution, based on the seventeenth-century books in which they had been taught, the unanimous course of decision after independence and down to the adoption of the Constitution [and] the writings of the two prime [drafters of] the instrument."

The role of courts in exercising judicial review is proper even though their decisions may not reflect public opinion at a given time. American government recognizes the utility of long-term restrictions on the power of legislative majorities to act, subject to an amendment to the Constitution, because American democracy is concerned not merely with effectuating the majority's will but with protecting minority rights. Further, federal judges in fact have a democratic imprimatur although they are appointed for life: Almost always drawn from the world of public affairs, they are appointed by the president and must be confirmed by the Senate. It is for these reasons that James Madison, the principal author of the Bill of Rights, said: "Independent tribunals of justice will consider themselves in a peculiar manner the guardian of those rights; they will be an impenetrable bulwark against every assumption of power in the Legislative or Executive."

Aggressive actions by independent courts in the enforcement of civil liberties has periodically provoked a variety of efforts to weaken judicial review. The abolitionists, dissatisfied with federal judges who protected the property rights of slaveholders, clamored for jury trials for alleged fugitive slaves; populists have long urged the election of judges; President Franklin D. Roosevelt sought to increase the size of the Supreme Court to bend it to popular will; Presidents Ronald Reagan and George Bush imposed restrictive ideological tests on those seeking judicial appointments; and bills have been introduced in Congress to limit the jurisdiction of the federal courts and to bar legal remedies necessary to enforce certain constitutional rights. Whatever the perceived short-term advantages of such schemes to one political group or another, the long-term effect would be the erosion of judicial review and a consequent undermining of civil liberty.

Legislatures and Nongovernmental Organizations

The centrality of courts to the constitutional plan must not obscure the important role that legislatures can play. Lawmakers can enhance or weaken civil liberty and, absent a declaration of unconstitutionality, their actions are final. On the positive side, during the 1960s Congress prohibited discrimination in employment, housing, access to public accommodations, and voting; it passed the Freedom of Information Act; and it created legal services for the poor. A few years later, it enacted a law to protect the privacy of personal information.

Legislatures can also impair civil liberties by ways other than restricting judicial review. In recent years, battles have raged in Congress over the Legal Services Corporation, abortion rights, the Voting Rights Act, school prayer, tuition tax credits to support private schools, the powers of the Central Intelligence Agency and the Federal Bureau of Investigation, and many other issues. In the 1980s, this legislative agenda reflected an intense national debate over the meaning and scope of civil liberties. Similar struggles can be expected in the current decade, including disputes over whether the United States should ratify international covenants protecting political and civil rights and those guaranteeing economic and social rights. These documents include many rights already guaranteed to Americans. As discussed above, others, primarily economic, should be viewed as aspirational in order not to dilute the concept of rights; as such, they would focus the government and the public on worthy objectives for a nation that prides itself on recognizing the dignity of each individual.

Whatever the forum in which rights are debated, the security of civil liberty requires trained professionals. Throughout American history, the services of paid lawyers have been supplemented by others who volunteer out of ideological commitment or a sense of obligation. In the United States, publicly supported legal services organizations and laws awarding attorneys' fees to prevailing plaintiffs in civil rights cases have encouraged the growth of a sophisticated bar that litigates constitutional issues. Private organizations such as the American Civil Liberties Union (ACLU) and more specialized groups such as the National Association for the Advancement of Colored People (NAACP) and the National Organization for Women (NOW) engage in litigation, legislative lobbying, and public education in order to advance constitutional rights. But these groups do not have the resources to provide adequate legal services for the mass of people. Only the government can do that. As long as the average person cannot obtain competent counsel there will be a blot on the American legal system.

The Unending Challenge

History shows that civil liberties must be defended again and again, in each generation. In 1925, it was necessary to defend the right of John Scopes to teach Darwin's theory of evolution in a Tennessee public school. In the 1980s, similar efforts were needed to defend against zealots who would teach biblical "creationism" in science classes.[65] Other examples of repetitive violations of civil liberties are police misconduct, school book censorship, and interference with free speech and assembly. For instance, civil liberties lawyers found it necessary to assert the constitutional right to march peacefully when Mayor Frank Hague banned labor organizers in New Jersey in the 1930s,[66] when Sheriff Bull Connor harassed civil rights demonstrators in Alabama in the 1960s,[67] when the Justice Department arrested antiwar demonstrators in Washington in the early 1970s,[68] and when the town of Skokie, Illinois sought to prevent neo-Nazis from peacefully demonstrating there in 1978.[69]

The lesson from these and other examples is that it is not enough for civil liberties to be proclaimed officially; to be effective, rights must also be implemented, on the ground, day by day.[70] In this way individuals are encouraged to exercise their rights and give them meaning. If rights are rarely used, they may erode and eventually may be lost.

Critical struggles lie ahead. For example, the right to free expression has come under intense pressure. The Supreme Court has ruled that the government can prohibit doctors from advising pregnant women who seek family planning advice from a government-financed clinic about the possibility of abortion,[71] and it has rejected claims by poor persons that sleeping in a public park to protest their condition[72] or begging for money in the New York City subways is protected expression.[73] The narrow majority by which it voided laws prohibiting desecration of the flag for political purposes,[74] coupled with the resignations from the Court of two leading civil libertarians, Justices William Brennan and Thurgood Marshall, suggests that these rulings could be reversed. The early 1990s also have seen attempted censorship in connection with grants to performance artists by the National Endowment for the Arts as well as criminal prosecutions of a museum director for exhibiting allegedly obscene photographs, a record store owner for selling an allegedly obscene "rap" album, and the "rap" group itself after it made a live performance. All these criminal defendants were found innocent or had their convictions annulled, but the threat of censorship remains. A different sort of threat to free expression has arisen as a result of successful efforts by some minority, women's, and homosexual groups to induce some universities, as part of their antidiscrimination programs, to promulgate "codes of conduct" which punish on-campus speech that offends certain sensibilities.

The government's heralded "war" on drugs and crime has led to massive violations of civil liberties which have not been redressed. In recent decisions the Supreme Court has restricted the scope of certain constitutional protections afforded crime suspects, upheld mandatory drug-testing of certain classes of government employees, and allowed highway checkpoints which detain all motorists to examine them for intoxication or drug use. The rising tension over urban crime, largely traceable to the prevalence of drugs, led a candidate for governor of New York in 1990 to advocate the use of armed citizen groups as vigilantes.

Among other current challenges are efforts to overturn a woman's right to procure an abortion, a right that already has been considerably narrowed; cutbacks in legal entitlements for poor people who are dependent on welfare payments and unemployment insurance; a weakening of religious liberty by the authorization of religious symbols on public property and the prosecution of Native Americans for using drugs for religious purposes as they have for centuries; and cutbacks on government assistance to racial minorities. Most ominously, the changing composition of the Supreme Court indicates that in coming years the judiciary will no longer be the bastion of individual liberty that many Americans have grown accustomed to expect.

The energetic defense of civil liberties is often thankless and frustrating, but it is essential to a free society. Strong and determined opponents have always used the rhetoric of patriotism and practicality to subvert liberty and to dominate the weak, the unorthodox, and the despised. Government efficiency, international influence, domestic order, and economic needs are all important in a complex world. But none is more important than the principles of civil liberties that are embodied in the American Constitution and Bill of Rights, reflecting a glorious tradition extending from the ancient world to modern times.

Notes

1. Korematsu v. United States, 323 U.S. 214 (1944).
2. Ex parte Milligan, 71 U.S. (4 Wall.) 2 (1867); Ex parte Merryman, 17 Fed. Cas. 144 (C.C.D.Md. 1861).
3. See L. Levy, Jefferson and Civil Liberties: The Darker Side (1963).
4. Quoted in 1 B. Schwartz, The Bill of Rights: A Documentary History 7 (1971).
5. Dred Scott v. Sandford, 60 U.S. (19 How.) 393 (1857).
6. 109 U.S. 537 (1883).
7. 163 U.S. 537 (1896).
8. Brandenburg v. Ohio, 395 U.S. 444 (1969).
9. Shelton v. Tucker, 364 U.S. 479 (1960); N.A.A.C.P. v. Alabama, 357 U.S. 449 (1958); Sweezy v. New Hampshire, 354 U.S. 234 (1957).
10. Roth v. United States, 354 U.S. 476 (1957); Miller v. California, 413 U.S. 15 (1973).
11. Chaplinsky v. New Hampshire, 315 U.S. 568 (1942). But see Rosenfeld v. New Jersey, 408 U.S. 901 (1972); Lewis v. New Orleans, 408 U.S. 913 (1972); Brown v. Oklahoma, 408 U.S. 914 (1972).
12. Rust v. Sullivan, 111 S.Ct. 1759 (1991).
13. Near v. Minnesota, 283 U.S. 697 (1931); New York Times Co. v. United States, 403 U.S. 713 (1971).
14. Metromedia, Inc. v. San Diego, 435 U.S. 490 (1981); Posadas De Puerto Rico Associates v. Tourism Co. of Puerto Rico, 478 U.S. 328 (1986).
15. Young v. American Mini Theatres, 427 U.S. 50 (1976); City of Renton v. Playtime Theatres, 475 U.S. 41 (1986).
16. Curtis Publishing Co. v. Butts, 388 U.S. 130 (1967); New York Times Co. v. Sullivan, 376 U.S. 254 (1964).
17. Burdeau v. McDowell, 256 U.S. 465, 477 (1921) (dissenting opinion).
18. In re Gault, 387 U.S. 1 (1967).
19. Cleveland Board of Educ. v. Loudermill, 470 U.S. 532 (1985). But see Arnett v. Kennedy, 416 U.S. 134 (1974).
20. Goldberg v. Kelly, 397 U.S. 254 (1970).
21. Shelly v. Kraemer, 334 U.S. 1 (1948); Brown v. Bd. of Educ. of Topeka, 347 U.S. 483 (1954).
22. Yick Wo v. Hopkins, 118 U.S. 536 (1886); Trans World Airlines, Inc., v. Hardison, 432 U.S. 63 (1977).
23. Craig v. Boren, 429 U.S. 190 (1976).
24. In re Griffiths, 413 U.S. 634 (1973); Sugarman v. Dougall, 413 U.S. 634 (1973); Graham v. Richardson, 403 U.S. 365 (1971).
25. Weber v. Aetna Cas. & Sur. Co., 406 U.S. 164 (1972); Levy v. Louisiana, 391 U.S. 68 (1968).

26. Baker v. Carr, 369 U.S. 186 (1962); Reynolds v. Sims, 377 U.S. 533 (1964).

27. Bowers v. Hardwick, 478 U.S. 186 (1986).

28. Youngberg v. Romeo, 457 U.S. 307 (1982); Schweiker v. Wilson, 450 U.S. 221 (1981).

29. EEOC v. Wyoming, 460 U.S. 226 (1983).

30. United States v. Paradise, 480 U.S. 149 (1987); Regents of Univ. of California v. Bakke, 438 U.S. 265 (1978) (dicta).

31. Johnson v. Transportation Agency, 480 U.S. 616 (1987); Schlesinger v. Ballard, 419 U.S. 498 (1975); Kahn v. Shevin, 416 U.S. 351 (1974).

32. Regents of Univ. of California v. Bakke, 438 U.S. 265, 407 (1978). 33. Calder v. Bull, 3 U.S. (3 Dall.) 386 (1798).

34. Lochner v. New York, 198 U.S. 45 (1905).

35. Shapiro v. Thompson, 394 U.S. 618 (1969); United States v. Guest, 383 U.S. 745 (1966); Edwards v. California, 314 U.S. 160 (1941).

36. N.A.A.C.P. v. Alabama, 357 U.S. 449 (1958).

37. Zablocki v. Redhall, 434 U.S. 374 (1978).

38. Griswold v. Connecticut, 381 U.S. 479 (1965).

39. Moore v. East Cleveland, 431 U.S. 494 (1977).

40. Roe v. Wade, 410 U.S. 113 (1973); Doe v. Bolton, 410 U.S. 179 (1973).

41. Bowers v. Hardwick, 478 U.S. 186 (1986).

42. Bowers v. Hardwick, 478 U.S. 186 (1986).

43. Cruzan v. Director, Missouri Dept. of Health, 110 S.Ct. 2841 (1990).

44. McCulloch v. Maryland, 17 U.S. (4 Wheat.) 316 (1819).

45. B. Cardozo, The Nature of The Judicial Process 17 (1921).

46. West Virginia Bd. of Educ. v. Barnette, 319 U.S. 624, 639 (1943).

47. Loan Ass'n. v. Topeka, 87 U.S. (20 Wall.) 655, 662–63 (1874).

48. Youngstown Sheet and Tube Co. v. Sawyer, 343 U.S. 579 (1952).

49. New York Times Co. v. United States, 403 U.S. 713, 730 (1971) (Stewart J., joined by White J., concurring); id. at 740–747 (Marshall, J. concurring).

50. INS v. Chadha, 462 U.S. 919 (1983).

51. Bowsher v. Synar, 478 U.S. 714 (1986).

52. Myers v. United States, 272 U.S. 52, 293 (1926) (Brandeis, J., dissenting).

53. Griffin v. Illinois, 351 U.S. 12 (1956).

54. Kramer v. Union Free School Dist. No. 15, 395 U.S. 621 (1969); Harper v. Virginia Bd. of Elections, 383 U.S. 663 (1966).

55. Boddie v. Connecticut, 401 U.S. 371 (1971).

56. See Cleveland Board of Educ. v. Loudermill, supra note 19.

57. Goldberg v. Kelly, 397 U.S. 254 (1970).

58. Dandridge v. Williams, 397 U.S. 471 (1970).

59. United States v. Kras, 409 U.S. 434 (1973).

60. San Antonio Ind. School Dist. v. Rodriguez, 411 U.S. 1 (1973).

61. Dandridge v. Williams, supra note 58, 397 U.S. at 485.

62. Reich, Arthur Garfield Hays Conference: The Proper Role of the United States Supreme Court in Civil Liberties Cases, 10 Wayne L. Rev. 457, 478 (Dorsen ed. 1964).

63. Scopes v. State, 154 Tenn. 105, 289 S.W. 363 (1927).

64. Marbury v. Madison, 5 U.S. (1 Cranch.) 137 (1803).

65. Aguillard v. Edwards, 765 F.2d 1251 (5th Cir. 1985); McLean v. Arkansas, 529 F. Supp. 1255 (E.D. Ark. 1982).

66. Hague v. C.I.O., 307 U.S. 496 (1939).

67. Shuttleworth v. City of Birmingham, 394 U.S. 147 (1969).

68. Laird v. Tatum, 408 U.S. 1 (1972).

69. Village of Skokie v. Nat'l Socialist Party of America, 69 Ill.2d 21, 373 N.E.2d 21 (1978).

70. See T. Becker & M. Feeley, The Impact of Supreme Court Decisions (2d ed. 1973).

71. Rust v. Sullivan, 111 S.Ct. 1759 (1991).

72. Clark v. Community for Creative Non-Violence, 468 U.S. 288 (1984).

73. Young v. New York City Transit Auth., 903 F.2d 146 (2d Cir. 1990).

74. Texas v. Johnson, 491 U.S. 397 (1989); United States v. Eichman, 110 S.Ct. 2404 (1990).

13

Civil Liberties in the United States: Changing Soviet Perspectives

Vasilii Vlasikhin

If we are to talk frankly, then better about something else.
(Gennadii Malkin, *Maximums and Minimums*)

" 'Who says that Americans are free?' Paid agents of Wall Street say this!"[1] Thus opens a book with the ominous title *American Gestapo*, published in 1950 in the Soviet Union. Nuances and subtleties aside, the Soviet vision of human rights in the United States could be reduced to this short formulation: the legally declared rights and freedoms of Americans do not exist in reality.

Americans Have Lost Their Rights

"Well, that is positively interesting," said the professor, shaking with laughter, "It seems no matter what you name here, it doesn't exist!"
(Mikhail Bulgakov, *The Master and Margarita*)

Authors of Soviet publications during the Stalinist years of the late 1940s and early 1950s looked across the Atlantic at the United States in the spirit of absolute intolerance engendered by the cold war. Soviet jurists naturally followed the "wise" thoughts of Comrade Stalin in their assessments of human rights in the United States and the west: "Previously, the bourgeoisie permitted itself some liberality. It defended bourgeois democratic freedoms and thus won for itself popularity among the people. Now not a trace is left of liberalism. There is no longer any so-called 'freedom of the individual.' "[2] The American bourgeoisie, imperialists, and monopolies had "trampled on individual rights and established for [themselves] a regime of police abuse and violence." All the state constitutions were "permeated with the spirit of racism and ignorance; they were all thoroughly reactionary."[3] American justice was "sinking completely into the morass,"[4] along with the writ of *habeas corpus*, which "had also ceased to act."[5]

At that time, American society really was living through difficult times. The cold war and anti-Soviet hysteria unleashed a political witch hunt, its edge directed against communists. The spirit of McCarthyism poisoned the political atmosphere. The House Committee on Un-American Activities feverishly pursued the exposure of "reds." The provisions of the Alien Registration Act of 1940 (the Smith Act) provided for criminal punishment for the propaganda of ideas supporting the violent overthrow of any governmental agency in the United States; it was directed against communists as bearers of ideas of revolutionary (including violent) transformation of capitalist society. Anticommunist laws were passed in the 1950s which, in effect, deprived the Communist party of the United States of the right to exist. This was, indeed, a dark page in the history of constitutional rights and freedoms in the United States. But was this evidence of "a beastly fascist regime" or a "rejection of any legality"?

"The reactionary debauch on an unprecedented scale" meant that throughout the history of the enforcement of the Smith Act against communists, 141 persons in all were indicted and twenty-nine of them served prison terms.[6] One hundred thirty-five persons subpoenaed to testify before the House Committee on Un-American Activities were found guilty of contempt of Congress for refusing to testify.[7]

Taking as one's yardstick a liberal constitutionalism, these figures present a gloomy picture—people were sentenced for their ideological convictions and for their membership in a political organization not favored by reactionaries. Their crime was their constitutionally founded refusal of self-incrimination. All the same, the question arises, if the convictions of 164 people amount to "reactionary debauch," "terror," "beastliness," and "fascism," then what words can be found to characterize the Stalin-Beria purging of millions?

Despite the evident progress of U.S. society in the democratization of political rights, the Soviet point of view on human rights in the United States continued in the post-Stalin period to base itself on the postulates of Stalin.

"Expose Relentlessly So-Called Rights and Freedoms in the United States"

> "Pardon!" answered Fagot, "I beg your pardon, but there is nothing to expose here, it's all clear."
> "Oh no, if you'll excuse me! The exposé is entirely essential . . ."
> (Mikhail Bulgakov, *The Master and Margarita*)

The post-Stalin period saw an enormous increase in the amount of literature about institutions of U.S. democracy and law, its system of justice and legal theory. A solid detachment of Americanists emerged. Analysis became more thoughtful and factual content more substantial. Propaganda-like criticism diminished.

Despite the considerable information about human rights in works on U.S.

government and law, the Brezhnev-Suslov ideological blinders worn by society as a whole determined as well the content of legal studies about the United States. The main result of this was tunnel vision, which excluded from view the rapid progress of the democratization of governmental structures in the United States at the end of the 1960s.

When President Jimmy Carter later launched a campaign in defense of human rights in the USSR and other socialist countries, the line on total exposure of the "class limitedness" of rights and freedoms in capitalist American, and the widespread revelation of the "attack of reaction on the rights of Americans" as well as their "wide-scale repression," acquired a new quality. After a certain delay, and on instructions of Soviet organs, a counterpropaganda campaign was launched. The decree of the Central Committee of the Communist Party of the Soviet Union "on the further improvement of ideological political educational work" (1979)—which L. I. Brezhnev called "a document of long-term validity"— pointed to the need to "expose the antipopular, antihuman essence of contemporary capitalism ... the real aspect of hypocritical defenders of rights and freedoms." This last passage I took from the introduction to my own book written in 1981.[8]

I take the above-mentioned Smith Act as an example simply because it was and remains a stalking horse of the exposers of the "reactionary essence" of U.S. law. Moreover, it related to the most cherished American right to freedom of expression concerning government policies. In 1957, the Supreme Court effectively paralyzed this law; in 1969, it extended the broadest legal guarantees of free expression to those who support views endorsing the overthrow of the U.S. system of government.[9] The Smith Act was dead in the United States but it continued to live on in the Soviet viewpoint of Americans' political freedoms.

Ten years later, in 1989, it was presented by eminent specialists as still being in effect[10] and was cited to justify a 1989 Soviet decree, later repealed, that continued to curb freedom of expression.[11] What is surprising from the point of political ethics is the fact that the Soviet law was so readily compared with a "reactionary, anticommunist" law that was at one time repeatedly labeled and exposed as such by Soviet communists themselves.[12] And it is not surprising at all that commentators cited a law that had not been in effect for more than thirty years and which American jurisprudence long ago threw on the scrap heap. Quite simply, here again the "Soviet viewpoint" surfaced.

American realities, when it comes to upholding citizens' rights and freedoms, of course have supplied no little material for Soviet exposés. But objectivity calls for a correct balance, which would be possible only through a thorough analysis of the reasons for not only the high level of fulfillment of Americans' rights and freedoms, but also their ongoing development. This author, who has carried on a study of American law, can remember no such works. Yes, and he himself yielded to the demands of the moment for an unfailing exposé at the expense of a thoroughgoing treatment of the subject.

A reader of these exposés, deprived of other information, could not but conclude that as a result of unceasing attacks against human rights in the United States, Americans must be absolutely deprived of rights. Only recently did the average reader learn that this was not so.

Individual Rights: Enduring Values

> To correctly judge nations one must study their general spirit, their vital principle, for only it, and not some character trait or other, can put them on the path of moral perfection and unceasing development.
>
> (Piotr Chaadaev, *Philosophical Letters* [1829])

The love of freedom is the vital principle of the American nation, the starting point for numerous theories of law. It shaped the nation, was the moving force of U.S. history, and defined the development of constitutional law and the principles and content of rights and freedoms. The judiciary, in landmark decisions regarding Americans' rights and freedoms, as well as political figures, activists, and organizations in the United States, took up the cause of defending rights.

The idea of the all-around protection of the freedom of the individual is melded in U.S. political and legal consciousness with the idea of the inherent autonomy of the individual. This seems to the author to be the foundation of U.S. constitutionalism, its principles and ideals. Thus the idea of the autonomy of the individual in the language of constitutionalism expressed a principle of popular sovereignty and a social contract of free, self-governing individuals with a government of their choice.

Among the principles of constitutionalism are those of limited government and the separation of powers. Limitations are put on government so as to prevent infringements on the freedoms and autonomy of the individual. The same purpose, the prevention of tyranny that follows from a concentration of power, is achieved horizontally through the separation of powers and vertically through federalism. Finally, a central place in a list of the traits of U.S. constitutionalism belongs to the principle of a person's inalienable and retained rights—once again, for the purpose of protecting the fundamental freedoms and autonomy of the individual.

There are a variety of sources and origins of American constitutionalism in the sphere of rights and freedoms: the theories of the ancient Greek philosophers; the natural law theory of inalienable rights derived from the philosophy of the European Enlightenment; religious and ethical norms and ideals; principles of the prerevolutionary, colonial American legal system including Roman law, English common law, and, in particular, such great landmarks in the history of British law as the Magna Carta of 1215, the *habeas corpus* act of 1678, and the Bill of Rights of 1689. These principles were brought together by the great American thinkers who stood at the ideological sources of the American Revolution.

Thomas Paine understood natural rights to mean all intellectual and spiritual rights, and the right of man to obtain well-being and happiness as long as their pursuits do not infringe on the natural rights of others.[13]

Because the theory of the natural rights of man flourished two and a half centuries ago and is often inseparable from metaphysical and theological doctrines, many American researchers do not acknowledge the theory of natural rights as the conceptual source of the rights of the individual and citizen in the present civilized world. However, many others, disturbed by the possibilities of attacks on the autonomy and freedoms of the individual which have been opened up by the technological century, again are discovering for themselves the moral and intellectual value of natural law: "theories of resistance to totalitarianism, theories of the self-realization of the individual, of political and legal progress of international brotherhood, all these, one way or another lead to the search for acceptable variants of natural law. . . . [T]he idea of natural law, resting on human nature, and looked at not in an ontological but in an historical and psychological perspective, and something to be realized in the future, is surprisingly popular in present day America. It gives one faith in the inevitability of political progress . . . ."[14]

The concept of natural rights not only affirmed freedom and autonomy of the individual, but also linked these with an individual's prosperity, that is, with the presence of property. "Life, Liberty, Property," the famous triad in John Locke's theory of natural rights, to this day are considered the precepts of capitalist democracy. The freedom of individuals through their economic independence is also one of the postulates of U.S. constitutionalism.

The American Constitution: Symbol
and Repository of Freedom

> The Constitution is our Mona Lisa, our Eiffel Tower, our Marseillaise.
> (Philip Bobbitt, *Constitutional Fate*)

The trail-blazing document of the revolutionary period was the Declaration of Rights passed by the legislature of Virginia on June 12, 1776, three weeks before the Declaration of Independence was issued by the Continental Congress. The first article proclaims in chaste style the natural essence of human rights which are "the basis and foundation of the government": "All men are by nature equally free and independent, and have certain inherent rights, of which, when they enter into a state of society, they cannot, by any compact, deprive or divest their posterity; namely, the enjoyment of life and liberty, with the means of acquiring and possessing property, and pursuing and obtaining happiness and safety." The primacy of the natural rights of the individual over the state was affirmed in the Declaration clearly and unambiguously.

In the elegant style of Thomas Jefferson, the Declaration of Independence asserting the right of the British colonies to independent statehood, had as its point of departure the natural origin of the rights of the individual and their primacy over the state: "We hold these Truths to be self-evident, that all Men are created equal; that they are endowed by their Creator with certain unalienable Rights; that among these are Life, Liberty and the Pursuit of Happiness. That, to secure these Rights, governments are instituted among men, deriving their just Powers from the Consent of the Governed . . . ."

The U.S. Constitution, adopted in 1787, did not contain any reference to inalienable rights. The founding fathers considered that natural rights do not need positive affirmation in the text of the fundamental law. A list of them could be taken as an exhaustive catalogue of rights and freedoms; this could lead to infringements on those rights not enumerated therein.

The Constitution contained guarantees of British origin—the right to trial by jury, the privilege of writ of *habeas corpus,* the prohibition on bills of attainder and *ex post facto* laws—as well as new principles, such as the refusal to grant titles of nobility and right of the citizens of each state to the same "privileges and immunities" granted to citizens of all the states.

The Constitution's preamble bears noting. "We, the people of the United States, in order to . . . establish Justice, insure Domestic Tranquility . . . promote the general Welfare, and secure the Blessings of Liberty to ourselves and our Posterity . . . do ordain and establish this Constitution for the United States of America." Scott Buchanan regards the preamble as a declaration of fundamental human ideals and values. It proclaims "truths which were fought for in the preceding revolution, the justness of which had been affirmed by the long experience of the deceptiveness of governmental authority. . . . They are formulated in the language of terse abstractions of the general good as a goal of the entire government: order, justice, peace and freedom. The authors of the Constitution knew that they were laying the foundation of an enduring tradition."[15]

But the absence in the fundamental law of the United States of a listing of federally affirmed rights and freedoms evoked sharp criticism of this document. Under the pressure of public opinion, the draft of amendments containing the principles of citizens' political and personal rights were proposed to the newly elected Congress in 1789. The first ten amendments to the Constitution, comprising the federal Bill of Rights, were ratified before the end of 1791.

The language of the Bill of Rights reflected Americans' deep-seated distrust of government, which they saw as inherently arbitrary and violative of rights. This idea was dictated by memories of the way the British Crown abused its political and religious opponents. The Bill of Rights is shot through with distrust of government: almost all the amendments making it up are written not in the form of positive rights possessed by citizens, but rather in the form of firm limits on the authority of government over the individual. The U.S. government does not give any freedom or rights; rather it limits its own capacity to infringe on them.

How strange it was to a Soviet person, still the child of a paternalistic state and prisoner of a statist consciousness, to read not "citizens have the right" or "the state guarantees freedom to the citizens," but "Congress shall make no law . . . no warrants shall issue . . . no person shall be held to answer . . . no state shall. . . ." These prohibitions are lost in a majority of its Russian translations. It seems that this reflects not simply errors on part of the translators, but also a conceptual misunderstanding of the nature of Americans' rights and freedoms. Thus the categorical proscription, "Congress shall make *no law*," in the Russian turns into the limp wording, "Congress will not make laws."[16] Taken as a whole, the principles proclaimed in these amendments established guarantees of the rights of the individual against governmental abuse which were utterly unknown in continental Europe at that time.

Fundamental law immediately and firmly occupied the top rung in the hierarchy of values of U.S. political culture. The cult of the Constitution is evident in the United States. It has become a sort of national symbol, an attribute of Americanism.

From a political point of view, the U.S. Constitution was undoubtedly created to protect the class interests of the young bourgeoisie, to defend freedom of private enterprise and the right of private property to the fullest possible extent. However, in the capitalist democracy of the United States, the right to own property and the freedom of private enterprise act as component elements of the American vision of freedom. Material well-being acts (and should act) as a means of realizing moral values, among them, the chief one—personal freedom.[17] The so-called average citizen may not be aware of the details of the judicial interpretation of the Constitution, and a majority of U.S. citizens know little of the specific content of its provisions. But "Constitution" symbolizes for the population a standard of justice and good. For this reason, the practical meaning of constitutional ideas and values has been a matter of heated political struggle between liberals and their opponents as to the meaning of those standards.

Human Rights, Historical Deformations, and Points of Achievement

> Let superficial philosophy howl about religious wars and bonfires of intolerance —we can only envy the fate of peoples who have given themselves over to the struggle of opinions, in bloody battles for the cause of truth, a whole world of ideas which we cannot even imagine, not to speak of throwing oneself into it, body and soul, as one may only dream about in our country.
>
> (Piotr Chaadaev, *Philosophical Letters* [1829])

Concepts of human rights and freedoms, as moral categories and as objects of the subjective moral judgment which underlies their legal formulation,[18] may be numbered among the forces shaping the history of the realization of human rights in the United States. Here it is appropriate to quote some relevant thoughts of Learned Hand, an eminent theorist of constitutional law and distinguished federal judge earlier in this century. He wrote, "I often wonder if we do not set too great hopes on the Constitution, the laws, and the Court. Believe me, these hopes are vain. Freedom resides in people's hearts; when it dies in the heart, no constitution, no law, no court can in any way help it. While freedom resides in the heart there is no need for a constitution, nor a law nor a court in order to protect it."[19]

Hand's reflections apply directly to that part of the U.S. political and legal culture marked by a long tradition of rejecting deviant ways of thinking and so-called unpopular convictions and opinions, strong traditions of conservatism, superpatriotism, conformism, and hostility to left-radical dissent. At no time in the history of the country did the U.S. government consider norms of the Constitution and the Bill of Rights to be absolute prohibitions on the limitation of citizens' rights and freedoms. At various times, both the U.S. Congress and the legislative and local government agencies of the states passed acts which infringed on the natural rights of the individual.

Neither the Constitution nor Bill of Rights ended slavery, protected against lynch mobs, or provided federal guarantees of voting rights. The regulation of procedures and conditions for realizing the important political right to vote was left to the discretion of the state governments. Such norms of law made it possible for the states to create a system of voting qualifications and conditions for exercise of the franchise which sharply limited the corpus of registered voters to the free, white, property-owning male citizens. Thus the majority of African-American people, women, and indigent persons were refused the right to participate in this basic part of the political process.

Throughout the entire history of the United States, in socially tense situations, the ideals of constitutionalism have given way to considerations of government policy.[20] (Norman Dorsen alludes to this in his chapter. Bertram Gross expresses in his contribution a critical view of the status, past and present, of U.S. citizens; many of his assessments are harsher than mine.) The bonfires of intolerance—political, ideological, racial and ethnic, and police—have constantly lit up the history of the United States. Many honest people became their victims. But these flames gradually forged firm guarantees of individual rights and freedoms such as are still unknown in many countries, including our own. From the end of the 1950s, the guidelines for judicial review (despite the eclecticism and fairly inconsistent norms created by the judiciary) were as a whole characterized by a liberal vision of the Constitution.

The preservation and expansion of legal guarantees of rights and freedoms cannot be explained only by the good intentions of the judicial elite. The actual fulfillment of the ideas of constitutionalism depends, to an enormous extent, on citizens themselves. It depends on how energetically and actively they defend these ideals from infringement by human intolerance. In this regard, Nat Hentoff writes: "When the Supreme Court makes a certain decision, the work of citizens only begins. When a specific decision encounters the resistance of the authorities (often carried out in disguised form) any concerned citizen may become a lay constitutionalist, locked in single combat with them. . . . In the opposite case, even a decision of the Supreme Court itself remains on the paper on which it was written."[21] Among these lay constitutionalists who worked their way through every judicial instance in the struggle for rights and freedoms were abolitionists, labor organizers and leaders, pacifists of different races and gender, and suffragists and their supporters. Staunch lay constitutionalists of the 1960s—antiwar activists, participants in the civil rights movement for African-Americans, and persons devoted to nonviolent protest—endured persecution, harassment, and police repression; and they achieved, through the courts, the recognition of their rights.

From the beginning of U.S. history, lay constitutionalists have had to protect their rights and freedoms from the infringements of reaction. "The Constitution will live as the charter of human freedom while there exist those who are endowed with the courage to defend it, with a breadth of view to interpret it, with a feeling of assurance to pursue it," said Justice William Brennan. To the extent that defenders of rights exist, so will there exist, with all the exceptions in practice, a regime of liberal democratic freedoms and rights in the United States.

What are the indicators of its historic progress?

Freedom of expression. In 1798 in the city of Newark, a certain Baldwin, a town drunk, watched the passing of President John Adams's carriage as it was saluted by sixteen muskets, and yelled out: "It's all the same to me if they shoot him in the behind."[22] Baldwin was convicted under the Alien and Sedition Act for the disrespect to the president. In 1971, the U.S. Supreme Court, in *Cohen v. California*, freed from criminal liability a person convicted of public obscenity directed against the government. A certain Cohen, a youthful activist and opponent of the universal conscription of the Vietnam War period, had been arrested for wearing a jacket inscribed with Fuck The Draft and convicted on the basis of a California law aimed at breaches of the peace, according to which "offensive behavior" constitutes a crime. However, other than the offensive slogan on the jacket, the behavior of the young man in a public place had been completely respectable, and the phrase that expressed his opinion could in no way produce the action it advocated. Reviewing Cohen's appeal after he had been sentenced to thirty days in jail, the Supreme Court established the principle that governments may not criminally prosecute a person for a public expression of "offensive words" if these words express a legitimate legal protest and do not provoke a violation of public order.

Thus, at the constitutional level, in the fulfillment of the First Amendment to the Constitution, U.S. jurisprudence supports the rule that freedom of expression presumes also the possibility of offensive and indecent expressions directed against the government, its agencies, its officials, and its flag, if by these actions a person wishes to express a protest or opinion regarding government policy.

During the 1960s and 1970s, participants in protest actions that involved the "Stars and Stripes" resorted to the most varied actions aimed at the flag. They burned the U.S. flag, stamped on it, tore it, hung it in unconventional ways, attached various signs and slogans to it, and made a phallic symbol out of it. All this the jurisprudence on the First Amendment to the Constitution considers constitutionally protected forms of expression. Freedom of expression is ruled to be of higher value than is patriotism.

Early in 1989 the author happened to witness a striking episode in this connection. An unusual exhibit was being shown at the Art Institute in Chicago. In a hall near the entrance on the floor there lay a U.S. flag with footprints on it. Desecration of the flag? The administration of the museum considered that this was an expression of the artist. A crowd of a thousand war veterans who came to the center with flags proudly raised on high considered it offensive and a desecration. The police arrived to keep order and arrested the patriotic demonstrators who tried to make away with the desecrated flag. The police, a government agency, defended the freedom of expression of the artist, the individual.

American constitutional law protects freedom of expression, even of those who reject the state and may publicly advocate, orally or in writing, the overthrow of the government. In 1969, in *Brandenburg v. the State of Ohio*, the Supreme Court ruled that persons may be held criminally liable only when their advocacy takes the form of incitement to specific violent acts against specific governmental institutions and if such actions may cause imminent lawless action. With this decision, the Court in effect annulled all state statutes forbidding subversive political slogans (laws on criminal anarchy and criminal conspiracy). The federal republic continues to exist, regardless of the fact that it gave full freedom to advocacy of its overthrow.

Two hundred years ago, freedom of the press in the United States was threatened not only by the short-lived federal Alien and Sedition act, but also by state statutes providing for criminal or civil liability for libel and broadly used by governments and private individuals against reporters and editors. Since the 1960s a punitive manipulation of the understanding of libel has been sharply limited in the United States. Until then this matter was decided by legislation in the states in such a way as in practice to make any imprecision in wording of the facts concerning an official possible grounds for bringing suit against the author or publisher of the offending publication.

In 1964, in *New York Times Company v. Sullivan*, the Supreme Court established the fundamental principle for applying libel law. For the first time, it defined a distinction between libel and protected expression. The plaintiff, Sullivan, was the police commissioner in Montgomery, Alabama. He had received an award of $500,000 in damages as a result of a newspaper advertisement that contained some inaccuracies in its criticism of police treatment of African-Americans. The Court ruled that when a publication concerns discussion of a socially significant question regarding the actions of governments and politicians, false statements do not constitute libel unless the allegedly libelous statement was made "with actual malice"; that is, with the knowledge that the statement was false or that it was made with careless indifference as to whether it was false or true.[23] The new standard of actual malice limited the ability of governments and politicians to bring suit for libel and gave mass media the right of error and freedom of judgment in the name of freedom of the press.

The United States has no government media censorship agencies. The only possibility of such kinds of censorship is for the government to petition in court to issue an injunction. The decision of the Court in 1971 in the *Pentagon Papers* case was of basic importance in this regard. Copies of these secret documents containing the results of the investigation by the secretary of defense into the question of U.S. aggression in Vietnam were leaked to the press by Daniel Ellsberg, who had once participated in their drafting. In mid-June 1971, *The New York Times* and, shortly thereafter, *The Washington Post* began to publish excerpts from these papers. The government immediately brought suit against the newspaper, demanding that the courts enjoin publication. Soon the federal courts were involved in what became the most heated constitutional litigation of our times.

In *New York Times Company v. United States* (1971) the Supreme Court found that the government did not make a convincing argument for issuing an injunction against publication of the papers. The Constitution gives the press the right to publish materials, whatever their source, free from prior censorship. In "extraordinary circumstances" the government may ask the court to forbid the publication of certain materials, but such circumstances were not discovered in this case; the court also did not find that the publication of the documents in question would cause "serious, direct, and irremediable harm" to the national security of the United States as the government had asserted. A decision in favor of the government could have established a precedent for expanding the scope of prior restraint in the future.

The right of peaceful assembly, demonstrations derives from the First Amendment right to peaceful assembly. In the case of *Cox v. New Hampshire* (1941), the Supreme Court affirmed the principle that the legislature may regulate the time, place, and forum for conducting a demonstration in public places for the purpose of maintaining order. The main conditions for conducting a demonstration are that it be peaceful, organized, and authorized by the city. The legal expression of this must be stated clearly to minimize the likelihood of arbitrary governmental response, and the decision must be free of ideological or political favoritism. Anything leading to a breach of the peace is ruled out.

Freedom of conscience is guaranteed to U.S. citizens via the complete freedom to profess any religion or to refuse to profess any religion at all, and by the full separation of church from state. Before the colonies became independent, taxes were assessed then to benefit established religious authorities. Today in the

United States, churches are not taxed and the state is forbidden from financing any form of religious activity. The United States has no government institutions conducting "affairs of religion." In public schools, religious teaching and Bible study are not permitted; the Supreme Court has ruled that even the reading of morning prayers in these schools is an unconstitutional act.[24]

Procedural rights of the individual in the U.S. system of criminal justice came in many ways to live up to human rights standards. In the first third of the last century the well-known jurist Joseph Storey, commenting on the Constitution, regarded the constitutional clause about due process of law as a second-order formality. But today a whole complex of requirements, principles, norms, and conditions of due process are recognized as following from or implied by constitutional provisions. The phrase "due process of law" appears twice in the Constitution, in the Fifth and Fourteenth Amendments. In the official commentary on the fundamental law, the explanation of the meaning of this phrase takes up nearly two hundred pages. Due process of law contains many-tiered, complicated protections against the injustice inherent in prosecutorial bias. It winds through the detention of the suspect, the judge's issuance of a warrant for arrest or search, the arraignment when the question of whether to release the accused on bail before trial is addressed, and the preliminary hearing of the case when the question of sufficiency of evidence to warrant binding over for trial is addressed by the judge. The indictment may follow and is in many cases the prerogative of the grand jury, an expanded panel of jurors which conducts a hearing on the question of probable cause for criminal indictment.

The arresting officer must inform a suspect that he or she has the right to remain silent. The suspect has the right to meet with counsel who may then be present at all interrogations *(Miranda v. Arizona* [1966]), and when the suspect lacks the means or refuses to employ counsel the court is required to provide a qualified lawyer for his or her defense *(Gideon v. Wainwright* [1963]). Failure of any officials to act according to these rules requires the court to refuse to admit evidence that was gathered during the period of omission, including confessions, and may result in dismissal of the charges altogether.

During the pretrial investigation, the suspect's lawyer is present for investigative activities involving the presence of the accused. Warrants for the sequestration of property, searches and confiscations, and professional activities equivalent to a search, such as wire-tapping, are signed by a judge and not the prosecutor. After arrest, a suspect must be given an arraignment before a judge. This can result in the granting of bail, jailing of the accused, or release until the trial date on the pledge of the accused to return to the court for trial.

The trial itself is conducted openly (only trials of minors are closed to the public); equal standing of the opposing parties in the case is the rule. The entire procedure, to the point of the rendering of the verdict by the jury, is controlled by the assumption that the accused is innocent until proven guilty. The accused's presence in the courtroom for the entire course of the trial is mandatory except in circumstances when the accused threatens violent behavior. No barriers surround the accused; a lawyer, not a guard, sits by the accused as personal counsel.

Because the principle of the presumption of innocence is so firmly embedded in the criminal process, the overwhelming majority of suspects are free pending their trials. Only those who are judged to pose a real threat to others, usually because of a prior criminal record, are detained. This author was present in federal court at the trial of a major Mafia figure. He stood indicted on more than forty criminal counts. When the court declared a mealtime recess, the defendant unhurriedly made his way toward the courtroom exit and went off with his lawyer to lunch in the small restaurant nearby.

The court hearing subjects the charge to long, scrupulous, and detailed examination. The question of guilt is established by a "jury of one's peers." This carries out the idea of citizen participation in the administration of criminal justice. Although juries do not always participate in every case, the institution of the jury trial continues to be one of the most important attributes of constitutionalism in the sphere of justice. It may take from three or four days to more than a week to select a jury for a given case. Evidence and witnesses' testimony are examined carefully by the prosecution and the defense, independently. In addition, the court is deluged by motions. Defendants have the right not to testify in any form, under the Fifth Amendment of the Constitution which gives them protection against self-incrimination. The accused may, however, testify voluntarily, and is then subject to cross-examination by the prosecution. The court is granted the authority, upon the agreement of the prosecution, to grant the witness—even if the witness is the accused—immunity from prosecution for those criminal episodes toward which voluntary testimony is directed.

The jury is responsible for weighing all the evidence presented in the courtroom. The judge is the final arbiter as to the actual presentation of any kind or amount of evidence to the jury. If evidence is ruled inadmissible because of violations of procedural rules, even if the evidence is crucial to the prosecution's accusations, the jury is not allowed to consider it in their deliberations. This is called the "exclusionary rule" and it is the judicial means employed against police abuse of power. It was prescribed by the Supreme Court in the decision *Mapp v. Ohio* (1961). Given the present prosecutorial inclination of the Supreme Court, however, the future of this decision may be in doubt.

The Supreme Court temporarily repealed the death penalty in the early 1970s, but it has been restored in thirty states for intentional murder under aggravated circumstances. Handing out a death sentence is an extremely complicated procedure, with the aim of preventing unjustified death sentences. [Norman Dorsen notes in his chapter the injustices inherent in the death penalty and the recent erosion of procedural safeguards in capital cases—Ed.]

When its authors wrote into the Bill of Rights a ban on cruel and unusual punishment, they had in mind torture, shackling, branding, beheading, and many other forms of medieval and painful punishment. Today, the constitutional ban on cruel and unusual punishment is used by convicted prisoners' attorneys and by civil rights organizations to improve prison conditions. Many prisons in the United States are overcrowded and conditions of detention are inadequate. When the courts find that such conditions constitute "cruel and unusual punishment," prison authorities are compelled to meet higher standards of treatment.

In 1988, this author visited the federal prison in Marion, Illinois as a member of a Soviet human rights group. Marion is the only category-six maximum security federal correctional institution in the United States. Prisoners there have committed crimes against the person while they are serving time in other prisons. The Marion prison has its own confinement regime. In the disciplinary unit, violent prisoners are kept in solitary confinement cells measuring approximately ten feet by seven feet. They contain one bunk with full bedding, a toilet and washbasin of stainless steel, a selection of toilet articles—lotions and deodorants included—a radio and a black-and-white television. The prisoners' lunch was fresh salad, bean soup with a dozen brussels sprouts, two small hamburgers with fried potatoes, condiments, tea, sugar, and chocolate cake. The standard monthly menu from the representative of the Bureau of Prisons of the Justice Department lists similar meals for all federal correctional institutions.

There are, of course, both institutional shortcomings and direct violations of rights in the U.S. criminal justice system. But when we in the former USSR wrote so much about them, it appears that we forgot about those typical U.S. legal structures and procedures intended to protect the rights and dignity of the individual against a powerful law enforcement apparatus. The Miranda warning, probable cause, rights to counsel and to bail, neutral and detached magistrates, juries of one's peers, the exclusionary rule, *habeas corpus*, the ban on double jeopardy, fair trials—behind these and other capacious abbreviations lie a host of legal protections that were not often translated into the Russian language.

Reproductive choice. In its decision in *Griswold v. Connecticut* (1965) the court lifted the legislative ban on the sale and use of contraceptives, citing an individual's constitutionally protected right to privacy. This expression (which does not have a sufficiently capacious analogue in either the Russian language or Soviet law) has found a place in U.S. constitutionalism as concerns the rights and freedoms of the individual, including what is left of the right to choice (to have abortions).

Equality

Constitutional equality of citizens is an ideal far from realization. The actual social and economic position of African-Americans, other racial and ethnic minorities, and women rules out any rosy depictions of American society. Yet the author is not pessimistic. In contrast to the slavery lasting until 1863 and the traditions and practices of racial segregation that began to be dismantled only after World War II, there are, today, civil rights laws to protect the rights, not only of African-Americans, but also of all other minorities. Conservative opposition is unflagging, but, beginning in the 1950s, the Supreme Court issued a number of decisions in a series of cases which greatly facilitated the liquidation of the most flagrant and legalized forms of racial discrimination. The equal protection clause of the Fourteenth Amendment expanded the criteria by which rulings of unconstitutionality could be made against state statutes that established segregation in public facilities. The Supreme Court annulled state laws forbidding interracial marriages and making miscegenation a crime and issued a series of decisions outlawing discrimination in hiring and admission to educational institutions. These last two issues remain at the forefront of political and judicial debate today, particularly as regards affirmative action programs. Affirmative action provides for a system of preference in hiring, admission to educational institutions, housing purchase, and so forth for citizens who belong to population groups that have suffered discrimination: African-Americans, other racial minorities, women, and the disabled.

Economic and Social Rights

We have at last reached that aspect of human rights in which U.S. society and constitutionalism are most vulnerable—that is, the question of guaranteeing economic and social rights. Under pressure of public opinion, Congress has undertaken from time to time attempts to affirm legislatively certain unrecognized and unprotected social and economic rights. But this kind of legislative action has turned out to be largely inapplicable in U.S. capitalist society.

Judicial lawmaking also has potential for guaranteeing to citizens certain economic and social rights. U.S. constitutional law doctrine knows an understanding such as "fundamental and basic rights and interests" of citizens. During the 1960s, the Supreme Court under Chief Justice Earl Warren expanded the understanding of fundamental rights, including not only those rights which were directly named in the Constitution, but also rights implied by it and following from its spirit. This interpretation of constitutional rights permitted the court to accept certain social and economic rights as fundamental and constitutionally protected. But the court held back from recognizing the vital human rights to work, to housing, to medical care, to education, and to social welfare as fundamental rights. Naturally, the reluctance to extend the concept of fundamental rights into the sphere of social-economic relations manifested by the liberal Warren Court has been even more clearly expressed in the activities of the conservatively reoriented Supreme Court.

As long as the United States refuses to recognize and guarantee social and economic rights, the exercise of political freedom of expression will often fail to produce intended results.[25] "We still have many people," William Brennan notes, "who don't enjoy the good things of our country . . . the gap between the rich and the poor appears to be growing. I suggest that we simply do not fully use our potential."[26] On the other hand, medical care is available to a majority of citizens —eighty-five percent—at reasonable cost, or free, because of state and private programs of medical insurance. Nor is it recognized that the largest share of the cost of education is met by scholarships, tuition grants, and other forms of financial aid to needy students, or that many unemployed are voluntarily so— and often are not recorded in the statistics on unemployment. The level of social and economic well-being in the United States is far from ideal but at a level which would appear ideal to most of my compatriots.[27]

Large corporate law firms expect their associates to work part time pro-bono (without payment) in the litigation for the protection of individuals' procedural and economic rights. A great number of private organizations are freely created and operate without hindrance to act in the political arena for the extension of legal guarantees of social, economic, and civil rights of Americans. Numerous societies and legal aid offices extend free legal help to indigent segments of the population. A great variety of legal defense organizations stand up for people's civil rights. Among the more prominent are the American Civil Liberties Union, the Center for Constitutional Rights, the National Lawyers' Guild, and the Legal Fund of the National Association for the Advancement of Colored People. Those available to defend the rights of the socially disadvantaged have at their disposal a very broad juridical instrument applied by a strong and independent legal community through strong and independent courts which are endowed with the authority of judicial review.

Political freedom is a sort of "propellant" for legal mechanisms. The author deeply believes that the stability and ongoing expansion of the legal guarantees of freedoms of political expression, of the press, and of meeting and association will eventually bring about the gradual development of legal guarantees of social and economic freedoms for Americans. The past experience of U.S. constitutional law justifies this prognosis. Out of the doctrine of fundamental and implied constitutional rights, the Supreme Court in the 1960s and later derived rights hitherto unknown in the letter of the fundamental law. Combining the Fourteenth Amendment clauses on due process of law and equal protection under the laws, the courts declared that the right to freely associate, to participate in the political process, to freedom of movement and choice of place of residence, and to freedom of information from government agencies, as well as many other vitally important human rights, are constitutionally protected rights.

As a whole, in the U.S. legal system, individuals have at their disposal a great variety of legal and procedural means for protecting or restoring their rights: the establishment of tort liability for various civil violations, the right to sue in court for a writ of *mandamus* or an injunction, the right to *habeas corpus*, and the right to bring suits in court for damages and for pain and suffering. All of these open up the procedures for appeal, including the possibility of initiating a constitutional review in the trial court—taking a case all the way to the Supreme Court. The potential for vigorous protection of rights is far from exhausted. As well, legislation appears to give constitutional protection to categories of persons hitherto unrecognized in many countries: the rights of the poor, the rights of apartment tenants, consumer rights, gay rights, the rights of the elderly and of children, and the rights of the homeless and the unemployed. Look at the proposals by one of the co-authors of our work, Bertram Gross, and his long list of organizations to protect rights. That is why this author views future human rights in the United States in an optimistic light.

I close with the words of Scott Buchanan: "We [Americans and former Soviets] must free our consciousness from stereotypes of the Cold War; we must really deeply concern ourselves with problems confronting both sides (the regulation of the process of technical development, which has gone out of control), by means of discovering new freedoms based on law. . . . The rediscovery of the kingdom of natural rights may possibly help us as well to love and benefit from the new world which is to come."[28]

Notes

Quotations from English-language originals are retranslations from the Russian, except in the case of official documents—Ed.

1. V. Minaev, *Amerikanskoe gestapo* (Moscow, 1950), 5.
2. J.V. Stalin, *Speech at the 19th Party Congress, 14 October 1952* (Moscow, 1953), 7.
3. A.A. Mishin, *Gosudarstvennyi stroi SShA* (Moscow, 1953), 8, 9, 36, 54, 68.
4. S.L. Zivs, *Reaktsionnaia sushchnost' ugolovnogo prava SShA* (Moscow, 1954), 4.
5. B.S. Utevskii, *Ugolovnoe pravo na sluzhbe anglo-amerikanskoi reaktsii* (Moscow, 1948), 20.
6. Nat Hentoff, *The First Freedom: The Tumultuous History of Free Speech in America* (New York: Delacorte, 1988).
7. K. Back, *Contempt of Congress* (New Orleans, LA: 1959), 181; cited in S.A. Chibiriaev, *Zakon Makkarrena i bor'ba za ego otmenu* (Moscow, 1975), 24.
8. V. Vlasikhin, *Sluzhba obveneniia v SShA: zakon i politika* (Moscow, 1981), 4.
9. *Yates v. United States*, 354 U.S. 298 (1957); *Brandenburg v. Ohio*, 395 U.S. 444 (1969).
10. "These provisions [of the Smith Act] are overtly intended to deal with and suppress representatives of communist and workers movements, fighters against class suppression, for the realization of bourgeois democratic promises so generously proclaimed in the Constitution of the USA and the Bill of Rights." K.F. Gutsenko, *Ugolovnaia iustitsiia SShA* (Moscow, 1979), 72.
11. In April 1989, the Presidium of the USSR Supreme Soviet issued an edict (later superseded) altering the USSR Law on State Crimes to read that punishment was prescribed for "advocacy of the overthrow [later published with the addition of 'violent'] of the Soviet State and social system." On the day the decree was published, newspaper commentaries hastened to assure society that the legislation of other civilized countries, including the United States, contained analogous norms restraining subversive expression. For example, the jurist, Academician Vladimir Kudriavtsev indicated in *Pravda* that the statutes of the United States including the Smith Act provide punishment for acts directed at the overthrow or elimination of the government of the United States, in particular by means of disseminating related printed materials. "Demokratiiu okhraniaet zakon,"

Pravda (April 11, 1989). See also Gennadi Ni Li, "Mnenie iurista," *Izvestiia* (April 10, 1989.

12. M.S. Savin, *SShA: pokhod protiv podlinnykh prav cheloveka* (Moscow, 1983), 54, 56. See also B.S. Krylov, *Vstupitel'naia stat'ia*, in Enn F. Dzhindzher, *Verkhovnyi sud i prava cheloveka v SShA*, trans. from the English (Moscow, 1981), 18.

13. *The Complete Writings of Thomas Paine*, 2 vols. (New York, 1945), vol. 1, 275–76.

14. Judith N. Sklar, *Legalism, Law, Morals, and Political Trials* (Cambridge, MA: Harvard University Press, 1986), 68.

15. Scott Buchanan, *So Reason Can Rule: Reflections on Law and Politics* (New York: Farrar Straus Giroux, 1982), 186.

16. *Konstitutsii burzhuaznikh stran*, vol. 1 (Moscow, 1935), 35; G.G. Boichenko, *Konstitutsiia SShA: tolknovanie i primenenie v epokhu imperializma* (Moscow, 1959), 223.

17. "The kernel of American formal culture," writes the political scientist Richard Merleman, "is shaped by our attachment to freedom, equality and private property . . . of these three values, personal freedom holds a special meaning for Americans." Peter K. Eisinger et al., *American Politics: The People and the Polity* (Boston: Little Brown, 1978), 268.

18. Alan Gewirth, "The Basis and Content of Human Rights," in J. Roland Pennock and John W. Chapman, eds., *Human Rights: Nomos XXIII* (New York: New York University Press, 1981), 120, 124.

19. Irving Dilliard, ed., *The Spirit of Liberty: Papers and Addresses of Learned Hand* (New York: Alfred A. Knopf, 1959), 144.

20. Vasilii A. Vlasikhin, "Political Rights and Freedoms in the Context of American Constitutionalism: A View of a Concerned Soviet Scholar," *Northwestern University Law Review*, 84, no. 1 (1989), 257–89.

21. Hentoff, 98.

22. Ibid., 83.

23. 376 U.S. 254, 280 (1964).

24. The Supreme Court's understanding of religion has expanded from a narrow, deistic definition into a much broader conception. In 1965, the Court recognized any sincere faith as "religious" and of equal significance with a faith in God. In 1970, the understanding of religion included any moral and ethical creed to which a person adheres with the force of traditional religious convictions. *United States v. Seeger*, 380 U.S. 163 (1965); *Welsh v. United States*, 398 U.S. 333 (1970).

25. Former U.S. Attorney General Ramsey Clark, a person with broad liberal views often publicly expressed, links political freedoms with social and economic rights: "No political freedom, no human rights, and even justice may be provided people who are deprived of economic rights. Human rights guaranteed in the Bill of Rights cannot be realized as long as economic rights are not." *Guild Notes* (September–October, 1982), 12.

26. *U.S. News and World Report* (January 8, 1990), 29.

27. When recently the average size of an elderly person's pension in the United States was $479 per month, in the USSR it was 89.2 (1990) rubles; the number of apartments and houses per thousand inhabitants in the United States was 380 and in the USSR 1,990. Furthermore, the average square meters of housing was 49 per capita in the United States but 15.2 in the USSR. Also, Americans spent $178 billion annually on education, while in the USSR the spending was $40 billion. See, e.g., Aleksandr Levikov, "Kuda idem," *Znamia*, no. 4 (1990), 157–59.

28. Buchanan, 320, 321.

14

U.S. Foreign Policy and Human Rights

Vladimir Kartashkin

Human Rights and U.S. Double Standards

Human rights have played a significant role in U.S. foreign as well as domestic policy. At the San Francisco founding meeting of the United Nations in 1945 the United States along with other great powers, the USSR, Great Britain, and China, sponsored the inclusion among the purposes of the United Nations listed in Article 1 of the U.N. Charter "to achieve international cooperation ... in promoting and encouraging respect for human rights and for the fundamental freedoms for all without distinction as to race, sex, language or religion." This statement had had no place in the preliminary proposals which had been adopted at the Dumbarton Oaks Conference in September 1944.

The U.N. Charter does not merely mention promoting and encouraging respect for human rights and basic freedoms. It obligates states to develop international cooperation for this purpose (Article 13 [b] and 55 [c]). Thus the U.N. Charter obligates states legally to protect basic human rights and freedoms of all without discrimination.

The official U.S. position on the binding force of the U.N. Charter, as on the international protection of human rights as a whole, shows inconsistencies and contradictions. This policy, as American scholars Thomas Buergenthal and Judith Torney write, can be termed at best a "tangle of contradictions often caused by incompatible considerations of domestic and foreign policy."[1] The Vienna Convention on the Law of Treaties specially provides that states may not cite their internal legislation to justify their failure to fulfill their international obligations (Article 27). The United States recognizes this generally acknowledged principle of contemporary international law with two reservations. First, U.S. courts do not recognize international obligations of the United States if they conflict with the Constitution. The Constitution is "the supreme law of the land." In a case of conflict between the country's international obligations and the

Constitution, the supreme law of the land has superior force. Second, international treaties may be implemented in U.S. internal law only when they are "self-executing"; that is, if their provisions are expressed so clearly and unambiguously that national agencies will have no difficulty in applying them. However, when such treaties are signed or ratified, the United States usually makes reservations to the effect that its norms are not self-executing. U.S. courts quite often cite these reservations and decline to recognize provisions of the U.N. Charter and of other international treaties that have been ratified by the United States as binding on them. Juviler points to Soviet isolationism on human rights before new thinking, and I suggest in this chapter further changes needed in the Soviet stance, but this stance of the United States is in its own way a persistent obstacle to the full realization of international human rights.

Soon after the adoption of the U.N. Charter, the U.S. State Department issued a special statement to the effect that this basic international accord imposes "no legal obligations to guarantee the observance of particular human rights and basic freedoms without distinction as to race, sex, language and religion."[2]

A California court in 1950 cited the U.N. Charter and the Universal Declaration of Human Rights (UDHR) when it declared a discriminatory state law to be illegal. This citation of international law to invalidate a state law alarmed some U.S. lawmakers. Senator Bricker of Ohio warned the Senate that if the principles of the U.N. Charter and the Universal Declaration were recognized by U.S. courts, then "thousands of federal and state laws will be automatically invalidated."[3] In 1952, Senator Bricker, with the support of fifty-eight other senators, proposed a constitutional amendment stating that no international agreement concluded by the United States shall have supremacy over national laws, unless Congress decides otherwise. During hearings on this amendment before the Senate Judiciary Committee, Secretary of State John Foster Dulles, speaking on behalf of President Eisenhower, assured the committee that the United States would not become a party to any international human rights accord which imposed legal obligations directly on citizens or whose purpose was to facilitate domestic social change. International treaties, Dulles said, embody the foreign policy of the country; they are contracts with foreign states made to further our national interests and guarantee that other powers will act to our advantage.[4]

Ensuing years brought no significant change in the position of legislators and the administration. The United States continues as before to refuse to become a party to most treaties that impose obligations to realize citizens' basic rights and freedoms. It has signed and ratified some less inclusive human rights treaties, but with reservations withholding recognition of them as self-executing.[5] The United States virtually ignored human rights in its foreign policy during the 1950s and 1960s. But the 1970s brought a significant change in human rights policy. During those years, public opinion in many countries demanded universal observance of the individual's basic rights and freedoms. Beginning in the mid-1970s, the United States has vocally and persistently declared the issue of human rights to be an important factor in its foreign policy. The inconsistencies in practice arise from conflicts between the views of advocates who agree with the UDHR that human rights are the basis of peace and justice, and skeptics, who assert that an active human rights policy may endanger national security.[6]

When seeking the Democratic party's nomination in 1976 as presidential candidate, Jimmy Carter proclaimed the defense of human rights to be one of the main planks of his foreign policy program. To a great extent, this seemed calculated to appeal to U.S. public opinion. The International Commission of Jurists report pointed out that setting the defense of human rights as a top priority for the future administration was a shrewd move on Carter's part. In this way he won the support of some liberals who had questioned the morality of U.S. foreign policy during the Vietnam War, the CIA's involvement in the Chilean military coup, and the Watergate scandals. At the same time, his sharp criticism of the Soviet Union appealed to conservatives. Carter's vision of the United States once again becoming a "beacon light for all mankind" through its promotion of basic and universal human rights standards sat well with the public[7] and thus played a part in his electoral victory.

Carter did not go beyond general pronouncements, important though these may have been at the time for the morale of human rights defenders in Argentina or the USSR. Much-publicized media events staged in Washington in 1977 around the signing, but not the ratification, of such international accords as the 1966 U.N. Human Rights Covenants remained yet another exercise in public relations without entailing any obligations for the United States.

To give the Carter administration its due, it did seek a more impartial foreign policy on human rights. It criticized violations of human rights not only in the Soviet Union but also in countries with which the United States was on friendly terms. But even this policy provoked conservative opposition. In 1975, a member of that opposition, the political scientist and future U.N. ambassador, Jeane Kirkpatrick, enunciated the doctrine named after her, according to which Carter's pressure on authoritarian friends of the United States because of their human rights violations ran counter to "the strategic and economic interests of the United States."[8] Those U.S. scholars and political figures who agreed with Kirkpatrick saw a foreign policy based on strategic interests to be more consistent and reliable than a more "pure" moral policy.

The Reagan administration followed the Kirkpatrick doctrine, giving its foreign policy a marked anti-Soviet bias. Elliot Abrams, one of the makers of U.S. human rights policy under President Reagan, said that the United States had "invented" a new conservative strategy in this field. It put additional emphasis on criticizing the policy of the Soviet Union and on using "quiet diplomacy" in relations with its allies concerning their human rights violations.[9]

This policy accorded with Ronald Reagan's declaration of a "crusade" against communism before the British Parliament in June 1982, in which human rights moved center stage. The U.S. administration set out on a program of conferences, research, exchanges, and funding which culminated in December 1983 with the creation of the National Endowment for Democracy—a private corporation financed from the federal budget. The endowment's aim was to contribute to the promotion of American standards of democracy all over the world. The actions of the fund, and of U.S. foreign policy as a whole, featured and anti-Soviet bias and interference in other countries' internal affairs.[10]

The Lawyers Committee for Human Rights assessed the Reagan administration's policy as mainly one of public accusations against its adversaries, the Soviet Union and other socialist countries [as communist countries called themselves—Ed.], while choosing to remain silent about violations of human rights in capitalist countries. This "double standard," the committee stressed, undermined the moral force of American human rights policy.[11] According to Professor Richard Falk of Princeton University, the promotion of human rights "often served as a propaganda vehicle." Falk called the policy of silence as to human rights in South Africa and other countries the "politics of invisibility," and the clamor around the violations of human rights in socialist countries, the policy of "supervisibility."[12] Since the end of the cold war, consistency in this regard should become easier and inconsistency ever more unjustified.

Intervention

To protect strategic and economic interests, the United States often resorted to armed force in the name of "humanitarian intervention," to defend "the lives and property of its citizens." On October 25, 1983, the United States invaded Grenada on this pretext. The U.N. rightly regarded this act of aggression to be a gross violation of international law, an infringement of the independence and sovereignty of this small Caribbean state. A U.N. General Assembly resolution, voted for by 108 U.N. members, including NATO allies of the United States, condemned the aggression and demanded the immediate withdrawal of foreign troops from Grenada. A few prominent U.S. experts on international law saw an act such as the Grenada invasion a source of "international tension, chaos and anarchy."[13]

But President Bush ignored such warnings. On December 20, 1989, he ordered American forces to invade Panama. One of the reasons for the invasion, Mr. Bush declared, was to "protect" U.S. citizens living there. There is no need to enumerate all the well-known cases of U.S. interference in the internal affairs of other countries on the pretext of "defending" human rights.

International Responsibility

Both Presidents Reagan and Bush repeatedly expressed concern over the violation of human rights in the United States itself. At the same time, they did not recognize any responsibility on their own parts or that of other countries to intervene on behalf of various human rights in the United States, though they assumed that responsibility with regard to other countries.[14] This situation changed dramatically at cold war's end, both in regional human rights meetings and during the failed coup of August 19 to 21, 1991, when the defenders of democracy welcomed the "interference" of President Bush and other leaders as a factor in their victory over reaction.

Modern international law holds that states are internationally responsible for how they treat their citizens. Individuals are becoming direct subjects of international law, with rights to seek international remedies against violations of their rights by their governments.[15] The United States has long regarded with disfavor any international monitoring of human rights within its borders. Monitoring bodies associated with various international human rights treaties that have not been ratified by the United States, such as the U.N. Covenant on Economic, Social, and Cultural Rights, the U.N. Convention on the Elimination of Discrimination against Women, the U.N. Convention on the Rights of the Child (not even signed by the United States), and the Covenant on the Elimination of all Forms of Racial Discrimination—lack jurisdiction over the United States. There have recently been some changes of the U.S. position on this matter, however. The United States has agreed to the creation of a system of monitoring countries' fulfillment of their international human rights obligations within the framework of the Conference on Security and Cooperation in Europe (CSCE). The western countries' proposals submitted to the CSCE meeting in Vienna in February 1987 supported the creation and a later evaluation of a permanent mechanism for monitoring the fulfillment of agreements on human rights and contacts. During the discussion of this proposal, it was decided that CSCE member states, including the Soviet Union and the United States, would exchange information and respond to each other's inquiries concerning violations of human rights. They agreed also to conduct bilateral meetings with an eye to resolving specific issues relating to the humanitarian and the human rights dimensions of the CSCE. Any nation could draw the attention of other CSCE members to any specific occurrences and situations.

A good test of nation-states' attitudes toward international protection of human rights is whether or not they have ratified the relevant international treaties. Today, a majority of countries are parties to the fundamental international agreements which set up appropriate monitoring bodies. However, the United States remains among those nations holding back—a situation which former Chief Justice Earl Warren called "sad" and "shameful," a situation mitigated only by the fact that the United States was not one of the fourteen countries who by 1973 had failed to ratify any human rights treaties at all.[16]

The Convention on the Prevention and Punishment of the Crime of Genocide was rejected five times by the U.S. Senate. Senators objected especially to Article 2 defining genocide—and not by chance. Many leading western public figures recognize that under that article the United States had been guilty of frequent acts of genocide against Native Americans, against African-Americans when it put down movements for equal rights and condoned lynchings, and against the peoples of Vietnam during the war there.[17] Not until 1986, forty years after the U.N. adopted the Genocide Convention, did the U.S. Senate ratify it. The president scrutinized the convention for two more years before signing it. The Genocide Convention obligates states who are party to it to pass implementing legislation. The U.S. Senate declared, however, that the United States would pass no implementing legislation or other measures forbidden by the Constitution. With this reservation, the Senate rejected one of the fundamental principles of international law, namely, that no nation may cite its internal legislation to justify nonfulfillment of a treaty.[18] Taken together, the Senate's reservations to the convention, as many senators remarked, "mutilate the document," "compromise" its ratification, "undermine the prestige" of the country, and turn the ratification into a "purely symbolic gesture," preventing the United States from using the convention as a valuable human rights instrument around the world.[19]

Several basic international human rights treaties—including the Convention on Economic, Social and Cultural Rights, the Convention on the Elimination of all Forms of Racial Discrimination, and the Convention on the Elimination of all Forms of Discrimination Against Women—have awaited Senate ratification for more than ten years and been loaded up with qualifications. According to the Lawyers Committee on Human Rights, "[T]he substantial weight of informed opinion views these proposed reservations, declarations and understandings, except those regarding free speech, as neither constitutionally necessary nor desirable."[20] These nonratifications have deprived the United States of a role in convention-monitoring procedures in the international community, and have limited one of the means of monitoring human rights fulfillment in the United States.

For New Approaches to Human Rights

I do not agree with the U.S. position, expressed by former Secretary of State George Shultz and some U.S. scholars, that progress in other areas of U.S.–Soviet relations depend on the fulfillment of human rights. Rather, I agree with *The New York Times* view that linking these problems hamper progress in both.[21]

Even while making human rights fulfillment the precondition for everything else, some U.S. scholars and statespersons strive, as they did many years ago, to give some rights priority over others. A considerable number of U.S. analysts distinguish three generations of human rights. In the first generation they place civil and political rights, which they call "negative" rights since individuals' enjoyment of them supposedly requires nonaction and noninterference on the government's part. They classify as second generation social and economic rights, which they call "positive" because their realization requires concrete governmental action. Many authors give civil and political rights top billing, as decisive, and they consider economic and social rights as "illusory" rights, asserting that ensuring these rights is impossible without encroaching on civil and political rights.[22] Moreover, there are attempts to arbitrarily set up hierarchies of rights and freedoms.[23]

The U.S. approach departs from that of most other countries and from the meanings of the Universal Declaration of Human Rights and U.N. Covenants on Civil and Political Rights and on Economic, Social and Cultural Rights; they all link the two groups of rights as interdependent and of equivalent importance. The U.S. approach appears in U.S. constitutional law and practice, and it was in the U.S. insistence during the drafting of the first treaties, on separate U.N. Covenants for these two groups of rights. It will be difficult for the United States to ratify treaties on the protection of economic social and cultural rights, according to James Green, because they are beyond the framework of rights contained in the U.S. Constitution.[24]

Despite their vital importance for individuals in their exercise of civil and political rights, economic and social rights have often come under attack in the United States as utopian and unattainable and as pretexts for curtailing civil and political rights. As the U.N. has itself acknowledged, most economic, social, and cultural rights may be realized only gradually, depending on the level of development and the available resources and population size in a majority of less developed countries.[25] Still, the U.N. Covenant on Economic, Social and Cultural Rights imposes obligations for their fulfillment only to the fullest extent of a nation's available resources.

In 1986, the U.S. State Department went beyond this qualifier to exclude economic, social, and cultural rights from its concern. It instructed its diplomatic and consular representatives abroad to omit the section on "economic and social situation" from their annual human rights reports on the countries in which they are stationed. In its note, the State Department stated, "The USA has consistently taken the view that economic and social 'rights' are aspirations rather than present obligations and as such are not included in our understanding of the meaning of the term 'internationally recognized human rights.' "[26] The United States is almost alone in this position.

Finally, the third generation of human rights are so-called collective rights, including the right to self-determination, the right to development, and the right to a healthy environment, plus an eclectic grab bag of contrived rights such as the right to sleep, the right not to be killed in time of war, the right to self-education, and the like.[27] Some U.S. experts quite correctly consider rights of peoples as human rights. The American international lawyer Louis Sohn writes: "International law recognizes not only the inalienable rights of individuals, but also certain collective rights, which are realized by individuals united together in large groups, including peoples and nations. These rights are human rights; the effective realization of collective rights is a precondition for the realization of other rights, both political and economic.[28]

Rights of peoples are basic human rights. They belong not to individuals but to the collective of persons forming a people or nation; they cannot be realized by a separate individual alone. In the course of advocating their rights as a people, the members of that people exercise also their individual rights (to freedoms of expression, of the press, of assembly, to participate in elections, and so forth).

Improving U.S.–Soviet Cooperation
for Human Rights

As noted in this volume, rights of nationalities remain an unresolved issue causing serious interethnic conflict. On the other hand, the time is ripe for a consensus on various problems among states with different social systems on problems, which until recently seemed impossible. Thus at the Paris meeting of the CSCE in June 1989 on the human dimension, the United States and Great Britain introduced a resolution obligating member states to permit their citizens full freedom to form political parties and other social organizations with their own independent programs.[29] This proposal was viewed by the USSR some other eastern European countries at the time as an attempt to interfere in their internal affairs and to foist on them values conflicting with socialism. Several months later, however, the situation had fundamentally changed. The introduction of multiparty systems in the USSR and other eastern European countries removed obstacles to adopting this and many other such proposals.

The significant recent progress in the international discourse on human rights widens the scope of concrete dialogue about really businesslike cooperation. These types of contacts are steadily expanding. Human rights questions have an important place as a ground of common interest (highlighted during the tense days of the August 1991 coup) in the former USSR's relations with the United States and other western countries.

The approach of the administration of President Bush to Soviet–American relations after its installation in January 1989 went through several stages. At first, the U.S. president reacted with caution to the policy of *perestroika* and democratization that was occurring in the USSR. The White House had its doubts about the depth and irreversibility of the changes taking place in our country. However, after a few months, when results of democratization became evident to the whole world—and also under pressure from Congress—George Bush stepped up contacts with the USSR. The expression "mutual benefit" gained popularity. The United States decided to increase cooperation with the USSR in a wide variety of spheres, from disarmament to human rights, provided that it benefited above all the U.S. side. Today, however, the expression "mutual benefit" is taking on new meaning of really mutually beneficial cooperation among equals.

One new form of that cooperation would be a joint human rights institute.

There, scholars and human rights activists could work on the issues of applying human rights worldwide, so as to create a true global human rights space. The institute would become a center for research and teaching in human rights and could arrange lectures on human rights for diplomats, teachers, military personnel, police, and health-care workers. A joint group of experts from the United States and the countries of the former USSR could assess the human rights situation in the United States and the former USSR and make recommendations for promoting respect and observance of human rights. This groups of experts could carry out comparisons of the countries' legislations and of their judicial and other guarantees of human rights.

Toward Cooperation for a
Common Global Home

1. Renunciation by the United States and the USSR* once and for all of the practice of creating "images of the enemy" of one another in our bilateral relations, taking politics and ideology out of their cooperation in all spheres including human rights. Moreover, human rights policy should proceed from an even-handed treatment of all states regardless of whether they are allies or belong to different social and economic systems. (This remains an issue for the 1990s.)

2. Recognition of the equal importance of the whole complex of rights: civil and political, economic, social and cultural, and the rights of peoples.

3. Ratification of all basic human rights treaties, without reservations, and recognition of the unconditional primacy of international law over national law. This requires bringing national law in line with the international obligations we have assumed.

4. Support for increasing the role of the U.N. and regional organizations in the sphere of human rights and increased participation in this activity.

5. Recognition of the mandatory jurisdiction of the U.N. International Court of Justice and provisions for giving it a greater part to play in the U.N. system.

6. Enhancement of the role of nongovernmental organizations and the monitoring of human rights around the world.

---

*Vladimir Kartashkin presented these six points to the Dialogue meeting in August 1989. In large part, they still hold. The first point's allusions to cold-war enmity and polarization show how far east–west relations further progressed by the time of the reactionary August coup two years later. The coup's failure two years later sped the breakup of the Soviet Union amidst deepening domestic crises and new threats to democracy. All this brought home the urgency of western cooperation—in the name of the U.N. purpose cited by this chapter's author: "To achieve international cooperation of an economic, social, cultural or humanitarian character, and in promoting and encouraging respect for human rights . . ."—with the dwindling Kremlin authority and with the Russian White House and the chancellories of a growing number of independent former Union republics.—*Ed.*

Notes

1. T.J. Buergenthal and F.Torney, *International Human Rights and International Education* (Washington, DC, 1976), 87.

2. Quoted from H. Lauterpacht, *International Law and Human Rights* (London, 1950), 149.

3. *Congressional Record* vol. 98, (Washington, DC, 1952), 911.

4. Cited from M. Moskovits, *Human Rights and World Order* (New York: 1958), 179.

5. Richard Lillich, ed., *U.S. Ratification of the Human Rights Treaties: With or Without Reservations?* (1981).

6. *Human Rights and U.S. Foreign Policy: the First Decade 1973–1983* (New York; American Association for the International Commission of Jurists, 1984), 6.

7. Ibid., 16.

8. Jeane Kirkpatrick, "Dictatorships and Double Standards," *Commentary* (November 1975), 34–35.

9. *U.S. News and World Report* (September 10, 1984), 38–39.

10. Tamar Jacoby, "The Reagan Turnabout in Human rights," *Foreign Affairs* 64, 5 (1986), 1076–86.

11. Lawyers Committee for Human Rights, *The Reagan Administration's Record on Human Rights in 1987* (New York, December 1987), 6, 22.

12. Richard Falk, *Human Rights and State Sovereignty* (New York, 1981), 10.

13. Francis Boyle, Abram Chayes, Clyde Fergusen and Richard Falk writing in *The American Journal of International Law* 78, 1 (1984), 133.

14. Falk, 4.

15. Myers S. McDougall and Michael Reisman, "International Law in Policy—Oriental Perspectives," in *The Structure and Process of International Law* (The Hague, 1983), 103–29.

16. Earl Warren, "It's Time to Implement the Declaration on Human Rights." *American Bar Association Journal* 59 (1973), 1257–60.

17. L. Le Blanc, "The Intent to Destroy Groups in the Genocide Convention: The Proposed U.S. Understanding," *The American Journal of International Law* 72, 2 (1984), 369–85.

18. *Case Western Reserve Journal of International Law* 10, 2 (1986), 277–82.

19. Ibid., 278.

20. Lawyers Committee, 37.

21. *The New York Times* (13 November 1986).

22. John Warwick Montgomery, *Human Rights and Human Dignity* (Dallas, 1986), 27.

23. Theodor Meron, "On a Hierarchy of International Human Rights," *The American Journal of International Law* 80, 1 (1986), 1–23.

24. James F. Green, *The United States and Human Rights* (Washington, 1956), 40.

25. Doc. U.N. E/CN⁴/1108/Add. 5, para 56.

26. *Status of U.S. Human Rights Policy*. Hearing before the Subcommittee on Human Rights of the Committee on Foreign Affairs, House of Representatives: One Hundredth Congress, first session (Washington, DC, 1987), 38–39.

27. Philip Alston, "Conjuring Up New Human Rights: Proposal for Quality Control," *The American Journal of International Law* 78, 3 (1984), 607–21.

28. Quoted in Richard N. Kiwanuka, "The Meaning of 'People' in the African Charter of Human and People's Rights," *The American Journal of International Law* 82, 1, 85.

29. Doc. CSCE/CDHP 33. Paris (20 June 1989).

30. Doc. CSCE/CDHP 17. Paris (16 June 1989).

15

A U.S. Comment on the Essay by Vladimir Kartashkin

David Forsythe

Vladimir Kartashkin has developed a historical interpretation concerning the United States and its policies on human rights that is essentially correct, although a few refinements can be offered here and there. His concluding ideas for the future are worthy of consideration, although some can be realized more easily than others.

As for his historical overview, many points are accurate despite the brevity imposed by space limitations. The United States does give priority to national laws when they clash with international standards, and the United States has indeed been reluctant to undertake numerous and specific legal obligations in the international human rights area—especially when they are supervised by international agencies. In this regard the United States lags behind most of its allies among the industrialized democracies. Especially are those in western Europe much more sympathetic both to *international* human rights standards and to their *supranational* interpretation. While the United States is more progressive in this regard than Japan, it remains far from emulating its western European colleagues.

Insofar as the western Europeans take the lead in trying to influence events in central Europe and the former Soviet Union, one can expect human rights considerations to exert considerable influence. Since Germany is the largest contributor of foreign assistance to that part of the world, and since the Germans seem to be taking the lead in linking human rights to foreign assistance, *and* since contemporary governments in central Europe and the former Soviet sphere seem to welcome that emphasis, U.S. hesitancy about international human rights would not seem to do serious damage to the struggle to institutionalize the practice of rights in that one region.

One might wish that Professor Kartashkin had paid more attention to the congressional role in the evolution of U.S. foreign policy and human rights. While he is correct to note that in the 1950s it was the Senate that pushed the

Bricker amendment which had the effect of pressuring the Eisenhower administration to eschew international human rights activity, it was the Congress, before Jimmy Carter, that in the 1970s insisted that more attention be paid to human rights abroad—and supposedly in the framework of international law and organization. Paradoxically, at different times the Congress both obstructed and advanced consideration of human rights in U.S. foreign policy. In certain respects, Carter was only adjusting to the new realities that existed when he assumed the presidency.

After Carter, Congress continued to insist on a relatively balanced approach to human rights questions, forcing the withdrawal of Reagan nominees for human rights positions, overriding presidential vetoes to impose sanctions on South Africa, and insisting that Reagan's allies in El Salvador give more consideration to human rights. U.S. policy on human rights abroad was neither totally determined by the executive, nor was that policy totally characterized by blatant double standards. Likewise, President Bush was confronted with an assertive Congress on such issues as human rights in China and Iraq.

At the same time, Professor Kartashkin is correct to note that Congress did nothing to alter the strained legal arguments by the executive branch that accompanied unilateral U.S. interventions in Grenada and Panama. These arguments, certainly insofar as they touched upon so-called humanitarian intervention for human rights reasons, merited much closer congressional scrutiny than transpired.

It may turn out to be the case that the United States will come to pay more attention to international human rights standards *within* its borders. In this regard pressures within the Helsinki (CSCE) process from the countries of central Europe and the former USSR may prove important. For example, the U.S. spokespersons in that process have repeatedly endorsed economic and social rights, not just civil and political ones. Should CSCE participants press the United States for implementation of socio-economic rights at home, starting perhaps with improved health care for the less fortunate, we might ironically see the CSCE play a role pushing for civil and political rights in the formerly Stalinist systems of eastern and central Europe.

It is likely that human rights, derived mostly from an international framework, will remain an important aspect of interstate relations in the northern hemisphere. Had the coup succeeded in Moscow in August 1991, U.S. and other western assistance and investment would have been curtailed—and rightly so—in the short and intermediate term.

This does not mean that "images of the enemy" can be regulated or abolished by governmental action. On the American side, such governmental action would run counter to traditions of individual liberty and free speech under the American Bill of Rights. Nor does it mean that by some magic formula anyone can transform the nativists in Washington who continue to attach qualifying understandings and reservations to human rights treaties. While there are many who oppose such nationalistic statements, especially in an interdependent world, there are perhaps even more who continue to be driven by a mythical American exceptionalism and who therefore prefer American autonomy to moral interdependence.

The long-term solution to these continuing problems on the American side is, however, precisely as Professor Kartashkin has stated: recognition of the validity of a complex of international rights, support for intergovernmental and nongovernmental organizations, and greater reliance on third-party interpretation of international law. All nations, not just the United States, will have sufficient difficulty in meeting these criteria.

Part 3

Toward the
Twenty-first Century

16

A Common Global Home

Vladimir Kartashkin

Toward a "World Legal Space"

The integration of all countries into a single world association is a basic idea of our times. Underlying it are not only economic but also historic, philosophical, religious, and a host of other factors. Economic cooperation gives a stimulus to interstate relations in all spheres; it makes it easier to develop contacts between people, to establish friendly ties, to solve problems of unemployment, to improve working conditions, and to realize basic human rights and freedoms.

The United States and all other members of the world community have a stake in close cooperation with the former USSR, in its transition to the market economy, and in preserving and strengthening its growing democratic institutions. A return to totalitarianism and dictatorship is much less likely since the victory of democratic over reactionary forces in the coup of August 1991. But further economic decline has already wiped out much of the post-coup euphoria, especially in the light of increasing ethnic communal tensions, and it could open the door to a more effective conspiracy that had learned the lessons of the failure of the "Gang of Eight." That would signal an end to the hopes of establishing a new world order and of guaranteeing human rights everywhere.

At present, especially favorable conditions exist for making a great leap forward to improve relations between states, to drastically reduce arms expenditures, and to reallocate the resources thereby freed up to meet the practical needs of humanity and to provide everyone with decent standards of living.

By the end of this century more than six billion people will be living on the territory of almost two hundred states. The character and system of international relations will have radically changed. Ideological conflicts are gradually fading away. All countries will be able to move forward with confidence toward the creation of a world market and, on its basis, a common human home or confederation of interdependent states.

Of course, all the members of the world community will continue to build their relations on respect for each other's sovereignty and independence. However, the meaning of sovereignty and independence will change fundamentally. The free exchange of information, the absence of customs barriers, and peoples' unimpeded movement across frontiers will characterize relations, not only among members of the European Economic Community, but beyond it.

International law will continually be enriched with new norms defining the legal rights of the individual in the world community. Differences in states' legal systems will remain; however, nations could reach, or progress toward, agreement on the meaning and realization of basic legal norms essential for human peace and development. The number of obligatory *jus cogens* norms would sharply increase.

Achieving an identity of all laws in the world community will be impossible, given the differences of social systems, of the national makeups of the populations, of cultural traditions, and of historical peculiarities. However, agreements have already been achieved which permit us to say with assurance that it will be possible to create a *global legal space* where similar and in some cases universal laws can operate, where generally accepted and concrete legal norms and rules regulating basic human rights and freedoms can be recognized.

At the present time, the movement toward convergence of legal principles and norms among the various countries of the world is concentrated basically in the sphere of civil and political rights. However, by the end of the present century, ever-increasing attention will be given to problems of employment, of housing, of the development of health-care systems, and of education and culture. The social and economic needs of everyone could be transferred up to the level of strictly enforced laws that are obligatory for all countries. These changes, of course, would not proceed at the same pace; there may be differences in development and in the definition of priorities. Witness in this regard the current scope of development of international cooperation in human rights. This cooperation has already gone through several stages—from individual agreements in which a few specific rights were regulated in general terms, to the conclusion of multilateral agreements which specify concrete obligations of governments to guarantee basic human rights and freedoms.

The stepping up of this cooperation at the present time is linked with the recognition of the priority of common human values over class values, the ending of the cold war, and the strengthening of a wide variety of ties between states. The common legal space which has been created in Europe has as its foundation a system of legal principles, norms and institutions, and mechanisms and procedures for guaranteeing and protecting basic human rights and freedoms. This common legal space can serve as a prototype for a future worldwide legal space.

Rule of Law

A global legal space would rest most securely on the rule of law such as has been achieved in many European countries. Among the countries with varieties of the law-governed state (*état de droit, Rechtsstaat*) are Austria, Italy, Spain, France, and Germany. Many fundamental elements and institutions—models of the law-governed state—are inherent in the system of common law of the United States, Great Britain, and the Scandinavian countries as well.

In the law-governed state, both government and society are subordinate to law and subject to legal regulation. There is rule of law in all spheres of social life, and the supremacy of law is inviolable. The basic principle and goal of the law-governed state is to guarantee the interests of the individual and the protection of basic human rights and freedoms. In fact, the individual should be the central concern of a state that is obligated to take all necessary measures to safeguard the individual's basic rights and freedoms.

Forming a community of law-governed states is a lengthy process—judging from the past experiences of the United States, Canada, and west European countries, it has been the work of centuries. In fact, some countries find themselves only at the very beginning of this road—or even only on its approaches. Only after this process is completed will it be possible to trace out the contours of the global legal space. It is built from the bottom up and the inside outward, though the international environment has played a big part too, as foreign responses to the attempted August 1991 coup pointed up.

The Supremacy of International Law

One of the essentials of the law-governed state is the supremacy of international law. Domestic means of legal defense in such a state are complemented by international ones—both regional and global. In this regard, both the United States and the countries of the former USSR face a number of significant decisions. In the Commonwealth of Independent States there is formal recognition of the priority of international laws over national law. In case of conflict between them, international law is supposed to prevail. However, in former Soviet as well as U.S. practice, until now international norms were not applied until they were transformed into national law. The countries of the former USSR, the United States, and the majority of other countries should lay out the international obligations they have assumed, not only formally but in practice, and should recognize the rights of their citizens to complain to national courts, basing their claims not only on national norms but also on international law.

Progress toward a single global legal space is inseparable from the improvement of the special agencies for monitoring countries' fulfillment of their obligations in the sphere of human rights, such as the Human Rights Committee under the U.N. Covenant of Civil and Political Rights, the U.N. Human Rights Commission, the Subcommission on Prevention of Discrimination and Protection of Minorities, the Commission on Women, and the commissions and courts of regional human rights systems. These commissions and courts work in contact with numerous nongovernmental monitoring, advocacy, and humanitarian organizations. In fact, a solid experience has already been accumulated as agencies for the international monitoring of human rights have developed through use. The basic purpose of such agencies has not been to coerce or to apply sanctions for nonfulfillment of obligations, but rather to monitor the fulfillment of international agreements. Another of the basic tasks of such agencies has been to render assistance to states in the fulfillment of their international obligations by making appropriate recommendations.

Progress toward a single global space must be accompanied by an increase of the authority of both global and regional human rights administrative organs. They must be given the right to issue concrete decisions that are binding on the states. Here it is especially important that all countries of the world community recognize the right of various international organs to investigate their citizens' complaints. At the present time, only two regional human rights courts are functioning—the European and the Inter-American. These bodies hear complaints of individuals and states and issue findings on them which are binding on the governments of the states.

A number of global agreements provide for the creation of an international criminal court to try persons who have committed international crimes. Among these are crimes against peace and humanity, war crimes, genocide, apartheid, and other crimes which are accompanied by mass and gross violations of fundamental human rights. Until such crimes are eliminated, we cannot even begin to create a world community of law-governed states. Now it is high time to found an international criminal tribunal to try persons guilty of criminal violations of human rights. Decisions of this court must be binding on all states of the world and the Security Council should be responsible for carrying them out. At present, the Security Council may not refuse to carry out decisions of the existing U.N. International Court, though its permanent members may employ the veto for this purpose.

It is time to expand the competence and increase the efficiency of the United Nations in the sphere of human rights. Many basic and auxiliary organs of that organization take up questions of human rights; they duplicate each other's work and make parallel decisions. In this regard, proposals to create the post of U.N. High Commissioner for Human Rights merit special attention. It would be the commissioner's responsibility to coordinate all the human rights activities of the United Nations.

A Bill of Rights for Our Interdependent World

At the present stage of the development of cooperation among nations, it is impossible to create either world law or world government. At the same time, we must today expand international cooperation and seek ways and forms for bringing the legal principles and norms of the various countries into closer accord and for creating new global international and regional human rights agencies. Our starting point for this should be the recognition of an ever more interdependent world.

We now confront problems of human survival. All humanity confronts such problems as the elimination of poverty, of sickness, and of malnutrition, as well as problems concerning the protection of our habitat and the solution to ecological problems. This calls for the common effort of the entire planet overstepping differences in social systems, and the willingness of the world community to place the solution to global problems above any particular sovereign rights and interests. Such an approach is especially needed if we are to achieve conditions in which individuals can develop to their full capacity and in which their rights and freedoms are to be fully guaranteed.

In the view of the interdependence of all societies in the contemporary world, it is high time countries agree to recognize a common set of international norms as legitimate and binding on all. The creation of a common global space should take as its starting point the general principles of international law and norms already inscribed in the Universal Declaration of Human Rights and in the Covenant on Human Rights, as well as in other international documents. These international standards of rights obligate the signatory states to follow such principles as self-determination of peoples and nations, the equality of all people without discrimination, equal rights for men and women, and culpability for criminal violations of basic human rights and freedoms, as well as many others.

These principles also provide the criteria for the legality of concrete human rights norms; the global legal space must be based in these principles. But the world has changed in fundamental ways since the adoption of these documents. For this reason, now is the time to draft a global or world bill of human rights—a charter for the twenty-first century. Such a document would require every state in the world to review its current national legislation, with the goals of eliminating departures from and contradictions to the charter's standards, filling existing gaps, and repealing obsolete laws. Only by such an approach will the way to creating a worldwide legal space be opened and a universal guarantee of basic human rights and freedoms be forged.

17

Goals for a Stronger United Nations

Bertram Gross and Vladimir Kartashkin

The cold war's end opens up golden opportunities for the genuine fulfillment of human rights. One of these opportunities is to take effective international action against the most dangerous enemy of human rights: war. During the cold war, the United Nations was seen in may respects as helpless in coping with any conflict that divided the two superpowers. Now that there is no longer even one superpower, the U.N. has begun to be more active—but on an on-again-off-again and highly underfunded basis—on development as well as on peacekeeping and peacemaking. It is also burdened by the heritage of declarations and treaties negotiated under the duress of the cold war and not related to the problems of the future. Yet neither major governments nor nongovernmental organizations (NGOs) are promoting open discussion on goals for action to protect, extend, and fulfill human rights and freedoms.

While individuals and groups are all, in Max Kampelman's words, "entering new worlds,"[1] many carry with them the intellectual baggage of old worlds. It takes time for most people to adjust to the cold war's ending. It is naturally difficult to realize how many U.N. actions that were previously regarded as impossible are now possible. Yet this possibility can become more probable if and only if enough people push governments and NGOs to do things previously stymied not only by the cold war but also by excessive nationalism. Such things take time to formulate and to carry out, so work on them should start at once.

One such step could be to reformulate the old 1945 concept of an international bill of rights.[2] In 1947, the case for doing this was stated by Professor R.W. Gerard:

> The particular codification of rights at any time will be imperfect and rapidly become less good. With any formulation should be included provisions for mandatory re-examination and reformulation at appropriate intervals.[3]

The present U.N. Charter (Chapter XVIII, "Amendments") provides a "re-examination and reformulation" mechanism. *If* we truly recognize the golden opportunities and huge obstacles arising from the cold war's end, *common sense requires that we plan to use that mechanism for both the U.N. Charter and the Universal Declaration of Human Rights.* At the very least, amendments are needed to recognize the principle that *"human rights problems,"* as stated by U.S. Ambassador Richard Schifter, *"should no longer be considered as essentially within domestic jurisdiction."*[4] They require some limits on national sovereignty. There are also important arguments for adjusting the permanent membership of the Security Council and abolishing the Trusteeship Council or converting it to a trusteeship for the protection of environmental rights.

In the light of these considerations, we focus on one major theme: open discussion of time-based goals for action to strengthen the United Nations. Such schedules, we suggest, emphasize *what is to be done (and undone) between now and the year 2000.* Flexible schedules could also be discussed for reinvigorating the human rights commitments of U.N. member states, the European Economic Community (EEC), the Council of Europe (COE), the Organization of American States (OAS), and the Organization of African Unity (OAU), and for improved monitoring by NGOs that communicate with each other more fully. The Conference on Security and Cooperation in Europe (CSCE) should give more attention to the creation of special bodies to deal with monitoring human rights violations. Legal mechanisms for the protection of human rights on the territory of the former USSR and in Asia must also be created.

Now that the cold war is over, it should be possible for business corporations, or their nonprofit subsidiaries, to obtain affiliation with the United Nations as fully recognized NGOs. Perhaps a conference of U.S. business enterprises, devoted to spelling out U.S. business rights and responsibilities, should be planned. Issues addressed at such a conference could include not only the right to property, but also the rights of managers, employees, and labor unions, together with specific rights and responsibilities with respect to the impact of business activities on the environment, on consumers, and on the people of other countries. Important examples of such statements can be derived from the more narrow provisions for the Sullivan principles on U.S. corporations operating in South Africa and the MacBride human rights principles that have already led to legislative proposals in at least nine U.S. state legislatures.[5] U.S. companies could thereby set an example for business organizations in other countries and for international business associations.

Other goals obviously need to be set. Some are implied by the work of the June 1993 U.N. International Conference on Human Rights. The U.N. Human Rights Commission and the various other U.N. human rights committees are already beginning to think of long-term schedules. This is also bound to happen in the new work of each specialized agency—the World Health Organization (WHO), the International Labor Organization (ILO), the Food and Agriculture Organization (FAD), the United Nations Education, Scientific and Cultural Organization (UNESCO), and so forth.

For example, WHO is already working on goals for the year 2000, focusing on epidemics, inoculation, water supply, and other vital public health measures. With more vision, WHO could move toward integrating the best aspects of health systems from different cultures (Euro-American medicine, Chinese medicine, Indian ayurveda, and so forth) while also dealing with the best of ancient and modern wisdom on nutrition and exercise. One can envision the regular assemblies of WHO as culminating in a world health assembly before the year 2000 to inaugurate a new decade of human health and vigor. We could work toward progress in combating not only contagious diseases (including AIDS) but also the major degenerative killers: cancer, heart disease, and stroke. We can begin to think of a higher quality of life for people, rather than longer life expectancy only.

Although a long life expectancy for the Security Council's present structure would not help to strengthen the United Nations, restructuring cannot be done overnight. Stronger roles for Japan and Germany (and possibly the EEC) are already emerging—not only financially, but also intellectually and culturally. It will take time to formalize these roles in terms of Japan's and Germany's participation as permanent or rotating members of the Security Council. Debate is already starting on larger roles for such other countries as India, Brazil, Nigeria, and Indonesia.

It may take longer, we fear, to fully review the work of the International Monetary Fund and the World Bank in the light of their actual and potential impacts on human rights and duties. Closer relations are needed among them and the Security Council, the General Assembly, ECOSOC, and the U.N. organs that deal with both human rights and development. Similarly, closer relations are needed among UNESCO, the ILO, and the Centre for Human Rights.

Unless the major NGOs build up the pressure, any of these goals could be unrealistically utopian. Obviously, new thinking is needed by every U.N. association (also needed is the creation of more such associations throughout the world). The same goes for every human rights association and network. Amnesty International is already talking about a human rights education project in third world countries which would focus more on preventive actions than on addressing violations that have already occurred.

Some people are interested mainly in short-term action. Others believe in making haste slowly, thinking of actions that may be possible only in the long run. Thought has already been given to naming the first ten years of the twenty-first century "The Human Rights Decade." This could be an historic move toward building what Myres S. MacDougal has called a "World Civic Order" based on respect for human rights.[6]

From now until the year 2000, many actions to bolster and more fully finance international agencies are bound to develop. Democratic debate on scheduling the most constructive actions will nurture the common awareness needed for the fulfillment of basic human rights and fundamental freedoms. It will be a part of the human rights education for a new world order championed by Charles Henry in the next chapter.

The following proposal is suggestive only. Its specifics, of necessity, deal with peacekeeping, the environment, and other U.N. activities essential to the promotion and protection of human rights. They are designed to inspire new thinking, intensive discussion, and alternative schedules for reinvigorating transnational institutions during the remaining years of this century.

A Discussion Draft of Possible Time-Based Goals

1993–1995

• Payments by delinquent nations (particularly the United States and Russia) of their debts to the United Nations; *additional funds* for human rights and election monitoring, human rights verifications, reparation of refugees, humanitarian aid for the starving, peacekeeping, peacemaking, and an expanded role for the Security Council and its military staff committee.

• Widely publicized U.S. hearings on the U.N. Covenant on Civil and Political Rights ratified by the United States in 1992, with full attention to the reservations that have been added.

• Ratification by all major countries of the Optional Protocol to the U.N. Covenant on Civil and Political Rights.

• Agreement by human rights organizations on a schedule for action on the U.N. pacts on economic, social, and cultural rights; on racism; and on discrimination against women; along with the major conventions proposed by the OAS, ILO, and UNESCO.

• Business and labor initiatives for education on personal, group, and corporate rights and the many duties and actions required for their fulfillment.

• Ratification by Russia and the United States of the Law of the Sea (thus far held up by U.S. opposition) and the negotiation and ratification of much-needed new environmental treaties.

• The appointment of a U.N. committee of experts to suggest the possible functions of a U.N. high commissioner for human rights, to draft the statutes of an international criminal court, and to suggest other ways and means to improve the activities of monitoring and promoting human rights by committees operating under U.N. covenants.

• Widespread distribution and discussion of the final report of the 1993 World Conference on Human Rights.

• NGO global conference on possible revisions in the U.N. Charter.

• Formal announcement by 1993, if possible, of major awards (funded by corporations, labor unions, foundations, or NGOS) of at least $100,000 (first prize), $50,000 (second prize), and $25,000 (third prize) in each of the following categories:

A. Poems or essays on human rights and responsibilities.

B. Essays on international military conversion to environmentally healthy civilian activities.

C. Musical compositions that might (in the mode of concerto, symphony, gospel, rock, jazz, or rap) herald the potentials (or horrors) that lie ahead.

Submissions of these works to be due in 1995. International juries to be selected under the auspices of the World Future Society, in consultation with the funding agency and UNESCO. Awards to be given in July 1996 at the Eighth General Assembly of the World Future Society, Washington, D.C.

1995 (The Fiftieth Anniversary of the U.N. Charter's Ratification)

• A general conference of the members of the United Nations for reviewing the Charter (in accordance with Article 109).

• U.N. queries on the strengthening of basic human rights and fundamental freedoms—to be sent to governments, transnational agencies, NGOs (including transnational corporations), and intellectual and cultural leaders. Results might be published by 1997, the fiftieth anniversary of UNESCO's 1947 query of philosophers on an international bill of rights.

1996–1998

• The appointment of the first U.N. High Commissioner for Human Rights, the creation of the International Criminal Court, and the restructuring of committees dealing with human rights under U.N. covenants.

• Ratification of amendments to the U.N. Charter by members of the United Nations, including all the permanent members of the Security Council.

1998 (The Fiftieth Anniversary of the Universal Declaration of Human Rights)

• Pastoral letters or other statements of moral commitment to the future of fundamental rights and duties by religious organizations or individual spiritual leaders.

• Completion of the first draft (together with alternative wordings) of a General Assembly resolution for a global bill of rights and duties. In addition to remedying defects, this resolution might recognize that the most dangerous enemies of human rights are war, poverty, starvation, oppression, and prejudice.

1999 (The Hundredth Anniversary of the First Hague Peace Conference)

• *Some schedules already call for the next Hague Peace Conference to be convened in 1999 under U.N. auspices.*

2000

• Adoption of the U.N. General Assembly resolution on a global bill of rights and duties. U.N. proclamation of the first decade of the twenty-first century as "The Human Rights Decade." Ratification by the major countries of a revised or amended U.N. Charter.

• Maturation of the Security Council's roles on human rights, humanitarian affairs, peacemaking, and peacekeeping. *U.N. recruitment of volunteers from among national armed services to supplement (and perhaps eventually replace) peacekeeping and peacemaking forces, with mature development of a U.N. doctrine governing the use of potential, threatened, or actual force.*

• Stronger U.N. and regional nonproliferation controls over nuclear, chemical, and bacteriological, and other weapons of mass destruction.

Notes

1. Max Kampelman, *Entering New Worlds* (New York: HarperCollins, 1992). Although a Hubert Humphrey Democrat, Ambassador Kampelman has headed many of the U.S. delegations at the Conference for Security and Cooperation in Europe. As head of the U.S. delegation to the Geneva negotiations on nuclear and space arms reduction, he has been called the father of the INF treaty. He now serves as Chair, Board of Governors, United Nations Association of the U.S.

2. "Under this document," stated President Harry Truman in his June 26, 1945 address on the U.N. Charter, "we have good reason to expect the framing of an international bill of rights. . . ." (Cyril Clemens, ed., *Truman Speaks, 1946*, [Kraus 1969], 56). Since then, the term has come to embrace only four documents: the Universal Declaration of Human Rights; the U.N. Covenant on Economic, Cultural and Social Rights; the U.N. Covenant on Civil and Political Rights; and the Optional Protocol to the Civil and Political Rights Covenant. The case for updating this concept appears in Vladimir Kartashkin's "A Common Global Home" (chapter 16 of the present volume).

3. R.W. Gerard, "The Rights of Man: A Biological Approach," in UNESCO, *Human Rights: Comments and Interpretations* (Allan Wingate, 1947), 209.

4. Richard Schifter, former Assistant Secretary of State for Human Rights and Humanitarian Affairs, at Geneva, 1991. This echoes President Truman's June 26, 1945 address: "We all have to recognize—no matter how great our strength—that we must deny ourselves the license to do always as we please. (Cyril Clemens, ed., *Truman Speaks, 1946* [Kraus, 1969], 56).

5. John Francis Burke, "The MacBride Principles: A Case of Human Rights," *Freedom Review* (March–April 1992), 9.

6. M.S. MacDougal, et al., "The World Process of Effective Power: The Global War System," in Myres S. MacDougal and W. Michael Reisman, eds., *Power and Policy in the Quest of Law* (Boston: Nijhoff, 1968), 353–414.

18

Human Rights Education for a New World Order

Charles Henry

The waning of the cold war has presented an unprecedented opportunity to advance the interests not only of the citizens of the former Soviet Union and the United States, but citizens of all the world. In fact, the leaders of both the former Soviet Union and the United States have recognized this opportunity by calling for a "new civilization" or a "new world order." If these statements are to move beyond the old world orders of imperialism and manifest destiny, they must address the concept of human rights. A "new civilization" or "new world order" must be based on fundamental human rights that are universally recognized and respected. If such a development is to occur, then human rights education must assume the status of a top priority for citizens of all countries.

It is often assumed that no one really objects to human rights education. However, the kind of human rights education referred to is generally a very narrow, rigid, and brief exposure to the Universal Declaration of Human Rights in a formal school setting. This type of human rights education will do little more to advance the prospects of a "new civilization" than have past efforts at exporting western constitutions to "underdeveloped" societies. A truly liberating human rights education must be seen as an instrument for empowering people and must arise from or at least involve their own cultural context. That is, many rights are "universal ideals" in the sense that they are widely known by elites in the world community; however, they cannot be accepted and acted upon by nonelites unless they are adaptable to or rooted in the unique cultures and resources of different societies. Human rights education, then, must play the mediating role in transforming these universally recognized ideals into practical instruments of empowerment at the individual and local level.

If we adopt this broader, more radical notion of human rights education we can see that there are likely to be significant obstacles to its implementation. Just as the Soviet–U.S. dialogue on human rights was often stalled over the question of economic and social rights versus political and civil rights, the implementation of a human rights education that empowers people will face serious opposition by those governments and private groups and individuals who profit from the denial of human rights to many. The first and most traditional objection to human rights education has come from local and national governments who declare that international standards threaten their authority and autonomy. The second obstacle to human rights education are those private groups and individuals (often men) who see such education as challenging their authority and autonomy in the family or at the workplace. A final obstacle to human rights education is its limitation to the classroom when in fact it should pervade the criminal justice system, the military, the union halls, and the corporate boardrooms. The battle for human rights education in itself is an empowering event because true education is a liberating experience. Those who object to human rights education recognize its power and therefore seek to control its definition, presentation, and use. This work seeks to challenge these definitions and their traditional presentation and use.

The National v. International Rights Debate

> Today, education is perhaps the most important function of state and local governments. Compulsory school attendance laws and the great expenditures for education both demonstrate our recognition of the importance of education to our most basic public responsibilities, even service in the armed forces. It is the very foundation of good citizenship. Today it is the principle instrument in awakening the child to cultural values, in preparing him for later professional training, and in helping him to adjust normally to his environment. In these days it is doubtful that any child may reasonably be expected to succeed in life if he is denied the opportunity of an education. Such an opportunity, where the state has undertaken to provide it, is a right which must be made available to all on equal terms.[1]

In its most important human rights case in the twentieth century, the United States Supreme Court in its 1954 *Brown* decision recognized the central role of the school in socializing the child and preparing the child for the workplace. In striking down school desegregation, the Court also recognized the central role of the state in providing for equal educational opportunity if any child is "to succeed in life." The *Brown* decision serves as a metaphor for our discussion of human rights education on at least three counts.

First, it was a decision reached by the courts. Thus, the arguments in *Brown* were framed in legal terms and debated by lawyers. Although the impact was society wide, nonlawyers had little opportunity to engage directly in the conflict. The Supreme Court is the least democratic body at the national level and its decision-making is done largely in secret. While one must applaud the Court for taking action when the Congress and the president hesitated, the lack of popular support or participation in the decision meant, in effect, that its implementation was ignored or resisted by large segments of the population. According to some, the Supreme Court went beyond the violation of the freedom to attend the same schools to question the effects of schooling. This shift to look at the results as a measure of the degree of equality had not been implied before and began to shift the burden of performance from the child to the school. For many, the Court confused the issue by making integration the measure of equality of education.[2] Whether this confusion could have been corrected by nonelite and nonlegal input is a matter of speculation.

Second, it is not coincidental that the *Brown* decision occurred at the height of McCarthyism in the United States. In the struggle for ideological supremacy at that time, the Soviet Union used the existence of separate and unequal "Jim Crow" schools in the United States to great effect with third world audiences. The Supreme Court, the president, and the National Association for the Advancement of Colored People (NAACP) were all aware of the influence of international politics on the case. However, this ideological struggle was not confined to the courts alone. In the state of Ohio, for example, schools were required to teach capitalism before exposing students to socialism. Florida specifically required a course entitled "Americanism and Communism," in which neither the teacher nor the textual material assigned to the course could "present Communism as preferable to the system of constitutional government and the free enterprise, competitive economy indigenous to the United States."[3]

Third, the ideological defense of capitalism has played a major role in domestic opposition to international human rights treaties. Conservative opponents of civil rights in the United States have used the threat of communist and socialist influence in both the pre- and post-*Brown* eras to defeat U.S. ratification of international human rights instruments. They have argued that such instruments as the Covenant on Economic, Social and Cultural Rights and the Covenant on Civil and Political Rights constitute violations of domestic jurisdiction. Frank Holman, president of the American Bar Association from 1948 to 1949, provides a classic example of such reasoning:

> I pointed out that if, in driving me from the airport, [someone] had unfortunately run over a negro child running out into the street in front of him, what would have been a local offense under a charge of gross negligence or involuntary manslaughter would, under the Genocide Convention, because of the racial differential, not be a local crime but an international crime and that [he] could be transplanted someplace overseas for trial.[4]

Such legal reasoning was used by Southern states to protect themselves from both national and international efforts to provide basic human rights to African-American citizens. By confining the struggle to the courtroom, conservative forces were able to delay significantly federal civil rights action and to this day have successfully delayed U.S. ratification of major international human rights instruments.

It is interesting to note that in the post-*Brown* era, conservatives have once again sought to limit the role of the federal government in providing equal educational opportunity. The Reagan administration sought to narrow the public sphere and limit the definition of what constitutes legitimate public interest. The block grant approach, for example, removed issues from the national level to the state level and lowered expectations of federal assistance. Individualization and privatization of the public interest attempted to redefine equality as choice, hence tuition tax credits and tuition vouchers were posed as solutions to the problem of inequality of education. The burden to produce was shifted back to the student. A wave of national educational studies focused on problems in the student-learning process including curricula, testing, planning, academic standards, length of the school year, and teacher certification. These conservative efforts emphasized a free market approach to education in which parents would receive vouchers to send their children to the best public or private school as measured by a new set of standardized national tests. This proposal, as well as many of the national educational studies focused on excellence rather than equality. Time and again, the message was raising standards and going back to the basics in order to compete in the world marketplace. Strikingly absent from these discussions was any link to a "new world order" and the need for human rights education.

Private v. Public Rights

In March 1991, Brazil's Supreme Court ruled that a man can no longer kill his wife and win an acquittal on the grounds of "legitimate defense of honor." The ruling ended a ten-year legal battle on behalf of thousands of murdered women whose husbands had claimed defense of their honor as justification for killing women accused of adultery. In the interior of the country, it was reported that it was easier and cheaper for a man to hire a gunslinger to kill his wife than to get a divorce and to separate the property. Although the "defense of honor" strategy had never been part of the legal code of Brazil, it had been used by lawyers to win acquittals in thousands of cases. Brazil's Supreme Court rejected the honor defense in a three-to-two decision.[5]

The Brazil decision raises a key question for human rights advocates: How can such a fundamentally flawed concept as "legitimate defense of honor" be permitted to exist until nearly the twenty-first century to deny the most fundamental of all human rights—the right to life. The answer involves looking at a number of obstacles that prevent us from giving the same status to human rights claims of the relatively powerless—women, children, and minorities—as we to the claims of the powerful—men, ethnic majorities, and corporations. These same obstacles prevent widespread knowledge or awareness of human rights.

Human rights, like public education, is a relatively new concept. Prior to the industrial revolution, there was little upward mobility and rights had little meaning apart from responsibilities. The master was responsible for the slave, the landlord for the serf, the father for the family. The weaker partner in these relationships had no standing in the community to claim equal rights. The right to rule itself was based on the power interests of dominant families or groups. Remedies for the violations of rights or responsibilities were sporadic at best and implemented by persons or institutions under the control of the most powerful in society.

Education, like rights, was a private matter for the family. Boys were trained to follow in the footsteps of their fathers, while girls, like their mothers, were often given the dual tasks of homemaking and economic labor. The few groups that might require some education beyond the home—merchants, for example— were taught in private or church-related schools. Thus, the family was directly responsible for the welfare and education of its members, and the community (nation) had no responsibility, hence no claims could be made on it.

For nearly three centuries, the notion of national sovereignty has been widely accepted. The rise of the nation-state has coincided with the industrial revolution. The acceptance of national sovereignty has grown along with the responsibility of national governments to provide for or adjudicate on the competing rights and claims of its citizens. Since the industrial revolution, the autonomy, stability, and security of the family has been replaced by the instability and relatively less personal security of a more mobile society. In the tradeoff, two institutions have come forward to replace the role of the family. In the economic sphere, the corporation has replaced the family as the unit of production. At the level of social welfare, including education, the nation-state has assumed various responsibilities once held by family members. In assuming these responsibilities, the nation-state has subjected itself to claims against it when these responsibilities are not met. It has also taken on the duty of providing remedies for the violations of rights in all spheres.

Much of the human rights activity in the United States has been directed toward the government. According to one author, an entire rights industry has developed to make claims on the government for the disabled, minorities, senior citizens, women, children, gays, the poor, the homeless, and so on.[6] The emphasis on governmental redress seems natural in a political system that allows the public to hold at least some government officials accountable for their actions. The focus on governmental action, however, has often served to obscure human rights abuses in the private sector.

Only in the last twenty years have Americans sought to hold corporations responsible for actions that negatively affect social welfare or individual rights. Perhaps beginning with Ralph Nader's attack on the lack of safety standards in the auto industry, there has been a gradual escalation of demands on corporations. Coinciding with the shift of nearly half of all women into the labor force, citizens have begun to demand such things as child-care facilities from their employers. Of course, the greatest recognition of the influence of private actions on the general social welfare has come with the rise of the environmental movement.

While citizens have challenged corporations on issues related to social welfare, there has been more reluctance to tackle issues related to economic rights. Legislation requiring notice of plant closures is illustrative of the minimal demands made in this area. The battle over quotas in the proposed 1990 and 1991 Civil Rights Act was really a debate over the responsibility of corporations to justify hiring practices that result in a disproportionate impact on women or minorities. The strong tradition of private property limits public support for claims against private industry. Ironically, the former Soviet Union went through the reverse process. A strong tradition of "public property" makes citizens of the countries of the former Soviet Union suspicious of privatization plans that could reduce their job security or lead to social injustice. At the same time, property concentrated in government hands destroyed economic incentives and led to corruption, mismanagement, and shortages.

In the Soviet system, economic planning shifted the responsibility for economic production and social welfare from the family to the state. In the United States, economic production is in private hands but responsibility for social welfare has been shifted to the state. Each system reduced the incentives for parental responsibility of children. Yet the home is the primary shaper of a child's identity and notions of right and wrong. In short, the family develops the child's basic character and hence its basic conception of human rights.

Human rights education must begin at home if the school is to have any impact on the development of human rights concepts in children. After all, children spend much more time out of school than in school. If the child is exposed to domestic violence and arbitrary decision-making at home, it is unlikely that the school can overcome these negative influences. These negative lessons, that the wealthier, stronger party is always right, are taught through the relationships of husband and wife or parent and child. Such lessons are easily transferred to personal relationships and political relationships between countries. [The next chapter develops this point.—Ed.]

A "new world order" must not recognize any private sphere that condones abuse of human rights. Education in human rights cannot be limited to the legal world of the judge. Human rights education cannot be limited to the public world of the government official. And human rights education cannot be limited to the school world of the teacher.

Formal v. Informal Human Rights Education

Efforts by governments at human rights education have lagged, despite their strong endorsement of the Universal Declaration of Human Rights in 1948. In proclaiming the Universal Declaration "a common standard of achievement for all peoples and all nations," the preamble to that Declaration urged that "every individual and every organ of society, keeping this Declaration constantly in mind, shall strive by teaching and education to promote respect for these rights and freedoms."

Various international covenants, treaties, and conventions since 1948 have stressed the importance of human rights education. Most recently, Article 16 of the draft Convention on the Rights of the Child calls for:

(a) the promotion of the development of the child's personality, talents, and mental and physical abilities to their fullest potential and the fostering of respect for all human rights and fundamental freedoms;

(b) the preparation of the child for responsible life in a free society, in the spirit of understanding, peace, tolerance, and friendship among all peoples, ethnic and religious groups;

(c) the development of respect for the natural environment and for the principles of the Charter of the United Nations;

(d) the development of respect for the child's own cultural identity and values, for the national values of the country in which the child is living, for civilizations different from its own, and for human rights and fundamental freedoms.

The various international and regional documents on human rights tend to stress formal education in the classroom. Student and parental concern over grades and tests often overshadows the important role of education in character development. There is no reason why every student cannot achieve excellence in moral education. In England and Germany, for example, students spend time comparing and contrasting the major faiths in the world. The Religious and Moral Education course for Zimbabwe's Junior Certificate speaks of students learning to accept responsibility to help others in the community.

Character development at the personal level cannot be separated from interpersonal relationships and civic education. One's identity is directly shaped by one's community. Thus, in Zimbabwe, the postcolonial government has introduced history syllabi and textbooks which are Africa-centered. It is at this level of the wider community that the student not only gains a sense of history but also comes to accept civic obligations and responsibilities. A discussion on the responsibilities of youth for example, might use documents from the Young Pioneers (of the former USSR) and the Boy Scouts (of the United States). It is also here that the student begins to see the dialectical or conflicting nature of many human rights. To what extent can the concept of individual liberty, for example, be accommodated by the notion of equality (as, for example, in the affirmative action debate)? At what point must the right to free speech be curbed to protect individuals or groups from slander or libel (as, for example, in the new university rules against racist speech)?

The final level of human rights education is societal and global in its dimensions. It incorporates both peace education and multicultural education and addresses such transnational concerns as energy and the environment. At this level, students confront the institutional and structural obstacles that often hinder or obscure the fulfillment of human rights. The comparative aspects of human rights and the international legal basis for human rights are foci for education at this level. Exposure to the work of such organizations as the International Red Cross and Amnesty International might give students a feeling of empowerment when abuses of human rights are revealed.

All three levels of education must be addressed when teaching about such contemporary issues as nationality and minority rights. At the personal level, students must have immediate and historical role models presented in a multicultural curriculum that shows famous people who have fought against discrimination and made contributions to society. At the interpersonal level, teachers must be aware that a student's level in interaction and responses—such as how much eye contact he of she finds comfortable, how receptive he or she is to group learning strategies, and his or her style of dramatic play or storytelling—are influenced by cultural factors. At the global level, students can be shown the influence of social structure on group progress by contrasting the success of the same racial or ethnic group in different societies. West Indians, for example, do much better economically and educationally in the United States than they do in the United Kingdom. Majority groups in some situations become minority groups in other situations or locations (the English-speaking Canadians in Quebec, for example). Education in human rights can be the glue that helps to tie together multicultural education, citizenship education, and global education.

Although there is a tendency to emphasize human rights education in the formal setting of the school, it must be made clear that human rights education and awareness must reach all corners of society. Education in human rights must be incorporated into the professional training of judges, lawyers, police, and social workers. The Brazilian state of Rio Grande de Sul, for example, passed a law in 1988 establishing the discipline of "Education on Human Rights" as part of the curriculum in the School of Police and in the School of Penitentiary Agents, as well as in the professional preparation course for the military police and others. Journalists need to be made sensitive to human rights issues and reports by the media, governmental bodies, and nongovernmental organizations should be regarded as opportunities to build public awareness of human rights.

Teachers must be trained not only to include material on human rights in their curricula but also to practice it in their classrooms. A democratic classroom, where each student is respected by all others and where the teacher designs and implements the instructional plan with the students, fosters an environment in which human rights are not only taught but remembered as well (skill development). Traditionally, the teacher presents the history leading up to the Universal Declaration of Human Rights and then asks the students to memorize its articles. Even if the student performs perfectly on an ensuing test, it is unlikely that he or she feels in any sense empowered by the experience. It is simply one more unit of material that produces teacher-talk, passive instruction in preset materials, mechanical drills, and punitive testing. In fact, such education usually generates student resistance because the process itself is disempowering.

Radical educators have suggested a kind of learning that deconstructs the conditioned habits of domination and resistance in teachers and students.[7] An example of this approach as it relates to human rights might be the educational guide on torture by governments which was prepared for high school students by Amnesty International. In one section of the guide, students were asked to read the testimonies of four victims of torture—from Hungary, Morocco, the USSR, and Paraguay—and then to express their feelings about what they had read. After discussing the "reasons" usually given by governments for torturing prisoners, the students were asked to think of examples from their own experience of fair and unfair interrogations. Examples could include being questioned by one's parents about why he or she was late home from a party, by somebody suspecting a student of stealing or lying, and by a teacher accusing a student of cheating or missing classes. This exercise enabled the students to empathize with prisoners undergoing unfair interrogation.

Another exercise demonstrates how easy it is to become a torturer. Students were told about an experiment conducted by Stanley Milgram to demonstrate how accustomed we all are to obeying authority. The aim of Milgram's experiment, in which one person was ordered to hurt another person more and more, was to find out at what point the person inflicting the pain would refuse to obey the experimenter and stop:

> Volunteers were told that the aim of the experiment was to test whether punishment improves the ability to learn. They were the "teachers." The "learner" was strapped in a chair behind a screen and had "electrodes" placed on his wrist. The volunteer "teachers" were not told the "learner" was, in fact, an actor and that his screams were tape recordings. The "teachers" were to punish him with an electric shock every time he made a mistake in his lesson. The generator was an impressive looking instrument with a range of switches from 15 volts to 450 volts and a set of labels going from "slight shock" to "moderate shock," "strong shock," "very strong shock," "intensive shock," and finally "XXX danger—severe shock."[8]

The results of the experiment were "shocking." Sixty-five percent of the volunteers were willing to give shocks up to 450 volts. When the "teacher" was placed in the same room as the "learner," however, obedience dropped to forty percent. In another version of the experiment, thirty percent of the volunteers were willing to force the "learners" hands down on a metal plate to receive the shock.

Of course, the purpose of the experiment was to show that it does not take an evil person to serve an evil system. People often find it easier to obey orders than to question authority. Such an example, reinforced by student recollections of situations in which they carried out orders they felt were wrong, are much more likely to be remembered and acted upon than, for instance, the memorization of international legal prohibitions of torture.

Professional and advocacy groups must move beyond mere dissemination of standards for human rights if such standards are to have an impact. Dominant institutions like the school and the press will always attempt to shape and control the message received by the public. In Mexico, for example, human rights activists have joined theater artists in taking their message to the streets and markets. In the first scene of a typical street drama, the actors play out a situation of oppression. Then a narrator explains to the public what happened and asks collaboration to change that situation of oppression. The actors then portray again the exact situation, but this time the public can jump in, saying "stop" and taking the place of the victimized person in the play. This process goes on until the situation of oppressor-oppressed is transformed into one of mutual liberation. Later, a discussion helps to resolve any problems, questions, and tension in the audience. Because the presentation involves the participation of the public in finding a solution, the human rights message makes more of an impact than a lecture on human rights standards.

In the United States, concerts and records by popular artists have been used to promote a variety of causes including human rights. During the last five years, the U.S. section of Amnesty International has established nearly 3,000 student groups at schools across the country, largely on the basis of its exposure to young people by popular artists. Of course, such concerts have now become a worldwide phenomenon.

Conclusion

In any society, education is both the major instrument of socialization to the status quo and the major danger to the status quo. Human rights education as sponsored and prepared by governments cannot be expected to be empowering for large numbers of people. Human rights education that is truly liberating must permeate every aspect of human relations. No one country or ideology can claim supremacy; rather, we might find some common ground from which to construct a more holistic and global approach to education in human rights.

Such a global approach would move beyond international standard-setting to a discussion of the political, economic, and social forces that work against the implementation of human rights. Until now, the scholarship on human rights has been dominated by legal scholars, philosophers, and psychologists. We must expand the discussion to include anthropologists, economists, and creative artists.

Sociologists might help us look at the role of the family in human rights education. For too long we have allowed the personal rights of one family member to dominate the personal rights of others. The consequences of human rights abuses in the family carry a price that the entire society must pay. Personal rights also carry with them personal responsibilities. [See Ch. 19.—Ed.]

Education in human rights must move out of the formal classroom setting to infuse every aspect of our institutional relationships. Neither the hidden hand of the marketplace nor the visible hand of government can be allowed to define our rights for us. Human rights education is something to be learned and relearned by living.

Notes

1. Derrick A. Bell, Jr., *Race, Racism and American Law* (Boston: Little Brown, 1980), 378–79.

2. Harold Cruse, *Plural But Equal* (New York: Morrow, 1987); Raymond Walters, *The Burden of Brown* (Knoxville, TN: University of Tennessee Press, 1984).

3. Marcus D. Pohlmann, *Black Politics in Conservative America* (White Plains, NY: Longman, 1990), 193.

4. Natalie Hevener Kaufman, *Human Rights Treaties and the Senate* (Chapel Hill, NC: University of North Carolina Press, 1990), 18.

5. James Brooke, " 'Honor' Killing of Wives is Outlawed in Brazil," *The New York Times* (March 29, 1991), B–9.

6. Richard E. Morgan, *Disabling America: The Rights Industry Run Amok* (New York: Basic Books, 1984).

7. Amnesty International USA, *Torture by Governments* (1984), 18.

8. Ibid., 30.

19

Roles of Women and Men: Integrating the Public and the Private

Riane Eisler

Time and time again in the twentieth century we have had to ask ourselves why, despite the great modern thrust for both freedom and equality, neither political nor economic rights have become firmly rooted. Why have reforms and revolutions carried out in the name of liberty and justice been only partly successful? Why are we chronically forced to defend gains we thought already made? And why, all over the world, are repression, torture, armed aggression, and terrorism so recurrent and so impervious to appeals of either reason or emotion?

Probing for answers to these questions leads in turn to two other questions which, once articulated, place these issues in a different and much larger context. How can people brought up in families where human rights are violated regularly be expected to respect the human rights of people outside their families? Can people brought up to accept such brutal practices as child and wife beating, genital mutilation, and the selective malnutrition of female children in their families realistically be expected to create a society free from torture, repression, warfare, and terrorism?

The simple answer is that they cannot. People who grow up in such families, or who are taught to acquiesce to such practices in other families for the sake of social convention, are in fact being effectively conditioned to accept human rights violations, in our homes, in our nations, and in our world. In other words, human rights violations in the private and public spheres are interrelated and only a new integrated approach to human rights can lead to real solutions to problems that otherwise seem unsolvable.

Fundamental changes in both human rights theory and action are urgently needed if we are to free ourselves at long last from destructive and dehumanizing traditions of domination in all parts of our globe. This chapter calls for a commitment on the part of the former USSR, the United States, and other countries to give priority to developing such a new approach. It proposes guidelines for a new partnership model for human rights: a new unified perspective that transcends the old polarities of a Soviet emphasis on economic equality and a U.S. emphasis on political freedom.

Toward an Integrated View of Human Rights

In a world where human rights are truly valued, the distinction between private and public cruelty, oppression, and discrimination—political or economic—would be seen as logically absurd. Yet many people still see private or family relations as separate and distinct, or at best as far less important than political and economic relations. This is the view that has shaped, distorted, and stunted the historical development of human rights theory and action.

At the very beginning, the modern movement for human rights was literally what it is still often called: the movement to protect the "rights of man." Philosophers such as John Locke in the seventeenth century and Jean Jacques Rousseau in the eighteenth century proposed the then-novel idea that a man has "inalienable rights." They never spoke of the same rights for women or children. Moreover, since their concern with despotism was limited to relations among men and men (more specifically, among free property-owning white men) in the public or political arena, they did not even address the question of despotism in the private or family sphere.

So while the "divine right of kings" to rule over their "subjects" was challenged in the seventeenth and eighteenth centuries, the also "divinely ordained" right of a man to be the "king" in the "castle" of his home was not. Women and children were not defined as individuals innately possessed of "natural rights" but as members of men's households, "naturally" to be controlled by men.[1]

It is true that there were women, such as Mary Wollstonecraft and Abigail Adams in the eighteenth century and Elizabeth Cady Stanton and Sojourner Truth in the nineteenth century, who argued that women too had human rights.[2] A number of men also made this point. In his article "The Subjection of Women," published almost two centuries ago, the English philosopher John Stuart Mill noted that "only when the most fundamental of the social relations is placed under the rule of equal justice" can a just society be realized. And in *The Origin of the Family, Private Property, and the State*, published shortly after Karl Marx's death, Friedrich Engels recognized family relations between women and men as the model for class oppression. But by and large, then as now, such views were noted only in passing and effectively banished to the intellectual ghetto of feminism.

Thus, the focus on the rights of adult free white males split "human rights" off from "women's rights" and later "children's rights." This in turn led to the accompanying distinction in human rights theory and practice between the "public" (or men's) world and the "private" world to which women and children were still generally confined by custom and sometimes also law.

Yet human society is based, first and foremost, on the relations between the female and male halves of humanity and on their relations with their sons and daughters. Our very first lessons in human relations (thus also in human rights) are learned not in the public but in the private sphere. This is where people learn to respect the rights of others to freedom from cruelty, oppression, and discrimination—or else it is where they learn cruelty, oppression, and discrimination.

Once we look at human rights from this unified perspective, the link between force-backed domination in the state and force-backed domination in the family becomes visible.

We can then see why, throughout history, regimes noted for their human rights violations, such as Hitler's Germany, Khomeini's Iran, Stalin's Soviet Union, and Zia's Pakistan, have made the return of women to their "traditional" or subservient place a priority. Or why in the United States the rightist-fundamentalist alliance backed Senator Laxalt's so-called Family Protection Bill that would have cut funding for battered women's shelters, in fact protecting a family structure where, through both law and force, male "heads of household" are free to exercise despotic control.

The connection between rigid male domination in the family and despotism in the state also helps explain the Moslem fundamentalist custom of not bringing men to trial for killing women in their families who are suspected of any sexual infraction. Rule by terror in the family buttresses a general rule by terror, be it international or within the state. In the despotic Roman Empire, as Engels noted, the male head of household had life-and-death powers, not only over his slaves but also over the women and children in his household. Similarly, under the English common law that developed during a time when monarchs relied so heavily on fear and force, husbands were legally permitted to beat their wives for disobedience—the well-known phrase, "rule of thumb" goes back to a legal reform decreeing that the stick a man used on his wife could be no thicker than his thumb.[3]

In other words, there is a systemic relationship between force-backed domination in the home and force-backed domination in the state. Moreover, as psychotherapist Alice Miller points out in her landmark book, *For Your Own Good: Hidden Cruelty in Child-Rearing and the Roots of Violence*, if we examine the childhoods of brutal despots like Adolf Hitler, we see yet another link between the institutionalization of domination based on cruelty and terror in childrearing and the institutionalization of domination backed by cruelty and terror in the state. The biographies of such demagogic archcriminals reveal that their cruelty—and particularly their cruel persecution of "inferior" or "dangerous" people, be they Jews in Germany, African-Americans in America, Armenians in Azerbaijan, or women in the fundamentalist Moslem world—is in large part rooted in the cruelty they experienced as children. It is a deflection to powerless people of their own rage against powerful fathers.

To be sure, not all people raised in such households go this route. But studies such as Adorno et al.'s *The Authoritarian Personality* have documented how individuals who participate in or acquiesce to authoritarianism, violence, and scapegoating in the state tend to be individuals from families where authoritarianism, violence, and scapegoating were also the norm.[4] In other words, such studies verify what common sense would tell us: that the link between cruelty, domination, and violence in the private sphere of the family and cruelty, domination, and violence in the political sphere is all too real.

The Public and Private Spheres

But, one might ask, should a government or international agency have the power to interfere in people's private affairs? Shouldn't what happens inside a family be free from outside interference? What about the right to privacy?

Certainly the right to privacy, or more precisely the right to protection from governmental interference with the right to privacy, is an important civil right. There is a right to protection from governmental interference in certain areas of personal choice and action, such as with whom one speaks and associates, whether to conceive or not to conceive, and whether to carry or not to carry a pregnancy to term. But these are *personal* rights, not family rights. They are individual rights even though they may involve personal choices and actions that characteristically take place within the family. Moreover, every society in fact interferes with internal family affairs through both custom and law. For example, the killing of one brother by another in the privacy of their home is regarded as a crime in both tribal custom and modern law.

But all too often customs and laws have been applied in a quite selective manner and have served to permit, rather than prevent, chronic violations of human rights. For example, Islamic laws still permit a man to have more than one wife and to divorce a wife simply by repeating "I divorce you" thrice. But women, who are often completely dependent on their husbands for economic survival, are not given the same right. As late as the nineteenth century (long after the Declaration of Independence proclaimed that all men have inalienable rights to life, liberty, and property), women in most American states had few if any political or economic rights. Upon marriage, they were legally divested of any right to control property, even including property they brought into the marriage. And only a few years ago, the Kenyan legislature refused to enact a law forbidding men from beating their wives because, as some members of the Kenyan Parliament argued, such a law would interfere with men's right to "teach their wives good manners."[5]

Even when there are laws on the books protecting women or children, they are often selectively enforced in ways that protect their violators from scrutiny and punishment. One example is the still widespread failure in much of the industrialized world (including the United States and the former Soviet Union) to prosecute men who beat their wives (despite laws prohibiting such batteries) on the grounds that these are "domestic" or internal family affairs. Another example is the practice by families selling girl children into prostitution or sexual slavery which, despite all the national laws and international conventions outlawing slavery, continues unabated in parts of the developing world (particularly Asia), largely because it is generally not prosecuted.[6]

So while there is much talk of protecting the family, the principle of noninterference in the private or family sphere is often used to maintain a particular kind of family: a patriarchally dominated family in which women and children have few if any individual rights; in which men may still dominate and hurt women with impunity, and parents may do the same to their children, and in which women and children have no recourse in either custom or law.

This is why the distinction between personal and family decisions is so critical. Clearly a person's right to make certain private decisions should be free from governmental interference. But that is not the same as immunizing family decisions—or more specifically, the decisions of those who wield power in a family—from public scrutiny and regulation. In short, *the protection of personal rights is not synonymous with noninterference in actions within the family. In fact, there often is a direct conflict between the two.*

It is only when we begin to apply one standard to violations of human rights, whether they occur inside or outside the family, that we see how the distinction between the public and private spheres has served to prevent the application of human rights standards to the most formative and fundamental human relations. We also see how this double standard not only has resulted in the failure to protect the rights of women and children but has also served to maintain the kind of family where both girls and boys learn to accept cruel and oppressive human relations in *both* the private and public spheres as the social norm.

The basic fact is that people learn how to behave in their families. Just as important, they learn what behaviors will be punished, or not punished and thus effectively condoned. And as long as acts of cruelty and brutality in people's families are condoned rather than condemned and prosecuted, not only will these continue from generation to generation but so also will acts of cruelty and brutality outside the family.

Traditions of Domination

Another argument against "outside interference" in family affairs is that the family is the repository of traditional religious, ethnic, and cultural values, and that neither laws nor governments, much less international agencies, should be permitted to interfere in these areas. But once again, the real issue beneath the rhetoric is not so much one of preserving religious or ethnic traditions but of preserving those traditions that maintain a particular form of familial and social organization. For from the very beginning, it has been precisely the re-examination—and rejection—of once hallowed cultural and religious traditions that has characterized the modern movement for human rights.

The first phase of the human rights movement was presaged by what at the time were fundamental changes in consciousness, as people gradually rejected the traditional idea that kings and noblemen have a divinely ordained or natural right to rule. This rejection of autocratic traditions was the basis of both the American and Russian revolutions. However, these autocratic traditions were staunchly defended by religious authorities and even by secular philosophers such as Edmund Burke, who argued that the doctrine of "the rights of man" would lead "to the utter subversion, not only of all government, in all modes, but all stable securities to rational freedom, and all the rules and principles of morality itself."[7]

Today, this kind of rhetoric is still being used by religious authorities and secular writers to oppose women's rights and children's rights. They would have us see women's and children's rights as subversive of the moral order, a threat to family and social stability, and, particularly in the developing world, to ethnic traditions.[8] Thus, the cry of interference with "ethnic traditions" is still being raised in defense of genital mutilations which kill, maim, and blight the physical and psychological health of millions of women and little children every year. Unlike male circumcision, with which these practices are sometimes erroneously equated, these are not simply ceremonial cuttings of skin. They include cutting off the clitoris (designed to deprive women of sexual pleasure, and thus presumably the desire to "stray") and/or cutting off the labia and tightly sewing up the vaginal opening, making sexual intercourse impossible and normal bodily functions painful until a larger opening is again cut upon marriage.

Due to the challenge by women's rights advocates across the world, a number of national leaders have condemned such practices.[9] Yet to date, despite the fact that ending torture is a major human rights priority, international human rights organizations have not taken a strong stand against genital mutilation—even though it is widely practiced on the African continent and in some parts of Asia, is estimated to affect more than ninety million women, and is being brought by immigrants into Europe and the United States.[10]

One might argue that genital mutilation is not a form of torture in the conventional legal-political sense of an instrument of political oppression to exact conformity and suppress dissent. But although the practice of genital mutilation is deeply embedded in religious rites and ethnic customs, its essential purpose is extremely political. It is a means of perpetuating male domination—indeed, male ownership—over women. Like the torture of political prisoners, it is a most effective means of breaking a person's spirit; it causes traumatic pain, even death, and afflicts its survivors with major physical and psychological problems for the rest of their lives. And it is a most effective instrument for exacting conformity and suppressing dissent precisely because the victim is socialized to accept it.

The idea that genital mutilation is justified in the name of respect for cultural traditions is not only horrifying but ludicrous. All institutionalized behavior, including cannibalism and slavery, are cultural traditions. And surely no human rights advocate would today dare to justify ethnic traditions of cannibalism or slavery on cultural or traditional grounds. Nor would any human rights advocate justify apartheid or segregation based on race in South Africa on the grounds that apartheid had become a cultural tradition during the years of white rule. Yet, segregation based on gender—still the norm in much of the Moslem world, including whole nations such as Iran, Saudi Arabia, Bangladesh, and Pakistan— is defended by both Moslems and non-Moslems on the grounds that it is a cultural tradition. This, even though gender segregation effectively bars one group (women, who in fact are half the population) from equal access to educational and employment opportunities and even freedom of movement.

Indeed, while no human rights advocate would think of justifying house arrest, few western human rights advocates take note of the traditional confinement or seclusion of women to special quarters, which is virtual house arrest. And while it is tempting to frame this issue in regional terms because the examples from the middle east and Africa are so striking, it is important to remember that segregation by gender is to varying degrees a universal problem. For example, the custom of segregating jobs into women's and men's work, with work assigned to women given lower status and pay regardless of requirements of technical skill, intellectual ability, or emotional sensitivity, has been a major factor in maintaining the subordination of women to men worldwide. Thus, in the former USSR, while there has been much emphasis on outside employment for women, the sad fact is that the occupations and professions where women are concentrated— from street cleaning to medicine (the latter of which in the United States is dominated by men and extremely lucrative)—are poorly paid. In the United States, despite legislation mandating equal opportunities for women, the same pattern prevails, and "feminine" occupations—which tend to focus on caretaking, cleaning, and nurturing—are not given high social or economic value.[11]

Truly shocking is the omission from conventional discussions of either economic or political rights of this pattern of economic discrimination against women, whose magnitude and whose injustice come into even clearer focus when we consider that both in the United States and the in Russia (as well as in most parts of the world) women work much longer hours than men do.[12] In the United States, the fact that women who hold outside jobs still do most of the child care and housework is commonly called the "double burden." In Russia and the other countries of the former USSR, it could properly be called the "triple burden" because women customarily spend long hours after their jobs standing in lines for food and other necessities, in addition to taking care of children and home.

Wife beating is also customary behavior both in the former USSR and in the United States (where, according to the U.S. Department of Justice, a woman is beaten every fifteen seconds).[13] It too is deeply ingrained in many cultural traditions, with study after study showing that it cuts across all national, racial, and socio-economic lines. This tradition of domestic violence, which blights the lives of so many millions of women worldwide, has been passed on from generation to generation precisely because men are *not* generally held accountable, much less prosecuted, for it.[14] Even the killing of women is in some cultures not prosecuted if it is by a male family member. And where statistics are kept by gender, they show that victims of family murders are overwhelmingly women and children. For example, in Austria in 1985 fifty-four percent of all murders were committed in the family, and women and children comprised ninety percent of the victims.[15]

Indeed, as Lori Heise writes in her article "International Dimensions of Violence Against Women," few phenomena are as pervasive, yet so ignored, as violence against women.[16] She also notes that much of this violence is justified by long-standing customs, such as the habit of men worldwide (including in the United States and in the countries of the former USSR) to use drunkenness as an excuse for beating their wives. And from the selective starving of girl children and bride burnings of India[17] to the fact that in the United States it is estimated that a woman is raped every six minutes,[18] this pattern of violence against women continues because it is still generally perceived as "normal," even by the victims themselves who have been socialized by their families to accept it. Thus, in the United States, rapes have begun to be more widely reported only in recent years, since in the past—as is still the case in many cultures today—the rape victim and not the rapist would be punished, under traditions that blamed women for "tempting men to sin" or for "not being at home where they belong."

In this connection, it is instructive to note that, very properly, the restriction by governments on foreign travel by their citizens has been soundly condemned by international human rights organizations. Yet the fact that millions of women (not only in Islam but in many other parts of the world) cannot travel anywhere without their husbands' permission is still rarely noted.

It is also instructive, and sobering, to realize how deeply ingrained traditions of cruelty to children have been—and how most human rights organizations are still conspicuously silent about even the most brutal forms of family violence against children. We have already seen how human rights violations such as genital mutilations, sale into prostitution and forced marriage, and starvation by their own parents affect children who happen to be born female. According to the latest estimates, twenty-five to thirty-eight percent of girls in the United States are sexually molested.[19] And both girls and boys all over the world are routinely subjected to beatings, with traditions of physical abuse still the norm rather than the exception in many places today.

In terms of the unified conceptual framework proposed here, it is also instructive—and predictable—that those who today in the United States support traditions of corporal punishment in homes and schools are the very same people who would return us to the "good old days" of religious intolerance and persecution, before the rights of men, women, or children became a social and political issue. It is ironic that the systemic connection between violence in the private and public spheres is more often recognized by those working against, rather than for, human rights. But it is also understandable, since these people draw from traditions of domination that span the entire spectrum of human relations, from family to tribe to state.

These traditional behaviors continue to be major obstacles to the modern movement for human rights. Like the submerged mass of an iceberg with only its tip in view, traditions of domination and violence in the private sphere support domination and violence in the more visible political or public sphere. This is why a unified theory of human rights encompassing both these inextricably interwoven spheres of life is today so urgently needed if we are to build a better society.

The Partnership Model
for Human Rights

Today, as never before in human history, the world stands at a crossroads. The well-trodden path of violence and domination—of man over woman, parent over child, nation over nation, and mankind over nature—leads to a world of totalitarian controls and nuclear or ecological disaster. The other road could take us to a new era of human partnership and peace: a world where our basic civil, political, and economic rights—including the right of all to protection from domination and violence and, just as urgently, to the protection of our natural environment from man's fabled "conquest of nature"—will at long last be respected.

In this chapter, I use the terms *domination* and *partnership* to describe two contrasting models of social organization.[20] In the dominator model, human differences—beginning with the differences between male and female—are automatically equated with inferiority and superiority. Those deemed "superior" (such as men) dominate, and those deemed "inferior" (such as women) are dominated. Hence human rights are, by definition, severely limited, as the whole system is ultimately held together by fear and force. By contrast, in the partnership model, differences—again beginning with the differences between women and men—are *not* automatically equated with inferiority and superiority. Here more "feminine" values such as caring, nonviolence, and empathy can in fact and not just rhetoric achieve social and economic precedence, since here men do not have to be socialized for domination and conquest. And here human rights can in fact and not just theory be protected in both the so-called private and public spheres.

New evidence from archaeology indicates that for thousands of years more peaceful and egalitarian societies oriented primarily to the partnership rather than dominator model; in other words, strong-man rule, be it in the family or the state, has not always been the human norm. A detailed discussion of these findings is beyond the scope of this chapter but can be found in my book *The Chalice and*

The Blade: Our History, Our Future, which also examines the two contrasting configurations of the dominator and partnership models in detail. (An overview of some salient features of both systems is shown in the chart.)

The point I want to emphasize here is that the modern human rights movement is part of the struggle to free ourselves from a dominator model of human relations. But the first phase of this movement only challenged the top of the dominator pyramid: domination in the public or political sphere. *The next essential step is the challenge to its base: domination in the private sphere of family relations, particularly in the day-to-day relations between women and men and parents and children.*

When viewed from this unified human rights perspective, the reasons why both capitalism and communism have to date been unable to bring about either real economic equality or political freedom can also be better understood. In the former Soviet Union, socialist ideals of equality were undermined by traditions of domination going back even beyond tsarist times. And in both "planned" and "free market" economies, the acceptance of economic injustice and domination in the family—such as the unjust work burden of both Russian and American women, who get less pay in the labor market and no pay at home—has conditioned both women and men to accept a larger economic system, be it capitalist or communist, where some people work less and get more, and others work more and get less. Indeed, it is unrealistic to expect either capitalism or communism to give full social and economic priority to health, education, and a clean environment as long as caring and cleaning, both inside and outside the family, continue to be devalued as "women's work."

Moreover, this perspective reveals the connection between a family system in which people are taught to obey unquestioningly those who are bigger and stronger and an authoritarian (dominator) political system, be it leftist or rightist, northern or southern. An acceptance of violence in family relations is likewise connected to an acceptance of violence in international relations.

The encouraging thing is that more and more people today are challenging traditions of force-backed domination. Not so very long ago, the traditional wisdom was "spare the rod and spoil the child." Today, we are beginning to recognize child beating as child abuse. It used to be a joke that "if rape is inevitable" a woman should "relax and enjoy it." Now rape is increasingly recognized for what it is, an act of aggression and violence. Like the painful and deforming foot-binding of girls in prerevolutionary China, female genital mutilations were once considered strange "ethnic customs." Today, they are increasingly recognized as brutal means of maintaining male sexual control over both the bodies and psyches of women. And increasingly, customs like the payment of a "bride price"—whereby women (often mere children) are sold by their own fathers into arranged marriages where they must not only bear a man children but often work uncompensated from dawn to dusk—are recognized for what they are: a form of slave trading.

The Dominator and the Partnership Models: Basic Configurations

Component	Dominator Model	Partnership Model
One: Gender Relations	The ranking of the male over the female, as well as the higher valuing of the traits and social values stereotypically associated with "masculinity" rather than "femininity."*	Equal valuing of the sexes as well as of "femininity" and "masculinity," or a sexually equalitarian social and ideological structure, where "feminine" values can gain operational primacy.
Two: Violence	A high degree of institutionalized social violence and abuse, ranging from wife—and child—beating, rape, and warfare to psychological abuse by "superiors" in the family, the workplace, and society at large.	A low degree of social violence, with violence and abuse not structural components of the system.
Three: Social Structure	A predominantly hierarchic† and authoritarian social organization, with the degree of authoritarianism and hierarchism roughly corresponding to the degree of male dominance.	A more generally equalitarian social structure, with difference (be it based on sex, race, religion, or belief system) not automatically associated with superior or inferior social and/or economic status.

*The terms "femininity" and "masculinity" as used here correspond to the sexual stereotypes appropriate for a dominator society (where "masculinity" is equated with dominance and conquest), and *not* with any inherent female or male traits.

†As used here, the term hierarchic refers to what we may call a *domination* hierarchy, or the type of hierarchy inherent in a dominator model of social organization, based on fear and the threat of force. Such hierarchies should be distinguished from a second type of hierarchy, which may be called an *actualization* hierarchy, for example, of molecules, cells, and organs in the body: a progression toward a higher and more complex level of function.

These are major changes in consciousness that could presage a fundamental advance in global respect for human rights. But changes in consciousness must be followed by legislative, juridical, and social action. And this is where a Russian-American partnership can make a critical contribution.

A Call to Action

In the last decade of the twentieth century, the United States and the former USSR moved to the threshold of a new era of cooperation. People in both countries began to recognize that violence does not resolve conflict and that we must work together to rethink and reformulate human rights theory as well as action. There was even talk (as one of the coordinators of Soviet-American human rights discussions, Bertram Gross, urged) of working toward the year 2000 as the dawn of "A Human Rights Century."

I too believe that we have the opportunity to move forward to a new phase in the global movement for human rights. But I am convinced that the groundwork for this must first be laid. This is why I am proposing two fundamental joint actions.

The first proposal is that the fundamental reformulation of human rights theory, to fully integrate the private and public spheres, should be a top priority in discussions on human rights. The goal will be to develop specific guidelines for governmental and nongovernmental agencies to follow in altering their charters, their policies, and, most important, their action agendas for an integrated (partnership) model of human rights.

The second proposal is that immediate international attention with U.S. and Russian backing should be given to a concerted human rights education campaign. The central aim of this campaign will be to demonstrate vividly the integral connection between violations of—or respect for—human rights in the public and private spheres.

The Reformulation of
Human Rights Theory

Many of the building blocks for a new partnership model for human rights are already in place. The United Nations Charter as well as numerous conventions and declarations have generally affirmed the dignity and worth of all persons without distinction as to race, religion, or sex. Most important, during the past two decades there have been two conventions that specifically deal with the human rights of the hitherto excluded majority—women and children—in *both* the private and public spheres.

The 1979 U.N. Convention on the Elimination of all Forms of Discrimination Against Women specifically and forcefully addresses the need to integrate women's rights into human rights in both theory and action. This convention was the first move beyond the spurious distinction between public and private spheres. Article 16, for example, specifically deals with "discrimination against women in all matters relating to marriage and family relations" and enumerates such "private" rights as the right "to decide freely and responsibly on the number and spacing of their children and to have access to the information, education, and means to enable them to exercise these rights." It requires recognition and enforcement of a woman's right "to choose a family name" and "a profession and an occupation." And in requiring protection for women's rights of "ownership, acquisition, management, administration, enjoyment and disposition of property," it directly challenges male economic control of the family.

Of major significance is also that this convention expressly addresses the issue of ethnic customs or practices that deny human rights to women. Article 5 asks that signatories "shall take all appropriate measures . . . to modify the social and cultural patterns of conduct of men and women with a view to achieving the elimination of prejudices and customary, and all other, practices which are based on the idea of the inferiority or the superiority of either of the sexes or on stereotyped roles for men and women."

Similarly, the U.N. Convention on the Rights of the Child, adopted by the General Assembly in 1989, focuses heavily on the private or family sphere. It addresses the social, economic, cultural, civil, and political rights of children and defines the obligations of parents and others to them. Article 19 deals with the protection of children from all forms of abuse, neglect, and exploitation by parents or others. Article 34 deals with the protection of children by the state from sexual exploitation and abuse. And Article 24, on health care, states as an aim the abolishment of "harmful traditional practices."

There are many other existing resources out of which to construct a new integrated framework for human rights. These include the United Nations conventions condemning slavery, UNESCO reports such as the 1975 report on prostitution "hotels" in Europe which documents the torture of women and their imprisonment in prostitution; the Forward Looking Strategies from the United Nations Decade for Women (1975–1985); the 1990–1995 System Wide Medium Term Plan for Women and Development; and the research of INSTRAW (the United Nations International Research and Training Institute for Women).

In addition, numerous nongovernmental organizations address the problems and rights of women and children. The International Women's Rights Action Watch (IWRAW) at the Humphrey Institute of Public Affairs at the University of Minnesota monitors, analyzes, and encourages law and policy reform in accordance with the principles of the U.N. Convention on the Elimination of all Forms of Discrimination Against Women. So do the Sisterhood is Global Institute in New Zealand and groups such as Women Living Under Muslim Laws International Solidarity Network in Grabels (Montpelier), France. Also important are publications such as *Women's International Network (WIN) News*, published in Lexington, Massachusetts, which has a regular section on human rights; Robin Morgan's anthology *Sisterhood is Global*; and Katarina Tomasevski's *Development Aid and Human Rights*, which stresses the need for taking into account human rights, and specifically the human rights of women, in development programs. Many organizations monitor the needs and problems of children: the United Nations Children's Emergency Fund (UNICEF); the Children's Defense Fund in Washington, D.C.; the Inter-American Children's Institute in Montevideo, Uruguay; and Defense for Children International–USA in New York, to name but a few. As well, a plethora of new organizations and conferences are collaborating with social action groups to broaden the definition of human rights to include reproductive rights, the right to literacy, and other rights enumerated in U.N. conventions which focus on the rights of women and children in both the private and public spheres. Among these are Lawyers for Human Rights in Pakistan; the Uganda Association of Women Lawyers; Citizenship Studies Information Action in Brazil; the International Interdisciplinary Congress of Women; and the European Inter-Parliamentary Symposium on the

Participation of Women in the Political Decision-Making Process.

Of particular importance is that the governmental reporting of human rights violations in the private sphere has also begun. In 1989, the U.S. State Department instructed its embassies to report the extent to which foreign governments tolerate or condone various forms of violence against women, including domestic or "private" violence. The Percy amendments, of 1974 and of 1973, mandated U.S. and international agencies to study the impact of development programs on women. By 1987, the Netherlands, Norway, Canada, Sweden, and Denmark had adopted policy guidelines requiring that appraisal reports of their foreign development aid include information about women, to ensure that funds are used in a manner that will protect and strengthen women's rights.[21]

In sum, a piecemeal reformulation of human rights theories, practices, and reporting methods to include women and children and integrate the private and public spheres is already underway. But what is urgently needed at this critical time is a new conceptual framework for this integration backed by the world leadership which a Russian–American partnership can provide.

Until now, in both the former USSR and the United States, the rights of women and children have been viewed, at best, as secondary. To its shame, the United States has not at this writing even ratified the U.N. Convention on the Elimination of all Forms of Discrimination Against Women. And while, to its credit, the USSR was among the first to do so, to its shame, it prosecuted, ridiculed, and even incarcerated in mental institutions women such as Tatyana Mamonova, who was forced into exile from her homeland for the "crime" of circulating materials calling attention to such women's issues as the almost total lack of effective contraceptives and the need for more day-care centers, better conditions in maternity wards and abortion clinics, protection from domestic violence, more effective enforcement of rape laws, and better paying jobs as well as pensions for older women.[22]

Clearly, if the United States and the former USSR are to work toward a new era for human rights, the United States must quickly ratify the Convention on the Elimination of all Forms of Discrimination Against Women, and all the republics of the former USSR must quickly move toward the implementation of its provisions—including official governmental backing to encourage the development of a strong movement for women's rights. All nations also need to protect their children from violence and abuse and in all other respects fully implement the U.N. Convention on the Rights of the Child.

In both words and deeds, the protection of human rights in the so-called private sphere must be made a top priority. Specifically, in relation to the current human rights discussions between representatives from the United States and the former USSR, it is essential that all meetings include in their agendas attention to the human rights of the majority: women and children. In addition, the year 1996 (just after the midpoint of the decade before the year 2000) should be dedicated to intensive research and publications on a partnership model of human rights—

culminating in a conference focusing on the integration of the public and private spheres. This project should seek active participation from human rights advocates, in particular advocates for women's and children's rights, from all over the world.

Human Rights Education

To be effective, human rights education must furnish people with the tools for recognizing human rights violations in our everyday lives and show how respect (or disregard) for human rights begins in our homes. To this end, an international human rights education campaign focusing on the integral connection between the public and private spheres should be a top priority for action and funding— not only for the United States and the countries of the former USSR, but for all nations and peoples.

Mass media (particularly television, films, rock music, and comics) bombard us with images of "entertaining" violence and abuse. Movies are X-rated (or even censored) if they contain nudity or sex. But movies, comics, rock videos, and television programs that are watched daily by millions of young people chronically show beatings, rapes, murders, and even dismemberment and torture —with women among the most frequent victims—effectively accustoming us to domination and violence as normal, and even "fun." Not only physical abuse, but psychological abuse, is marketed as "entertainment" in television situation comedies where canned laughter is coupled with acts that hurt, humiliate, and ridicule others, thus further teaching us to be insensitive to people's feelings and rights. The fact that such violent and abusive "entertainment" is proliferating and spreading to all parts of the globe is a symptom of dominator resistance to the strong contemporary partnership thrust of which the international human rights movement is such an important part. All around us—in the Middle East, Africa, Asia, Latin America, as well as inside both the former Soviet Union and the United States—dictators and would-be dictators threaten to wrest from us even those gains already made. Moreover, in a world threatened as never before by nuclear and bacteriological warfare and terrorism, a mass media education campaign focusing on the human right to live free of violence—be it in our immediate families or the family of nations—may be a requisite for survival.

International human rights education is already being promoted by the United Nations Information Office on Human Rights, which is conducting a campaign aimed at broadening general public awareness of rights and remedies by disseminating information on international standards and redress procedures. Defense for Children International–USA has initiated a Children's Rights Education Project aimed at junior high schools and high schools, with textbooks and curriculum materials for the United States, Canada, Europe, and Latin America. Many women's organizations all over the world are working to make women more aware of their rights and recourse in both the private and public spheres. A proposal to designate a Decade of Human Rights Education (DARE) is currently being circulated in many nations, including the United States and the countries of the former USSR. According to the proposal activists from the human rights, education, and grassroots communities would be brought together in order to educate and empower people to take effective action to realize their human rights at all levels.

These are all steps toward an international human rights campaign. But once again, what is now urgently needed are specific guidelines to ensure that the human rights of the majority—women and children—are in this effort central, and not, as in the past, peripheral.

The dedication of 1994 as the United Nations Year of the Family highlights the need for a major human rights education campaign aimed at transcending the double standard for the human rights of women and children and the political and economic rights for men. One of its main aims is to support and strengthen the family.

But what kind of family do we want to support and strengthen? If it is a dominator family in which women and children have few if any rights, the prospects for human rights—in *both* the private and public spheres—are grim indeed. If it is a partnership family in which the rights of all members are fully recognized and implemented, there is good reason for long-range hope.

It is on this note of hope for the future that I close this chapter. I am convinced that people *can* learn to change both attitudes and behaviors. Indeed, we see evidence of this around us every day. The fact that today Americans and the peoples of the former Soviet Union are joining hands to work on strengthening global human rights is in itself proof that changes *can* happen, sometimes in an amazingly short time.

Notes

1. For an in-depth discussion of historical antecedents to the split between the private and public spheres, as well as for more detailed citations, see R. Eisler, "Human Rights: Toward an Integrated Theory for Action," *Human Rights Quarterly* vol. 9 (August 1987), 287–308.

2. For example, at the first United States Women's Rights Convention in 1848 (the same year Marx and Engels issued the much better known Communist Manifesto), Elizabeth Cady Stanton adapted the U.S. Declaration of Independence as a Women's Rights Manifesto by adding to it two critical words: "We hold these truths to be self-evident: that all men *and women* are created equal. . . ." ("Seneca Falls Declaration of Sentiments," in M. Schneir, ed., *Feminism: The Essential Historical Writings* [New York: Random House, 1972], emphasis added).

3. For a discussion of the English and American common law affecting women, see R. Eisler, *Dissolution: No Fault Divorce, Marriage, and the Future of Women* (New York: McGraw Hill, 1977). See also W.B. Blackstone, *Commentaries*, 19th London ed. (Philadelphia: Lippincott, 1908).

4. T.W. Adorno, E. Frenkel-Brunswik, D. Levinson, and S.R. Nevitt, *The Authoritarian Personality* (New York: Harper & Row, 1950).

5. *Time* Magazine report quoted in *Women's International Network (WIN) News* vol. 5, (Autumn 1979), 42.

6. A pioneering work on this subject is K. Barry, *Female Sexual Slavery* (New York: Avon, 1979).

7. Edmund Burke, quoted in A. Castel, *An Introduction to Modern Philosophy* (New York: MacMillan, 1946), 425.

8. For example, in the Kenyan debate on a bill that would have required reforms in traditional violence against women as well as polygamy, one of the legislators, Kimunai Arap Soi, charged that the bill was "very un-African." (*Time* Magazine report quoted in *WIN News* vol. 5 [Autumn 1979], 42). But as the Kenyan women's magazine *VIVA* observes: "There is nothing 'African' about injustice or violence, whether it takes the form of mistreating wives and mothers, or slums, or circumcision. Often the very men who . . . excuse injustice to women with the phrase, 'It is African,' are wearing three-piece pin-stripe suits and shiny shoes." (Quoted in L. Heise, "International Dimensions of Violence Against Women," *Response* vol. 12 [1989], 8).

9. Among African nations that have begun to take measures against the continuation of genital mutilation are Egypt, Kenya, and Sudan where in 1979 the Khartoum Seminar organized by the World Health Organization (WHO) recommended the eradication of these practices.

10. A groundbreaking work on this subject is F.P. Hosken, "The Hosken Report: Genital and Sexual Mutilation of Females," *WIN News* (1982, 1984). Hosken's quarterly *Women's International Network (WIN) News* has a regular feature on genital and sexual mutilations. At a World Health Organization-sponsored conference in Dakar, Senegal in 1984, groups joined together to form the Inter-African Committee (IAC) to abolish female circumcision and to dispel the ignorance and myths that perpetuate this practice, such as the false belief that the Koran demands female genital mutilation.

11. In the United States, comparable worth legislation and lawsuits have begun to address this issue of the devaluing of caretaking, cleaning, nurturing, and other "women's work," but progress is still very slow.

12. According to the United Nations, globally, women put in two thirds of the world's work hours, but earn only one-tenth of what men earn, and own only one-hundredth as much property (*1985 State of the World's Women Report*, compiled and written on behalf of the United Nations by New International Publications, Oxford, England).

13. Bureau of Justice Statistics, *Preventing Domestic Violence Against Women* (Washington, DC: U.S. Department of Justice, August, 1986).

14. Recent studies from the United States and Canada verify this, showing that when men are prosecuted and jailed for domestic violence (as people routinely are for violence against friends or strangers), this acts as a deterrent. See for example R.A. Berk and P.J. Newton, "Does Arrest Really Deter Wife Battery?" *American Sociological Review* vol. vol. 50 (1985), 253. The experience in Minneapolis, where husbands are prosecuted and jailed, also showed the importance of holding men legally accountable for violence against their wives or lovers.

15. C. Bernard and E. Schlaffer, "A Case Study of Austria," *Proceedings of the Expert Group Meeting on Violence in the Family with a Special Emphasis on its Effects on Women* (Vienna, Austria, December 8–12, 1986), U.N. Document BAW-EGN–86-CS.15.

16. L. Heise, "International Dimensions of Violence Against Women," *Response*, vol. 12 (1989).

17. "The Lesser Child: The Girl in India," a report prepared by the government of India to mark South Asia's Year of the Girl Child 1990, has recently verified how truly horrible and heartbreaking the situation of women in India is. For example, it reports

findings of UNICEF that twenty-five percent of girls in India die before the age of fifteen because of systematic patterns of neglect, discrimination, and sometimes infanticide due to their gender. (B. Crossette, "25% of Girls in India Die by Age 15, UNICEF Says," *The New York Times* [October 5, 1990]).

18. Federal Bureau of Investigation, *Uniform Crime Report* (Washington, DC: U.S. Government Printing Office, 1988).

19. E.S. Blume, *Secret Survivors: Uncovering Incest and Its After Effects in Women* (New York: John Wiley and Sons, 1990), xiv.

20. See R. Eisler, *The Chalice and The Blade: Our History, Our Future* (San Francisco, CA: Harper & Row, 1987) and R. Eisler and D. Loye, *The Partnership Way: New Tools for Living and Learning* (San Francisco CA: HarperCollins, 1990).

21. Congresswoman Patricia Schroeder, co-chair of the Congressional Caucus for Women's Issues, has proposed trade sanctions against countries that violate U.S. standards for the treatment of women, just as there have been trade sanctions against the way South Africa treated blacks. (Shroeder's testimony before the House Subcommittee on Human Rights and International Organizations, as well as an interview with her, appeared in *USA Today*, March 27, 1990). Fran Hosken has also noted that implementation of the Percy amendments has been very slow by both the United States Agency for International Development and the United Nations agencies. She proposes to make United Nations agencies and others, such as the World Bank, subject to equal employment legislation in order to increase the number of women working for the agencies, especially in decision-making positions. (Private communication from Fran Hosken, October 18, 1990.)

22. For an English-language collection of some of Mamonova's writings, see T. Mamonova, *Russian Women's Studies: Essays on Sexism in Soviet Culture* (New York: Pergamon Press, 1989). An excellent update on the abominable situation of family planning in the Soviet Union as well as most of Eastern Europe (with the notable exceptions of Czechoslovakia, East Germany, and Hungary), with correspondingly very high rates of abortion, is J.L. Jacobson, "Out From Behind the Contraceptive Iron Curtain," *Worldwatch* vol. 3 (Sept.–Oct. 1990).

20

A Healthier United States

Bertram Gross

> The health of nations is more important than the wealth of nations.
> (Will Durant, *What Is Civilization?*)

From time immemorial, people in positions of great power have done what they could to protect their health. They have also taken measures to protect the health —and thereby maintain the productivity—of livestock, wives, employees, and slaves. In this sense, the health of nations has generally been the foundation of the wealth of nations.

The United States is a superpower in which the improving health of many people has helped make it the wealthiest country in world history. This process of becoming healthier has been measured through averaged-out indicators on rising life expectancy and declining disease rates. For health-food faddists, "health" may refer to granola, yogurt, or food that doesn't taste good. Then there are the various ideas suggested by such terms as "mental health," "environmental health," and "preventive medicine" or "preventive health." More broadly, health has also been used to refer to well-being. This suggests a combination of satisfactory, exhilarating, benign, and relaxing feelings and activities. Let's put it this way:

> The health of a nation is advanced when every person has the opportunity to fully enjoy, exercise, and utilize under the rule of law all his or her human rights—civil and political, economic, social, and cultural, and environmental —in an atmosphere free from monopoly and open or tacit sexism, racism, religious prejudice, and homophobia.

In the United States, as pointed out in chapter 10, many people have enjoyed a large measure of this opportunity while many others have suffered tragically from the denial, violation, or delegitimation of such rights. One does not have to be ill, disabled, hungry, homeless, jobless, abused, discriminated against, or deprived of political and nationality rights to know that the "human rights and fundamental freedoms" in the Universal Declaration of Human Rights of 1948 are still being grossly violated throughout the world, including the United States.

Looking ahead to the end of the twentieth century and the dawn of the twenty-first, one should recognize that new and old forms of empire or tyranny (including "repressive corporatism" and "friendly fascism") will always be a threat. Yet there are also great opportunities for the world to move along the path of nonviolent campaigns against the enemies of human rights: concentrated power, poverty, hunger, disease, environmental destructiveness, ignorance, prejudice, repression, nationalist extremism, dangerous and dehumanizing technologies, and violence of all sorts including war itself.

As before, persons and groups in the United States (nongovernmental and governmental) can be expected to play major roles in responding to these challenges while also holding back the tides of tyranny and empire. Any serious list of "what is to be done" and "who is to do it" can never come from a scholar's pen. It would have to emerge, rather, from democratic debate in homes, workplaces, religious organizations, and legislative bodies throughout the country. My own contribution is merely to emphasize a few matters that might contribute to such debate.

Fulfilling Human Rights Declarations

Despite the end of the cold war, the U.S. government has not yet ratified major human rights covenants and conventions that its own representatives often took the lead in formulating. The Senate Foreign Relations Committee has become the burial ground for the most basic human rights covenants proposed under the auspices of the United Nations, the International Labor Office, and the Organization of American States. Since a two-thirds vote is required before any such treaties become law, presidential initiative is essential. This requires a schedule of well-organized hearings in which pro and con opinions, together with proposed reservations and definitions, can be thoroughly discussed.

A possible schedule for such hearings might be:
* 1993: The Convention Against Torture and Other Cruel, Inhuman, or Degrading Treatment or Punishment; and The Convention on the Rights of the Child
    * 1994: The International Covenant on Economic, Social, and Cultural Rights
    * 1995: The Convention on the Elimination of all Forms of Discrimination Against Women
    * 1996: The International Convention on the Elimination of all Forms of Racial Discrimination
    * 1997: The American Convention on Human Rights

With enough initiative on the part of human rights organizations, members of Congress, and presidential candidates and presidents, this schedule could be compressed—along with basic treaties on arms reduction and nonproliferation—into a shorter time span. In the meantime, persons, groups, and organizations need not wait for formal ratification. Rather, they should take the most fundamental provisions of these legal documents as moral imperatives, guiding their daily action in every locality of the country.

Economic Opportunity #1: Poor People

Before World War II, President Franklin D. Roosevelt proclaimed the south as "Economic Opportunity Number One." The logic was clear. Still suffering from the ravages of the Civil War, the southern states were more agricultural than industrial. Their vast numbers of poor people, both white and black, contributed too little to the purchasing power needed for the development of modern industry both in the south and elsewhere. Fifty years later, with major strides in health care, education, industrial development, and agricultural mechanization, the south is in many respects an entirely different place.

Today, the poor people in this country—in the south, north, midwest, and west—could well be regarded as "Economic Opportunity Number One." Despite their heterogeneity, they constitute an enormous reservoir of underdeveloped purchasing power, skills, and moral values. Naturally, putting this reservoir to use would require some modifications in the traditional structures of power and privilege and in managerial tradition. It would also provide the indispensable infrastructure for transcending legalistic declarations and making basic human rights and fundamental freedoms more of a reality in the daily life of everyone.

We versus Them

On many aspects of human rights, the Left seems bereft, the Middle muddled, and the Right not always right—or wrong. Indeed, it is rather silly to classify people or ideas along any simplistic continuum from radical to liberal to conservative to reactionary. As David Boaz of the Cato Institute points out, Americans "are too complex to be forced into the Procrustean bed of the liberal-conservative dichotomy."[1] The democratic leadership required for a healthier United States and for its contribution to the dawn of a human rights century requires—as in all spiritual matters—strange bedfellows.

Note

1. David Boaz, preface to Maddox and Lillie, *Beyond Liberal and Conservative: Reassessing the Political Spectrum* (Washington, DC: Cato Institute, 1984).

21

Negative Duties Toward All, Positive Duties Toward Some

Henry Shue

The Family of Basic Rights

There are many pointless debates over the priorities to be assigned different clusters of rights, especially over the priority of economic, social, and cultural rights on the one hand and civil and political rights on the other. The most striking general feature of basic human rights, of which events continually remind us, is their strong interdependence. The basic rights are a mutually supportive family, and no one of them can thrive in isolation from the others.

It might seem possible for economic rights, for example, to be provided for in the absence of provisions for civil and political rights. It might be thought that, even though no right of free expression which would allow people to complain as much as they needed to was guaranteed, people might nonetheless be guaranteed adequate food and shelter. This is imaginable—it simply is not very likely in the real world. A government could conceivably be so dedicated to honoring the economic rights of its people that it would promptly create, allocate funds to, and indefinitely maintain institutions to guarantee that those who are unable to feed and shelter themselves would not be left to suffer. Such a government, however, would need to consist of people so principled that they would not only act on principle in the absence of political pressure to do so but also resist all the economic and political pressures to act otherwise. Even when loud voices advocated maximum production, and no one advocated adequate nutrition for the aged who were no longer economically productive, the needs of the aged would be provided for in spite of the fact that this was not the most efficient use of resources. In a world governed by such wonderfully principled leaders, who spontaneously implement human rights, there would perhaps be no particular need for the institutions and processes that are ordinarily the guts of rights fulfillment. Yet obviously that utopian world is not our world, and in this one we do need institutionalized, not personalized, protections for rights.

If we try to imagine the mirror-image—a government that carefully implements civil and political rights while ignoring economic, social, and cultural rights—the problem is somewhat different but no less serious. As we noted above, civil and political rights are normally needed in order to bring about the fulfillment of economic rights. Economic rights are needed in order to enjoy, or to put to any use, civil and political rights. This reflects more than the mere truism that if a homeless person has frozen to death on the street, she cannot make any use of, say, free speech, because she is dead. That is true (which is the great thing about truisms!). The more important point is that even those whose economic rights are not so totally unfulfilled that they are dead or physically debilitated will quite reasonably be too obsessed with somehow finding food and shelter for themselves and their families to make any significant use of, say, a right of free expression or a right to vote. Someone working two poorly paid jobs because she has no other choice if she is to feed the children may still drag herself into the voting booth and cast a ballot. But if she dropped out of school in order to go to work before she learned to read very well, or if she is so tired that when she picks up the newspaper she immediately dozes off, she does not have a right to vote or a right to free expression in a form that has any value for her. I would say that she does not genuinely enjoy these political rights: while she has them on paper, in her life they mean nothing because the lack of basic economic rights has distorted and dominated her life, making political rights, for her, unusable. These generalities have concrete implications.

Will the Market Take Care of Everything?

A market is a tool. For the purpose for which it is designed, it is an excellent—indeed, the best known—tool. Markets do not, however, serve all purposes or solve all problems. A perfect market is a splendid form of decentralized communication about economic demand, and it is the best method known for efficient allocation of resources among alternative uses. The impersonal mechanism of a perfect market could quickly and accurately communicate changes in the effective demand for various products so that resources could be moved from the production of goods that are less in demand to the production of those in greater demand. A market, however, is a theoretical abstraction that is never fully embodied in reality. This fact does not, of course, distinguish it from other abstractions, including abstract ideas of human rights, and it is not the familiar market failures to which I want to call attention.

If the outcome under consideration is, for example, productive work, the most efficient distribution of food (that is, the distribution that would result in the most productive work) between a group of healthy young adults and a group of frail, aged adults would certainly be an allocation by which most of the food went to the two productive youths. Since the productive youths would normally be earning considerably more income than the no-longer productive old people, in a food market the youths would be able to bid up the price of food until it reached a level at which they could indeed afford to buy more of it than the older people could buy. So the market would indeed yield an efficient allocation which provided the bulk of the food to the (younger) more productive people who could earn more and pay more for it. Because active people burn more calories than inactive people, it is not wrong in principle for the younger, more active group to get more and the older, less active group to get less—provided the older pair get enough. Suppose, however, that at some particular time the supply of food is so small that if the older pair get significantly less than half of it, they will not in fact have enough.

In theory, the rise in the price of food should signal to farmers that the demand for food had increased, and farmers should increase the supply by planting more. It is instructive here to note two respects in which the real world is different from the theoretical market. First, in reality, even when responses to increased demands come, they often come only after long delays. In a nation that has a one-crop single growing season, the earliest that the supply can be increased is one year after the increase in demand. The farmer who sees this autumn that wheat is fetching a higher price cannot respond until next spring's planting which, if the weather is good, may produce a greater supply next autumn. In between autumns there is a winter: What happens to our groups of old people who have been priced out of the food market during the winter? Second, within the global economy there is nothing remotely resembling a free market in agricultural products. The Common Agricultural Policy (CAP) of the European Community, for example, artificially increases production in France and Germany to such an enormous extent that food prices all over the world are artificially depressed. The CAP prevents any international market from functioning in several major food commodities. Our groups of old people may have to survive quite a few winters before the price of food rises enough to stimulate greater production where they live.

What does this show? It shows that if we want to be sure that our group of old people have enough to eat between now and the time when the real market in fact does what the theoretical market can do, we must make extramarket arrangements to guarantee them the food: we must grant them a right to food whenever they are unable to obtain it through the market. If the market works, we will have attained the best outcome, and we will not need to fall back upon this right. But the right needs to be provided so that there is something to fall back upon.

The underlying principle here is important. Whatever our real purposes are, it always makes more sense to attain them efficiently than it does to attain them inefficiently. Doing something inefficiently means wasting resources that could have been used for something else. There is nothing good to be said about inefficiency. However, considerations of efficiency should never dictate to us which purposes to have. It is misguided to do A rather than B only because we can do A more efficiently than we can do B, especially if it is vital that B should be done and optional whether A should be done. Once we have chosen our purposes, however, we should pursue them as efficiently as we can. But the efficiency with which a purpose can be attained is only one of many considerations relevant to the decision whether to attain it. It is much easier to get food into the hands of healthy productive young people who can pay the market price than it is to get it into the hands of old and infirm people with inadequate incomes. The first decision we have to make, then, is whether or not it is essential that old people should be able to survive—and survive with a little dignity—even after they are no longer able to contribute to the economy. If it must be done—if food must be delivered to them one way or another—it is only sensible to do it in the most efficient way we can. If the most efficient way we can do this is not particularly efficient, that is genuinely regrettable. The price may nevertheless be a price we must pay if we are not going to discard our old people like worn-out machines. It is only rational to welcome efficiency—and so to welcome any tools like markets that give us efficiency—but we must still tell the market what purposes we want it to serve for us. We must decide which rights people should be guaranteed. Then we should use the market when we can and go beyond it when we must.

Efficient markets require the real possibility of unemployment, which means in practice that they require some unemployment. If inefficient firms cannot go "belly up," no matter how inefficient they are, the resources of which they are making relatively poor use cannot be moved to another firm that will use the resources more effectively. If firms go out of business, the jobs they offered disappear. What is supposed to happen to the workers who were in those jobs? Are they supposed to go "belly up" too? Of course not; even in terms of the efficiency of the market one does not simply discard "human capital"—which has been expensive to educate and train—the instant it is idle. The point, however, is that it does not matter what efficiency would dictate on *this* score: "human capital" ought not ever be discarded, because human capital consists of human beings, and human beings have rights. There are lots of reasons to try to hold down the amount and length of unemployment, but however much unemployment may occur, arrangements should be made for all the unemployed to live with dignity during the whole of the time they are unemployed. These arrangements, in their turn, should be designed to be as efficient as they can be. What should *not* be considered is any argument that says that resources devoted to support the unemployed could be used more efficiently for some other purpose. That argument uses the consideration of efficiency to settle purposes; it gets the priorities backward. Rights come first, and efficiency follows.

Must Human Rights Be
Excessively Individualistic?

One of the deepest worries expressed about concepts of human rights has been that they are individualistic to the extent of being antisocial. I would like to examine this issue at greater length. How individual are individual rights? Or rather, how individual must they be? We obviously may construe them in more and less individualistic ways, and have done so. Plainly, the same individual rights are assigned to different individual persons, and those individual persons each have their own rights. You have a right not to be assaulted, and I have a right not to be assaulted. If I am assaulted, my right, but not your right, is violated. Individual rights are separately countable and separately protectable. In many places, men but not women, whites but not blacks, and rich but not poor are safe from assault. And putative rights of different kinds would pit individuals directly against each other. If there were a right to the unlimited accumulation of property, there could be no right to food, for the right of a helpless child to food would conflict with the right of an affluent adult to maximize her or his wealth.

Perhaps individual rights are merely individual conflicts expressed in a form that one will find either more civilized or more disguised, depending upon how much conflict one takes to be ineradicable; but a form that nonetheless leaves individuals fundamentally on their own and in competition with each other. The structure of rights may merely provide rules for the conflict. In the end, perhaps, theories of individual rights are simply the just-war doctrine for the war of all against all. Just as systems of legal rights transfer fights between individuals from alleys, where brawn dominates, to courts, where the wealth to hire the cleverest lawyer dominates, systems of moral rights may only transform struggles over X into struggles over the right to X. I think, however, that while this is sometimes all the story and often some of the story, it is not always all the story.

Rights as Social Guarantees

The concept of rights is as essentially contested as any concept is (one should not pretend that there is a consensus about everything). Much is at stake in how rights are conceived—in whether, for example, rights to liberty are taken to have supreme priority over all other rights, and whether rights are thought to be divisible into negative ones and positive ones. Rights are by no means thought of in only one way, even among people who are in some sense proponents of rights. I want to set out parts of one way to conceive of rights, which I think is continuous with the tradition even while extending it in some respects.

Rights can be understood as social guarantees; or better, as systems of social guarantees. Any given right in the system will in practice be much more valuable to some people than to others because the respective circumstances of the individuals vary. We guarantee to each other that we will not attempt to deprive each other of the objects of the rights, that we will protect each other against third parties who attempt such deprivations, and that we will assist each other when protections fail and deprivations occur. These guarantees, then, can be expressed as duties not to deprive, duties to protect, and duties to assist. I believe that every right has these three kinds of correlative duties, which range from negative duties to positive duties; if this is correct, then the attempt to divide rights rather than duties into positive and negative is misguided.

I have argued for this tripartite analysis of correlative duties elsewhere.[1] Not everyone bears every kind of correlative duty toward everyone else who has a given right, but for each person's right there is an assignment of correlative duties which, usually through a division of moral labor, provide for the fulfillment of the right. Toward most people I bear only negative duties. I could not possibly bear positive duties toward *most* people—there are five billion of us, after all, not to mention future generations. Someone, however, must bear positive duties toward each right of each person or that right is unfulfillable even in principle—if the duties correlative to it have not been assigned, the "right" is empty.

Critical questions arise, then, about who is included within any given system of social guarantees—of rights. People toward whom no one bears some of the duties correlative to rights are outside the system. Most people probably believe, for example, that they have positive duties only toward compatriots—that duties to protect and duties to assist stop at national borders. While I think this degree of priority for compatriots is arbitrary and groundless, difficult issues arise about inclusion or membership in any one system of rights. Here, however, I want to leave aside the controversies about the explicit boundaries of systems of rights and examine what a system of social guarantees is like for those who clearly participate in it.

Rights are still individual in the sense that it is individuals who bear them, and they can be, for example, left unprotected for some individuals and protected well for others. Police protection for many rights in the United States is better in the suburbs than it is in the ghetto. If such an inequality in the protection of rights is tacitly accepted by those whose rights are well-protected, then those who receive inadequate protection are being implicitly but effectively excluded from the system of social guarantees—their streets are being treated as "no-man's lands" or, at best, as internal colonies where only some rights are guaranteed. Once again, while I think implicit exclusion from the system, like explicit exclusion, is extremely important, I want here to concentrate upon the nature of the relationships among those who clearly are within a single system of rights, however large or small one thinks such systems actually are.

Within the society of those who share social guarantees of the kind that give substance to rights, everyone will have negative duties toward the others: duties not to deprive others of whatever they have rights to. (Negative duties may even be acknowledged toward explicit or implicit outsiders.) It is not the case, however, that everyone in the system need have positive duties toward everyone else. It is necessary only that for each right of each person in the system, someone in the system have the positive duties essential to the full enjoyment of that right by that person. For the right not to be assaulted, for example, the normal assignment of the duty to protect goes to the local police (even though for much household violence this has not proven to be effective). For subsistence rights, such as the right to food, some believe that the duty to assist falls primarily upon the national government and its welfare system and secondarily upon local volunteers; and others believe the priority of responsibility is reversed. Some questions about the assignment of duties are fundamentally moral issues, and others are largely questions of efficiency. Irrespective of exactly how the particular assignments of duties are made, however, in a society in which the participants enjoy rights, the correlative duties would have been systematically taken care of.

This means that there is reciprocity of responsibility between any one person and the rest. The reciprocity may not be individual-to-individual: you may be assigned some duties toward me that I do not have toward you (because, say, you are younger and stronger than I am). Nevertheless, for one person who is genuinely part of the society, the others—more or fewer of them as appropriate—have duties to fulfill rights, and the person in question has duties toward the others—negative duties toward all and positive duties toward some.

Now, what I have just described is the minimum machinery for a functioning system of rights. The rights are as individual as they can be, but the overall arrangement is deeply social. The system of rights does not strike me as "individualistic" in any respect that would give good reasons for objection. I suspect that individual rights look most objectionably competitive ("individualistic" in the sense of egoistic or atomistic) if, as often happens, no serious attention is paid to the correlative duties or, especially, to patterns of assignments for the correlative duties. If one simply thinks of rights as being somehow claimed against the world but not against any individuals or institutions to whom the relevant duties have been assigned, then it appears that various rights-bearers are really scrambling around trying to get someone to pay attention to their rights and, in that confused situation, are no doubt competing with each other for attention. This lack of arrangements would certainly make a struggle over alleged rights to X look a lot like a simple struggle over X.

One can almost say that it is the duties that are correlative to rights which make rights social. If having rights were merely a matter of individuals running around claiming things—even with good reasons—rights would indeed constitute an individualistic and, very likely, competitively egoistic struggle. What makes rights social is the fact that in any meaningful system of rights, duties are assigned among individuals and institutions who, at least for the most part, acknowledge the assignments. We—those of us within the society of shared rights—guarantee certain things to each other: those things are the objects of the rights we recognize.

The most basic guarantees, of course, are unconditional. It is not that individuals are entitled to enjoy their rights only if they fulfill their duties toward other people, although some sanctions for failures to perform duties take the form of deprivations of the same or different rights (as when someone who violates the right to physical security by assaulting another is deprived of liberty by being jailed). Some fundamental rights (like the right to physical security), however, are unconditionally guaranteed; for example, those who assault are not assaulted as their punishment (any more than those who kill should all be killed).

Content Against Form

Rights come as social institutions (and the principles that inform those institutions). The existence of rights is the implementation of a complex practice of assignments of duties into a moral division of labor among individuals and institutions. Functioning rights are far from being collisions of atomistic individuals; at least, the form of rights-fulfilling institutions pulls toward cooperation and interdependence. Yet the respective contents of particular rights may war with the form.

It is one of the great truisms of political theory that the right to liberty does not include permission to harm others. Insofar as this is a matter of physical or bodily harm, the point can be put more clearly and positively by saying that the right to physical security has equal priority with the right to liberty. At least equal priority: in practice, civilized societies punish convicted criminals with deprivations of liberty but not with torture, whippings, or other deprivations of bodily integrity, which suggests that in our considered judgment the right to physical integrity takes priority over the right to liberty in a manner to which liberal theories blind us. Be that as it may, it is clear that if our right to liberty was construed to include, say, a husband's right to "discipline" his wife with physical beatings, that right would conflict with the right of everyone, including wives, to physical security and bodily integrity. Such a patriarchal right to liberty and our current version of the right to physical security would obviously throw husbands and wives (and children) into conflict. This situation would be worse than "individualistic" and more like hostile. In spite of the extraordinary numbers of battered wives in many societies, no one seems ready to provide a theoretical defense of this expanded (for husbands) version of the right to liberty.

Other conflicting rights have those who defend them in principle. People still sometimes defend a right to the unlimited accumulation of private property (minus even John Locke's proviso of "enough and as good left in common for others"). Naturally, it is not usually called a "right to unlimited accumulation"— it is said to be part of the meaning of liberty. Other people, including myself, defend subsistence rights, such as the right to food, which, for example, entitle those who are helpless to defend themselves to protection against developers (public and private, local and transnational) whose development schemes would destroy those people's ability to feed themselves.

The purpose here is not to examine critically the case for either of these two putative rights. It is to note that a system of rights that incorporates both of these rights would indeed incorporate the existing conflict between disrupted peasants and disrupting developers. The developers would now be attempting to enjoy their putative right to accumulate wealth, and the peasants would be attempting to enjoy their putative right not to be deprived of subsistence. The two rights are, however, in conflict: it is impossible for both rights actually to be respected. A system of rights containing a right to unlimited accumulation as well as a right to subsistence has indeed merely redescribed and relocated a conflict between the respective groups of individuals with the assertion of the supposed rights.

My suggestion is the fairly obvious one that such a "system" of rights is not a system. That is, where an account of rights incorporates an existing conflict, in effect with one right to represent each party in the conflict, the account is simply not finished. Further argument is required until a coherent set of rights has been specified. One requirement of a coherent account of rights is surely that all the rights can be enjoyed, and all the duties fulfilled, by all their respective bearers.

I do not mean to suggest that this is easy. Apparent conflicts of rights are on all sides—rights of immigrants versus rights of natives, rights of children versus rights of parents, and on and on. Nevertheless, either the conflicts are susceptible to some reasonable and principled resolution, or theories of human rights are indeed merely one more reflection of individual conflict. My own hope is that theories of rights, far from merely restating individual conflicts, are one tool for dealing with them.

Note

1. Henry Shue, *Basic Rights: Subsistence, Affluence, and U.S. Foreign Policy* (Princeton: Princeton University Press, 1980), Ch. 2; and Henry Shue, "The Interdependence of Duties," in Philip Alston and Katarina Tomasevski, eds., *The Right to Food*, International Studies in Human Rights (Dordrecht: Martinus Nijhoff, 1984), 83–95. On the allocation of duties among individuals, see Henry Shue, "Mediating Duties," *Ethics* 98, 4 (July 1988), 687–704.

22

Rethinking Rights Without
the Enemy

Peter Juviler

From One Enemy to Many

Our dialogue on human rights has occurred during change more sweeping than at any time since the international breakdown and totalitarian buildup after World War I. *The* enemy, rampant communism, has disappeared as a threat. The world will no more be divided into "superpowers and their satellites."[1]

During the euphoric fall of the Berlin Wall on November 9, 1989, it may have seemed that, as John Lennon once dreamed, "the world will be as one." If even the border guards could be friendly, then at last humans could "act toward one another in a spirit of brotherhood," as the Universal Declaration of Human Rights (UDHR) admonishes us to. Already universalized on the paper of pacts and constitutions,[2] human rights seemed closer to actual realization.

But the darkness lingers beyond noon. The ninth of November 1989 was also the fifty-first anniversary of the violent anti-Jewish *Kristallnacht*, and the semi-anniversary of the Tbilisi massacre in the republic of Georgia. Two years later, Georgia was freer—from Moscow—but a troubled dictatorship with home-grown violations. As cold war restraints on freedom disappear, multiple adversaries appear in place of *the* enemy, spreading violence and new nuclear threats to the former USSR.

Looking back over this book, I am prompted to leave the reader with questions about the way we think about human rights. The questions are framed in terms of the connection between human rights and two goals they long have been supposed to serve: people's security and people's self-determination, within communities of rights and responsibilities.

The Changing Meaning of Security

Security means the absence of danger or threat. It rests on the realization of human rights. "[T]he recognition of the inherent dignity and of the equal and inalienable rights of all members of the human family," the UDHR affirms, "is the foundation of freedom, justice and peace in the world. . . . Disregard and contempt for human rights have resulted in barbarous acts."

The disintegration of *the* enemy and the democratization following on this would seem to bring security closer. But as Alexis de Tocqueville saw in the 1830s, democratization after long repression brings a threatening crisis. These days, in place of *the* enemy of rights, we confront four threats to security: ethnic strife, the breakdown of new democracy into local despotisms, the center's loss of tight control over nuclear weapons, and the nonrealization of economic and social rights to a minimum of dignified existence.

Both ethnic conflicts and material deprivations are aggravated by leaders' corruption and political ambitions which cause them to cheat and to incite their citizens against one another, playing on long-held grievances.[3] Economic and political breakdown have produced a paroxysm of generalized insecurity for almost everyone in almost all the countries of the former USSR. The security of the rest of the world as well depends on surmounting this insecurity with real gains after years of lost time.

As long as the U.S. government treats economic and social rights only as "aspirations," security will continue to crumble away at home in a welter of poverty, violence, crime, and un- or underemployment. As Bertram Gross reminds us in chapter 10, Franklin Roosevelt long ago pointed out that poverty destroys freedom and security.

Self-Determination

While the liberation of human beings in the former USSR has plunged them into insecurity and conflict, Vladimir Kudriavtsev and Elena Lukasheva write in chapter 8 that they are "convinced that the crisis wracking our society cannot be overcome without the liberation of human beings," without their "self-determination." This cannot be postponed for better, quieter times. In their view, which I share, the denial of self-determination, not its exercise, lies at the root of their society's crisis—and I would add, America's own crisis as well.

Self-determination means one's freedom of choice in the pursuit of identity and interests, as an active participant, within the bounds of one's obligations to the community and of respect for the rights of others. The contest over individual rights to self-determination in the United States continues—over the meaning and priorities of, for example the right to privacy of choice versus the right to life and the right to affirmative action versus equal protection under the law. The lack of constitutional guarantees to economic and social rights at minimum levels of dignified existence jeopardizes individual self-determination, including all democratic rights. Successor states of the former USSR are coming to recognize the hitherto unfamiliar and internationally almost ignored human right to private property. The Soviet and Russian Declarations of Rights of 1991 endorse the right to private property, as a guarantee of an individual's freedoms. Appearing also in the Copenhagen final CSCE (Conference on Security and Cooperation in Europe) document in 1990, the right to private property should be considered for wider insertion in charters of human rights. Whatever the evils of capitalism, they won't be cured simply by obliterating private property.

We should think of self-determination not only in terms of individual rights and the collective rights of peoples in overseas colonies, but in terms of solidarity rights and other collective rights as well. A "solidarity right," as Philip Alston and others use the term, is a right whose violation or protection directly affects all inhabitants of a country, a region, or the world, whether they claim that right or not. One of these is the right to peace.[4] It needs to be pressed and reaffirmed along with existing international rights of noncombatants during internal war. Many people recently forgot about these rights in former Yugoslavia and parts of the former USSR. The right to development is generally associated with claims of the third world, or developing countries, on the first.[5] We'll be hearing now more from the underdeveloped successor states of the former USSR on this. The right to a healthy environment is recognized in Article 29 of the Soviet Declaration of Rights along with a right to compensation for damage to health or property caused by pollution. Both the recognition and the realization of this right, Andrei Sakharov and others have told us, are central to humanity's survival and development.

Whereas individual rights are claims to equality and other entitlements within the civic community, collective rights are rights to a distinct community identity.[6] Distinct communities, from the Amish people, peacefully settled in Pennsylvania, to the embattled Armenians in Azerbaijan, assert such rights to be distinct in their identity and, sometimes, their governance.

The virtual nonrecognition of collective rights to ethnic self-determination within existing multiethnic states is not surprising. The assertion of those rights has brought instability and massive violation of individual rights. Yet a growing opinion has it that although contradictions may arise between individual rights and collective rights to self-determination (such as claims of the Estonians and Latvians to survival as an ethnic group), the recognition of both individual and collective rights and their reconciliation are indispensable in multiethnic societies. I would argue that denying recognition to collective rights is futile and counterproductive in the long run.

Speaking in New York,[7] Elena Bonner challenged the experts and politicians to reconcile ethnic rights to self-determination with the "inviolability of frontiers." Simply rejecting collective rights out of hand won't make the problem go away. If collective rights to self-determination—through cultural or political autonomy, or in special cases separation—are to be recognized as human rights, of course, this must preclude their exercise at the expense of the rights of other individuals or groups.

Perhaps some tentative guidelines will help toward meeting Elena Bonner's challenge: First, self-determination means not necessarily or only the right to secession–full independence, though in some instances strong cases can be made for this; self-determination may be also realized at many levels of free choice, from cultural to full local autonomy (sovereignty).[8] Second, recognizing the rights of ethnic groups to self-determination is a way to hold a civic community (a country) together, but only if such recognition comes promptly and is fully extended to minority rights, individual and collective; denying the right to self-determination in the name of preventing a "stampede to independence," may set off that very stampede unless other bonds of civic community hold the country together.

In sum, all human rights contribute to the realization of the basic human right of self-determination by individuals and communities. Human rights have developed through three generations, as political rights, economic-social-cultural rights, and—still to be adequately recognized—solidarity rights and collective rights. Changes in society and in attitudes, technology, and medicine raise unresolved issues of self-determination, which are bound up with the struggle for such rights as the rights of national minorities; women's and children's rights; the rights of gays; the right to informed reproductive choice, the right to die, and the right to life (as regards abortion, euthanasia, and the death penalty); and issues of rights posed by biogenetic engineering. The exercise of each generation of rights is a form of self-determination and depends on the other generations of rights. Their fulfillment by the twenty-first century requires new cooperative efforts.

Human Rights Associations

On the immediate agenda is the expansion and strengthening of the ragged network that is called the "human rights movement." This suggests:

1. more international and domestic support for monitors and advocates of human rights as the violations pile up and become more difficult to monitor and head off in the multipolar world;

2. a broader self-image of the human rights movement, or human rights community, to include activist monitors and lobbyists in NGOs (nongovernmental organizations), humanitarian workers in PVOs (private volunteer organizations), scholars, journalists, lawyers, diplomats, writers, artists, feminists, and civil rights adherents;

3. not more "coordination"—which would cause the fragmented movement (and such it always will be) to wither—but more "communication" so that it flourishes through exchanges of human rights information and annual reports[9] and thinking on such issues as we have raised in this dialogue;

4. setting up human rights associations (HURAs).[10] The idea for such a common meeting ground originated in this dialogue. It was well received by a growing number of activists and scholars in North America and the former USSR. To start with, there could be a North American Human Rights Organization, as well

as republic and regional HURAs in the successor states of the former USSR.

As for expanding international dialogue on human rights and the future, it will continue beyond this book, come what may.

Notes

1. Vaclav Havel, president of Czechoslovakia, on the *McNeil Lehrer News Hour*, February 2, 1990.

2. Louis Henkin, *The Age of Rights* (New York: Columbia University Press, 1989).

3. Henry Steiner, "The Youth of Rights" (Review of Henkin, *The Age of Rights*), *Harvard Law Review* 104, 4 (1991), 917–35.

4. Philip Alston, "The Legal Basis of a Right to Peace," *Peace Review* 4, 3 (1991), 223–27; Bertram Gross, "Power, Rights and Peace," Ibid., 7. The right to peace is implied in Article 28 of the UDHR: "Everyone is entitled to a social and international order in which the rights and freedoms set forth in this Declaration can be fully realized." Nowhere do the UDHR or the International Bill of Rights (the UDHR and the 1966 U.N. Covenants on Civil and Political Rights and Economic, Social and Cultural Rights) name a right to peace. International peace is proclaimed as a right of peoples in the African (Banjul) Charter on Human and Peoples' Rights (1981), Article 23–1, reprinted in Albert P. Blaustein, Roger S. Clark and Jay A. Sigler, *Human Rights Sourcebook* (New York: Paragon House, 1987), 637, and the Declaration of the Rights of Peoples to Peace, General Assembly Resolution 39/11 of November 12, 1984. Katarina Tomasevski, "The Right to Peace after the Cold War," Ibid., 14–22.

5. Russell Lawrence Barsh, "The Right to Development as a Human Right: Results of the Global Consultation," *Human Rights Quarterly* 13, 3 (1991) 322–38.

6. Douglas Sanders, "Collective Rights," *Human Rights Quarterly* 13, 3 (1991), 368–86; James Anaya, "The Capacity of International Law to Advance Ethnic or Nationality Rights Claims," Ibid., 403–11.

7. Association of the Bar of New York, October 22, 1991.

8. A basic introduction to issues of self-determination is Hurst Hannum, *Autonomy, Sovereignty, and Self-Determination: The Accommodation of Conflicting Rights* (Philadelphia, PA: University of Pennsylvania Press, 1990).

9. Bertram Gross, "Towards a Human rights Century," *Human Rights Quarterly* 13 (1991), 387–95.

10. Peter Juviler, "HURA for a Human Rights Community: A Proposal," Ibid., 396–402.

Index

For Product Safety Concerns and Information please contact our EU
representative GPSR@taylorandfrancis.com
Taylor & Francis Verlag GmbH, Kaufingerstraße 24, 80331 München, Germany

www.ingramcontent.com/pod-product-compliance
Lightning Source LLC
Chambersburg PA
CBHW071840270326
41929CB00013B/2059